Cosmopolitan Elites

Cosmopolitan Elites

Indian Diplomats and the Social Hierarchies of Global Order

KIRA HUJU

Great Clarendon Street, Oxford, OX2 6DP,
United Kingdom

Oxford University Press is a department of the University of Oxford.
It furthers the University's objective of excellence in research, scholarship,
and education by publishing worldwide. Oxford is a registered trade mark of
Oxford University Press in the UK and in certain other countries

© Kira Huju 2023

The moral rights of the author have been asserted

All rights reserved. No part of this publication may be reproduced, stored in
a retrieval system, or transmitted, in any form or by any means, without the
prior permission in writing of Oxford University Press, or as expressly permitted
by law, by licence or under terms agreed with the appropriate reprographics
rights organization. Enquiries concerning reproduction outside the scope of the
above should be sent to the Rights Department, Oxford University Press, at the
address above

You must not circulate this work in any other form
and you must impose this same condition on any acquirer

Published in the United States of America by Oxford University Press
198 Madison Avenue, New York, NY 10016, United States of America

British Library Cataloguing in Publication Data
Data available

Library of Congress Control Number: 2023935894

ISBN 978-0-19-887492-8

DOI: 10.1093/oso/9780198874928.001.0001

Printed and bound by
CPI Group (UK) Ltd, Croydon, CR0 4YY

Links to third party websites are provided by Oxford in good faith and
for information only. Oxford disclaims any responsibility for the materials
contained in any third party website referenced in this work.

Acknowledgements

Although I have chosen to keep their names off the pages ahead, this book owes its very existence to the diplomats, politicians, and foreign policy experts in Delhi and Bangalore who granted me interviews. Even when our conversations touched on heavy topics or when securing them seemed to involve inordinate amounts of awkward networking and impenetrable logistics, the interviews were a pure pleasure to conduct. I will have more theoretical and methodological things to say about the magnanimity and warmth that characterized many of the interviews later on. For now, I would simply like to offer this: However individual readers might feel about different elements of the book, it was written from a place of great regard for India's diplomats, many of whom work with tremendous creativity and resolve in the face of the vast inequalities that structure Indian society and the world at large.

Andrew Hurrell took me under his wing as a supervisee when I first came to Oxford as an MPhil student in IR in 2015. Ever since, he has encouraged me to ask bigger questions and to see broader patterns. Without him, this book would not have addressed itself to the impossibly complex theme of global order, on which he himself has so eloquently written. In a discipline that perhaps tends towards epistemological subcultures, he has always urged me to expand the audience I hope to be writing to. Since I first walked into his book-spangled study as a wide-eyed graduate student with fierce convictions and an attendant penchant for preaching to the choir, I have grown into the academic I am in large part due to his gentle pushbacks, ambitious analytical horizons, and continuing guidance.

Kate Sullivan de Estrada approaches Indian foreign policy through a judicious engagement with social contexts that much of Indian IR carelessly papers over, and a healthy analytical irreverence towards the field's 'nat-sec uncles' and social exclusions. I have been fortunate to learn from her research and supervision since I began my DPhil programme in 2017. She has been my go-to person for working through delicate research ethics dilemmas, bringing order into my theoretical chaos, and bouncing off ideas that more conventional academics may have discouraged but she always found a way of tying back to the discipline's core questions. She has helped me make sense of the

vi ACKNOWLEDGEMENTS

fraught domain of Indian IR that she herself navigates with a rare combination of analytical precision and moral integrity.

Kalypso Nicolaïdis has been my unofficial mentor, sometime employer, forever role model, and friend since she first taught me to 'decenter' IR during my MPhil degree. She convinced me that IR could be a much more creative field of inquiry than conventional methods training had disciplined me into believing. She has been generous in offering me opportunities to work and network, as well as to jointly reflect on the role of academics in the world and the role of women in academia. She has offered perceptive comments on several drafts of the work found in this book and has shown more faith in the project than I ever did.

This book is a result of countless conversations and debates, many of which I will fail to do justice here. As examiners for my DPhil viva, I was fortunate to have Iver Neumann and Polly O'Hanlon, both of whom practise an admirable balance between being intellectually generous and analytically exacting. Against more conventional advice from earlier readers of the DPhil dissertation to moderate and narrow my analysis, Polly pushed me to be more explicit and expansive on questions of both gender and caste. Iver's Bourdieusian expertise has tightened up the sociological concepts of this book. His delightful mentorship has introduced me to a wider research community working on sociological IR and diplomatic studies. His lyrical flair has encouraged me to try and mitigate against the dryness that sometimes plagues academic writing—though never his.

For reading versions of this work, sharing their intuitions and complaints, and thinking out loud with me, I am also thankful to Sidharth Bhatia, Nicolas Blarel, Adil Hossain, Deepak Nair, Avinash Paliwal, Andrew Payne, Camille White, and Suraj Yengde. For their constructive comments on my paper presentations, I am thankful to the participants of Leiden University's Workshop in Political Science in May 2021 as well as Oxford's South Asian Political Thought Seminar in June 2021 and the Modern South Asian Studies Seminar in May 2022. For helping me with the labyrinthine quests of obtaining an Indian research visa, winning permission to enter the archives, and trying to know the right people in Delhi, I want to thank Martin Bayly, Jukka Holappa, Happymon Jacob, and Lion König.

Two further academics deserve special mention. Rahul Rao, who was one of the first academics to see any sense in the hazy outlines of my research interests back in 2017, has been generous with his time and helpful in his thoughts on the role of Dalit and Muslim diplomats in particular.

Sankaran Krishna read the entire manuscript with unparalleled precision, creativity, and good humour. He has known where to push me further and when to ask me to pause and reflect. While I have long admired his unflinching work on South Asia, postcolonialism, race, and caste, I was not prepared to be met with the mentorship and largesse that he has shown towards me and my work. We share a certain disappointment with how Indian IR has developed, who it addresses itself to, and what it stays silent on. To the extent that I have been able to attend to some of these gaps and silences, I owe a debt of gratitude to his pioneering work and generous counsel.

Delhi is an exasperating, seductive, and relentless city. For making it feel like home, gracing me with their friendship, fixing a roof over my head, offering their very South Delhiite social capital in service of this research, rescuing me after a rabid dog's bite, or showing me their favourite spots in town for books, jazz, boxing, and cold brew coffee, I am grateful to Poornima Katyal, Rohit Pillai, Moumita Mandal, Thomas Mathai, Khushi Singh Rathore, Satyajit Sarna, Pushkar Thakur, as well as Raag Yadava and his generous parents. In Bangalore, I have long been fortunate to know, debate, and go on adventures with Vitor Antão, Oliver Roshan Louis, Krittika Vishwanath, as well as Mihir Rebello, who is greatly missed. I remain grateful, too, to friends whose social identities mean that their names are best kept off a public list of acknowledgements. All these individuals made an exacting research project a pleasure to pursue. Theirs is an Idea of India worth fighting for.

Contents

List of abbreviations	xi
Introduction: Actually existing cosmopolitanism	1
Who are the cosmopolitan elite?	7
Rethinking diversity and difference	11
Cosmopolitan theory, cosmopolitan practice	20
Analytical boundary-making	23
Outline of the book	27
1. Method: Power, pluralism, and privilege	30
The politics of universality	31
Liberal neutrality and the question of difference	32
Power past the postcolonial	35
The social codes of elite belonging	38
A sociology of silences	43
A lexicon of distinction and domination	43
The diplomatic cleft habitus in India	47
Unfaithful readings	51
Caste as a category of distinction	56
Positionality and method	64
Reading silences	65
Saying diversity, practising sameness	70
Conclusion	76
2. Genealogy: Balliol and Bandung	78
The genealogy of a cleft	80
The founders	80
The education of an (anti)imperial elite	84
Race and belonging in European international society	91
The postcolonial metamorphosis	97
The radical potential of postcolonial reordering	97
Brave old world	102
Conclusion	111
3. World-making: Protest and protocol	113
A revolution unfinished	115
Third World difference	115
The practice of postcoloniality	119
Reversing the moral gaze	122

The cosmopolitan standard of civilization	124
Sisir Gupta's paradox	125
The cultural capital of constructive ambiguity	132
Provincializing European international society	136
Non-universal cosmopolitanism	139
Cosmopolitanism and power	140
Caste and race in international society	143
Conclusion	153
4. Representation: Cosmopolitan elites, domestic Others	**155**
Elite reproduction, disrupted	157
Corps d'élite	157
Selection as exclusion	165
Deregulated ambitions	169
The standard bearers	177
Presence and presentation	177
Who has merit?	182
The segregation of social capital	189
Cosmopolitanism as an elite aesthetic	192
The cosmopolitan club	192
Diversity as decline	199
Conclusion	202
5. Pedagogy: Making diplomats in India	**204**
A pedagogy of two worlds	205
From the Raj to the Taj	208
The Discovery of India	214
Democratization and its discontents	222
To the manner born	223
Democratization as appropriation	227
The diplomatic autodidacts	231
Conclusion	236
6. Interregnum: The end of the cosmopolitan elite?	**238**
Misfires in a post-Western world	239
A much-belated elegy	240
Postcolonial afterlives	245
Saffronizing the Foreign Service	248
Trading solidarity for saffron	249
Hindutva as everyday diplomatic practice	252
(Inter)nationalism reconsidered	254
Adaptation and resistance	257
The cosmopolitan elite turned domestic Other	263
Conclusion	267

Epilogue: A world of difference 270
    Heirs and pretenders in Naya Bharat 275
    Difference and recognition in global order 280
    The once and future cosmopolitans? 284

Bibliography 291
Index 311

List of abbreviations

BJP	Bharatiya Janata Party
CSE	Civil Service Examination
FSI	Foreign Service Institute
IAS	Indian Administrative Service
ICS	Indian Civil Service
IFS	Indian Foreign Service
IIT	Indian Institute of Technology
IIM	Indian Institute of Management
IMF	International Monetary Fund
IPS	Indian Police Service
IR	International Relations
MEA	Ministry of External Affairs
NAI	National Archives of India
NMML	Nehru Memorial Library and Museum
OBC	Other Backward Castes
RSS	Rashtriya Swayamsevak Sangh
SC	Scheduled Caste
ST	Scheduled Tribe
UN	United Nations
UNSC	United Nations Security Council
UPSC	Union Public Service Commission

Introduction

Actually existing cosmopolitanism

A cosmopolite is a premature universalist, an imitator of superficial attainments of dominant civilizations, an inhabitant of upper-caste milieus without real contact with the people.

Ram Manohar Lohia

Cosmopolitans are the only tribe who seem convinced that they do not belong to one. And yet membership in the club of cosmopolitans comes with its own social codes, cultural rules, and entry requirements. It assumes familiarity with dominant beliefs and manners, a resume enabled by exposure to an elite transnational class consciousness. Cosmopolitanism also has its constitutive Other: those whose membership in the cosmopolitan club has been declined on political, cultural, or social grounds. It exists in an unequal world defined by hierarchies of nationality, class, race, gender, religion, and caste.

This is a book about belonging. More specifically, it asks what it takes to belong among the cosmopolitan elite in international society. To answer this question, I am 'worlding' cosmopolitanism. 'Worlding' concepts, as Geeta Chowdhury writes in a tribute to Edward Said, involves 'historicizing them, interrogating their sociality and materiality, paying attention to the hierarchies and the power–knowledge nexus embedded in them.'[1] Concepts such as cosmopolitanism are not ethereal. They produce, legitimate, and make sense of social realities. They must, therefore, be taken very seriously—even if never, as I will argue, at face value. Worlding seemingly settled concepts often reveals a disconnect between our analytical or ethical priors on the one hand and lived experience on the other. It also permits us to query the social processes that give rise to the oxymoron inherent in the very term 'cosmopolitan elite' itself—a term which pairs equality with elitism and toleration with exclusion.

This book does not engage in pure political theorizing, indulging the conventional notion of cosmopolitanism as an *egalitarian ethic*. Instead, it borrows from sociology to consider cosmopolitanism as an *elite aesthetic*. This sociological move throws up a host of questions. What social characteristics

---

[1] Geeta Chowdhry, 'Edward Said and Contrapuntal Reading: Implications for Critical Interventions in International Relations', *Millennium* 36, no. 1 (1 December 2007): 105.

Cosmopolitan Elites. Kira Huju, Oxford University Press. © Kira Huju (2023). DOI: 10.1093/oso/9780198874928.003.0001

2 INTRODUCTION: ACTUALLY EXISTING COSMOPOLITANISM

mark somebody out as an elite member of the cosmopolitan club, and how does one sign up? Where is cosmopolitanism learned and who teaches it? How does an exclusive elite practise cosmopolitanism, with its world-embracing inflections and ostensible regard for difference? And, more specifically: how have India's cosmopolitans sought to leverage their cultural capital to find social parity in a politically unequal world?

In asking these questions, the book narrates the birth, everyday life, and fracturing of a Western-dominated global order from its margins. It does so by examining career diplomats of the elite Indian Foreign Service, many of whom were present at the founding of this order, set out to remake it in the name of an anti-colonial global subaltern,[2] but often ended up seeking status within its hierarchies through social mimicry of its most powerful actors. In interrogating how Indian diplomats learned to live under a Westernized order, the book also offers a sociologically grounded reading of what might happen in spaces like India as the world transitions past Western domination. Equally: what happens to the received habits of Westernized cosmopolitanism as India is ever more deeply engulfed in Hindu nationalist readings of identity? Indian diplomats have been neither straightforward insiders nor complete outsiders in the global club of cosmopolitans, finding themselves at the intersection of complex international and domestic hierarchies. The ambivalence of their status is instructive as we seek to make sense of the revolt against the much-maligned cosmopolitan elite who have been entrusted with the governance of our so-called liberal order. The challenge is to figure out how to listen, and, most crucially, to whom.

Each chapter drives us closer towards an uncomfortable conclusion: cosmopolitanism, as it has actually been performed, can stifle precisely the kind of diversity that political theory tells us cosmopolitanism ought to celebrate. This paradox complicates the stories we tell ourselves about global order and the supposedly pluralistic and liberal international society that underlies it. Indeed, the stale binary between 'cosmopolitan' and 'closed', which liberal internationalists believe to represent the primary struggle of our time, is the

---

[2] 'Subaltern', a term originally developed by Antonio Gramsci, refers to a position of subordination, be it in terms of caste, class, gender, race, language, or culture. In the context of Subaltern Studies, a South Asian historiographical project with its roots in the 1980s, the emphasis on the subaltern sought to critique and dislodge the elitist bias of much of South Asian historical writing, and to draw out 'subaltern' perspectives instead. Cognizant of Gayatri Spivak's admonition against using the term too laxly, it is used in this book not so much as an analytical tool as much as a rhetorical device, intended to capture the sense among Indian diplomats that they ought to be a 'voice for the voiceless'. This is, in itself, a deeply ironic move, suggesting that Spivak's famous question, 'Can the subaltern speak?', is here answered in the negative, as a diplomatic elite is called to speak on the behalf of the subaltern. See Gayatri Chakravorty Spivak, 'Can the Subaltern Speak?', in *Marxism and the Interpretation of Culture*, ed. Gary Nelson and Lawrence Grossberg (Basingstoke: Macmillan, 1988), 271–313.

wrong one. Instead, I suggest that we ask in which ways cosmopolitan elites themselves can propagate a 'closed' and narrow reading of belonging in the world.

Cosmopolitan Elites is a double intervention: it examines the often-flawed orthodoxies through which we understand Western-led global order and develops a close reading of Indian diplomats, who have a long, distinguished history of going against the predictions and prescriptions of many Western foreign-policy commentators. The Indian Foreign Service—also known as IFS(A)—is the elite-trained cadre of career diplomats who dominate the most crucial positions at the Ministry of External Affairs (MEA). My approach to the Foreign Service is that of critical sociological inquiry. This involves deep engagement with the practices and conventions of the Service, embedded in the rich domestic context as well as the changing international landscape it finds itself in. Instead of drawing the Indian diplomatic corps as a technocratic entity endowed with bureaucratic responsibilities and shared knowledge—an 'epistemic community' in Adler and Haas' conventional sense[3]—I consider the Indian Foreign Service as a space of intra-institutional elite contestation. The Service is a site of world-making, in which meanings and practices of cosmopolitanism are produced, renegotiated, and resisted. This is a book about the everyday life of Westernized order, global international society, and order-making, narrated through Indian diplomats.

We must do better at thinking about India and where it sits in the world, past simple bifurcations and mechanistic prognoses of its rise. As India's economic, military, and diplomatic power gathers apace and the 'Indo-Pacific' consolidates itself as a popular geopolitical construct in an ever-more evidently post-Western world, our scholarship—especially that produced in the epistemic and geographical 'West'—must move beyond binary debates on whether India will be 'on our side'. In fact, some of the puzzlement around India's rise is arguably down to the proclivity of prominent commentators to ridicule Indian diplomats for defying the commentators' expectations, prescription masquerading as description. India's rise is no simple geopolitical story of ascension or a narrative about a post-liberalization economic boom— the dominant register in which India is cited and debated.[4] The prominent scholarship on India's rise has a habit of pushing immeasurable elements out

---

[3] Emanuel Adler and Peter M. Haas, 'Conclusion: Epistemic Communities, World Order, and the Creation of a Reflective Research Program', *International Organization* 46, no. 1 (1992): 367–390.

[4] See e.g. C. Raja Mohan, *Crossing the Rubicon: The Shaping of India's New Foreign Policy* (New Delhi: Viking, 2003); Harsh V Pant, 'A Rising India's Search for a Foreign Policy', *Orbis* 53, no. 2 (2009): 250–264.

4 INTRODUCTION: ACTUALLY EXISTING COSMOPOLITANISM

of the frame, its currency a litany of 'objective standards' that might predict India's diplomatic behaviour by calculating the precise coordinates of its solidifying military, economic, or institutional capacities.[5] This analysis often ends up saying curiously little about India itself—or about how Indian diplomats have made sense of their country's shifting status in global order.

Underlying much of the commentary on rising India is the implicitly prescriptive hope that India may finally be socialized into behaving 'normally' in international society—even as the boundary conditions of normalcy are never ontologically defined or epistemologically justified. Accordingly, Indian diplomats are celebrated for any signs of shedding their 'anti-Western ideologies in favour of a pragmatic foreign policy'[6] and reprimanded whenever they seem to stay their anticolonial course. India's uncooperative manoeuvring is read not as a developing country defending itself against hegemonic Western institutions but simply as embarrassingly dissonant with its newfound status as a superpower. Harsh Pant has charged Indian diplomats with 'intellectual laziness and apathy',[7] and Sunila Kale castigates their 'lofty ideals of anti-imperialism'.[8] India should abdicate its anachronistic moralism and engage with the international system as though it had already arrived at the insiders' club. Or as Edward Luce, writing from his vantage point as South Asia Bureau Chief for the *Financial Times*, wryly remarked in 2007: 'It would be tempting to conclude that India is rising in spite of its diplomacy.'[9] Sumit Ganguly said the quiet part out loud when he entitled an article of his 'India's Foreign Policy Grows Up',[10] as though India's critical reading of an unequal world was little more than a fictional never-neverland it had better mature out of. Whether it be India's objections to the various manifestations of US hegemony or its resistance to a common platform on climate diplomacy, Indian deviations from a global liberal script are inevitably interpreted as irresponsible breakouts from a rational norm.

---

[5] Sanjay Baru, 'Strategic Consequences of India's Economic Performance', in *Globalization and Politics in India*, ed. Baldev Raj Nayar (New Delhi: Oxford University Press, 2007), 321–345; Bharat Karnad, *Why India Is Not a Great Power (Yet)* (New Delhi: Oxford University Press, 2015); Daniel Markey, 'Developing India's Foreign Policy "Software"', *Asia Policy* 8, no. 1 (2009): 73–96; Mohan, *Crossing the Rubicon*; Ashley J Tellis, 'India as a New Global Power: An Action Agenda for the United States', *Carnegie Endowment for International Peace*, 2005, Washington, DC.

[6] C Raja Mohan, 'Rising India: Partner in Shaping the Global Commons?', *The Washington Quarterly* 33, no. 3 (2010): 133–148; David M. Malone, *Does the Elephant Dance? Contemporary Indian Foreign Policy* (Oxford: Oxford University Press, 2011), 53.

[7] Pant, 'A Rising India's Search for a Foreign Policy', 262.

[8] Sunila S. Kale, 'Inside Out: India's Global Reorientation', *India Review* 8, no. 1 (2009): 57.

[9] Edward Luce, *In Spite of the Gods: The Rise of Modern India* (Abacus Books, 2007), 288.

[10] Sumit Ganguly, 'India's Foreign Policy Grows Up', *World Policy Journal* 20, no. 4 (2004): 41–47; Karnad, *Why India Is Not a Great Power (Yet)*; Mohan, *Crossing the Rubicon*.

INTRODUCTION: ACTUALLY EXISTING COSMOPOLITANISM   5

There is an intellectual error behind the argument about a potential 'normalization' of Indian diplomacy, whereby India might be persuaded to enter the conventional halls of 'normal', non-cultural diplomacy espoused by Western counterparts. The opposite is true, in fact: the Indian example points to the limits of the 'supposed universality of the modern regime of power' overall—exposing the strange idea that the West can or should act as a placeholder for universality and neutrality in world affairs.[11] India is not an exception to a blueprint grounded in human nature (classical realism), some structural logic of power politics (neorealism), or the celebrated ideals of unfettered global interdependence (liberal internationalism). It is, rather, an example of the limits of the very idea of the universal. Its quest to find its place in the world brings to the surface the historically contingent, socially stratified, and deeply hierarchical rules of elite belonging in a Western-dominated global order.

India is also an entry point into a broader debate about global order and its margins. *Cosmopolitan Elites* re-evaluates contemporary global order through a close, critical reading of its unsteady founding, unacknowledged hierarchies, and implicit social codes. Something has been missing in the mainstream telling of this order, which assumes universally, appeals to neutrality, and builds its arguments about inclusivity by citing a formal lack of barriers to entry. The 'non-Western challenge' to incumbent institutions, as well as the rise of populist and nativist forces, can only make sense when studied through the underlying battles for status, forms of mimicry and resentment, and social tensions that have accompanied implicitly Western forms of order-making from its very beginnings. Indeed, liberal order must be read as Western-dominated order—and as such, any meaningful account of anti-liberal challenges from the margins must contend with the ways in which deeper, long-running processes of colonial dependence and postcolonial hierarchization gave shape to global order today.[12] It is this equation that India's example so lucidly reveals. For ultimately, questions of belonging at the margins force us to consider the boundary conditions of global order-making itself.

---

[11] Partha Chatterjee, *The Nation and Its Fragments: Colonial and Postcolonial Histories* (Princeton: Princeton University Press, 1994), 13.

[12] See e.g. Amitav Acharya, 'Race and Racism in the Founding of the Modern World Order', *International Affairs* 98, no. 1 (2022): 23–43; Gerrit W Gong, *The 'Standard of Civilization' in International Society* (Oxford: Clarendon Press, 1984); Gerrit W Gong, 'Standards of Civilization Today', in *Globalization and Civilizations*, ed. Mehdi Mozaffari (London: Routledge, 2002), 77–97; Edward Keene, *Beyond the Anarchical Society: Grotius, Colonialism and Order in World Politics* (Cambridge: Cambridge University Press, 2002); Kalypso Nicolaidis et al., 'From Metropolis to Microcosmos: The EU's New Standards of Civilisation', *Millennium* 42, no. 3 (1 June 2014): 718–745.

6 INTRODUCTION: ACTUALLY EXISTING COSMOPOLITANISM

Much has been made of just how flawed Francis Fukuyama's[13] reading of the End of History was at the end of the Cold War. What matters here is how, in his naïve reading of belonging, Fukuyama gave little thought to the political and psychological indignities wrought by mimicry of the West. As Ivan Krastev observes of the 'post-1989 Imitation Imperative' which compelled the former Soviet bloc to adapt itself to an increasingly homogenizing, Westernizing order: 'The imitation of moral ideals, unlike the borrowing of technologies, makes you resemble the one you admire but simultaneously makes you look less like yourself at a time when your uniqueness and keeping faith within your own group are at the heart of your struggle for dignity and recognition.'[14] Castigating the hubris of post-Cold War liberalism, Krastev insists that such mimicry was always 'emotionally taxing and transformative.'[15] He draws on philosopher René Girard to argue that imitation—as inhibitor of self-realization and perpetuator of dependency—breeds psychological trauma. Mimicry promises parity but entrenches hierarchy. The imitator living at the End of History is constantly thrust into comparisons with the Western 'original', being cajoled into accepting 'the right of Westerners to evaluate their success or failure at living up to Western standards.'[16] This is not an aspirational exercise but a repressive pattern of power, fixing the course of history into a liberal teleology that the non-Western world is forever playing catch-up with. Krastev turns Fukuyama on his head. The Age of Imitation is not irredeemably uneventful, as Fukuyama predicted; rather, the imitator's 'existential shame' renders the whole order fundamentally unstable.[17] There is an unmistakable prescience to Krastev's prognosis to anyone reading his work in the volatile interregnum the world finds itself in.

Yet the bitter mimicry performed across the former Soviet bloc after the fall of the Berlin Wall is but one reflection of a much deeper pattern of unequal belonging under liberal global order. As I think about Indian diplomats finding their footing in a Westernized world in the wake of decolonization, it strikes me that performances of Western-oriented mimicry are more geographically spread, of older origin, and more deeply experienced. Mimicry of the self-confessedly liberal West began much before 1989, conditions life in a tremendous expanse of the postcolonial world beyond Europe, and transcends forms of political and institutional imitation to encompass deeply intimate,

---

[13] Francis Fukuyama, *The End of History and the Last Man* (London: Hamish Hamilton, 1992).
[14] Ivan Krastev and Stephen Holmes, *The Light That Failed: A Reckoning* (London: Penguin Books, 2020), 9.
[15] Krastev and Holmes, 11.
[16] Krastev and Holmes, 74.
[17] Krastev and Holmes, 13.

everyday performances of elite status. The fraying of today's Western-led order must be critically examined not only through its most obvious populist adversaries in Europe in the contemporary era, but through a careful analysis of how this order has always been contested, reinterpreted, and often resentfully mimicked at its global margins.

Who are the cosmopolitan elite?

It does not come naturally to a discipline like IR to think of Indian diplomats as possible members of an exclusive insider club of cosmopolitans. With much of the conversation on exclusion and belonging fixated on important debates on colonial imbalances and race,[18] it rarely occurs to us to look for traits of privilege *inside* places like India. The broader social scientific inquiry into elites, too, tends to assume that elites are 'white, Protestant, and male'.[19] The analytical convergence between whiteness and elites renders 'non-white' elites conceptually invisible, their social characteristics and everyday performances of eliteness understudied. To see the elite nature of the dominant factions of the Indian Foreign Service, we must first sever the analytical equation between elites and whiteness in international politics. The Westerncentrism of our social imagination also means that the way we envision the cosmopolitan elite is missing a category of enormous social consequence to over a billion people: caste. This is an omission that the book seeks to rectify as it develops caste into a crucial form of identity in the creation of a cosmopolitan elite under global order.

The subliminal tendency to imagine the 'cosmopolitan elite' as residing in the West has flattened the debate on the nature of this elite. It may also be part of the explanation for why diplomats from places like India are so easily understood simply as diplomatic underdogs, despite bearing such stark sociocultural resemblance to elites elsewhere. In Western readings of how power operates, our reflexive recourse has been to an imagery of India that stresses the structural disadvantage of a nation lacking in economic and social resources. As a space, India is ordered into the geopolitically disadvantaged Global South; as

---

[18] See e.g. Errol A Henderson, 'Hidden in Plain Sight: Racism in International Relations Theory', *Cambridge Review of International Affairs* 26, no. 1 (2013): 71–92; Alexander Anievas, Nivi Manchanda, and Robbie Shilliam, *Race and Racism in International Relations: Confronting the Global Colour Line, Interventions* (London; New York, NY: Routledge, Taylor & Francis Group, 2015); Robert Vitalis, *White World Order, Black Power Politics: The Birth of American International Relations, United States in the World* (Ithaca: Cornell University Press, 2015).

[19] Shamus Khan, 'The Sociology of Elites', *Annual Review of Sociology* 38, no. 1 (2012): 373.

8 INTRODUCTION: ACTUALLY EXISTING COSMOPOLITANISM

an evaluative threshold, it is associated with the oppressed majorities of the world.[20] These classifications produce ill-fitting analytical straitjackets. Many of the most widely cited Western commentators on Indian diplomacy have converged around the notion that there is something strange about the way in which Indian diplomats negotiate, the sense of entitlement they exhibit even as they represent a materially subordinate state with scant geopolitical leverage, and the penchant for philosophical debate and argumentative eloquence they prefer over what Western commentators have arbitrarily defined as more 'rational' diplomatic behaviour for them.[21] These traits are seen as anthropological oddities, as illogical diversions from 'normal' diplomacy for a country like India. And yet in many ways, this is precisely how we might expect members of an elite club of confident cosmopolitans to behave, as they seek to prove their belonging to fellow cosmopolitans abroad.

We need a more nuanced reading, therefore, of India's place in the world, as well as of the place of Indian elites in the cosmopolitan club. The Indian Foreign Service lies at the intersection of a complex set of hierarchies, among them not only national, civilizational, racial, or material divides that structure the world of formal states, but also the hierarchies of class, gender, religion, and caste which operate domestically and transnationally. Indian diplomats have often been marginalized in a materially unequal and racialized world, but many of them have also historically, as members of India's dominant classes and castes, sought to reinforce hierarchies that legitimate their own dominance. This complex set of hierarchies underpins the ambivalence of the elite status of Indian diplomats, reflecting both a postcolonial ethic of egalitarianism and an investment in many old hierarchies. The question of their 'insider status' in international society is a fraught one.

Studying members of the cosmopolitan elite as products of both international and domestic hierarchies allows us to reconsider their nature. These intersecting hierarchies matter greatly for who gets to call themselves a cosmopolitan, how cosmopolitanism is talked about, and the ways in which the cosmopolitan club operates. They are also messy. How are we to make sense of the social position of an Oxbridge-educated upper-caste officer from Delhi, who spent a decade feeling spoken down to by Europeans whenever serving abroad? Or, by contrast: what does it mean for a Dalit

---

[20] See David Blaney and Naeem Inayatullah, 'International Relations from Below', in *The Oxford Handbook of International Relations*, ed. Christian Reus-Smit and Duncan Snidal (Oxford: Oxford University Press, 2008), 663.

[21] See e.g. Stephen P. Cohen, *India: Emerging Power* (Washington, DC: Brookings Institution Press, 2001); Malone, *Does the Elephant Dance?*

diplomat, at the very bottom of India's caste system, to seek membership of the cosmopolitan elite—a club that diplomats might seemingly have privileged access to, but one which has traditionally not been a space for lower-caste Indians? These transnational intersections of power, voice, and position reveal the finer, underlying rules of elite belonging among the cosmopolitan elite.

Out of the ambivalence of elite membership emerges a central tension in how Indian diplomats envision the world. An awkward balancing act animates the order-making of India's diplomats: despite a genuine desire to strive towards a postcolonial international society founded on diversity, difference, and the symbolic representation of a global subaltern, there coexists a lingering belief in a caricature-like notion of a white, European-dominated homogenous club, to which Indian diplomats feel a social imperative to belong. Indeed, even as these diplomats passionately contest Western hegemony and its attendant ideals in their world-making, they also continually engage in social behaviours that betray a longing to be recognized as elite members of a Westernized elite, in whose hierarchies of race and class they hope to ascend.

This is, therefore, a story of how a geopolitically and racially marginalized collective of diplomats have sought to belong in the cosmopolitan club—and of how this project of belonging brings the club's hierarchies, hypocrisies, and political limits into sharp relief. Many among the Indian Foreign Service claim membership of the cosmopolitan elite—but thinking through what it means for them to perform this membership forces us to rethink what the cosmopolitan elite actually looks like and who gets to belong within it.

For cosmopolitanism operates inside this balancing act not as a set of world-embracing principles upholding an equal, tolerant, or liberal global order—as an *egalitarian ethic*. Rather, it is a social standard that presumes cultural compliance, diplomatic accommodation, and social assimilation into upper-class Western mores—an *elite aesthetic*. In the everyday lives of Indian diplomats, cosmopolitanism becomes a new 'standard of civilization' which they must continually enact to secure their status as worthy participants of a Westernized order, in which some members are more equal than others. This is not the cosmopolitanism of ideal theory but rather that of lived reality in a particular corner of the world. And yet the socially situated lived reality of cosmopolitanism—what I call 'actually existing cosmopolitanism'—is not to be relegated into the world of case studies or particularistic works on Indian diplomacy. Understanding actually existing cosmopolitanism matters for all the ways in which it has normalized a set of power hierarchies and bred social resentments, which are increasingly destabilizing the legitimacy of the world that cosmopolitan elites have sought to govern.

10   INTRODUCTION: ACTUALLY EXISTING COSMOPOLITANISM

Those suspicious of metastasizing Western dominance in a formally pluralistic global order have often detected new incarnations of the old 'standard of civilization' in Western-led inventions like the international human rights regime or the Bretton Woods idioms of 'good governance', which some believe to demarcate an old civilized–barbarian divide in more polite language.[22] Yet if it once was European powers who employed a colonial 'standard of civilization' 'to defend their domination of non-European societies, to stand in judgment of their social practices',[23] in a formally postcolonial order, Indian diplomats themselves have come to think of the elite performances of cosmopolitanism as a kind of new standard of civilization, according to which they judge themselves and their colleagues. This standard is not formally imposed on Indian diplomats by Western fiat but instead operates through a process of cultural self-policing. In this process, dominant upper-class and upper-caste members of the Foreign Service impose a standard of civilization against internal Others, including those of lower class and caste status, who are continuously stigmatized as insufficiently cosmopolitan for their supposed inability to imbibe the correct elite aesthetic. Belonging in the club of cosmopolitans becomes an internally enforced standard of civilization, which governs India's engagement with the world even under the formally equal rules of liberal order.

The cosmopolitan imperative comes with its own social codes of belonging, set of rules, governing ideals, and appropriate modes of thought and being—but its continued performance also provokes resentment on the part of Indian diplomats, who seem to only find recognition in the implicit hierarchies of international society if they adhere to these dominant prescriptions. What the case of Indian diplomats makes apparent is that the most resilient re-enactment of a standard of civilization in postcolonial international society might not have to do with explicit policy regimes or even happen by Western imposition. It is not only a question of global power imbalances but also of exclusionary performances and embodied practices in the diplomatic everyday—perpetuated by Indian diplomats in their relations amongst each other. The dominant standard of civilization that governs liberal global order

---

[22] Branwen Gruffydd Jones, '"Good Governance" and "State Failure": The Pseudo-Science of Statesmen in Our Times', in *Race and Racism in International Relations*, ed. Alexander Anievas, Nivi Manchanda, and Robbie Shilliam (Routledge, 2014); Gong, 'Standards of Civilization Today'; Barry Buzan, 'The "Standard of Civilisation" as an English School Concept', *Millennium: Journal of International Studies* 42, no. 3 (June 2014): 576–594; Keene, *Beyond the Anarchical Society: Grotius, Colonialism and Order in World Politics*.

[23] Andrew Linklater, 'Process Sociology and International Relations', *The Sociological Review* 59 (2011): 49.

functions through the need to prove one's belonging among the cosmopolitan elite.

The cosmopolitan aesthetic survives because it serves two functions: firstly, of social recognition in international society and secondly, of domestic elite reproduction. It is a sorting mechanism whereby the Indian Foreign Service elite have sought parity among the global club of diplomats and decision-makers by sending their most suave, cultured, and educated—that is, cosmopolitan—members to represent India in key positions abroad. This seeking of international parity has had the perverse effect of cementing domestic inequalities: the cosmopolitan aesthetic legitimizes the continued domestic reproduction of the traditional diplomatic elite, who use it to argue for their own unique ability to act as India's representatives. That is, the cosmopolitan aesthetic perpetuates the domestic dominance of officers who can harness their familiarity with upper-class, Westernized manners of a bygone white world to secure their own institutional position. Diplomats who match elite markers associated with the Indian upper-classes, higher castes, and Anglophile circles can leverage their compatibility with 'worldly' elite markers of distinction against those who do not. This legitimates sociocultural hierarchies at home in the name of social recognition abroad. Colonial entanglements produced the cosmopolitan aesthetic; postcolonial socialization and domestic power structures sustain it.

As such, the performance of elite cosmopolitanism exposes the unequal rules of belonging in a formally pluralistic but socially stratified international society. How is it that cosmopolitanism—theoretically the quintessential placeholder for broadly liberal ideals like tolerance, inclusion, diversity, and difference—also sociologically signifies a transnational elite aesthetic, premised on club-like gate-keeping and social exclusion? Is there not an inherent lexical paradox between the world-embracing inflections of 'cosmopolitanism' and the very notion of an 'elite' to whom its propagation is entrusted? By continuously asking what it takes to belong among the cosmopolitan elite day to day, the book makes sense of the genealogy and reproduction of this paradox.

Rethinking diversity and difference

Much of the research for this book involved long hours spent with Indian diplomats of various titles and identities—either face to face or indirectly, through a careful perusal of records they have left behind in the archive.

12 INTRODUCTION: ACTUALLY EXISTING COSMOPOLITANISM

In more standard academic parlance: I build my arguments on the back of 85 semi-structured interviews as well as extensive archival research among the personal papers and oral history transcripts at the restricted archival section of Nehru Memorial Museum and Library (NMML) and the Ministry of External Affairs division at the National Archives of India (NAI), between January and June 2019 in New Delhi and Bangalore. Of the interviewees, 80 were career diplomats, one was a Bharatiya Janata Party (BJP) affiliate working for the MEA, and two were Indian foreign-policy experts. Of the career diplomats, 33 personally served under the current Prime Minister, Narendra Modi, while 47 had retired by the time of his swearing-in ceremony in May 2014. The interviews also included some former ministers and current or former members of the *Rajya Sabha*, India's Upper House of Parliament, some of whom were once career diplomats, too.

Through critical engagement with these sources, I challenge mainstream readings of global order in four ways, adjusting our analytical gaze for a sharper focus on its everyday hypocrisies and hierarchies. Firstly, the book adopts a critical sociological sensibility—this is global order narrated not through its high principles or explicit institutions, but through quotidian gestures, practices, tastes, and manners. With the analytical sensibilities of reflexive sociology, inspired by the French sociologist Pierre Bourdieu, *Cosmopolitan Elites* reads global order through themes of belonging, domination, performance, pride, shame, status, stigma, mimicry, and assimilation. The Bourdieusian emphasis on *habitus* highlights the embodied nature of global orders, excavating social logics that escape scholars sketching out the broad contours of world-historical developments. The tenor in which diplomatic life is recorded into the annals of history rarely allows for internal contestations, subtle institutional imbalances of voice, or quotidian depictions of symbolically significant gestures which are either unavailable or imperceptible to traditional narrators of diplomatic history.

A Bourdieusian treatment, by contrast, lets us interrogate social logics that never make it into the history books, since such histories tend to reproduce dominant narratives propagated by dominant actors. The book also asks questions that diplomatic historians may not find it worth their time asking. Indeed, much can be learned by studying what Bourdieu called *doxa*—that which is so commonsensical to actors and those who study them as to become naturalized as an obvious way of being. It is precisely in studying the self-narrated dispositions, beliefs, and tastes of diplomats, and the social hierarchies into which they order themselves, that so much is revealed about international society, too. Throughout this book, everyday enactments of elite status are continuously tied back to larger questions of a hierarchically ordered, racialized, classed, gendered, and caste-segregated international society.

In a Bourdieusian treatment of the world, the very concepts through which we understand social orders are embedded in a set of social hierarchies that give them meaning. There is no purely *abstract* understanding of cosmopolitanism—only one rooted in particular power structures that sustain a *situated* reading. A sociological approach allows us to take concepts of political theory or moral philosophy and ask how they are actually understood, contested, and reproduced in the everyday of diplomatic life. This is what I call 'actually existing cosmopolitanism'. How Indian diplomats live out their understanding of cosmopolitanism stands in stark contrast to the benign abstractions that have animated the theoretical study of cosmopolitanism in the West. This is a deep disconnect, with both analytical and empirical consequences for our ability to make sense of India's place in the world and its own sense of Self. The intellectual canon of International Relations (IR) has—quite rightly—been critiqued as particularistic, parochially European or Western, resolutely illiterate in questions of race, and complicit in the normalization of an unequal world.[24] My epistemological counteroffer is not to devise a more 'truly universal' theory but to embrace the socially embedded nature of concepts. This is the essence of 'worlding' the terms we use. I am therefore interested in asking what the everyday enactments of 'actually existing cosmopolitanism' among Indian diplomats can tell us about the quest for elite belonging in the world—not because they hold a universally germane lesson, but because they point to the very limits of universalistic thinking.

Secondly, India's ambivalent status within international society disrupts the lazy metaphors and expedient heuristics that characterize much of the contemporary commentary on a global order in peril. To study global order through Indian eyes is itself, still, a rarity—a rarity which, when indulged, confounds many premises that underpin Western work on global order. That is to say: understanding Indian's relationship with global order matters far beyond India itself. For India does not fit neatly into the prevalent binaries of the current liberal debate on global order, which habitually positions 'upholders' against 'challengers', 'insiders' against 'outsiders'. Often, the existential threat is considered exogenous and novel: a populist outsider entering a formerly

---

[24] See e.g. Amitav Acharya, 'Advancing Global IR: Challenges, Contentions, and Contributions', *International Studies Review* 18, no. 1 (2016): 4–15; Sankaran Krishna, 'Race, Amnesia, and the Education of International Relations', *Alternatives* 26, no. 4 (1 October 2001): 401–424; Robbie Shilliam, *International Relations and Non-Western Thought: Imperialism, Colonialism and Investigations of Global Modernity* (London: Routledge, 2010).

14 INTRODUCTION: ACTUALLY EXISTING COSMOPOLITANISM

collegiate club, a rising power disrupting rules it is culturally determined to misunderstand.[25] This framing crowds out any sincere engagement with the longstanding fault lines, hierarchies, and anxieties which have underlain the thin veneer of polite cosmopolitanism. It is the very ambivalence of India's place in the world that unsettles imprecise narratives about who and what is threatening the stability of the current global order.

This book analyses India's ambivalence through a critical dissection of the racialized, civilizational, class, and caste hierarchies that have long underpinned its complex engagement with the world. Indeed, what makes the case of Indian diplomats so compelling is precisely the futility of trying to pin down some fixed 'essence' of the Indian diplomat, nation, or ethos. India has been marked by its postcoloniality and marginalization in world affairs, assuming the mantle of a pioneer of decolonization and leader of the dispossessed.[26] Yet postcolonial India also grew out of the cultural remnants and inherited ideals of empire, with an elite interpreter class shaped by its formative entanglements with the British. As a result, Indian diplomats are more conversant in the conventions and idioms of 'the West' than many in the West itself. Against the backdrop of this paradox, India's diplomats are now having to contend with India being talked of as a rising power, with all the political expectations and cultural priors that come with such discourse.

At home, the nation has long been held together by a secular, socialist creed that honours India's vast internal diversity, but has been presided over by a remarkably homogenous upper-caste elite. The Hindu nationalist challenge, consolidating since the election of Prime Minister Narendra Modi in 2014—which purports to challenge this elite—is not about making the ruling classes, diplomats, and high functionaries of the state more representative of the underlying diversity of the country. Rather, it is about substituting one narrow conception of elites, built on Anglophile class signalling and educational standing, for another, built on civilization unity and Hindu supremacy. Hybridity and tensions mark India's diplomatic identity and its approach to

---

[25] For a historiographical critique of a rendering of liberal order that treats the 'liberal' Western core as structurally distinct from the 'illiberal' periphery, see Partha Chatterjee, *I Am the People: Reflections on Popular Sovereignty Today* (New York: Columbia University Press, 2019).

[26] I use the (rightly) contested term 'Third World' partly because the numerology brings it into cultural contrast with the 'First World' that defined European international society, partly because, as originally coined by the French anthropologist Alfred Sauvy, it bore reference to the 'third estate' of the disenfranchised and oppressed, and partly because it functions as a kind of metonym for the various forms of solidarity forged by Indian diplomats across the postcolonial world, through the Non-Aligned Movement, and throughout what would later, in a more technocratic register, come to be called the 'Global South'. The chapters also discuss the empirical and ideational limits of the 'Third World' for the Indian Foreign Service itself. For terminological evaluations, see e.g. Leslie Wolf-Phillips, 'Why "Third World"? Origin, Definition and Usage', *Third World Quarterly* 9, no. 4 (1987): 1311–27.

the world throughout—forcing us to differentiate our reading of global order more skilfully.

Indeed, it seems that only the unquestioned equation of liberal order-making with a club of benign Western nations has allowed the debate on rising India to be framed as a debate about whether India is likely to behave like a 'responsible power'[27]—the unspoken assumption remaining that this responsibility be defined by and owed to Western powers. An influential example of this derivative discourse is a Chatham House report from January 2021,[28] which relegates India to the company of Turkey, Russia, and Saudi Arabia as part of the 'difficult four' with whom 'we' will struggle to uphold global order, and which decries India's 'long and consistent record of resisting being corralled into a "Western camp"'.[29] Such simplified readings of India's place in the world have led to pessimistic prognoses of its unwillingness to cooperate with incumbent powers on climate diplomacy, democracy promotion, global economic governance, and international security.

Underlying these laments is the implicit assumption that all forms of ambivalence towards, resistance to, and renegotiations of liberal order are prima facie illegitimate, reactionary, or dangerous. There is also an insinuation that 'we' in the West are merely interested in maintaining a fair and equal system, and that 'we' have done a good job of it so far. Both assumptions are flawed. Instead, the terms of the liberal internationalist debate on 'responsibility' deserve to be the subject of sociological study themselves. Indeed, they are studied in the pages to come as an example of broader processes of normative order-making and the maintenance and normalization of Western dominance.

Thirdly, the book deals with real, complex people. This is not a story of individuals neatly ordered into ideal types, groups, or nations sectioned off into mutually exclusive ideological archetypes. There are no card-carrying defenders of liberal order, set against its enemies; no caricatured sketches of sovereigntist traditionalists, Nehruvian modernists, or Hindu revisionists that do battle against each other as members of some abstracted taxonomy. Given space and respect in confidential interviews, Indian diplomats will

---

[27] Xenia Dormandy, 'Is India, or Will It Be, a Responsible International Stakeholder?', *Washington Quarterly* 30, no. 3 (2007): 117–130; Malone, *Does the Elephant Dance?*; Amrita Narlikar, 'Is India a Responsible Great Power?', *Third World Quarterly* 32, no. 9 (2011): 1607–1621.

[28] Robin Niblett, 'Global Britain, Global Broker' (Chatham House, 11 January 2021), https://www.chathamhouse.org/2021/01/global-britain-global-broker.

[29] For a close, critical reading of the Chatham House report, see Kate Sullivan de Estrada, 'The Liberal World Order Is Yet to Free Itself from Imperial Bias, as a Report that Dubs India a "Difficult" Country Reveals', *The Indian Express*, 15 January 2021, https://indianexpress.com/article/opinion/columns/the-liberal-world-order-is-yet-to-free-itself-from-imperial-bias-as-a-report-that-dubs-india-a-difficult-country-reveals-7146640/.

16 INTRODUCTION: ACTUALLY EXISTING COSMOPOLITANISM

reveal just how internally torn they are on a delicate set of cultural and political questions.

In fact, the Indian Foreign Service is a particularly apposite site for the research methods of interviewing. Firstly, the close-knit Foreign Service is defined by its remarkable smallness. At roughly the same size as the diplomatic corps of the island state of Singapore, it enjoys a distinctly elite reputation, with officers holding considerably more individual sway in the day-to-day conduct of diplomatic life than diplomats of most other nations. This smallness also means that interviews present themselves as a particularly viable method for both capturing a broader bureaucratic ethos and identifying salient social fault lines within it. Furthermore, in stark contrast to somewhere like the United States where most senior ambassadorships are reserved for political appointees and ruling-party donors,[30] barring individual exceptions, there is no established tradition of lateral appointments in India.[31] Career diplomats scale the very heights of Indian diplomacy. This makes it possible to capture the lived realities of diplomatic life from the junior-most officer to the most senior echelons of the Indian diplomatic machinery by interviewing career officers.

The book gives the stage to eloquent, thoughtful, self-critical, and candid individuals grappling with competing impulses and desires, occupying roles in a myriad of hierarchies. There is an implicit sense of 'intersectionality' to the way I study Indian diplomats; that is, different forms of identity and marginalization intersect to produce very different experiences of the world.[32] There are women or lower-caste diplomats navigating questions of diplomatic representation in a world designed in their absence, fierce feminists who declare themselves avid supporters of a Hindu nationalist Prime Minister, internationalists who recognize the inherent Westerncentrism of their own commitments, Third World nationalists who long for recognition for their Oxbridge liberal arts education and French pronunciation, self-professed secular socialists deriding the presence of lower-caste colleagues, and celebrated Foreign Secretaries who spent their career feeling like underdogs because their rural roots or accented English marked them out as cultural misfits in international society. Their perpetual ambivalence about their own place in India and the world

---

[30] Iver B. Neumann, *At Home with the Diplomats: Inside a European Foreign Ministry* (Ithaca: Cornell University Press, 2012), 132.

[31] Devesh Kapur, 'Why Does the Indian State Both Fail and Succeed?', *Journal of Economic Perspectives* 34, no. 1 (2020): 31–54.

[32] For the seminal work on intersectionality, see Kimberle Crenshaw, 'Mapping the Margins: Intersectionality, Identity Politics, and Violence against Women of Color', *Stanford Law Review* 43, no. 6 (1990): 1241–1299.

is culturally rooted, institutionally embedded, and analytically crucial for a mature understanding of the social hierarchies of global order. This is not a book of caricatures but rather of complex characters, torn between conflicting ideals and sometimes wonderfully inconsistent in their reasoning, just as we all are. Even as the book moves towards a broader set of conclusions, this is global order narrated in the first person.

In fact, although many scholarly interviews with Indian diplomats have taken place before, there are no precedents for the conversations around several difficult topics, such as caste relations inside the Foreign Service, the way internal hierarchies guide diplomatic duties, the deep performative desire of Indian officers to live up to a Europeanized imagery of a cosmopolitan diplomat, or the rise of Hindu nationalism inside the Service. The often devastating personal experiences of social stigmatization and elite mimicry among Dalit diplomats, for example, set the interviews apart from the typecast of 'elite informants' that IR is accustomed to.

Fourthly, the book suggests that we rethink which hierarchies matter for an understanding of the workings of international society—and systematizes the study of one such hierarchy in IR. It moves beyond the West–non-West binary which is popular in studies of rising and incumbent powers, but only ever seems to capture national status competition. By problematizing the idea that national lines demarcate the primary expressions of difference in the world, we are pushed beyond some binary heuristics that are popular in the study of places like India. Instead, the book analyses a much broader set of hierarchies in the making of global order, prominent among them race, class, gender, and caste. These hierarchies are present in each chapter, as their intersections underpin India's engagement with the world and its diplomats' entanglements in diplomatic culture over the decades. Nations are not obvious, perennial wholes, sustained on one true 'national ethos' or a 'national character', which it is the job of IR to tease out and place in comparative perspective against other, equally cohesive national wholes. Attempts at locating some sort of national authenticity not only downplay the complexity of social structures but also bury underneath a veneer of unity the social hierarchies that order the unity into its unequal parts.

In other words, this is also not traditional 'IR from below', in the sense of situating colonial powers or incumbent nations against a subjugated or marginalized 'rest'.[33] In the coming pages, the great battles are fought not only

---

[33] Blaney and Inayatullah, 'International Relations from Below'.

18 INTRODUCTION: ACTUALLY EXISTING COSMOPOLITANISM

between 'West' and 'non-West',[34] former colonizer and the formerly colonized, the oppressor and the oppressed. They are just as crucially fought inside individual states and their diplomatic services, where, as in India, different understandings of international society have spawned different prescriptions for what diplomacy ought to be. It is a core conceptual contention of the book that what is missing in the popular postcolonial and subaltern accounts of IR is the study of an intersecting set of hierarchies, national as well as international, transnational, and subnational. While colonial dependencies—both material and immaterial—matter, Sankaran Krishna warns us that 'binary categories such as black/white, Western/nonWestern, and Global North and South tend to draw our eyes away from the complexities within each of them and desensitize us to ways in which they are themselves hierarchized'.[35] This warning must certainly be heeded when dealing with Indian diplomats.

However marginalized Indian diplomats have been in a racialized, unequal world, many of them have sought to reproduce hierarchies of class, caste, and gender within the Foreign Service itself. The cosmopolitan standard of civilization is shown throughout the book as being used domestically by the elite factions of the Foreign Service against internal Others—lower-caste or lower-class Indians, rural recruits, vernacular speakers, sometimes women—not seen as adhering to the codes of cultural capital expected in international society. It is this tragic intermingling, whereby marginalized members of international society can suffer under domination abroad while themselves domestically dominating others in the name of elite cosmopolitanism, that complicates our story. To understand the resistance to or turn away from cosmopolitanism is also to understand whose identity is legitimated by a commitment to it. It is to grasp the various intersecting hierarchies that support the social expression of our supposedly liberal, tolerant, or cosmopolitan ways. National lines of difference matter, but so do lines of, say, class, gender, or education. The book also introduces a further line of difference into the study of IR, which hitherto has been absent: caste.

---

[34] The book uses the vocabulary of 'the West' in full recognition of its many epistemological inadequacies, political implications, and theoretical as well as empirical blind spots—mostly, perhaps, because it is a term repeatedly used by Indian diplomats themselves. It is nonetheless important to remain alive to the ways in which discourses of 'the West' have built themselves up in naturalized opposition to an often undifferentiated 'rest' or 'Other'. In fact, it is precisely these processes of naturalization that this book itself examines. For a critical reading of 'the West' as an analytical category, see e.g. Stuart Hall, 'The West and the Rest: Discourse and Power (1996)', in *Race and Racialization: Essential Readings*, ed. Tania Das Gupta et al., 2nd edition (Toronto: Canadian Scholars' Press, 2018), 85–93.

[35] Sankaran Krishna, 'A Postcolonial Racial/Spatial Order: Gandhi, Ambedkar, and the Construction of the International', in *Race and Racism in International Relations: Confronting the Global Colour Line*, ed. Alexander Anievas, Nivi Manchanda, and Robbie Shilliam (London: Routledge, 2014), 139.

Breaking a disciplinary silence, the book theoretically and empirically develops caste into a crucial form of social, transnational hierarchization in diplomacy. An omnipresent axiom in Indian anthropology and sociology, caste presents itself as the very opposite in IR: a loud absence and telling omission. The word itself rarely appears in mainstream works, while the thorough *Oxford Handbook of Indian Foreign Policy* safely relegates caste to a chapter on colonial-era military organization.[36] Even in critical works dedicated to dismantling the discipline's Eurocentric and statist biases—with words like race, class, and gender emblazoned in the titles—caste remains neglected.[37] Indian IR might think of itself as marginal when measured against the 'mainstream' of a Westerncentric discipline, but it engages in analytical marginalizing itself. Tying its silences to social positionality, Krishna has suggested that 'the Indian variant of the discipline of International Relations is a (un)critical part of the hegemony of a certain upper-caste, middle-class view of the world and India's place in it.'[38] The absence of caste in Indian IR, therefore, is no accident. The diplomatic historian Vineet Thakur's[39] exceptional attention to caste in his perceptive biography of League of Nations delegate V.S. Srinivasa Shastri is yet to be replicated in more systematic accounts of caste in the IR work done on independent India.[40] Marking a promising break with our disciplinary silence, a nascent collaborative project led by Pavan Kumar, Kalathmika Natarajan, and Vineet Thakur on caste and diplomacy will be an intellectual boon for Indian IR in the years ahead.

Meanwhile, more mainstream works by Western scholars that do mention caste tend to do so in introductory sections that lay out India's peculiar idiosyncrasies, and often essentialize caste, along with exotic notions like karma, as a semi-mythical, ancient drag on Enlightenment modernity.[41]

---

[36] David M. Malone, C. Raja Mohan, and Srinath Raghavan, *The Oxford Handbook of Indian Foreign Policy* (New Delhi: Oxford University Press, 2015).

[37] Geeta Chowdhry and Sheila Nair, *Power, Postcolonialism and International Relations: Reading Race, Gender and Class* (London: Routledge, 2002).

[38] Krishna, 'A Postcolonial Racial/Spatial Order: Gandhi, Ambedkar, and the Construction of the International', 141.

[39] Vineet Thakur, *India's First Diplomat: V.S. Srinivasa Sastri and the Making of Liberal Internationalism* (Bristol: Bristol University Press, 2021).

[40] A welcome exception comes from historian Kalathmika Natarajan, whose archival work on the caste and class inflections of postcolonial Indian passport policy conceptualizes caste as central to Indian readings of 'the international'. Kalathmika Natarajan, 'The Privilege of the Indian Passport (1947–1967): Caste, Class, and the Afterlives of Indenture in Indian Diplomacy', *Modern Asian Studies* First View, no. Online (11 July 2022): 1–30.

[41] Cohen, *India*, 120–23; Andrew Latham, 'Constructing National Security: Culture and Identity in Indian Arms Control and Disarmament Practice', *Contemporary Security Policy* 19, no. 1 (1998): 147; George Tanham, 'Indian Strategic Culture', *The Washington Quarterly* 15, no. 1 (1992): 130–31.

20 INTRODUCTION: ACTUALLY EXISTING COSMOPOLITANISM

These silences and simplifications obscure the role of caste in the world-making of Indian diplomats. And yet the political taboo of caste is foundational to the project of postcolonial sovereignty itself. As M.S.S. Pandian theorizes: 'the very domain of sovereignty that nationalism carves out in the face of colonial domination is simultaneously a domain of enforcing domination over the subaltern social groups such as lower castes, women and marginal linguistic regions, by the national elite.'[42] Understanding caste in the context of the Indian Foreign Service matters because caste-based hierarchies, perceptions, notions of diplomatic representation, and even recruitment and promotion practices have fundamentally shaped the sociology of the Service. Equally, India's reading of international hierarchies, elite belonging in the diplomatic club, and its understanding of anti-discrimination diplomacy at the UN have all been shaped by caste. Through its conceptual and methodological innovations around caste, then, the book contributes to a less Eurocentric way of 'doing sociology' in IR, as well as to a more nuanced understanding of the hierarchies that shape order-making outside the West.

Cosmopolitan theory, cosmopolitan practice

This is a book about cosmopolitans, more so than about cosmopolitanism. Yet it grows out of a commitment to critically examine the latter, and as such, theoretical inquiries into cosmopolitanism are by no means inconsequential to it. I am also convinced that the self-evidence with which we often think about and act upon cosmopolitan principles is deceptive. As Dipesh Chakrabarty, Homi K. Bhabha, Sheldon Pollock, and Carol Breckenridge write, cosmopolitanism is not 'some known entity existing in the world, with a clear genealogy from the Stoics to Immanuel Kant.'[43]

Of course, we can delineate some prevalent themes. Theoretically, cosmopolitanism declares the moral insignificance of borders: our universe of moral duties and obligations should not be bounded to a particular nation or community but should rather take humanity as its referent object.[44] In ideal theory, cosmopolitanism is an ethic of international equality which 'elaborates a concern with the equal moral status of each and every human being and creates a bedrock of interest in what it is that human beings have in common, independently of their particular familial, ethical, national and religious

---

[42] M. S. S. Pandian, 'One Step Outside Modernity: Caste, Identity Politics and Public Sphere', *Economic and Political Weekly* 37, no. 18 (2002): 1736.

[43] Sheldon Pollock et al., 'Cosmopolitanisms', *Public Culture* 12, no. 3 (2000): 577.

[44] Rahul Rao, *Third World Protest: Between Home and the World* (Oxford: University Press, 2010), 5.

affiliations'.[45] It espouses coexistence and respect for the Other, and in its institutional garb, has only become conceivable as a guiding principle of international life because, as political philosopher Thomas Pogge argues, 'all human beings are now participants in a single, global institutional scheme—involving such institutions as the territorial state and a system of international law and diplomacy'.[46] As famously defended by Kwame Anthony Appiah, cosmopolitanism is—in theory—at ease with difference and cognisant of the local: 'we value the variety of human forms of social and cultural life; we do not want everybody to become part of a homogeneous global culture; and we know that this means that there will be local differences (both within and between states) in moral climate as well'.[47] Cosmopolitanism can be emancipatory, if pursuing the dignity of the individual means going against the existing social order.[48] These are themes that align cosmopolitanism with classically liberal thinking. Other cosmopolitanisms are possible. Indeed, a great variety of cosmopolitanisms can be envisioned, many of them neither liberal nor Western: Muslim, Hindu, and Christian cosmopolitanisms speak to religiously sanctioned universal solidarities, Marxist cosmopolitanism conceives of a global community of the proletariat, and so on.[49]

Yet the problem, for Chakrabarty and his co-authors, is that 'most discussions of cosmopolitanism as a historical concept and activity largely predetermine the outcome by their very choice of materials'—the mere act of beginning with the Stoics and Kant, or indeed with Marx or Muhammad, already tells us how we will end up conceiving of cosmopolitan practice and thought.[50] We find what we were looking for; our chosen thinkers and terms prearrange the outcome of our theorizing. The authors propose another way: 'What if we were to try to be archivally cosmopolitan and to say, "Let's simply look at the world across time and space and see how people have thought and acted beyond the local."'[51]

This is the curiosity and indeterminacy that I brought to my encounters with Indian diplomats. This is also the kind of analytical innocence that led me to stumble upon a very different way of practising cosmopolitanism at the margins of global order. The elite factions of the Indian Foreign Service speak of themselves—proudly—as cosmopolitans. This is a concept they themselves

---

[45] David Held, *Cosmopolitanism: Ideals, Realities and Deficits* (Cambridge: Polity, 2010), x.
[46] Thomas W Pogge, 'Cosmopolitanism and Sovereignty', *Ethics* 103, no. 1 (1992): 51.
[47] Kwame Anthony Appiah, 'Cosmopolitan Patriots', *Critical Inquiry* 23, no. 3, (1997): 621.
[48] Kwame Anthony Appiah, *Cosmopolitanism: Ethics in a World of Strangers* (London: Penguin, 2007).
[49] Appiah, 'Cosmopolitan Patriots', 619.
[50] Pollock et al., 'Cosmopolitanisms', 585–586.
[51] Pollock et al., 585–586.

22 INTRODUCTION: ACTUALLY EXISTING COSMOPOLITANISM

use to describe their own sense of their role in the social spaces they occupy in India and in the world. Yet the cultural habits and quotidian exclusions of the cosmopolitan elite I am concerned with in this book are neither entirely intuitive nor in any way inevitable. There is nothing preordained about this elite's existence, social mores, or expressions of status. Indeed, it seems from conversations I have had, overheard, or been recounted to that other Asian diplomats—even from nations formerly colonized by the British—often find their Indian colleagues' penchant for Anglophilic manners, cultural references, and upper-class affectations rather alien.

There is also a significant disconnect between cosmopolitanism as political theory and cosmopolitanism as a social aesthetic here: Appiah's theoretical respect for local difference is superseded by the Foreign Service's social disdain for those who fail to meet the amorphously global markers of the cosmopolitan aesthetic. These disconnects between theory and practice, as well as these misalignments between universal conceptions and local expressions, is why I am 'worlding' cosmopolitanism. We must first acknowledge that expressions of cosmopolitanism vary in space and time, then study why and how particular expressions become dominant and naturalized. Only then can we consider the purpose and value of cosmopolitanism in a global age of instabilities and divisions—and maybe imagine it anew.

The question, then, is how cosmopolitanism has come to denote such a politically unambitious and socially narrow project among Indian diplomats. How does cosmopolitanism become read as a denouncement of the vernacular and instead come to signify the attainment of a globalized standard of elite comportment? So prevalent are such connotations in our social imagination now across the globe that the very notion of a cosmopolitan elite conjures up caricatured depictions of a class cast adrift from the world it claims to embrace. Critical political theorists have repeatedly levelled claims of 'cosmopolitan arrogance' against the very idea that cosmopolitanism is, in fact, egalitarian.[52] In such critiques, cosmopolitanism stands accused of being unduly harsh on vernacular ideologies that emphasize non-universal attachments to family, community, religion, or nation; its adherents are also suspected of disguising their parochially Western and irredeemably neo-imperialistic views as neutral universal goods.[53] Insofar as cosmopolitanism ends up reproducing instead of contesting existing power structures, I also agree with Rahul Rao

[52] Luis Cabrera, *The Humble Cosmopolitan: Rights, Diversity, and Trans-State Democracy* (New York, NY: Oxford University Press, 2020), 8.
[53] See e.g. Gurminder K Bhambra, 'Whither Europe? Postcolonial versus Neocolonial Cosmopolitanism', *Interventions* 18, no. 2 (2016): 187–202; Farah Godrej, *Cosmopolitan Political Thought: Method, Practice, Discipline* (Oxford University Press, 2011); Christine Helliwell and Barry Hindess,

that 'the contemporary praxis of cosmopolitanism relies on, and reinforces, the existing distribution of power in the international system.'[54] Critical political theory can helpfully point to the abstractions of liberal cosmopolitanism as deceptively apolitical and impartial. What it cannot tell us is how the politics, partialities, and power asymmetries of 'actually existing cosmopolitanism' play themselves out in particular corners of the world.

I suggest that studying this narrowing of the cosmopolitan imagination requires a sociological sensibility. Appiah writes that 'the favourite slander of the narrow nationalist against us cosmopolitans is that we are rootless.'[55] My concern is the inverse: it is the refusal of many self-ascribed cosmopolitans to recognize that they most certainly do have roots that bothers me analytically and socially. The cosmopolitan elite of this book has very specific historical, political, geographical, and sociocultural roots. It is their unwillingness to acknowledge these roots that breeds resentment among those whose roots lie elsewhere. We are concerned here with the genealogies of elites, the themes of status, stigma, difference, and mimicry, domestic contestations for power and prestige. We must ask what it looks like, day to day, to be a 'citizen of the world' in an at once domestically elitist and globally marginal space like the Indian Foreign Service. This book does not revisit the debate on cosmopolitanism as it has been fought on normative or ideological grounds. Rather, it moves the debate onto sociological terrain.

Analytical boundary-making

Indian diplomats have been the subject of critical analysis before, some of which this book draws upon. We have Kate Sullivan de Estrada's careful analysis of exceptionalist narratives among Indian foreign-policy elites,[56] Mélissa Levaillant's historical-institutionalist examination of the Foreign Service's organizational practices and management styles,[57] and Deep K. Datta-Ray's poststructuralist analysis which, controversially, concludes that Indian

---

'Kantian Cosmopolitanism and Its Limits', *Critical Review of International Social and Political Philosophy* 18, no. 1 (2015): 26–39; Chike Jeffers, 'Appiah's Cosmopolitanism', *The Southern Journal of Philosophy* 51, no. 4 (2013): 488–510; Anthony Pagden, 'Stoicism, Cosmopolitanism, and the Legacy of European Imperialism', *Constellations* 7, no. 1 (2000): 3–22; Rao, *Third World Protest*.

[54] Rao, *Third World Protest*, 7.

[55] Appiah, 'Cosmopolitan Patriots', 618.

[56] Kate Sullivan 'Exceptionalism in Indian Diplomacy: The Origins of India's Moral Leadership Aspirations', *South Asia: Journal of South Asian Studies* 37, no. 4 (2014): 640–655.

[57] Mélissa Levaillant, 'The Contribution of Neo-Institutionalism to the Analysis of India's Diplomacy in the Making', in *Theorizing Indian Foreign Policy*, ed. Mischa Hansel, Raphaëlle Khan, and Mélissa Levaillant (Abingdon: Taylor & Francis, 2017), 160–181.

24 INTRODUCTION: ACTUALLY EXISTING COSMOPOLITANISM

diplomats 'make for the antithesis of modernity.'[58] There has also been commentary on India's diplomatic style, characterized in most accounts by intense status consciousness, intellectualized moralism, and a tendency to argue from self-evident rights rather than acquired capabilities.[59] Writing in a historical register, scholars like Vineet Thakur and Pallavi Raghavan have explored the bureaucratic legacies of the Raj in the organization and policies of the MEA,[60] while Swapna Kona Nayudu has chronicled the lived experience of old-school Nehruvians in the very early years of the Foreign Service,[61] and Martin Bayly has delineated a colonial-era genealogy of Indian international thought, with some key figures becoming Indian diplomats following Independence.[62] By comparison, mine is at once a more quotidian and a more social inquiry. It is quotidian in its interest in seemingly small, everyday habits, tastes, and dispositions, and yet deeply social in that it systematically roots the quotidian in a set of structural hierarchies that underpin India's engagement with the world.

Since the lived experiences of Indian diplomats are on display, it is worth emphasizing that this book queries social processes of exclusion for the specific purpose of understanding the construction, reproduction, and contestation of a dominant habitus among Indian diplomats. Hierarchies manifest themselves in various ways, many of which bear on the conduct of diplomacy but some of it which are primarily felt as personal indignities. The chapters consider several ways in which hierarchies of caste, class, religion, and gender produce the diplomatic habitus, often allowing a cascade of anecdotes to point towards larger patterns. However, this is not an exhaustive Human Resources report about all the possible ways in which sexism, casteism, classism, religious chauvinism, or other forms of discrimination play themselves out in the lives of

---

[58] Deep K. Datta-Ray, *The Making of Indian Diplomacy: A Critique of Eurocentrism* (Oxford: Oxford University Press, 2015), 31.

[59] Manu Bhagavan, 'India and the United Nations, or Things Fall Apart', in *The Oxford Handbook of Indian Foreign Policy*, ed. David M. Malone, C. Raja Mohan, and Srinath Raghavan (New Delhi: Oxford University Press, 2015), 605; Cohen, *India*, 23; Malone, *Does the Elephant Dance?*, 271; Amrita Narlikar, 'Peculiar Chauvinism or Strategic Calculation? Explaining the Negotiating Strategy of a Rising India', *International Affairs* 82, no. 1 (2006): 66; Amrita Narlikar and Aruna Narlikar, *Bargaining with a Rising India: Lessons from the Mahabharata* (Oxford: Oxford University Press, 2014), 71; Sullivan 'Exceptionalism in Indian Diplomacy'.

[60] Vineet Thakur, 'The Colonial Origins of Indian Foreign Policy-Making', *Economic and Political Weekly* 49, no. 32 (August 2014): 58–64; Pallavi Raghavan, 'Establishing the Ministry of External Affairs', in *The Oxford Handbook of Indian Foreign Policy*, ed. David Malone, C. Raja Mohan, and Srinath Raghavan (Oxford: Oxford University Press, 2015), 82–91.

[61] Swapna Kona Nayudu, '"India Looks at the World": Nehru, the Indian Foreign Service & World Diplomacy', *Diplomatica* 2, no. 1 (2020): 100–117.

[62] Martin J. Bayly, 'Lineages of Indian International Relations: The Indian Council on World Affairs, the League of Nations, and the Pedagogy of Internationalism', *The International History Review* 44, no. 4 (4 July 2022): 819–835.

officers (although there would arguably have been enough interview material from many generous, brave diplomats for such an account, too).[63]

In fact, a focus on explicit discrimination would be analytically counterproductive. As women and Dalit officers often pointed out, many of those who engage in everyday forms of marginalizing their less powerful colleagues are often the loudest self-declared advocates of gender equality or caste blindness in the Service.[64] I also sensed a scarcity of solidarity among diplomats of marginalized backgrounds beyond their own experience of ostracism. Many Dalit men were convinced that women were playing up gender discrimination, while upper-caste women believed lower-caste officers to be exaggerating the problem of caste in the Service. There was no diplomatic sisterhood that could erase hierarchies of class and caste among female officers. There were female diplomats who were deeply unhappy about the increasing officer intake from rural households, where these women feared bourgeois notions of feminism may not yet have taken root. A study of how diplomats perceive their own world must consider these divergent interpretations of hierarchy, but it cannot get bogged down in adjudicating competing truth claims between individual officers as a referee.

Institutional path dependencies and the capacity constraints of a severely under-staffed Service mean that individual Indian diplomats have unusual autonomy and flexibility in the day-to-day conduct of Indian diplomacy.[65] Yet not all members hold equal sway. This is, specifically, an analysis of the career diplomats of the IFS, not the MEA. While the MEA is the ministerial institution mandated to manage India's foreign policy, the IFS is the body of career diplomats whose officers staff much of the MEA.[66] The Foreign Secretary who runs the IFS is an administrative head, while the Foreign Minister in charge of the MEA is a political one (although both positions are, in fact, politically appointed). The Foreign Secretary is always a career diplomat and the IFS itself only encompasses individuals who enter through a centralized examination, undergo joint training, and rise through the ranks in accordance

---

[63] Most standard IR is heteronormative and illiterate in questions of sexuality; and most diplomatic work itself follows not only masculine but heteronormative scripts. While I encountered some practices and identities among Indian diplomats that I interpreted as queer, I have chosen to keep them out of this book. For a characteristically creative reading of what it might look like 'to queer' Indian diplomacy and diplomats, see Rahul Rao, 'The Diplomat and the Domestic: Or, Homage to Faking It', *Millennium* 45, no. 1 (1 September 2016): 105–112.

[64] Interview 15, March 2019; Interview 71, May 2019.

[65] Manjari Chatterjee Miller, 'The Un-Argumentative Indian? Ideas about the Rise of India and Their Interaction with Domestic Structures', *India Review* 13, no. 1 (2 January 2014): 7–8.

[66] MEA, 'Indian Foreign Service: A Backgrounder', accessed 6 August 2020, https://www.mea.gov.in/indian-foreign-service.htm.

with their examination performance, seniority, and perceived talent. These socializing practices make it more meaningful to study IFS officers specifically, instead of stretching the analysis to involve lateral hires, seconded officers from other Civil Services, and fixed-term consultants, all of whom are also found at the MEA. So strong is the sense of organizational superiority and insularity, in fact, that a more junior IFS officer will usually chair a meeting if a non-IFS officer is formally their senior, one recently retired officer recalled.[67]

The focus on career diplomats of the IFS—also known as IFS(A)—similarly excludes officers of the IFS(B), a clerical branch whose members work as stenographers and assistants, and who are not shaped by the elite recruitment, training, working practices, and camaraderie of the diplomatic ranks of IFS(A). Their outsider status and lack of elite vetting and training have created what one millennial IFS(A) officer called 'another kind of caste system', within which trained diplomats largely keep to themselves instead of socializing with IFS(B) officers.[68] This is a long-held divide, once captured by Foreign Secretary T.N. Kaul (1968–1972): 'The most glaring division between "A" and "B" grades was even more prevalent in our Missions abroad where the two lived in two separate and water-tight compartments, as in the Indian Railways.'[69] It has therefore been with open dismay that the elite IFS(A) has observed the trend, accelerating over the past decade as the IFS struggles with its small size, of IFS(B) officers attaining diplomatic rank, on occasion even making Ambassador.[70] In fact, a crucial component of the declinist narrative of old-school diplomats fearing the end of an Indian age of enlightened cosmopolitan elites is precisely the fact that supposedly inferior, untrained, and less culturally suitable Indians from the Home Services and the IFS(B) are slowly making their way up the ranks at the MEA. Focusing on the core elite diplomatic cadres of IFS(A) makes it possible to trace shared organizational practices, philosophies, and procedures, while also saying something about the exclusionary cultural processes of elite formation itself.

---

[67] Interview 55, May 2019.
[68] Interview 82, May 2019.
[69] 'Ministry of External Affairs and the Foreign Service', manuscript, T.N. Kaul, undated, page 6. Miscellaneous Articles by T. N. Kaul. Speeches/Writings by Him, S. No. 141. T. N. Kaul Individual Papers, NMML.
[70] Telegraph India, 'Steno Envoy Sparks "Caste War"', 9 June 2012, https://www.telegraphindia.com/india/steno-envoy-sparks-caste-war/cid/410209.

Outline of the book

Each chapter of this book offers its own answers to the same set of animating questions: how have Indian diplomats sought to secure recognition as members of the global cosmopolitan club, and how has this quest shaped the ways that they have imagined the world? How is international society reproduced, shaped, and contested at the margins, and what does this tell us about liberal order itself? What emerges out of these inquiries is not only a deeper understanding of the often ridiculed and seemingly paradoxical behaviour of Indian diplomats but also a commentary on the nature of actually existing cosmopolitanism. The chapters bear witness to the inadequacies of cosmopolitanism as an emancipatory project and analyse the historical processes that have rendered it a programme of social exclusions.

Chapter 1 is a theoretical and methodological reflection on how to think more imaginatively and inclusively about global order. It provides a critical reading of both liberal internationalist and postcolonial accounts of global order. It then proposes a set of alternative analytical tools, involving reflexive sociology, critical archival work, a subaltern anti-technocratic sensibility, and autoethnographic interview methods. Drawing on self-critical experiences of fieldwork, it introduces the sensibilities of reflexive sociological thinking and lays the methodological groundwork for a systematic treatment of caste in diplomatic studies and IR.

Chapter 2 writes an embodied origin story of India's fraught engagement with international society. It shows how the ambitious Nehruvian project of postcolonial solidarity and Third World reconstruction was, from the very founding of the Foreign Service, deeply intertwined with a narrower reading of 'worldliness' and the codes of cosmopolitan class signalling inherited through socialization under the British Raj. It locates this story in the elite educational and bureaucratic conditions of empire and analyses the lived experience and autobiographical narrations of native Indian Civil Service (ICS) officers as they are socialized into imperial bureaucracy through training at Oxbridge. It bears witness to the soul-searching on status, race, and class of young future officers, as they train to imbibe the idealized image of a sophisticated, cosmopolitan colonial officer, all the while seeking to prove their allegiance to a radical anti-imperial project of Indian Independence. It then argues that the desire to belong in upper-class, white international society did not dissolve at Independence. Instead, a dual ideal for an Indian diplomat was institutionalized into the very structures of the postcolonial Indian Foreign Service:

an officer attuned to the anti-imperial, solidarist demands of postcolonial diplomacy, yet proudly conversant in the elite conventions and networks of a white European world. This is the genealogy for how a truncated and heavily hierarchical reading of cosmopolitanism became normalized among Indian diplomats.

Chapter 3 asks what kind of world Indian diplomats have envisioned and how they have sought to navigate their place within it. It analyses their deep ambivalence towards the conventions, debates, and hypocrisies of Western-dominated global order, in which the elite factions of the Service partake with a performative fluency but also some resentment at their own desire for mimicry. Indeed, the chapter demonstrates how the cosmopolitan imperative has interfered with India's efforts at proposing a radically different order, founded on Third World solidarity, anti-imperialism, and a rejection of the very idea of an enlightened elite club governing international society. The chapter also considers the place of caste and race in international society, asking how these fraught categories of identity relate to the dual Indian project of belonging among the exclusive cosmopolitan club and envisioning a more equal world.

Chapter 4 uses Indian debates around diplomatic recruitment, promotion, and the so-called 'democratization' of the Foreign Service to establish how cosmopolitanism operates domestically as an elite aesthetic. Tying cosmopolitanism to domestic hierarchies, the chapter shows how, instead of transcending private loyalties, as political theory tells us cosmopolitanism does, cosmopolitanism in the Indian diplomatic imagination is stored in an elite habitus and its attendant forms of cultural and social capital. Against the professed ideals of democratization, the chapter shows how the more 'authentically Indian' or 'representative' diplomats miss out on promotions and prestigious postings, rarely find a place in the existing webs of social capital that reproduce old hierarchies, and fail to fundamentally alter the ideal of a cosmopolitan diplomat, against which officers continue to be measured. Repeatedly, self-described cosmopolitans of the Foreign Service speak the language of diversity while engaging in practices of social exclusion, in which internal Others are marked by their inability to imbibe the cosmopolitan aesthetic, and thus also by the impossibility of being recognized as equal members of international society.

Chapter 5 considers how Indian diplomats are made. It shows how the over seven decades of Indian diplomatic training constitute an ongoing attempt at reproducing, managing, and re-appropriating an ideal cosmopolitan officer—while also analysing the ongoing anxieties around Indian authenticity and subaltern representation. From an earlier postcolonial anxiety about making 'real' Indians out of suspiciously worldly elites, Indian diplomatic training now coalesces around the concern that future diplomats may be excessively 'authentic' and insufficiently comfortable in the wine-drinking club of elite diplomats. The chapter examines both the official project to instil a certain habitus in diplomatic probationers during mandatory institutional training and the lonely autodidactic attempts by self-professed outsiders—female and lower-caste recruits in particular—to mimic the dominant, supposedly more worldly officers of the Service outside official training hours.

Chapter 6 finds Westernized global order and its attendant forms of belonging fraying. It considers how the twin transformation of India's growing global stature in an increasingly 'post-Western' world and its changing domestic power constellations are producing what Bourdieu called *misfires*: occasions on which a dominant habitus has outlived the conditions in which it was originally assembled. The backlash against cosmopolitan elites in Indian political discourse and inside the Service itself must be thought of in this twin context: against a backdrop of global changes on the one hand and shifting political alliances inside India on the other. To this end, the chapter first considers changes brought about by the dawn of an ever-increasingly 'post-Western' world in the early twenty-first century, asking whether they could signal the possibility of a more inclusive, democratized understanding of cosmopolitanism, liberated from its earlier colonial confines. It then attempts a first sketch of an understudied development: the effects of 'saffronization' on the Foreign Service—that is, the takeover of the Service by the forces of Hindu nationalism since 2014, and the ways in which diplomats have sought to navigate and resist these changes. If there was an opening, with the dawn of a 'post-Western' world, to move towards a more expansive or inclusive way of doing cosmopolitanism, the Hindu nationalist project signals a wholesale rejection of the very idea.

The **Epilogue** considers what a reflexive sociological reading of Indian diplomats tells us about a wider set of questions about cosmopolitanism, diversity, and domination under Western-led order. It elaborates on the limits of a liberal understanding of recognition that focuses purely on formal admission, considering instead the importance of the social recognition function of actually existing cosmopolitanism. It asks whether some rendition of the cosmopolitan ideal can—or ought to—be salvaged, and how it might be reimagined for the sake of a more genuinely pluralistic world.

1

Method

Power, pluralism, and privilege

International societies do not naturally emerge out of a set of power differentials like a logically sound solution to a fixed equation. Much as Benedict Anderson said of domestic communities, international societies, too, are imagined: they are constructed imageries of a joint community and culture which the imaginers see themselves as part of.[1] 'Imagined' does not mean fragile—in fact, social constructions of international society often outlast significant historical shifts in the underlying material structures, living a sort of cultural afterlife. It does not mean ethereal either, for our imageries are never innocent of power. Instead, imageries of international society tie themselves to national pecking orders and politics: they reflect and legitimate not only particular global structures but also domestic hierarchies. They contain social codes for belonging on who gets to be an insider, in what kind of international society, and on whose terms. In other words: they express the social hierarchies of global order. The power to imagine a social order is profound, and who is allowed to set the prevalent imagery matters. The question, then, is not only what international society looks like, how it operates, or when it changes, but also, crucially: *whose* international society is it? Whose is it to imagine into being? Whose is it to define and dominate?

In sociologizing the study of international society, this chapter rethinks questions of membership and belonging in it. It considers how we might think about the emergence and nature of the social order now under challenge and where the 'cosmopolitan elite' features in this order. A sociological sensibility allows us to have a more embodied discussion about why, despite an imperial Western concern that decolonization would splinter international society into unmanageable diversity,[2] postcolonial diplomacy has in fact continued being played out in the shadow of a deep, historically rooted, and socially

---

[1] Benedict Anderson, *Imagined Communities: Reflections on the Origin and Spread of Nationalism* (London: Verso, 1991).
[2] Tim Dunne, *Inventing International Society: A History of the English School* (Basingstoke: Palgrave Macmillan, 1998).

Cosmopolitan Elites. Kira Huju, Oxford University Press. © Kira Huju (2023). DOI: 10.1093/oso/9780198874928.003.0002

expressed desire to conform to dated standards of European international society. Critical of the false promise of universality in liberal internationalist interpretations of international society but also partially dissatisfied with the postcolonial challenge to them, I suggest that we recast the narratives of belonging and membership that have accompanied decolonization across the globe.

Such a recasting requires its own conceptual scaffolding, one borrowed from outside of IR. To tell the story of Indian diplomats in the world, I push into reflexive sociological thinking, sketching out the importance of questions of membership, hierarchy, status, and mimicry. Descending from the rarefied heights of grand ideological debate and sweeping systemic analysis, I take my cue from the French sociologist Pierre Bourdieu's fascination with the subtle everyday practices that sustain social orders. Having introduced the sociological concepts that will shape the analysis in the pages to come, the chapter considers how questions of positionality—both of the researcher and the researched—must shape our methods. This means asking ourselves questions not only about global order and India, but about who we think of as reliable narrators on these themes. How are we to make sense of the power imbalances that shape not only the world, but the academic work done on it?

The politics of universality

When we talk about the cosmopolitan elite, we are telling ourselves particular stories about the historical evolution, cultural constitution, and social rules of international society. Many stories in this genre revolve around decolonization, the significance it ought to be afforded, and the rupture it occasioned in how international life is ordered. Certainly, decolonization is pivotal in any story that involves India, born as it was out of the anti-imperial project of Indian Independence in 1947. What decolonization began or ended is less obvious, however. The classic understanding is that decolonization marked the end of the old colonial standard of civilization, which once employed a set of cultural and political standards to segregate the world into those with the right to govern it and those who would be governed. With decolonization, 'Third World struggles' would replace the standard of civilization with an 'idea of a plurality of civilizations that face one another as equals'.[3] A reimagined world—and the tripled number of states now claiming formal

---

[3] Andrew Linklater, 'Process Sociology and International Relations', *The Sociological Review* 59, no. 1 (2011): 49.

32 METHOD: POWER, PLURALISM, AND PRIVILEGE

sovereign equality within it—needed to contend with struggles for racial equality, cultural liberation, economic justice, and recognition of the diversity that now defined the enlarged society of states.[4] It was to be built on the democratization of global governance, reflective of Third World solidarity, constructed against the image of everything that had come before. It was to be democratic, diverse, and open to the expressions of difference from once marginalized quarters. This suggested a cultural restructuring: a brave new international society that had outgrown the old, born out of decolonization and its radical potential. Out of this promise of democratization and diversity, many narratives of global order have spawned.

Liberal neutrality and the question of difference

One story about membership in today's international society that is popular in Western elite discourse is liberal internationalism, a close cousin of liberal institutionalism and its attendant theories of liberal order. Unique in the history of international politics, liberal internationalists argue, the formally equal institutions of the modern era have suspended with any 'discriminatory obstacles to the admission of states of culturally diverse backgrounds'.[5] Where once there was a standard of civilization, there now exists a technocratized world of global interdependence, not even conversant in the cultural language of civilization and empire. Borrowing the axiom of neutrality from liberal political theory, liberal IR theorists have postulated that the state-sanctioned institutions of the post-war global order are plain frameworks of objective rules and procedures, which regard the cultural affinities of their members with absentminded disinterest. Liberal order can even survive systemic power shifts, precisely because it shows no interest in the cultural credentials of its members: it exhibits 'an unusual capacity to accommodate rising powers' since its 'sprawling landscape of rules, institutions, and networks provide newer entrants into the system with opportunities for status, authority, and a share in the governance of the order'.[6] In other words, there are no explicit rules of belonging under liberal order: once you are in, you are equal, have status, and

---

[4] Andrew Hurrell, *On Global Order* (Oxford: Oxford University Press, 2007), 47.
[5] Christian Reus-Smit, 'Cultural Diversity and Global Order', *International Organization* 71, no. 4 (2017): 861.
[6] G. John Ikenberry, *Liberal Leviathan: The Origins, Crisis, and Transformation of the American World Order* (Princeton: Princeton University Press, 2011), 345.

shape institutions just like everybody else. While it is common in both realist[7] and critical circles[8] of IR to question the optimism of liberal international-ists, less has been said about the liberal reading of diversity that underlies its understanding of belonging.[9]

The benevolent self-conception of liberal internationalists has long rested on a reading of international relations that emphasizes negative freedom. The ensuing laissez-faire reading of diversity postulates that life under liberal order is democratic, pluralistic, and diverse because there are no formal barriers to expressions of difference. Since the official nature of liberal order is 'open' and 'rules-based', it can accommodate any kind of actor regardless of its internal characteristics. The institutions of liberal order have an explicit neutralizing function: they exist to shave off any cultural excesses that might come in the way of rational positive-sum-maximizing. In other words, liberal inter-nationalism solves the question of diversity by trivializing it. Liberal leaders, alongside scholars like Daniel Deudney, John Ikenberry, Anne-Marie Slaugh-ter, and Andrew Moravcsik, have made a point of celebrating as a prime virtue the fact that the current order was built to defang difference, not express it. Struggles for recognition, demands for equality, and the desires and anxi-eties of world-making—all these are reinterpreted as technical 'preferences' to be tactically bargained with. In its idealized vision of itself, liberal interna-tionalism practises diversity through a seeming disinterest in identity. Liberal world-ordering does not express diverse identities, it seeks to achieve *a win over identity*.

This liberal account of diversity beautifies radical divergences of power. Its language of neutrality is not liberating—it shields power from view but does nothing to democratize its distribution. The rhetoric of neutrality, interdependence, and institutions suggests a benign transactional reality in which international politics is premised on bargaining on roughly equal terms. The inadvertent equation of 'like units' with 'equal units' glosses over the irreducibly hierarchical nature of international institutions as well as the stark power asymmetries embedded in their very architectures. It assumes that identities exist separately of power. Similarly, the inclusion of

---

[7] See e.g. John J. Mearsheimer, 'Bound to Fail: The Rise and Fall of the Liberal Global Order', *International Security* 43, no. 4 (2019): 7–50; Patrick Porter, *The False Promise of Liberal Order: Nostalgia, Delusion and the Rise of Trump* (Hoboken (New Jersey): John Wiley & Sons, 2020).

[8] See e.g. Duncan Bell, *Reordering the World: Essays on Liberalism and Empire* (Princeton: Princeton University Press, 2016); Adom Getachew, *Worldmaking after Empire: The Rise and Fall of Self-Determination* (Princeton University Press, 2019); Inderjeet Parmar, 'The US-Led Liberal Order: Imperialism by Another Name?', *International Affairs* 94, no. 1 (2018): 151–172.

[9] For a seminal, if lonely, exception, see Reus-Smit, 'Cultural Diversity and International Order'.

34   METHOD: POWER, PLURALISM, AND PRIVILEGE

subaltern or 'non-Western' voices in a shared liberal dialogue with the powerful presupposes the former's ability to articulate their subject position within the dominant liberal vocabulary.[10] Since the liberal lexicon does not allow space for cultural difference, the notion of liberal principles as the neutral backbone of a shared global order is simply assumed. That is: liberal assumptions become universal, the participation in liberal world-making an exercise among equals. What is missing, therefore, is any meaningful questioning of how marginalized actors can express difference under liberal hegemony.[11] The culture of the dominant West becomes universal culture, but the rules of liberal neutrality dictate that these origins cannot be spoken of.

Indeed, the neutrality claims of liberal theorizing mask the specificity of their geographical origins. This evasion points to a larger silence—and liberalism's false promise of universality. For, upon closer inspection, the purported universals of Western world-making appear parochial: elevated onto a theoretical plane and purified of any trace of their origins through a process of abstraction, these universalized claims nonetheless remain constructs uprooted from specific political, cultural, and social contexts.[12] Ours has been a discipline 'which speaks partially, but which has assumed and declared universally', gazing at the world from the perspective of the West.[13] The Western-dominated discipline of IR has generously elevated the Hobbesian state of nature from a provincial account of papal hegemony and the English Civil War into an established truth of international life and generalized from the experience of European state formation into a blanket account of sovereignty.[14] Having done this, it has turned around to declare all states 'like units' operating under culture-neutral rules. That which was abstracted from the particular is proclaimed resistant to the partialities of space and time; that which owes its judgement to a dominant position in the world is announced blind to bias because of the rigour of one's chosen method. The infamous English School

---

[10] See Kimberly Hutchings, 'Dialogue between Whom? The Role of the West/Non-West Distinction in Promoting Global Dialogue in IR', *Millennium* 39, no. 3 (2011): 639–647.

[11] For a liberal attempt at grappling with whether liberal order exhibits imperial traits, see G. John Ikenberry, 'Reflections on "After Victory"', *The British Journal of Politics and International Relations* 21, no. 1 (1 February 2019): 14–15.

[12] See e.g. Amitav Acharya and Barry Buzan, eds, *Non-Western International Relations Theory: Perspectives on and beyond Asia* (London: Routledge, 2010); Sankaran Krishna, 'Colonial Legacies and Contemporary Destitution: Law, Race, and Human Security', *Alternatives* 40, no. 2 (2015): 1–17; Robbie Shilliam, *International Relations and Non-Western Thought: Imperialism, Colonialism and Investigations of Global Modernity* (London: Routledge, 2010).

[13] Stephen Chan, 'Seven Types of Ambiguity in Western International Relations Theory and Painful Steps towards Right Ethics', in *The Zen of International Relations: IR Theory from East to West*, ed. Stephen Chan, Peter Mandaville, and Roland Bleiker (London: Palgrave Macmillan UK, 2001), 77.

[14] Navid Pourmokhtari, 'A Postcolonial Critique of State Sovereignty in IR: The Contradictory Legacy of a 'West-Centric' Discipline', *Third World Quarterly* 34, no. 10 (2013): 1775.

defence that 'it is not our perspective but the historical record itself that can be called Eurocentric'[15] becomes a tautological inevitability of its own theoretical premises.

The liberal conception of global order, too, has presupposed a universal good—an open-minded, tolerant, cosmopolitan collection of common principles—without ever asking how these principles land across the globe and how they are actually perceived or practiced.[16] The evolution of liberal thinking is intimately intertwined with empire and the legitimating theories that Britain in particular produced to justify its domination over territories outside Europe.[17] The 'manifest Eurocentrism' of classical liberal thinking, which tied itself to visions of empire between the nineteenth century and the Second World War, has shifted shape to what John Hobson calls 'subliminal Eurocentrism': the language of civilization versus savagery has been 'whitewashed', as it were, into seemingly more universal binaries, such as 'tradition versus modernity', in which tropes of modernity connote the crowning achievements of the liberal project.[18] Yet the theoretical validation of certain historical experiences and cultural commonplaces is not an obvious exercise in discovery or an innocently descriptive method. Rather, it reflects back to us the very imbalances of power we ought to be studying. The task is therefore to 'provincialize Europe'[19] and 'decentre' Western IR[20]—not by folding 'non-Western experience' into the liberal mainstream but by asking how this experience unsettles the liberal telling of global order.

Power past the postcolonial

'Provincializing Europe' is something postcolonial theory does well. As such, it might seem that all that needs to happen for us to fix the cultural blind spots of liberal theorizing is for us to adopt a postcolonial research paradigm. 'Provincializing Europe' in a study of Indian diplomats does not mean that we look

---

[15] Hedley Bull and Adam Watson, *The Expansion of International Society* (Oxford: Clarendon Press, 1984), 2.

[16] For a thoughtful critique of liberal institutionalists, see e.g. Beate Jahn, 'Liberal Internationalism: From Ideology to Empirical Theory—and Back Again', *International Theory* 1, no. 3 (2009): 409–38.

[17] Bell, *Reordering the World*.

[18] John M. Hobson, 'Re-Embedding the Global Colour Line within Post-1945 International Theory', in *Race and Racism in International Relations*, ed. Alexander Anievas, Nivi Manchanda, and Robbie Shilliam (Routledge, 2014), 83.

[19] Dipesh Chakrabarty, *Provincializing Europe: Postcolonial Thought and Historical Difference* (Princeton: Princeton University Press, 2008).

[20] Nora Fisher Onar and Kalypso Nicolaïdis, 'The Decentring Agenda: Europe as a Post-Colonial Power', *Cooperation and Conflict* 48, no. 2 (2013): 283–303.

36 METHOD: POWER, PLURALISM, AND PRIVILEGE

elsewhere, entirely outside Europe. Rather, it means that we look at the ways in which Europe—an imagined Europe, Europe as metonym—has played a role in how Indian elites situate themselves in the world. Insofar as imageries of 'Europe' or 'the West' reflect a particular memory of the colonial experience, one is reminded of Dipesh Chakrabarty's meditation on the mental creation of Europe, which was always a joint exercise between colonial Britain and Indian elites:

> I was aware that there were and still are many Europes, real, historical, and fantasized. Perhaps the boundaries between them are porous. My concern, however, was the Europe that has historically haunted debates on modernity in India. This Europe was made in the image of a colonizing power and [...] the making of such a Europe was not an act of Europeans alone. This Europe was, in the sense in which Lévi-Strauss once used the word, a founding 'myth' for emancipatory thought and movements in India.[21]

The postcolonial challenge to liberal internationalism is indispensable. At the same time, a traditional postcolonial sensibility sometimes sees hierarchy in a way that ends up obscuring as much as it reveals.[22] My concerns here are twofold: firstly, postcolonial accounts often offer too narrow and innocent a reading of who has power; secondly, they propose an impossible ethical threshold, which only accepts a total rejection of 'the West' as its basis.

Firstly, postcolonial theorizing locates domination in a very particular place: in the relationship between the colonizer and the colonized, the Western and the non-Western, the Global North and the Global South.[23] In so doing, postcolonialism implicitly accepts a state-centric reading of power in today's world of nation states—it is, after all, nation states that are the carriers of old colonial injustices today. This is not always a productive instinct. The postcolonial diagnosis is keenly aware that the universalizing language of liberal internationalism is predicated on unspoken hierarchies of power and voice—but, in its keen attention to colonial hierarchies, it often neglects other forms of domination. What is lost in a postcolonial telling of membership and belonging are the complex ways in which hierarchies of nationality, race, class, gender, and—crucially for us—caste intersect to

---

[21] Chakrabarty, Provincializing Europe, xiv.

[22] For a broader critical reading of how postcolonial theory analyses hierarchies and structures, see Rosalind O'Hanlon and David Washbrook, 'After Orientalism: Culture, Criticism, and Politics in the Third World', Comparative Studies in Society and History 34, no. 1 (1992): 141–167.

[23] Important exceptions exist. For example, Spivak discusses the internal domination techniques of postcolonial elites in: Gayatri Chakravorty Spivak, 'Scattered Speculations on the Subaltern and the Popular', Postcolonial Studies 8, no. 4 (2005): 475–486.

produce international society. There is a wealth of social hierarchies and cultural expressions that structure the social fabric of international society that do not organize themselves into national or imperial wholes. As Sankaran Krishna observes, even if postcolonial work sometimes moves beyond the colonial dichotomy to questions of gender or class, hierarchies that usually escape the lived experience of Indian postcolonial scholars themselves are rarely discussed: 'Postcolonial studies, in its many variants, have remained perhaps excessively focused on the East–West encounter framed with a nationalist cartography, and inadequately sensitive to the encounter between, on the one hand, upper-caste elites, and, on the other, tribals and Dalits, within the Indian society itself.'[24] Thinking about hierarchy as intersectional expands and refines the definition of domination popularized by postcolonial thinking. It also forces us to be more critical of attempts at diversifying international society simply by including more 'non-Western' voices.

Secondly, the postcolonial ethic presupposes an impossible threshold that can only be met by expunging all things West from one's polity. There is a sense in much of postcolonial literature that the only ethical response to the hierarchies of colonial order is to revolt, reject, or unlearn in toto[25]—hence Partha Chatterjee's question: 'Can nationalist thought produce a discourse of order while daring to negate the very foundations of a system of knowledge that has conquered the world?'[26] The division of the world into a standard and its antithesis—West and non-West—valuably exposes a power imbalance. It points our attention towards the fact that the latter is expected to position itself in the world through a negative prefix, a declaration of what it is not, or of what it has failed to become—*not* the West. Yet this division also presupposes a hermetically sealed and uncontaminated Otherness, entirely separate and different from 'the West'. This only serves to reify essentialist, nativist demands for indigenous 'authenticity' that can be neatly separated from foreign influence.[27] It presumes that the West corrupts, while virtue is found in rejecting it. It places moral questions at the border between West and non-West, inviting us to reject the power-political predations of the former in favour of the emancipatory potential of the latter.

---

[24] Krishna, 'Colonial Legacies and Contemporary Destitution: Law, Race, and Human Security', 2.
[25] Dipesh Chakrabarty, 'Legacies of Bandung: Decolonisation and the Politics of Culture', *Economic and Political Weekly* 40, no. 46 (2005): 4812–4818.
[26] Partha Chatterjee, *Nationalist Thought and the Colonial World: A Derivative Discourse?* (London: Zed Books, 1986), 42.
[27] Pinar Bilgin, 'Thinking Past "Western" IR?', *Third World Quarterly* 29, no. 1 (2008): 7.

An absolutist project of negation reflects neither the realities nor the ambitions of how Indian diplomats have sought to navigate the space between colonial vestiges and postcolonial structures. Indian diplomats are, by profession, embedded in global orders directly implicated in colonial histories. They have also often found it necessary, convenient, or even desirable to signal fluency in the mores of this old world. As a way of reimagining international society, then, the postcolonial ethic of rejection leaves little room for ambivalence and subtle contradictions, which are the very stuff that Indian diplomacy is made of. Learning to live under a Western-dominated order has been a project involving loud rejections and forceful protest, yes—but it has also called forth a set of emotive coping mechanisms, strategies for reconciling mutually contradictory social codes, and assimilationist impulses that have allowed Indian diplomats to skilfully navigate a world of Western making.

Indian diplomacy cannot afford the strict binary, for it is constituted precisely by the ambivalence between West and non-West, insider and outsider. Speaking to notions of the Self that emerged under colonial rule, Ashis Nandy has emphasized that 'India is not non-West; it is India'[28]—it is not a mere 'counterplayer or antithesis' to the West, its entire identity constructed as a negation. This is not to deny that colonialism was fundamental to the way that the local elite came to see its place in the world. Indeed, Nandy locates the insistence on this binary precisely among the Indian elite exposed to the everyday operations of empire and among the contemporary 'heirs to this colonial memory'. It is, however, to push back on the notion that the ethic of the Self can be captured through a reactive binary alone: 'The imposed burden to be perfectly non-Western only constricts his [sic], the everyday Indian's, cultural Self, just as the older burden of being perfectly Western once narrowed—and still sometimes narrows—his choices in the matter of his and his society's future.' There is no pristine sense of uncontaminated Self to which any Indian ought to 'return'. The moral questions around mimicry and revolt are subtler than such a binary reading allows for.

The social codes of elite belonging

With its emphasis on the porosity of colonial binaries and its preoccupation with caste and other forms of hierarchy, this book will engage with postcolonial readings but often moves beyond their core epistemic commitments.

---

[28] Ashis Nandy, *The Intimate Enemy: Loss and Recovery of Self under Colonialism* (New Delhi: Oxford University Press, 1983), 73.

Neither liberal internationalist nor postcolonial scholarship offers an entirely satisfactory account of the social hierarchies of global order. What would it look like to get at our questions as a sociologist might, instead?

There is a social subtext to how anxieties about sameness and difference have animated much of the seemingly theoretical debate on difference, diversity, and decolonization. To ask our questions in a sociological register means, first, to query the meaning of these anxieties and to locate them in a broader structural framework. Both those celebrating and lamenting decolonization around the middle of the previous century assumed that the sheer diversity expressed in a newly postcolonial, pluralistic world would become a defining feature of international life. The British were alarmed enough to set up a committee—the British Committee, established in 1959—to analyse the chaos about to be unleashed upon the world by the creation of self-governing entities outside of Europe.[29] The understanding was that decolonization marked the end of the standard of civilization and posed a threat to the cultural cohesion that had underlain the European project of world-ordering, rendering the world ungovernable.[30] The rules of the club of civilized nations were threatened—the rules, in other words, of elite belonging.

What does it take to find a sense of belonging in international society? Barry Buzan has argued that, in the wake of decolonization, 'questions of membership in, and conditions of entry to, international society largely disappeared.'[31] This argument assumes that entry into international society is a one-off occurrence performed by a unitary state actor as its sovereignty is formally recognized by other members of the Westphalian club. By contrast, I argue that membership in international society is, in fact, a continuous and domestically contested performance of belonging. Seeking membership involves a recurring set of behaviours and dispositions aimed at finding recognition (membership in international society is about rehearsed social belonging). The navigation strategies employed by Indian diplomats to scale the hierarchies of international society are embodied and socially produced. Furthermore, these behaviours not only divide the world along national lines but also reveal which groups within a nation, a culture, or diplomatic service get to be recognized as legitimate insiders (membership in international society is tied to domestic hierarchies). Elite belonging becomes a domestically grounded but internationally attuned performance.

---

[29] See e.g. Dunne, *Inventing International Society*.
[30] Hedley Bull, *The Anarchical Society: A Study of Order in World Politics* (London: Macmillan, 1977), 31–32.
[31] Buzan, 'The "Standard of Civilization"', 585.

40 METHOD: POWER, PLURALISM, AND PRIVILEGE

The unequal and deeply social rules of performing one's belonging are encoded in the very nature of how we have come to think of the origins and nature of 'international society'. For all the language of universality, international society, as it came to be conceived in the nineteenth century, was more accurately understood as a 'European family of civilized nations'.[32] In the European imagination, 'civilization' never appeared in the plural, standing instead in singular opposition to the alleged savagery outside.[33] This civilizational understanding of order was underwritten by a standard of civilization that differentiated the supposedly superior European club of 'international' society, which could meet the cultural and political standards of belonging, from the colonies and other subordinate entities outside it which could not.[34] This standard legitimated the notion that the barbarian, backward societies outside Europe were, rightfully, colonies governed by Europe, having not satisfied its conditions for admission into the European club. International society was produced through an uneven encounter with non-European 'Others', not by 'expanding'—as the euphemistic language of the English School of IR would have it—like a world-historical bulldozer into a cultural vacuum.[35]

The colonial history of international society is also the history of class relations, spread across the globe and projected onto colonial dependencies from within Europe's social order. Classical diplomacy, shaped by traditions and precedents born in Renaissance Europe, was founded on an 'aristocratic etiquette for world ordering'.[36] Early European diplomatic elites were bound together by a certain cultural cohesion nurtured by the homogenous backgrounds of the 'aristocratic international', as princelings of noble families conducted much of European diplomacy amongst their own,[37] their 'shared aristocratic outlook' nurturing a collective culture of diplomacy.[38] The evolution of aristocratic manners in the eighteenth and nineteenth centuries divided European societies into civilized and barbarian constituencies along a class

---

[32] Hurrell, *On Global Order*, 41.

[33] William A. Callahan, 'Nationalising International Theory: Race, Class and the English School', *Global Society* 18, no. 4 (October 2004): 315.

[34] Buzan, 'The "Standard of Civilization"'.

[35] Barry Buzan and Richard Little, 'The Historical Expansion of International Society', in *Guide to the English School in International Studies*, ed. Daniel M. Green and Cornelia Navari (New Jersey: John Wiley & Sons, 2013), 59–74; Callahan, 'Nationalising International Theory'; Gong, 'Standards of Civilization Today'; Keene, *Beyond the Anarchical Society: Grotius, Colonialism and Order in World Politics*; Nicolaidis et al., 'From Metropolis to Microcosmos'.

[36] Callahan, 'Nationalising International Theory', 305.

[37] Christer Jönsson and Martin Hall, *Essence of Diplomacy* (Basingstoke: Palgrave Macmillan, 2005), 131.

[38] Adam Watson, *The Evolution of International Society: A Comparative Historical Analysis* (London: Routledge, 1992), 250.

hierarchy, and colonial conquest used the measures of aristocratic etiquette to divide the world between civilized European insiders and non-European barbarian Others. Crucially, the aristocratic air of classical European diplomacy would go on to survive the gradual replacement of aristocrats with career professionals, as new entrants into the diplomatic world became 'aristocratic by absorption.'[39]

This class-connoted European exercise of world-ordering gave birth to what we now often think of, simply, as universal expectations in diplomacy. This is not to make the ontological claim that only Europe is a historical site in which diplomatic custom emerged—if anything, European diplomatic tradition itself was formed through close encounters with Ottoman and Chinese diplomatic practice in particular.[40] Even the hereditary elitism of European diplomacy was predated by about a millennium by the Indian diplomatic dictum, captured in Kautilya's seminal work on Indian statecraft, the *Arthashastra*, that envoys should be 'born of high family.'[41] Diplomacy has multiple roots. The claim here, rather, concerns the ways in which diplomatic history has come to be understood across the world. It is to observe the absolute centrality that European diplomatic history has claimed for itself, and the way this centrality would later come to shape how even non-European diplomatic communities understood their craft as rooted in European tradition. In former colonies, of course, this reference takes on deep political importance, with the former barbarians of Eurocentric narratives essentially internalizing Europe's understanding of its standard of civilization.

Cultural uniformity was foundational to the myths of international society. Not unlike the civilizational thinking of the nineteenth century, classical English School writing, emanating from an inescapably European angle in the wake of decolonization, believed that the existence of an international society had been made possible by the existence of a common culture.[42] This culture could be predicated on vast value systems—Christianity, Europe, Western civilization—or it could be understood to rely on a shared transnational culture nurtured by a specialized class of homogenous diplomatic elites.[43] This

---

[39] Robert J. Moore, *Third World Diplomats in Dialogue with the First World: The New Diplomacy* (London: Macmillan, 1985), 16; In fact, European diplomats would even frequently be bequeathed titles of nobility upon reaching a certain bureaucratic rank. See Iver B. Neumann, 'The Body of the Diplomat', *European Journal of International Relations* 14, no. 4 (2008): 671–695.

[40] Iver B. Neumann, 'A Claimed Originary Site: Europe', in *Diplomatic Sites: A Critical Enqiry* (Oxford: Oxford University Press, 2013).

[41] Kautilya, *The Arthashastra* (New Delhi: Penguin Classics India, 2000), 98.

[42] Martin Wight, *Systems of States* (Leicester: Leicester University Press, 1977), 46.

definition ruled out any possibility of, say, an 'Indian civilization' on par with a European equal: to join international society was to join civilization, and to join civilization was to imbibe a European system of symbols, etiquette, and manners.[44] This was an international society whose defining cultural features were premised on the exclusion of most of the world. The question of elite membership sustains the rules of belonging: who is seen as part of international society, who as a barbarian outside its civilizational gates, and what does it take, culturally and socially, to gain entry?

Against a long history of colonial conquest and class cohesion, decolonization could have marked a revolutionary moment of hierarchical reordering. It could have delivered a democratization of international society. And yet, what is striking is not the anticipated triumph of the new but the unanticipated persistence of the old. The expectation of a large shift in attitudes, manners, cultural presentation, and ideals significantly underestimated the stickiness of internalized international social orders and the cultural grammar that expresses them. Decolonization was supposed to transform the basic tenets of international society, but social orders are slow to adjust and even harder, it seems, to unlearn.

Therefore, understanding how diversity and difference can be expressed in international society requires a move away from interpreting formal rules of entry, in favour of a focus on implicit social rules of elite belonging. For pluralism is not only about official governing principles like self-determination or normative principles like formal equality. The lived reproductions of international society are performed by diplomats who embody and reveal its everyday hypocrisies and disciplining effects. This, in many ways, is the story of Indian diplomats, expected to imbibe an elite cosmopolitan aesthetic which, far from reflecting a pluralistic international society, takes its cues from colonial imagery, aristocratic European diplomacy, and the class-consciousness of a once-white governing elite. It is precisely the cultural grammar of supposedly pluralistic international society that has in fact regulated and censored the self-expression of Indian diplomats and the kind of Indian difference they feel capable of representing. To better grasp the social mechanisms by which membership and belonging play themselves out in this order, we must move beyond the standard lexicon of IR. We must look at the quotidian practices which sociologists have long made it their vocation to understand.

---

[43] Hurrell, *On Global Order*, 40.
[44] Norbert Elias, *The Civilizing Process (Vol. 1: The History of Manners)* (Oxford: Basil Blackwell, 1978).

A sociology of silences

A lexicon of distinction and domination

An accidental Bourdieusian, the famous Indian Ambassador K.M. Panikkar once acknowledged in 1960 that '[i]n India, more than in most countries, national culture had been the monopoly of the higher classes'.[45] Indian diplomacy has reflected a similar monopoly, as upper-class, upper-caste Anglophone elites have shaped how India engages with the world. Diplomatic power, then, is the power of outward representation over domestically competing but equally legitimate representational claims about what culture is and who has it. In India, this power has been exercised by an Anglophile elite restricted in its domestic reach but invested in a deep engagement with foreign audiences. Culture and power are not two different modes of argument; they are inseparable.

The sensibilities of Pierre Bourdieu, the French sociologist renowned for his interrogation of the social nature of elites, allow us to think about power, culture, and identity in tandem. Against a runaway poststructuralism invested in the possibilities of deconstruction, Bourdieu believed that practices and ideals are tied to social position, while also being acts of social positioning themselves.[46] Social orders and cultural conventions are maintained neither through constant physical coercion nor by ideological fiat; they are sustained through the subtle perpetuation of certain practices, the valorization of certain tastes and worldviews over others, and the quiet assimilation of society into structures that reflect the preferences, perceptions, and priorities of dominant groups.

Culture matters—but it matters within unequal societies shaped by those with the resources to define it. Symbolic struggles over the legitimate definition of culture are a dimension of the broader struggles for dominance.[47] Dominant groups shape the very categories in which a society comes to speak of itself. This is not token authority over semantics: it is a 'worldmaking power', allowing some actors to set the 'legitimate vision of the social world and of its divisions'.[48] Such seemingly commonsensical moves legitimate forms of differentiation, notably between 'the groups which produce the principles and the

---

[45] K. M. Panikkar, *Common Sense about India* (London: Macmillan, New York, 1960), 162.
[46] Pierre Bourdieu, *Distinction: A Social Critique of the Judgement of Taste (1984)*, trans. Richard Nice (London: Routledge, 2010).
[47] Bourdieu, 86.
[48] Pierre Bourdieu, 'What Makes a Social Class? On the Theoretical and Practical Existence of Groups', *Berkeley Journal of Sociology* 32, no. 1 (1987): 13.

groups against which they are produced'.[49] As such, even abstract definitions have social consequences, as the conversations about 'merit' or 'social graces' inside the Indian Foreign Service will show.

The right to produce concepts is deeply political since the bearer of this right holds power over how meaning is accorded in the social world. How meaning is accorded, in turn, becomes the basis on which different groups are represented within a culture, and on which these groups are mobilized and demobilized.[50] Identities and power must always be considered together, too. Identities express positionality, and as such, taking them seriously requires taking seriously the social conditions that produce one's position in society. A fundamental prerogative of dominant classes is their power to articulate their own identity, while a group lower down a hierarchy is 'forced to shape its own subjectivity from its objectification' by the more dominant.[51] An analysis of unequal power structures does not preclude an analysis of culture and identity—it necessitates one.

This is also why the end of coercive colonialism did not spell the end of a social standard of civilization: in the absence of formal imposition, implicit social codes of belonging have continued to structure social life. By extension, a sociological reading of belonging under liberal order begins with the recognition that an order need not be equal simply because it is has no formal rules of exclusion—nor neutral simply because its dominant actors fail to interrogate their own positionality. Indeed, it is the very normalization of certain rules as universal that has allowed the cosmopolitan elites to obfuscate the specificities of their own identity, while seeing deviations from the liberal script as aberrations rooted in the exotic identities of its detractors.

What does a Bourdieu-inspired lexicon consist of? In the conversations I conducted for this book, diplomats repeatedly emphasized the importance of 'having a kind of manner' or 'quality', an unspecified air that surrounded the best diplomats but could not be captured in a laundry list of characteristics[52]—in other words, a certain kind of *habitus*. Habitus is the largely preconscious embodiment of dispositions that make up the individual. These dispositions—tastes, thoughts, bodily postures, and ways of being—are socially produced, being 'the result of the internalization of external structures'.[53] Habitus 'is

---

[49] Bourdieu, *Distinction*, 481.

[50] Bourdieu, 481.

[51] Pierre Bourdieu, *The Bachelors' Ball: The Crisis of Peasant Society in Béarn* (Chicago: University of Chicago Press, 2008), 198.

[52] Interview 9, March 2019; Interview 39, April 2019.

[53] Pierre Bourdieu and Loïc Wacquant, *An Invitation to Reflexive Sociology* (Chicago: University of Chicago Press, 1992), 18.

not something natural, inborn: being a product of history, that is of social experience and education, it may be changed by history, that is by new experiences, education or training (which implies that aspects of what remains unconscious in habitus be made at least partially conscious and explicit).[54] Bourdieu once explained habitus as the sum of 'the mental structures through which [individuals] apprehend the social world'.[55] But habitus—as 'the social made body'—also has a corporeal dimension, expressing itself in the way the body is carried and presented.[56] It approximates what old-guard diplomats repeatedly referred to as proper ways of 'carrying oneself'. In the world of diplomacy, where representation is at the core of the enterprise, the diplomat is both a symbol and a living embodiment of the ideals of the nation. In the words of IFS founder K.P.S. Menon paying homage to Dr Sarvepalli Radhakrishnan's record as Indian Ambassador in Moscow in 1949–1952: 'what counts more in a diplomat is not what he does but what he is'.[57]

A dominant habitus signals belonging in a social order's elite. It serves an exclusionary purpose, denoting that which does and does not belong. It 'marks, produces, and organizes a distinction between those whose tastes are regarded as "noble" because they have been organized and legitimated by the education system, and those whose tastes, lacking such markers of nobility, are accorded a more lowly status'.[58] Dispositions must be denaturalized in this analysis: what we think are personal preferences, worldviews, or mere 'matters of taste' are inculcated through social position. It is telling that Bourdieu was conceptually indebted to Norbert Elias'[59] psychological thinking on the 'civilizing process', which Elias saw as a historical evolution of the manners that distinguished a 'civilized' person at a given moment in history[60]—a colonial assumption which sometimes appears in the thinking of Indian diplomats, too. Habitus marks the boundaries of legitimate culture and 'correct' aesthetics, opinions, and tastes. There is nothing trivial about diplomacy's 'petty rituals and ceremonies of power'[61]—they become objects of study in themselves.

---

[54] Pierre Bourdieu, 'Habitus', in *Habitus: A Sense of Place*, ed. Jean Hillier and Emma Rooksby (Aldershot: Ashgate, 2002), 29.

[55] Pierre Bourdieu, 'Social Space and Symbolic Power', *Sociological Theory* 7, no. 1 (1989): 18.

[56] Bourdieu and Wacquant, *Invitation*, 127.

[57] K.P.S. Menon, 'Our President as Diplomat (an Undated Newspaper Article)', n.d., 'Writings by him', S. No. 43, K.P.S. Menon papers, NMML.

[58] Tony Bennett, 'Introduction to the Routledge Classics Edition', in *Distinction: A Social Critique of the Judgement of Taste*, ed. Pierre Bourdieu (Routledge, 2010), xix–xx.

[59] Elias, *The Civilizing Process*; Norbert Elias, *The Germans: Power Struggles and the Development of Habitus in the Nineteenth and Twentieth Centuries* (Cambridge: Polity, 1996).

[60] Deborah Reed-Danahay, *Locating Bourdieu* (Bloomington: Indiana University Press, 2005), 104.

[61] James Der Derian, *On Diplomacy: A Genealogy of Western Estrangement* (Oxford: Basil Blackwell, 1987), 114.

46   METHOD: POWER, PLURALISM, AND PRIVILEGE

Successfully performing the desired habitus requires *capital*—societal resources, or sociological currencies, so to speak, which can be mobilized to gain and maintain one's place in a hierarchy.[62] *Cultural capital* is about intangible assets like skills, manners, knowledge, competences, and style.[63] It expresses itself in a familiarity with spheres of dominant culture and thus also in a certain cultural confidence. Those with high cultural capital, abiding by habits and customs of the upper strata in society, have the resources to symbolically dominate a broader culture. We can think of those with cultural capital as having mastered the rules of the game—indeed, of having in many ways invented and then monopolized them. Holders of cultural capital are most accustomed to expressing themselves in society's dominant idiom. They have grown up feeling entitled to take up space in social settings. Cultural capital is institutionalized through education, held in the form of credentials and certificates, but also through the dispositions that the educational environment imparts. The stamp of elite schooling, for example, endows its holder not only with a degree certificate but also with the embodied cultural capital that comes with personifying a certain 'type'—behaving, looking, and talking like someone who attended an elite institution.

Different forms of capital are often mutually reinforcing, and so cultural capital allows its holder to acquire *social capital*. Bourdieu defined the term as 'the sum of the resources, actual or virtual, that accrue to an individual or a group by virtue of possessing a durable network of more or less institutionalized relationships of mutual acquaintance and recognition'.[64] Think of classic Old Boys' Clubs that bind generations of privately educated men together as they monopolize the upper echelons of politics, bureaucracy, or business— or, in the case of Indian diplomats, the networks that elite schools like Delhi University's iconic St Stephen's College weave into being.

Finally, a *field* is a hierarchically ordered, relatively autonomous space in which a set of actors operate and struggle for power.[65] Each field is defined by the kind of habitus and capital that are considered desirable within it.[66] Across different spheres of their lives, actors occupy a variety of fields, all of which reflect different kinds of power relations. A field's implicit rules may

---

[62] Pierre Bourdieu, 'The Forms of Capital (1986)', in *Cultural Theory: An Anthology*, ed. Imre Szeman and Timothy Kaposy (Oxford: Wiley-Blackwell, 2010), 82.

[63] Bourdieu, 82–84.

[64] Bourdieu and Wacquant, *Invitation*, 119.

[65] Nikko Kauppi, 'Transnational Social Fields', in *The Oxford Handbook of Pierre Bourdieu*, ed. Thomas Medvetz and Jeffrey J. Sallaz (Oxford: Oxford University Press, 2018), 186.

[66] Antonin Cohen, 'Pierre Bourdieu and International Relations', in *The Oxford Handbook of Pierre Bourdieu*, ed. Thomas Medvetz and Jeffrey J. Sallaz (New York: Oxford University Press, 2018), 202–204.

escape outsiders—'within a field, people fight to the death over things that are imperceptible to those who find themselves in the next room', as Bourdieu dramatically described.[67] This leaves plenty of room for interpretation—as Peter Jackson wryly notes, Bourdieu is rarely caught explaining the concept exactly the same way twice.[68] A 'locus of struggle' for position,[69] fields are settled to varying degrees, depending on the level of consensus around the appropriate kinds of habitus and capital.[70] Those who do not embody the dominant habitus may cultivate a 'resignation to the inevitable' and in so doing will end up underwriting structures that disadvantage them.[71] Alternatively, they might seek to join the dominant group by acquiring the expected habitus. They can also rebel: should the dominated seek to join the dominant group without striving after the dominant markers of distinction, they have put into play the very principles by which the field operates.[72] In fact, most fields, at some point, become battlegrounds for struggles 'between the heirs and the pretenders'[73]—struggles that abound in the chapters to come, too.

The diplomatic cleft habitus in India

After Independence in 1947, a tortured duality of two imageries of international society confronted Indian diplomats. One was an inherited conception of a caricature-like notion of a white, European-dominated society akin a homogenous club, born out of colonial hierarchies. The other was a vision of a radically different postcolonial international society envisioned as its negation, founded on diversity, difference, and the symbolic representation of the subaltern. Independence did not mark the departure of the old world and the arrival of a new one. Instead of a transition, we find the coexistence of two seemingly paradoxical worlds: the colonial as well as the postcolonial. As the cultural theorist Stuart Hall writes, 'what we are dealing with is not two successive regimes but the simultaneous presence of a *regime and its*

[67] Pierre Bourdieu, *On the State: Lectures at the Collège de France, 1989–1992*, trans. David Fernbach (Cambridge: Polity Press, 2014), 318.

[68] Peter Jackson, 'Pierre Bourdieu, the "Cultural Turn" and the Practice of International History', *Review of International Studies* 34, no. 1 (2008): 167.

[69] Pierre Bourdieu, 'The Specificity of the Scientific Field and the Social Conditions of the Progress of Reason', *Information (International Social Science Council)* 14, no. 6 (1975): 19–20.

[70] George Steinmetz, 'Bourdieusian Field Theory and the Reorientation of Historical Sociology', in *The Oxford Handbook of Pierre Bourdieu*, ed. Thomas Medvetz and Jeffrey J. Sallaz (New York: Oxford University Press, 2018), 611.

[71] Bourdieu, *Distinction*, 373.

[72] Steinmetz, 'Bourdieusian Field Theory', 612.

[73] Bourdieu quoted in Didier Bigo, 'Pierre Bourdieu and International Relations: Power of Practices, Practices of Power', *International Political Sociology* 5, no. 3 (September 2011): 240.

after-effects.[74] Insofar as postcolonialism is supposed to signify 'the way one configuration of power, institutions and discourses, which once defined the social field, has been replaced by another', there is nothing conclusively *post* about the colonialism that structures the social codes of international society. For 'colonialism persists, despite the cluster of illusory appearances to the contrary'.[75]

Indian diplomats' complex reading of their own place in these two different visions of international society animates how they behave, argue, carry themselves, and conceive of their work as diplomats. The tension between the two imageries—which we might loosely think of as *fields*—has informed diplomatic recruitment, training, and institutional culture in South Block since Independence.[76]

Consequently, what emerged post-Independence was also a very particular kind of dominant habitus among Indian diplomats: a *cleft habitus*, perched between old, elitist 'worldliness' on the one hand and postcolonial 'authenticity' on the other. The Indian diplomat, in the words of one former Grade I Secretary was 'a bundle of contradictions'.[77] The ideal Indian diplomat was capable of meeting classical expectations of an eloquent, Oxbridge-educated, well-read imperial gentleman, while also credibly embodying Third World subalternity and Indian difference. Torn dualities are a recurring theme in Bourdieu's thinking. As somebody of 'low social origin' planted into the highbrow world of French boarding schools and academia, Bourdieu conceptualized his own social awkwardness into the cleft habitus—'inhabited by tensions and contradictions'.[78] The theme of tensions and contradictions was also prevalent in how Bourdieu spoke of local elites in colonized countries, whom he saw as occupying an 'ambiguous location between two social conditions':[79] moulded by colonialism's unequal power relations, caught between 'two mutually alienating universes' of colonizer and colonized,[80] and compelled to anxious attempts at continually reconciling this 'duality of social regulations'.[81]

---

[74] Stuart Hall, *Familiar Stranger: A Life between Two Islands* (London: Penguin Books, 2017), 24.

[75] Hall, 24.

[76] I sometimes refer to the Foreign Service by this colloquial metonym, which alludes to the original and main building in which the MEA and the diplomats of the IFS work in Central Delhi.

[77] Interview 33, April 2019.

[78] Pierre Bourdieu, *Sketch for a Self-Analysis*, trans. Richard Nice (Cambridge: Polity, 2007), 100.

[79] Bourdieu, 56–57.

[80] Pierre Bourdieu and Abdelmalek Sayad, 'Colonial Rule and Cultural Sabir', *Ethnography* 5, no. 4 (2004): 164.

[81] Bourdieu's French expression translated in Julian Go, 'Decolonizing Bourdieu: Colonial and Postcolonial Theory in Pierre Bourdieu's Early Work', *Sociological Theory* 31, no. 1 (March 2013): 59.

My thinking on the Indian diplomatic cleft habitus is conceptually indebted—but not particularly faithful—to Bourdieu's original conceptualization. The cleft habitus of the Indian diplomat contains a world of embodied tensions: between ideals of colonial homogeneity and postcolonial diversity, desires for conformity and for protest, class-connoted conceptions of elite cosmopolitan culture and subaltern Third World solidarity. It expresses two very different impulses in the construction of a postcolonial Indian diplomatic programme in a formally pluralistic but deeply Western-dominated world.

On the one hand, rethinking and democratizing diplomatic representation was paramount for a young postcolonial nation: a representative body of diplomats was to be a reflection of the ideational commitments that came with an embrace of postcolonial and emancipatory ideals, freed of the exclusionary bureaucratic elitism that had characterized the British Raj.[82] And yet, on the other hand, there is a persistent imagery of European international society which appears in the self-narrations of Indian diplomats across generations. This imagery is, at its root, a colonial legacy sustained by Indian attempts at imbibing the old-fashioned manners and ideals of a deeply racialized international society once 'defined by elite white men'.[83] Bourdieu's claim that matters of taste and demeanour are fundamental to the constitution of a dominant habitus is borne out most clearly in this classical, colonial imagery of international society, which emphasized etiquette, eloquence, protocol, sound judgement, and questions of tact and comportment.[84] It was a field in the most explicit of Bourdieusian terms: 'a small society with its own rules of conduct, its own courtesies and what is more, its own prejudices and exclusions'.[85] In this club, the 'aristocratic tradition brings to the cult of power—to be found in every nation state—the discipline of good taste'.[86] This international society, in other words, was 'society according to Jane Austen rather than according to Max Weber'.[87]

The ensuing cleft habitus, containing within it the social codes for two very different kinds of worlds, has been most successfully performed by the 'St Stephen's type' which dominates the Foreign Service's cultural hierarchy. This cohort, made up of left-leaning liberal arts graduates of the prestigious St Stephen's College of Delhi University, has traditionally managed to perform

---

[82] Interview 1, February 2019; Interview 19, April 2019; Interview 48, May 2019; Interview 49, May 2019.

[83] Callahan, 'Nationalising International Theory', 318.

[84] Neumann, 'The Body of the Diplomat', 674; Jackson, 'Pierre Bourdieu, the "Cultural Turn" and the Practice of International History', 169.

[85] S.L. Roy, *Diplomacy* (New Delhi: Sterling, 1984), 142.

[86] Moore, *Third World Diplomats*, 17.

[87] Callahan, 'Nationalising International Theory', 318.

the classical markers of Anglophone elitism, while also espousing Nehruvian, Third Worldist worldviews. Its existence has been made possible by a coming together of various hierarchies of class, caste, gender, and education, since the products of this elite School are usually also products of upper-class families, English schooling, and mostly upper-caste spaces. Their capital is convertible: graduates depart St Stephen's not only with an official qualification but the air of somebody who has attended the College (cultural capital) and the connections that come with it (social capital).

This habitus regulates the everyday performance of Indian diplomacy. It empowers and disempowers diplomats based on their ability to imbibe it. At home, the felt imperatives imposed by it underpin debates about diplomatic recruitment and cadre management, guide the pedagogies of diplomatic training and the socialization of diplomats, and underlie the thinking on what kind of diplomats India values and elevates into the highest positions. Out in the world, the habitus has borne its imprint on how Indian diplomats have sought to navigate global order, whose struggles they have chosen to champion, how they have thought of big categories like hierarchy or status, and in which ways they have seen themselves as either marginalized or buoyed in the cosmopolitan club of diplomats.

It is worth pointing out that all diplomats straddle competing demands, trying to find a balance between assimilating into a global culture and differentiating themselves as representatives of a particular nation with its own mores. What is intriguing about the Indian Foreign Service is not this rather conventional tension between 'home and the world', as Tagore's 1916 classic novel would have it,[88] whereby the ideals of home and the world are in tension but seem to have some stable meaning. Rather, for Indian diplomacy, the radical ambivalence is about what this global culture itself looks like. It is at this international level, between 'two worlds'—the colonially tainted and the postcolonially conceived—that the crucial cleft is perched. There is no clear, singular reading of the world that Indian diplomats live by; rather, they travel between two often contradictory imageries of international society. It is here that so much of the tension in Indian world-making is located. The connection between *homes* and *worlds,* each in the plural, comes about as these two very different readings of the world are reflected in two very different interpretations of how domestic life itself should be ordered—either to match the socioculturally exclusive and Westernized script of global order or to express at home the diversity and equality that a postcolonial world expresses.

---

[88] Rabindranath Tagore, *Home and the World* (Penguin Books India, 2005).

The continued force of the cleft habitus—which, as I will argue, animates Indian diplomats to this day—is a product of both subconscious embodiment and social hierarchy. Ostensibly old structures of domination persist in the face of political change precisely by expressing themselves through the habitus, which is the product of long, structurally embedded and embodied processes of socialization, and as such often beyond the reach of the 'weapon of consciousness'.[89] Therefore, the continued duality through which Indian officers perceive ideals of representation is a reflection of the stickiness of old structures and the often subconsciously carried colonial legacies which have culturally survived the formal end of empire. Yet the Indian Foreign Service must also be seen as a scene of social struggle. Thus, the reproduction of cleft habitus is also the product of social investment on the part of dominant officers, who can harness their familiarity with classical expressions of European elite diplomacy to secure their own social position. Those who match certain elite markers associated with the Indian upper-classes, higher castes, and Anglophile liberal arts graduates can leverage their own compatibility with 'worldly' elite markers of distinction against those who do not. What emerges is a dual social disposition—perhaps even a paradoxical one. It reflects both a postcolonial ethic of egalitarianism and a self-serving investment in the representational ideals of aristocratic European international society.

Unfaithful readings

This book thinks with, beyond, and against Bourdieu, offering an unfaithful reading of his sociology as well as the ways in which it has previously travelled into IR. The language of habitus and capital, so readily familiar even outside of sociology, has an intuitive quality to it that makes the study of elites feel almost instinctive. At the same time, this is not a 'Bourdieusian' book in any deeply doctrinaire sense. It borrows lightly from Bourdieu to think through thoughts that Bourdieu himself never had. In fact, the very notion of a chronically complex Self—a perpetual cleft habitus—would have sat uneasily with a sociologist for whom the cleft habitus was a perversion of sorts. Bourdieu's theorization only allowed for the hybridities of a cleft as a condition of transition from one uniform habitus to another. It was always the painful product of a transition incomplete, revealing an individual yet to make an adjustment into a new order. The coming chapters take the cleft to represent a tension, too,

---

[89] Pierre Bourdieu, *Masculine Domination* (Cambridge: Polity, 2001), 39.

52 METHOD: POWER, PLURALISM, AND PRIVILEGE

but acknowledge more hybridity, instabilities, and complexity in how notions of the Self are sustained than Bourdieu, ever the structuralist, might have. Hybridity is assumed, not pathologized.

Indeed, there is no *solution* to the diplomatic cleft habitus, unlike Bourdieu's transitory understanding of the term implies. Rather, what we find is the cleft's *institutionalization* into structures and processes of the Indian Foreign Service. Instead of being ironed out or fixed, the cleft habitus becomes normalized, internalized, customary. The ambivalence is never solved; it is managed. How this management unfolds is a productive way of analysing change in identities and dispositions in Indian diplomacy over time.

My reading of hierarchy also departs from Bourdieu's rather singular focus. Reflecting on the wider analytical relevance of his seminal *Distinction: A Social Critique of the Judgement of Taste*, Bourdieu conceded that much of his original argument pertained specifically to the socio-cultural currents of 1960s France.[90] Primarily preoccupied with class, Bourdieu's treatment of racial and colonial hierarchies as well as gendered difference has been scrutinized for its essentialist argumentation which often failed his own demand that scholars practise 'epistemological vigilance' about their own subject position—unlike with class, Bourdieu sometimes slides into uncritically assuming, instead of critically deconstructing, the social primacy of whiteness and maleness, for example.[91] Yet it is certainly possible to move beyond class relations in France using the Bourdieusian lexicon, as the meticulous ethnography of caste in Indian engineering education by the anthropologist Ajantha Subramanian so richly illustrates.[92] Similarly, for sociologist Surinder S. Jodhka, fluency in English is an Indian example of cultural capital 'acquired through one's caste and class habitus',[93] while Arpita Chakraborty is developing a feminist Dalit standpoint theory using Bourdieu's theorizing of symbolic violence.[94] What is required is, once again, an expansion of the conceptual remit of hierarchy.

---

[90] Bennett, 'Introduction', xxi.

[91] See e.g. Beate Krais, 'Gender, Sociological Theory and Bourdieu's Sociology of Practice', *Theory, Culture & Society* 23, no. 6 (November 2006): 119–134; Edward Said, 'Representing the Colonized: Anthropology's Interlocutors', *Critical Inquiry* 15, no. 2 (1989): 205–225; Kerry Woodward, *The Relevance of Bourdieu's Concepts for Studying the Intersections of Poverty, Race, and Culture*, ed. Thomas Medvetz and Jeffrey J. Sallaz, vol. 1 (Oxford: Oxford University Press, 2018); Tara J. Yosso, 'Whose Culture Has Capital? A Critical Race Theory Discussion of Community Cultural Wealth', *Race, Ethnicity and Education* 8, no. 1 (March 2005): 69–91.

[92] Ajantha Subramanian, *The Caste of Merit: Engineering Education in India* (Cambridge, Mass.: Harvard University Press, 2019).

[93] Surinder S. Jodhka, 'Ascriptive Hierarchies: Caste and Its Reproduction in Contemporary India', *Current Sociology* 64, no. 2 (2015): 9.

[94] Arpita Chakraborty, '"Symbolic Violence" and Dalit Feminism: Possibilities Emerging from a Dalit Feminist Standpoint Reading of Bourdieu', *International Feminist Journal of Politics*, 21 October 2021, 1–19.

I also depart in some of my analytical emphasis from the kind of work that IR scholars have previously produced by engaging with Bourdieu. Pioneering interdisciplinary thinking has been advanced by scholars such as Rebecca Adler-Nissen,[95] Didier Bigo,[96] Iver Neumann,[97] and Vincent Pouliot,[98] with a wide-ranging oeuvre covering NATO-Russia relations, individual Foreign Ministries, diplomacy as a 'meta-field', international practices, and European integration. My own approach departs from the general tenor of this work in three ways: it is not pitched at the level of the nation state, it develops an anti-technocratic bend, and it sets its sights on actors that the largely Eurocentric study of Bourdieusian IR has previously neglected. Firstly, a discipline that is primed to prioritize the national has instinctively gravitated towards scholarly interpretations of *national* habitus. In Vincent Pouliot's Bourdieusian reading of NATO-Russian diplomacy, the 'Russian habitus' is something which captures how 'diplomats and state representatives come to embody the state in practice', and the analysis rests on the premise that 'there typically exists a body of dispositions that similarly characterizes members due to their shared history'.[99] With its state-centred focus, this depiction assumes that the diplomatic representatives of a country are shaped primarily by common national institutions, histories, and experiences. It postulates a broadly unitary diplomatic essence, uncontested and equally performed by each member of the diplomatic corps.

By contrast, my reading of Indian diplomats emphasizes the unarticulated internal hierarchies inherent in any 'national habitus'. For me, Indian diplomacy is not a natural derivative of Indian national culture at large. In fact, any attempt at framing the conversation in such terms risks reproducing nationalistic, even nativist, tropes about Indian authenticity.[100] The limits of a national reading of habitus lie not only in promoting cultural stereotypes but in uncritically allowing certain actors to speak for the nation. Indian diplomats are positioned at the intersection of internal and international hierarchies, even

---

[95] Rebecca Adler-Nissen, 'The Diplomacy of Opting Out: A Bourdieusian Approach to National Integration Strategies', *Journal of Common Market Studies* 46, no. 3 (2008): 663–684; Rebecca Adler-Nissen, 'On a Field Trip with Bourdieu', *International Political Sociology* 5, no. 3 (2011): 327–330.

[96] Didier Bigo, 'Pierre Bourdieu and International Relations: Power of Practices, Practices of Power', *International Political Sociology* 5, no. 3 (September 2011): 225–58; Didier Bigo, 'The Globalization of in(Security)', *Cultures Conflits* 58, no. 2 (2005): 3–3.

[97] Neumann, 'The Body of the Diplomat'; Neumann, *At Home with the Diplomats*.

[98] Vincent Pouliot, *International Security in Practice: The Politics of NATO-Russia Diplomacy* (Cambridge: Cambridge University Press, 2010); Vincent Pouliot and Jérémie Cornut, 'Practice Theory and the Study of Diplomacy: A Research Agenda', *Cooperation and Conflict* 50, no. 3 (2015): 297–315.

[99] Pouliot, *International Security in Practice*, 87–88.

[100] N. C. Behera, 'Re-Imagining IR in India', *International Relations of the Asia-Pacific* 7, no. 3 (21 May 2007): 359.

if the various distinctions of class, caste, gender, or race are often invisible to dominant actors and those who study the world through them. I find a kindred spirit of sorts in Iver Neumann, who has analysed the classed and gendered scripts of the Norwegian Foreign Ministry[101]—even if his deep participatory ethnographies, involving years immersed in the daily lives of Norwegian diplomats as a fellow officer, are not something that my outsider status or mixed success in landing Indian research visas would ever have allowed for.

In India, it is not only that the famous 'IFS type'—'elite, English-speaking, Anglicised and urbane'[102]—fails to meaningfully represent a 'national habitus'. It also does not speak for all of the Foreign Service—it merely culturally dominates it. The Service is home to Indians from very different walks of life. Yet it is predominantly the 'IFS type' who chronicle their own existence in memoirs, find international recognition, and establish themselves as household names in public debate and interviews with academics. How a culture is conceived and presented is a question of who within it is seen as embodying the correct habitus. In fact, insofar as habitus is a mechanism of exclusion, the way that the internal elite of the Indian Foreign Service carries itself happens precisely in opposition to some of the 'lesser' diplomats of the Service—against less distinguished fellow Indians. Our understanding of the diplomatic habitus, then, depends on who within the diplomatic corps is given a voice.

What is more, the dominant group of liberal upper-caste diplomats interviewed for this book repeatedly distinguished the India they hoped to embody from the Indian nation as they actually saw it, elevated above its rough edges and supposedly more regressive social attitudes. The connection between nation and its representation is never obvious and always socially produced. A 'national habitus' can never be given or fixed, only approximated through purposeful socialization: as Chapter 5 discusses, one prevalent critique of India's diplomatic elites has been that the upper echelons of the Foreign Service have, if anything, been insufficiently 'Indian', and therefore in need of being inducted into proper Indianness during diplomatic training.

Secondly, I adopt a distinctly anti-technocratic perspective on Bourdieu. As Médéric Martin-Máze has observed, what sometimes gets lost in translation from Bourdieu into IR is a quintessentially Bourdieusian sense of struggle: an analysis not of polite disputes between diplomatic equals or policy disagreements among professionals, but of the symbolic violence that underpins social

---

[101] Neumann, *At Home with the Diplomats*.
[102] Sullivan 'Exceptionalism in Indian Diplomacy', 646.

relations.[103] There are, of course, notable exceptions—Matthew Eagleton-Pierce's *Symbolic Power in the World Trade Organization,* for example, dissects the quiet diplomatic dominance of the Industrial North at the expense of poorer Southern nations in a formally equal organization.[104] Yet in much of Bourdieusian IR, there is a certain expectation of equality and unity of purpose between actors, perhaps owing to the elite technocratic nature of the groups being studied. This technocratic tendency crowds out Bourdieu's preoccupation with the ubiquitous reproduction of hierarchies, obfuscating the themes of struggle and inequality that defined so much of Bourdieu's original sensibility.

Mine is not a postcolonial Indian rendition of the British 'official mind'— 'largely free from undue external influence and guided by its own memories, traditions and values'[105]—that ran the imperial operation from Whitehall.[106] This is also why I do not treat the Indian diplomatic corps as an 'epistemic community' tied together by shared expert knowledge[107] or as a 'community of practice' developing a shared repertoire of explicit competences.[108] I seek to do the very opposite of drawing the diplomatic elite as an entity with hermetically sealed technocratic or national traditions: I recognize Indian diplomats as actors with complex positions in various hierarchies of empire, class, gender, religion, and caste that cut across Indian and international society alike.

Thirdly, Bourdieusian IR has occupied itself principally with research subjects in the West. This book marks the first time that Indian diplomacy—or South Asian diplomacy more broadly—is analysed through a Bourdieusian lens. Together with Deepak Nair's masterly examination of ASEAN diplomacy and practices of face-saving, it is one of the very few Bourdieu-inspired projects on diplomacy to have been written up on the world outside the West at all.[109] Broadening the geographical reach of Bourdieusian IR is a way of decentring Europe in the sociological work that IR produces. More concretely,

---

[103] Médéric Martin-Mazé, 'Returning Struggles to the Practice Turn: How Were Bourdieu and Boltanski Lost in (Some) Translations and What to Do about It?', *International Political Sociology* 11, no. 2 (1 June 2017): 203.

[104] Matthew Eagleton-Pierce, *Symbolic Power in the World Trade Organization* (Oxford: Oxford University Press, 2013).

[105] J. Darwin, 'Imperialism and the Victorians: The Dynamics of Territorial Expansion', *English Historical Review* 112, no. 447 (1997): 625.

[106] Ronald Robinson and John Gallagher, *Africa and the Victorians: The Official Mind of Imperialism* (London; New York: Macmillan: St Martin's Press, 1961).

[107] Adler and Haas, 'Conclusion: Epistemic Communities, World Order, and the Creation of a Reflective Research Program'.

[108] Etienne Wenger, *Communities of Practice: Learning, Meaning, and Identity* (Cambridge: Cambridge University Press, 1999).

[109] Deepak Nair, 'Saving Face in Diplomacy: A Political Sociology of Face-to-Face Interactions in the Association of Southeast Asian Nations', *European Journal of International Relations* 25, no. 3 (2019):

56   METHOD: POWER, PLURALISM, AND PRIVILEGE

the Eurocentric accents of existing Bourdieusian IR have also shaped the very concepts in which it trades. As such, social categories like caste have yet to enter its lexical universe—an introduction that must now follow.

Caste as a category of distinction

If we are to make sense of caste as a social category in a Bourdieusian universe of meaning, we must first establish some common ground on how to think about caste as a phenomenon. This is especially true for readers outside South Asia and for self-professedly caste-blind upper-caste liberals, who are unlikely to have spent much time thinking about caste at all. It bears emphasizing, then, that caste is not a mystical religious doctrine to be banished by rational thought or a secular creed—if this were so, it would arguably have made its exit by now. Writing in *The Discovery of India* in 1946, future Prime Minister Jawaharlal Nehru was convinced that '[c]onditions of life have changed and thought-patterns are changing so much that it seems impossible for the caste system to endure'.[110] Much like the Fukuyaman 'end of history', the eschatological prognosis for an end of caste put far too much faith in the triumph of liberalism, democracy, and secularism, falsely assuming that their logics were inimical to caste. Instead of declaring caste obsolete, we must confront its manifestations inside modernity itself.

Caste is a category of identity with enormous implications for cultural, social, economic, and political relations. In its South Asian garb, it is a form of social stratification characterized by the hereditary transmission of an entire life path, including status in a hierarchy, occupation, and forms of social interaction and exclusion.[111] While thousands of endogamous groups called *jatis* exist across India, the diplomats I interviewed usually ordered themselves into the conventional four-tier *varna* system that catches the various subgroups in an overarching scheme of hierarchy: Brahmins (ritual experts and scholars), Kshatriyas (warriors), Vaishyas (traders), and Shudras (labourers).[112] Outside the varna fold are Dalits (also colloquially known as the Untouchables, or officially addressed in government parlance as the Scheduled Castes), who have traditionally performed 'polluting' duties for caste Hindus. Caste hierarchies

672–697; Deepak Nair, 'Sociability in International Politics: Golf and ASEAN's Cold War Diplomacy', *International Political Sociology* 14, no. 2 (1 June 2020): 196–214.

[110] Jawaharlal Nehru, *The Discovery of India (1946)* (New Delhi: Penguin Books, 2004), 264.

[111] John Scott and Gordon Marshall, 'Caste', in *A Dictionary of Sociology* (Oxford: Oxford University Press, 2009), 64.

[112] Romila Thapar, *Early India: From the Origins to AD 1300* (London: Allen Lane, 2002), 63.

may be stark in India, but the caste system is not a self-evident, uncontested whole.[113] The modern place of caste in Indian society is intensely debated among scholars and citizens alike, who disagree on its origins, salience, and the appropriate methods for redress.[114] The oeuvre of minute anthropological case studies cautions against undue generalizations, as status rankings among castes and sub-castes shift over time and space, shaping cultural, political, social, and religious practices in a myriad of ways.[115]

A hierarchical system originally based on notions of purity and pollution developed in ancient Hindu legal scriptures like the Manusmriti,[116] the caste system took on more formalistic traits from the late nineteenth century onwards, as brahminical elites collaborated with British colonial officials to draw up census data and anthropological work which simplified caste relations, gave them legal standing in colonial law, and codified brahminical dominance.[117] The colonial machinery itself became intertwined with the upper castes, as some Brahmin families came to be regarded as 'Civil Service families', suitable for the ICS by descent and cultural compatibility with British bureaucratic norms.[118]

In 1950, the Indian Constitution intervened in the caste constellations of the newly sovereign nation, banning the practice of Untouchability in Article 17 and making caste one of the illegal forms of discrimination outlined in Article 15.[119] Articles 16(4) and 335 put India on a path to repairing historical inequities by instituting the world's largest programme of affirmative action, known in India as the reservations system. Reservations, which the Foreign Service is bound by, guarantee representation in public and educational

---

[113] Arjun Appadurai, 'Is Homo Hierarchicus?', *American Ethnologist* 13, no. 4 (1986): 753.

[114] André Béteille, 'The Peculiar Tenacity of Caste', *Economic and Political Weekly* 47, no. 13 (March 2012): 41–48; Satish Deshpande and Mary E. John, 'The Politics of Not Counting Caste', *Economic and Political Weekly* 45, no. 25 (2010): 39–42; Nicholas B. Dirks, *Castes of Mind: Colonialism and the Making of Modern India* (Princeton: Princeton University Press, 2001), 286–288.

[115] Dipankar Gupta, *Interrogating Caste: Understanding Hierarchy and Difference in Indian Society* (New Delhi: Penguin Books, 2000); Lucia Michelutti, '"We (Yadavs) Are a Caste of Politicians": Caste and Modern Politics in a North Indian Town', *Contribution to Indian Sociology* 38, no. 1–2 (2004): 43–71; M.N. Srinivas, *Social Change in Modern India* (Berkeley: University of California Press, 1966); Divya Vaid, 'Caste in Contemporary India: Flexibility and Persistence', *Annual Review of Sociology* 40, no. 1 (2014): 391–410.

[116] Jodhka, 'Ascriptive Hierarchies', 1–2.

[117] Ram Bhagat, 'Census and Caste Enumeration: British Legacy and Contemporary Practice in India', *Genus* 62, no. 2 (2006): 121–24; Thomas R. Metcalf, *Ideologies of the Raj* (Cambridge: Cambridge University Press, 1997), 119.

[118] L. Shanthakumari Sunder, *Values and Influence of Religion in Public Administration* (Los Angeles: SAGE, 2011), 237; C. A. Bayly, *The Local Roots of Indian Politics: Allahabad, 1880–1920* (Oxford: Clarendon Press, 1975).

[119] Gautam Bhatia, 'Horizontal Discrimination and Article 15(2) of the Indian Constitution: A Transformative Approach', *Asian Journal of Comparative Law* 11, no. 1 (2016): 87–109.

58 METHOD: POWER, PLURALISM, AND PRIVILEGE

institutions to the previously most marginalized communities.[120] The Constitution pledged 15% reservations for the Scheduled Castes (SCs—Dalits) and 7.5% reservations for the Scheduled Tribes (STs—indigenous peoples or Adivasis).[121] For all their radical potential, reservations have historically done little to threaten the core of Indian power structures, especially since the quotas often went unfilled for lack of candidates or interest in upholding constitutional provisions.[122] Until the 1980s, only low-level menial positions across the national bureaucracy consistently met their reservation targets, arguably defeating their very purpose. This disconnect is in line with anecdotes from the Foreign Service—one faintly amused diplomat, speaking of the 1950s, did not 'think we worried too much about quotas.'[123]

Although the iconic constitutional lawyer, scholar, freedom fighter, and Dalit campaigner B.R. Ambedkar had asked that caste-based reservations be observed for only a decade, and the Foreign Service still considered them a 'short-term measure' in the mid-1960s,[124] they not only continue until this day but have been expanded. A fiercer public response followed the so-called Mandal agenda, when the Indian Government, in accordance with recommendations of the 1980 Mandal Commission Report, implemented reservations for the 'Other Backward Castes' (OBCs) in 1992.[125] Comprising marginalized sub-castes of Shudras, OBCs were assessed to constitute 52% of the Indian population, but given the legal limit of 50% for overall reserved seats for any institution, the figure for OBC reservations was fixed at 27%.[126] Controversially, the new reservations included historically marginalized but now politically dominant communities like the Yadavs of Uttar Pradesh and Bihar and the land-owning Kalingas of Andhra Pradesh. The changes met with violent nation-wide upper-caste protests[127]—although, once again, only about

---

[120] 'Appendixes V and VI with All Scheduled Castes and Scheduled Tribes Eligible for Reservations Listed by State. Union Public Service Commission Notice No. F/5/49/540EI', 12 February 1955, 'Recruitment of Candidates for the Indian Foreign Service on the Results of the Competitive Examination Held by the UPSC in 1954*l*. FSP/55, Part I, NAI.

[121] Christophe Jaffrelot, 'The Impact of Affirmative Action in India: More Political than Socioeconomic', *India Review* 5, no. 2 (2005): 182.

[122] Jaffrelot, 177.

[123] Interview 18, April 2019.

[124] K.P. Saksena (Research Assistant, MEA), 'Memo: Draft Declaration on the Elimination of All Forms of Religious Intolerance', 18 September 1964, 'Draft Declaration on the Elimination of All Forms of Religious Intolerance', F/UI/151/62, NAI.

[125] K. C. Suri, 'Competing Interests, Social Conflict and the Politics of Caste Reservations in India', *Nationalism and Ethnic Politics* 1, no. 2 (1995): 238.

[126] Jaffrelot, 'Affirmative Action', 182.

[127] Kancha Ilaiah Shepherd, *Buffalo Nationalism: A Critique of Spiritual Fascism* (Calcutta: Samya, 2012), 66; Suri, 'Competing Interests', 235–238.

half these seats have been filled across Government Services.[128] Another jolt to the system arrived after my interviews. In a move that some progressive campaigners believe to herald the gradual erosion of caste-based affirmative action in India, the Union Council of Ministers in January 2019 signed off on a 10% reservation in government and educational institutions for the 'Economically Weaker Section' (EWS) of upper-caste Indians—complicating the public debates about caste and class in India further.[129]

Indeed, caste and class are both distinct and intertwined.[130] As one rather undiplomatic officer from a 1960s batch controversially contended, bad officers 'generally came from poorer backgrounds', and since 'caste inequalities are very closely tied with economic inequalities', caste status often works in the Service as a proxy for who might fit the dominant habitus.[131] The most structurally salient difference lies in the question of mobility: while it is theoretically possible to change class, caste is a 'closed system of stratification'—a birth-based marker fixed for life.[132] While upper-caste Indians find themselves overwhelmingly among the highly-educated professional classes and lower-caste Indians in lower-class occupations, there does exist, for example, a small Dalit bourgeoisie.[133] At the same time, such Dalits tend to work in reserved positions in Government, where they are pejoratively referred to as the 'creamy layer' of the oppressed, and are rarely received as equals by upper-caste colleagues. Caste therefore conditions not only the likelihood of finding oneself

---

[128] The Times of India, '20 Years after Mandal, Less than 12% OBCs in Central Govt Jobs', *The Times of India*, 26 December 2015, https://timesofindia.indiatimes.com/india/20-years-after-Mandal-less-than-12-OBCs-in-central-govt-jobs/articleshow/50328073.cms.

[129] This new reservation category encompasses those with an annual family income of less than ₹8 lakh (US$10,000), who do not belong to the SC/ST/OBC community. The argument in favour of this amendment suggests that caste-based reservations have discriminated against Indians who are marginalized in society for economic rather than caste-based reasons. Those who are against the amendment have pointed out that, since the stipulated income threshold applies to essentially all but the top 1% of earners in the country, we should think of the amendment as effectively creating a caste-based reservation for relatively well-off upper-caste Indians. In November 2022, the Supreme Court of India upheld the constitutional validity of the change, meaning that about 60% of positions in government and educational institutions will now be reserved. These changes complicate debates on the future of caste-based reservations, on who is seen as worthy of affirmative action, and on how caste and class are to be understood together. They will also be shaping the caste and class dynamics of the Foreign Service in decades to come. For a constitutionally grounded critique of the broadly popular amendment, see the following article by a senior advocate at the Supreme Court: KS Chauhan, 'How the EWS Judgment Has Failed the Indian Constitution', *The Indian Express* (blog), 10 November 2022, https://indianexpress.com/article/opinion/columns/how-the-ews-judgment-has-failed-the-indian-constitution-8259525/.

[130] André Béteille, *Caste, Class and Power: Changing Patterns of Stratification in a Tanjore Village* (New Delhi: Oxford University Press, 2012), 187.

[131] Interview 30, April 2019.

[132] Gupta, *Interrogating Caste*; Henri Stern, 'Power in Modern India: Caste or Class? An Approach and Case Study', *Contributions to Indian Sociology* 13, no. 1 (1979): 67.

[133] D. Shyam Babu, 'Caste and Class among the Dalits', in *Dalit Studies*, ed. Ramnarayan S. Rawat and K. Satyanarayana (Durham: Duke University Press, 2016), 244–46.

high up on the class ladder but also the likelihood that one is accepted there upon arrival. The bitter debates about this so-called creamy layer, which the Foreign Service has long conducted out of the view of researchers, are an example of why caste and class cannot be considered analogous categories, and why caste matters on its own terms.

Bourdieu was insistent that identities must always be rooted back into material and social conditions; caste is a case in point. Against profound economic and political change in the over seven decades of Independence—and many more years of liberal prognoses about its imminent demise—caste remains 'a reality that shapes opportunity structures, status differences and cultural values in contemporary India'.[134] Caste has survived by adaptation, expressing itself through systemic, resilient forms of socioeconomic inequality, institutionalized imbalances of power and privilege, and cultural attitudes across society.[135] It has sorted itself into enormously tangible institutions, from state organs, labour relations, and marriage to civil society organizing and political parties.[136] This is why it is imperative that caste not be reduced to a 'state of mind' to be banished by a liberal attitude (as many upper-caste interviewees were keen to do). An aspirational Dalit cannot inventively imagine themselves out of structural inequality any more than a progressive Brahmin can claim to live in a casteless reality.

Yet just as caste reflects stark structural hierarchies, it is also at home in a Bourdieusian world of subtle expressions, distinction, and habitus. As one self-ascribed caste-blind Brahmin diplomat argued, caste was also about 'a value system, education, linguistic abilities'.[137] In Vineet Thakur's biographical treatment of India's celebrated pre-Independence delegate to the League of Nations, V.S. Srinivasa Sastri is read as a 'cultured Brahmin', who finds acceptance in diplomatic circles through his impeccable English and familiarity with markers of upper-class sociability.[138] A similar subtlety and pervasiveness characterize how caste appears throughout this book. The inclusion of caste

---

[134] Jodhka, 'Ascriptive Hierarchies', 2.

[135] S. R. Charsley and G. K. Karanth, *Challenging Untouchability: Dalit Initiative and Experience from Karnataka* (New Delhi: Sage, 1998); Dipankar Gupta, 'Caste and Politics: Identity over System', *Annual Review of Anthropology* 34, no. 21 (2005): 409–427; Clarinda Still, ed., *Dalits in Neoliberal India: Mobility or Marginalisation?* (London: Routledge, 2015).

[136] Tridip Ray, Arka Roy Chaudhuri, and Komal Sahai, 'Whose Education Matters? An Analysis of Inter-Caste Marriages in India', *Journal of Economic Behavior & Organization* 176 (2020): 619–633; Lloyd I. Rudolph and Susanne Hoeber Rudolph, 'The Political Role of India's Caste Associations', *Pacific Affairs* 85, no. 2 (2012): 5–22; Suryakant Waghmore, 'Community, Not Humanity: Caste Associations and Hindu Cosmopolitanism in Contemporary Mumbai', *South Asia: Journal of South Asian Studies* 42, no. 2 (2019): 375–393.

[137] Interview 43, April 2019.

[138] Thakur, *India's First Diplomat: V.S. Srinivasa Sastri and the Making of Liberal Internationalism*, 8.

into a study of Indian diplomats involves reckoning with the upper-caste construction of the diplomatic habitus and the largely brahminical origins of the Indian Foreign Service, examining how caste underpins the diplomatic elite's conceptions of international society, analysing the demographic changes in caste relations and the role of reservations in diplomatic recruitment over the decades, and evaluating the role of caste in the socialization of diplomatic probationers.

A study of caste relations in the Indian Foreign Service will, to some extent, reflect wider patterns in Indian society. Yet the Service is also historically a comparatively progressive space in which caste has been a taboo, manifesting itself not so much in outright political discrimination as subtle cultural marginalization. As Dalit diplomats and those sympathetic to their situation repeatedly emphasized, most upper-caste officers—fiercely anti-casteist in their political principles—rarely acknowledge the subtler prejudices they hold.[139] Even those who welcome reservations tend to view social justice and world-class diplomacy as mutually exclusive goals, so that 'there will be a price to pay' for the professional upliftment of the lower castes, as one retired upper-caste officer warned.[140]

To understand the social context against which caste operates in the Foreign Service, we must understand how the liberal upper castes—members of which constitute the traditionally dominant group of the Service—have historically ordered caste into their universe of social meaning. These upper castes have distinguished themselves as proponents of secularism. However, as with all ostensibly universal concepts, 'secularism' has a meaning in Indian parlance that bears only passing resemblance to the term's usage in the West. Instead of shrinking the space for the sacred in public life reminiscent of French *laïcité*, Indian secularism, crucially against the backdrop of Partition, has been about 'the recognition and acceptance of difference', so that 'the question of secularism has been posed as a question of pluralism, or of tolerance between diverse religious and cultural communities'.[141] Juxtaposed to Gandhi's religiosity, Nehru himself held a 'lifelong aversion to religion as practiced by common

---

[139] Interview 45, April 2019; Interview 49; Interview 54, May 2019; Interview 71; Interview 75, May 2019; Interview 85, May 2019.

[140] Interview 12, March 2019; The same argument was also made in: Interview 1; Interview 3, March 2019; Interview 7, March 2019; Interview 9; Interview 16, March 2019; Interview 18; Interview 19; Interview 23, April 2019; Interview 24, April 2019; Interview 31, April 2019; Interview 35, April 2019; Interview 36, April 2019; Interview 56, May 2019; Interview 57, May 2019; Interview 69, May 2019; Interview 70, May 2019; Interview 85.

[141] Gyanendra Pandey, 'The Secular State and the Limits of Dialogue', in *The Crisis of Secularism in India*, ed. Anuradha Dingwaney Needham and Rajeswari Sunder Rajan (Duke University Press, 2007), 157.

62 METHOD: POWER, PLURALISM, AND PRIVILEGE

people', as T.N. Madan has argued, and what emerged was a constitutional compromise—not the expulsion of a force that could hardly be legislated out of existence, but a 'secular state in terms of religious pluralism'.[142] The liberal compromise on secularism came with a silence that developed around caste.

By the time Nehru's Congress Party took power in 1947, the institution of caste was seen in the political circles of the freedom struggle as an international embarrassment. 'We isolate ourselves in castes, with the result that it is a unique Indian habit which does not prevail anywhere else in the world', Nehru despaired in a speech in the Lok Sabha, India's Lower House of Parliament, on 17 September 1953.[143] Caste had become a phenomenon to be concealed, especially so from the rest of international society, of which Indian liberals were keen to become equal, respected members. In the idiom of liberal neutrality, these elites sought to distance themselves from—instead of meaningfully addressing—the question of caste.[144] Their opposition to caste discrimination manifested itself not so much in anti-casteist campaigning as in a careful omission of caste from permissible discourse.[145] Caste was a taboo precisely for those whose caste identity placed them at the zenith of the hierarchy, and whose lack of exposure to the indignities of caste discrimination allowed them to think of caste in the past tense, as happening elsewhere. Caste in the imagination of the liberal upper castes, as M.S.S. Pandian writes, 'always belongs to someone else; it is somewhere else; it is of another time'.[146]

What emerged out of this idiosyncratic liberal erasure of caste was a form of elite secularism. A culturally homogenous upper-caste elite—distinguishing itself by an overt commitment to a secular, inclusive India—could 'render invisible its own ascriptive markers' of privilege by denouncing talk of caste as divisive.[147] The silence on caste not only allowed the secular elites governing India to remain firmly brahminic in social make-up, it also permitted the state itself to be 'rendered brahminic in the name of secularism'.[148]

Liberal castelessness won one of the most crucial 'struggles about the meaning of the social world', as Bourdieu would have it.[149] The liberal intelligentsia

---

[142] T.N. Madan, 'Whither Indian Secularism?', *Modern Asian Studies* 27, no. 3 (1993): 683.

[143] Jawaharlal Nehru, *Jawaharlal Nehru's Speeches, Vol. 3: 1953–1957* (New Delhi: Publications Division of the Ministry of Information and Broadcasting of the Government of India, 1958), 244.

[144] Gail Omvedt, *Dalit Visions: The Anti-Caste Movement and the Construction of an Indian Identity* (Hyderabad: Orient Blackswan, 2006), 14.

[145] Kancha Ilaiah Shepherd, *Why I Am Not a Hindu: A Shudra Critique of Hindutva Philosophy, Culture and Political Economy* (1996) (Calcutta: Samya, 2002), 49.

[146] Pandian, 'One Step Outside Modernity', 1735.

[147] Satish Deshpande, *Contemporary India: A Sociological View* (New Delhi: Viking, 2004), 71.

[148] Shepherd, *Buffalo Nationalism*, 79.

[149] Bourdieu, *Distinction*, 481.

embodied by figures like Nehru did its utmost to convince religious communities that in political life, the individual was the basic unit of the nation, with communal affinities suspended in favour of a common, unified 'Indianness'.[150] There was also a certain sophistication to secularism: it distinguished India from its theocratic neighbour Pakistan, as well as from the culturally inferior 'bigoted rednecks' of the old American South, as one former officer once stationed at India's Texas consulate sneered.[151] Note how the *social* hierarchies of global order exert themselves over *political* ones: political superpower status does not afford social elite status to just any American in the eyes of a self-styled Indian cosmopolitan elite, if they fail to abide by the intersubjectively imagined markers of elite sociability. In India, secularism not only signified a more inclusionary reading of the nation; it was also an emblem of a more enlightened, educated, and worldly domestic elite. This air of enlightenment was purchased at the expense of an open debate about caste.

Indeed, the manner in which liberal upper-caste elites have delegitimized debates around caste as 'communal' and 'divisive', making 'not seeing caste' the most acceptable way of dealing with caste inequality, is a prime example of what Bourdieu meant regarding the symbolic power of the dominant to define the social world. The lower castes are read out of the Indian grand narrative, as Suraj Yengde writes in his autobiographical account of Dalit life in India: 'I am constantly seen and judged as the Other. I am forced to live in the world as though I am secondary, and the Brahmin and his universality are primary'.[152]

The luxuries of 'not seeing caste' are reserved for the upper castes. The lower castes may not speak of caste, but they see it every day. This duality of personally professed caste blindness and structurally enforced caste vision gives us what M.S.S. Pandian thinks of as 'two competing sets of languages' of caste: 'One talks of caste by other means; and the other talks of caste on its "own terms"'.[153] One is the realm of evasive euphemisms and liberal declarations of equality, the other a direct encounter with all the prejudice that caste blindness claims to abolish by refusing to acknowledge. These are two very different ways of talking—or staying silent—about caste. They often remain private or expressed in hushed tones. Neither language has found utterance in existing literature on Indian diplomats. However, they each feature in this book, as diplomats of different caste affiliations confront and evade caste hierarchies inside the Indian Foreign Service. It is against this duality that the claims about

---

[150] Christophe Jaffrelot, *Religion, Caste and Politics in India* (London: Hurst, 2011), 5.
[151] Interview 26, April 2019.
[152] Suraj Yengde, *Caste Matters* (New Delhi: Penguin Random House India, 2019), 40.
[153] Pandian, 'One Step Outside Modernity', 1735.

64 METHOD: POWER, PLURALISM, AND PRIVILEGE

castelessness, secularism, and the cultural capital of the upper castes should be read in the pages ahead.

Positionality and method

How should we think not about Indian diplomats per se but the way we come to know anything about them? There are many good reasons to be sceptical of whatever can be retrieved in the archive or during interviews—indeed, such scepticism is what forms the methodological core of reflexive sociology. Can one really learn anything of substance by talking to individuals whose careers are premised on smoothing out rough edges and persuading an interlocutor of the truth of any matter, however implausible or unpopular? Is there not a self-censorship that permeates whatever documents have made their way into an officially sanctioned archive? The epistemological status of the primary sources was cause for scepticism even among the interviewees themselves: while individual officers seemed convinced that they personally were rendering the world in the most truthful terms, they were equally unconvinced that colleagues could match their candour and objectivity. And yet it seems to me that Ashok Kapur's old lament on the impossibility of studying Indian diplomats—'unfortunately the attitudes that really deserve analysis cannot be documented'[154]—is all too pessimistic.

The archival records and personal conversations do not serve to provide 'external validity' in a traditional sense: they offer valuable insight not *despite* their subjective and situational nature, but *because of* it. This is as true of the historical utterances unearthed from the archives as it is of contemporary discourse. The anonymity of the interviews allowed for unexpectedly frank conversations, so that the interviews often provided deeper insights on contested topics than the archival or autobiographical record. Yet since we are concerned with intersubjectively held beliefs and conceptions, it does not necessarily matter whether interviewees were expressing deeply held convictions or convenient heuristics. After all, reactions to intersubjective 'truths' can range from 'a deeper internalization of dominant notions to a more cynical or pragmatic conformity', suggesting considerable elasticity in how individuals convey or conceal their relationship to dominant narratives.[155] The question, rather, is whose subjectivities are canonized—and thus rendered objective,

---

[154] Ashok Kapur quoted in Shashi Tharoor, *Reasons of State: Political Development and India's Foreign Policy under Indira Gandhi, 1966–1977* (New Delhi: Vikas PubHouse, 1982), vii.

[155] Eagleton-Pierce, *Symbolic Power*, 53.

reliable, and normal. Who is allowed to narrate themselves, who is narrated by others? Whose account is seen as commonsensical, whose as politically motivated or biased? In other words, whose identity and worldviews have been neutralized into facts about Indian diplomacy?

Reading silences

The written record is often as instructive a guide for what it says as for what it does not say. The genre of autobiographical writing on Indian diplomacy is a well-cited canon on how 'the Indian diplomat' thinks about the world, how this diplomat is best trained, what the institutional culture of Indian diplomacy looks like from within, what we ought to make of the 'democratization' of the Foreign Service, and which individuals in the Service's history we ought to admire. The autobiographical corpus traces back to diplomats originally brought up in the Indian Civil Service (ICS)—India's first Foreign Secretary, K.P.S. Menon (1948–1952), in *Many Worlds Revisited: An Autobiography*, reflects both on his career in the IFS and his prior life within colonial bureaucracy.[156] This corpus encompasses works by well-regarded former Foreign Secretaries[157] as well as more light-hearted impressions of diplomatic life, such as Ambassador B.K. Nehru's *Nice Guys Finish Last*,[158] and more methodical works, such as the meticulous review found in Foreign Secretary J.N. Dixit's *Indian Foreign Service: History and Challenge*[159] and the prolific writings on global diplomatic processes by Ambassador Kishan Rana, still teaching diplomacy in his 80s.[160]

One form of silence in this kind of work is outright official censorship—a ministerial memo from 7 December 1961 confirms that K.P.S. Menon had received prime-ministerial permission to publish *The Flying Troika*, provided he amended the manuscript's commentary on Ambassador and Nehru's sister

---

[156] K.P.S. Menon, *Many Worlds Revisited: An Autobiography* (Bombay: Bharatiya Vidya Bhavan, 1981).

[157] Rajeshwar Dayal, *A Life of Our Times* (New Delhi: Orient Longman, 1998); J.N. Dixit, *My South Block Years: Memoirs of a Foreign Secretary* (New Delhi: UBS Publishers, 1996); Muchkund Dubey, *India's Foreign Policy: Coping with the Changing World* (New Delhi: Orient BlackSwan, 2016); Subimal Dutt, *With Nehru in the Foreign Office* (Calcutta: South Asia Books, 1977); Y.D. Gundevia, *Outside the Archives* (Hyderabad: Sangam Books, 1984); Triloki Nath Kaul, *Ambassadors Need Not Lie: Some Aspects of India's Foreign Policy* (New Delhi: Lancer International, 1988); Maharaja Krishna Rasgotra, *A Life in Diplomacy* (Gurgaon: Penguin/Viking, 2016).

[158] Braj Kumar Nehru, *Nice Guys Finish Second: Memoirs* (New Delhi: Viking, 1997).

[159] J.N. Dixit, *Indian Foreign Service: History and Challenge* (Delhi: Konark Publishers, 2005).

[160] See e.g. Kishan S. Rana, *Inside Diplomacy* (New Delhi: Manas, 2000); Kishan S. Rana, *The 21st Century Ambassador: Plenipotentiary to Chief Executive* (New Delhi: Oxford University Press, 2005).

66 METHOD: POWER, PLURALISM, AND PRIVILEGE

Vijaya Lakshmi Pandit, IFS Officers' Conduct Rules, and some unhelpfully sharp comments on US President Dwight D. Eisenhower and John Foster Dulles, his Secretary of State.[161] Yet a more pernicious silence is that which does not involve a conscious act of censure but rather a socially conditioned absence of voice. This is the fundamental shortcoming of the autobiographical canon of Indian diplomacy: it reflects and reinforces the power imbalances within the Foreign Service itself.

In fact, a note on this canon quickly becomes a miniature exercise in sociological inquiry in its own right. The Indian Foreign Service is narrated and projected outward from the vantage point of those privileged enough to claim 'not to see' gender, caste, or class in how their Service operates. Autobiography seems to be a genre usually reserved for upper-class, almost exclusively upper-caste men. In memoirs, diplomats mention their upper-caste credentials even at a post-Independence political moment when secularism was the elite's supposed creed—but only when the diplomat is a Brahmin. Foreign Secretary M.K. Rasgotra begins a narration of his upbringing by noting that he was born into a Dogra-Brahmin family,[162] while Vijaya Lakshmi Pandit opens the chapter on her life story by confirming in the very first sentence that the Nehrus were Saraswat Brahmins—a contextualization meant to place the family of Kashmiri Pandits where they belonged on the map of Indian caste hierarchies.[163]

Accounts from the openly expressed perspective of lower-caste officers and reservation recruits are missing entirely—not merely because of their underrepresentation in the Service's upper echelons but also because of the stigma of lower-caste origins. We can envision what such accounts may have looked like, if they in any way approximated the rare 1997 memoir *An Untouchable in the IAS*, in which Balwant Singh of the 1959 batch catalogues his five years of failing to 'adjust' to life in the IAS—which Singh calls a 'sanctuary' for the upper castes, hostile to Dalits as 'unwelcome intruders'.[164] Much of the time, however, there is no space for Indian writing on the world that acknowledges the caste positionality of the writer, unless that position is brahminical. 'It is not words of dialogue in the public, but moments of despair in the private, that the Indian modem offers the lower castes', as M.S.S. Pandian writes—'It demands

---

[161] V.H. Coelho (MEA), 'Memo Attached to a Letter from R.K. Nehru to K.P.S. Menon, 9 December 1961', 7 December 1961, Individual Correspondence, K.P.S. Menon Papers, NMML.

[162] Rasgotra, *A Life in Diplomacy*, 42.

[163] Vijaya Lakshmi Pandit, *The Scope of Happiness: A Personal Memoir* (London: Weidenfeld and Nicolson, 1979), 27.

[164] Balwant Singh, *An Untouchable in the I.A.S.* (Saharanpur: B. Singh, 1997), 9.

and enforces that caste can live only secret lives outside the public sphere.[165] The coming chapters commit to paper such private moments of despair, which lower-caste diplomats shared in interviews, often seemingly for the first time.

Analogously, the autobiographical canon of Indian diplomacy is composed almost exclusively by men. For over 70 years of Indian Independence, the only autobiography by a female diplomat was by Vijaya Lakshmi Pandit, who never joined the Service as a rank-and-file officer.[166] Female diplomats have certainly authored books on Indian diplomacy—recent examples include former Foreign Secretary Nirupama Menon Rao publishing on Indo-China relations[167] and former Ambassador to the EU Bhaswati Mukherjee witing on Indo-EU relations.[168] They have, however, abstained from autobiography or commentary on their Service. I rejoice at a very recent break with this pattern. After some years of promising a published English edition of her diary-like recounting of diplomatic life in Hindi, Madhu Bhaduri, of the 1968 batch, brought out *Lived Stories* at the end of 2021.[169] A narrativized journey told through comical incidents, curious anecdotes, and carefully considered impressions, Bhaduri's account takes aim at the Foreign Service's once discriminatory hiring and firing practices, even as she moves beyond the confines of gendered experience to marvel at the many absurdities and challenges of diplomatic life lived across the world. One hopes that Bhaduri's example inspires women of the Foreign Service to enter the autobiographical genre so prolifically practised by male colleagues.

This imbalance means that the Service's gender relations are publicly narrated from the perspective of male commentators. In an influential 1984 book on the institutional development of the Indian Foreign Service, Jeffrey Benner declared that since the discontinuation of discriminatory marriage rules in the early 1980s, any barriers to female diplomats' advancement have arisen from 'pre-recruitment family attitudes rather than on-the-job bias'.[170] Similarly, commenting on the emerging cadre of female diplomats married to male colleagues,[171] former Foreign Secretary Dixit decides that they have 'performed

---

[165] Pandian, 'One Step Outside Modernity', 1739.

[166] Vijaya Lakshmi Pandit, *The Scope of Happiness: A Personal Memoir* (London: Weidenfeld and Nicolson, 1979).

[167] Nirupama Rao, *The Fractured Himalaya: India, Tibet, China 1949–62* (New Delhi: Penguin Viking, 2021).

[168] Bhaswati Mukherjee, *India and the EU: An Insider's View* (New Delhi: Vij Books, 2018).

[169] Madhu Bhaduri, *Lived Stories* (New Delhi: Orient BlackSwan, 2021).

[170] Jeffrey Benner, *Structure of Decision: The Indian Foreign Policy Bureaucracy* (New Delhi: South Asian Publishers, 1984), 55.

[171] Since it is illegal for same-sex couples to marry in India, the official record speaks of and sees only heterosexual relationships.

68   METHOD: POWER, PLURALISM, AND PRIVILEGE

their functions as Foreign Service wives without any reticence or complexes'.[172] The female perspective on Indian diplomacy is consistently narrated by men, for whom the very existence of alternative experience would, it appears, be proof of a 'complex'. The male diplomat is an implicit standard against which reasonable behaviour is measured. It will scarcely come as a surprise to the reader that women diplomats themselves were voluble on the question of gender relations in the Service during interviews—and rarely shared the male narrative canonized in published works on Indian diplomacy.

It is often not so much obfuscation as ignorance that has skewed the diplomatic canon. One senior officer who has published widely on Indian diplomacy spoke to me proudly of a 'Service of peers' who were 'aristocrats of the bureaucracy' but equal among themselves.[173] This is also the mood in which much of the autobiographical record on the Service is written. A very different picture emerges when one takes the time to listen to the Service's lower-caste, lower-class, or female officers, many of whom regarded their more privileged colleagues' noble talk and published writing on this 'Service of peers' with considerable frustration.

Archival records at the NMML and the NAI were an occasional treasure trove of scattered signs which sometimes closed gaps in this narration from the top of the Service. On the face of it, these documents can be extremely dry or procedural in tone—mostly diplomatic cables, employment figures and policy outlines, budgetary documents, external and internal responses to Parliamentary Questions and queries from external interest groups, unorganized descriptive records on the entry of women and reservation recruits into the Service in the first four decades, as well as personal letters between career diplomats and political leaders. The data on caste is scattered and sometimes self-contradictory. Ad hoc letters sent by the MEA to Missions and departments requesting information on the number of reservation-recruits in their midst, so that the Ministry may comply with parliamentary inquiries on the Service's caste composition, attest to the fact that the Service was never fully in command of its own caste statistics.[174] Furthermore, while constitutionally mandated reservations have ensured that caste is a bureaucratic category of interest, and the NAI houses some early anecdotal findings on the representa-

---

[172] Dixit, *Indian Foreign Service*, 298.
[173] Interview 6, March 2019.
[174] See e.g. 'MEA Circular Requesting IFS(A) and (B) Officers to Self-Identify as SC/ST', 18 March 1968, Parliament Questions: Information regarding members of Scheduled Castes + Tribes in the IFS, F/Q/FSI/125/2/68, Part II, NAI.

tion of women, there is little by way of public statistics or ministerial dispatches on another taboo of a secular Service: the question of religious minorities.

Yet much more was retrievable from the archive than was assumed by the many academics and practitioners whose response to my interest in the archives was one of sardonic commiseration. Some of the NMML's material in particular is candid and self-critical, presumably because much of the correspondence was never intended for public consumption. At times, the most telling section of an argument is its casually thrown-in subordinate clause, the most profound part of an utterance its implicit underlying assumption, and the loudest matter a peculiar absence of certain themes where one would expect them to be addressed. The archival hunt for silences required months of work pouring over documents which seemed to have nothing to do with the Foreign Service—for it is here that one often finds, after days of nothing to report, that thematic slips of the tongue, hasty handwritten commentary on official documents, and complaints offered in confidentiality to one's colleague afford a glance into the inner workings of the Service.

Together, autobiography and the archive offer rich opportunities for understanding Indian diplomacy. And yet the very act of committing thoughts to paper invites a level of conscious and unconscious censure that is palpable to a reader familiar with the social milieu in which the writing took place. It also raises the bar on who and what will be heard. While all published writing is smoothed, perhaps even flattened out, in the process of editing, diplomatic writing is unusually curated, so that 'questions about the selection and organisation of information, and considerations of power and access shaping the archive, are especially pregnant'.[175] One response, as outlined by historian Bérénice Guyot-Réchard in her work on Indian diplomacy, is to cultivate a distinctly critical disposition, attentive to the melee of motivations, partialities, and imbalances of power. This is a disposition that the book practises throughout. The other response is to lessen the monopolistic hold of autography and the archive—and the inherent inequalities of class, caste, religion, and gender that it reinforces—by finding ways of studying alternative diplomatic voices. This was an essential ambition underpinning my personal conversations with Indian diplomats.

---

[175] Bérénice Guyot-Réchard, 'Stirring Africa towards India: Apa Pant and the Making of Post-Colonial Diplomacy, 1948–54', *The International History Review* 44, no. 4 (2022): 895.

70 METHOD: POWER, PLURALISM, AND PRIVILEGE

Saying diversity, practising sameness

Much of this book is based on meandering conversations, mostly with its very subjects: Indian diplomats. These anonymous in-person interviews lasted about an hour on average but ranged from the rare 40-minute interview to several conversations that stretched over three to five hours. They were transcribed by hand and, apart from a few cases where interviewees requested otherwise, were also saved on a phone's voice recorder. I do not consider them as pieces of forensic evidence, sanitized through attempts at analytical de-personification. Instead, they are 'autoethnographies': 'commentaries and analysis by informants on their own sociocultural milieus',[176] whose inbuilt biases and partial perspectives are not a problem to be remedied but a resource to be cherished.

The interviews in this book are always anonymous but never positionless. Much of the research on elite institutions in IR functions on an implicit equation of confidentiality with obscurity, 'to the point that elementary social characteristics of the agents too often disappear, at least to the reader, behind anonymity'.[177] This move divorces worldviews and habitus from the social positions that underpin them, erecting a false façade of neutrality and reducing differences of perspective into matters of personal preference. Technical anonymity gave space for diplomats to express what they would not have done under their own names. Making all interviewees anonymous (instead of only anonymizing upon request) ensured that no one rendition would hold more gravitas simply because it was, for example, attributable to a publicly renowned individual, such as the seven Foreign Secretaries interviewed. Yet even without a name, the book still records 'a position, a past, and identity'.[178] It has omitted some anecdotes and rare combinations of social markers that are so specific as to render the officer's identity obvious, but it does retain pieces of identity pertinent to the arguments being made. Seniority, education, class, familial background, gender, caste, and religion all feature at various points. Names do not matter but social context does.

The very process of negotiating access to interviewees merits some sociological observation, embedded as it was in the same social structures and conventions that the book studies. Securing appointments with high-level officers, sought-after ministers or prominent thinkers was undeniably and

---

[176] Reed-Danahay, *Locating Bourdieu*, 130.

[177] Cohen, 'Pierre Bourdieu and International Relations', 222.

[178] Anna Leander, 'The Promises, Problems, and Potentials of a Bourdieu-Inspired Staging of International Relations', *International Political Sociology* 5, no. 3 (2011): 299.

undeservedly abetted by my affiliation as a doctoral candidate to the University of Oxford—and to Balliol College in particular, which once trained the lion's share of Oxford's Indian student body and the mention of which elicited approving nods of recognition from elderly diplomats, entangling the interview process in the colonial legacies being studied. Generally, the interviews occurred through a process of snowballing—one interviewee recommending another—which was helped by established conventions inside the Service. Firstly, the principle of batch solidarity (camaraderie between officers of the same annual intake) meant that interviewees could confidently nominate their peers as the next interviewee, as declining would be considered bad form. Secondly, adherence to bureaucratic hierarchy (even if arguably less rigid than in the Home Services) ensured that seniors could request their juniors to grant interviews—even in the case of one retired officer recommending another.

Who recommended whom as an interviewee, as somebody worthy of being spoken to? Which types of diplomats socialize with one another, and how do they situate themselves in the hierarchies of their Service? As one Additional-Secretary sardonically noted, 'like begets like'—there was a certain 'typology' that emerged from taking recommendations from some of the most prominent diplomats.[179] This could result in only encountering officers who fit the dominant habitus. 'People will keep pointing you to people who are articulate', one elite-schooled Under-Secretary remarked, thus creating a process of snowballing that 'perpetuates certain social biases'—this she said before generously drawing up a clandestine catalogue of recommended interviewees from more heterodox backgrounds.[180] A focused counterbalancing of snowballing effects was required throughout, in fact, including explicitly requesting interviewee recommendations from social groups underrepresented in the snowballing suggestions—women, lower-caste diplomats, people without a liberal arts education, officers from outside the metropolitan centres, those with unconventional biographies for an IFS officer. It was instructive to observe what happened whenever I asked a well-established diplomat to recommend somebody outside the 'typology': most ended up recommending reservation recruits, and those without influential parents or an impressive liberal arts degree, even when I had offered no defining characteristics for what I thought might constitute the 'typology' or its antithesis. Even if it is rarely spelled out in the presence of outsiders, Indian diplomats have an instinctive sense of the hierarchies that organize the social life of the Foreign Service.

[179] Interview 7.
[180] Interview 59, May 2019.

72 METHOD: POWER, PLURALISM, AND PRIVILEGE

What is revealed and obscured when diplomats talk? Anonymity relaxed the boundaries of acceptable speech far beyond the standards that governed written material. One retired Dalit officer noted that most diplomats from marginalized backgrounds had learned never to articulate their alienation in the Service—'they just cope with this social arrogance.'[181] What was striking, then, was the impatience with which officers from all kinds of backgrounds peeled back taboos. The lively ongoing debate around reservations, for example, is not replicated in written sources on the Foreign Service. Often diplomats would also formulate their thoughts in telling expressions, making side comments, or reacting to certain topics in ways that spoke to a theme even when no grand declarations were issued. This will become especially pertinent by Chapter 6, when diplomats speak to the changes in diplomatic life after the election of the Hindu nationalist Prime Minister Narendra Modi in 2014.

This does not mean that interviews were some unobstructed doorway into the souls of diplomats; for taboos come in all shapes and sizes. While women were lavishly generous in their recounting of life as a female diplomat, questions relating to religious identity were either diplomatically diverted or answered by emphasizing that religion had never been a topic of conversation in the Service (at least, that is, until 2014).[182] Hindu officers habitually deflected from conversations on religion, Muslim officers would rarely engage in conversation about their place or numbers in the Service, while Sikhs and Christians seemed to have afforded little thought to what their religious identity might mean to them as diplomats. Some feared that critical comments on the more representative batches would be seen as 'casteist or classist' (something nobody wanted to be seen as).[183] Although the vast majority of upper-caste officers volunteered that their upper-caste colleagues harboured 'a very strong sense of resentment'[184] towards reserved-category officers (who felt it[185]), they all declared themselves free of such baggage. One outspoken Dalit officer drew an unpopular analogy: 'it's like racism—since it's now taboo and not *kosher* to say certain things out loud any more', it has become harder to discern where his colleagues stand.[186] 'With caste, with gender, it's all the same: it's there, just subtle', an upper-caste female colleague expanded.[187]

---

[181] Interview 54.
[182] Interview 3; Interview 7; Interview 9; Interview 20, April 2019; Interview 25, April 2019; Interview 26; Interview 72, May 2019; Interview 74, May 2019.
[183] Interview 33.
[184] Interview 7; Similar sentiments were also expressed in Interview 41, April 2019; Interview 19; Interview 45.
[185] Interview 54; Interview 67, May 2019; Interview 71; Interview 75.
[186] Interview 71.
[187] Interview 63, May 2019.

POSITIONALITY AND METHOD   73

There was no singular pattern to how marginalized members of the Foreign Service narrated their own subject position. Some officers who had entered the Service through reservations, for example, would declare their own caste status outright, others spent hours discussing the Service's hierarchies before easing themselves into more personal experiences, while yet others never revealed their identity, which was only known to me if I had happened to find written records for their particular batch during my hours in the archives. Claims around membership could be declaratory: 'he certainly didn't belong' was the commiserating assessment of an upper-caste officer of her Dalit colleague—and 'that was normal'.[188] Yet in the everyday life of caste in Indian diplomacy, questions of belonging were usually more embodied: diplomats drew the lines around their own tribes by imposing standards of habitus and capital upon each other, adjudicating access and membership on the basis of social and cultural ideals.

Opinions withheld are one thing—yet many attitudes and assumptions do not offer themselves up as conscious products to be shared or guarded in the first place. This raises the question of reflexivity—both on the part of those being studied and on the part of those studying them. Reflexivity involves a sort of 'socioanalysis' that considers the social order within which interviewees make their comments,[189] while also demanding constant self-reflexivity on my own part.[190] The positionality of the interviewee expresses itself on a spectrum of self-reflexivity. On one end is a *discourse of familiarity*, which 'leaves unsaid all that goes without saying'.[191] We might think of these givens as the ideational consensus that underwrites the field. For the interviewee, much of what fascinates the interviewer is not even worthy of the question being posed. Yet it is precisely the unquestioned that is often most revealing. Classic thinkers on diplomacy repeatedly offer claims such as 'common sense is the essence of diplomacy'.[192] Bourdieu called this *doxa*—'all that which is taken for granted',[193] representing 'a particular point of view, the point of view of the dominant, which presents and imposes itself as a universal point of view'.[194] The dominant are often oblivious to the historical struggles that have produced

[188] Interview 46, May 2019.
[189] Pierre Bourdieu, *Outline of a Theory of Practice* (Cambridge: Cambridge University Press, 1977), 18.
[190] Pierre Bourdieu, *The Craft of Sociology: Epistemological Preliminaries* (Berlin: Walter de Gruyter, 1991), 250.
[191] Bourdieu, *Outline*, 18.
[192] Harold Nicolson, *Diplomacy*, 3d ed. (Oxford University Press: Oxford, 1963), 20.
[193] Bourdieu, *Outline*, 166.
[194] Pierre Bourdieu, 'Rethinking the State: Genesis and Structure of the Bureaucratic Field', trans. Samar Farage and Loïc Wacquant, *Sociological Theory* 12, no. 1 (1994): 15.

74 METHOD: POWER, PLURALISM, AND PRIVILEGE

the current consensus they preside over. Thus, it is precisely the commonsensical nature of many popular assumptions that make them paramount for the maintenance of systems of power.

On the other end of the spectrum, an *outsider-oriented discourse* involves 'learned reconstruction of the native world'.[195] Interviewees 'produce a discourse' for the researcher, self-theorizing their utterances as a kind of interpretive courtesy—or as an instrument for controlling the narrative. Yet since people rarely follow plain rules in their behaviour or overt principles in their thinking, interviewees are forcing a structured rationalization upon themselves ex post facto.[196] There is, consequently, a certain affectation to articulating embodied knowledge: 'As soon as he [sic] reflects on his [sic] practice, adopting a quasi-theoretical posture', Bourdieu forewarns, 'the agent loses any chance of expressing the truth of his [sic] practice'.[197] This concern with overintellectualization is perhaps doubly heightened in the presence of India's well-read diplomats. Diplomats are, by profession, experts at framing their utterances with foreign audiences in mind. It emerged that Indian diplomats were also discerning consumers of the academic work done on themselves—work which might structure their own rationalizations as they engage with academics. In fact, four interviewees expressed doubts about being interviewed at all, following their experience of speaking with two well-known academics whose subsequent publications they felt had misrepresented Indian diplomatic thinking.[198] Being alive to these two modalities of discourse—familiar and outsider-oriented—requires unrelenting analytical vigilance, to which I can only pledge myself as having constantly aspired.

If it matters what interviewees 'talk about' and 'talk from',[199] it also matters who they talk *to*. It is not just which questions are asked but who is asking them. How does an interviewee order the interlocutor into their own social universe of hierarchies and allegiances? To some diplomats, a young European woman studying a country so far outside her own inherited social milieu seemed to come across as harmless, perhaps even culturally innocent, or politically naïve. I was particularly conscious of the caricatured impression I must have given off for a few weeks following the colour-throwing Holi festival in March, as I awkwardly walked into one interview after another in my accidentally bright

---

[195] Bourdieu, *Outline*, 18.
[196] Reed-Danahay, *Locating Bourdieu*, 131.
[197] Pierre Bourdieu, *The Logic of Practice* (Palo Alto: Stanford University Press, 1990), 91.
[198] Interview 1; Interview 6; Interview 12; Interview 59.
[199] Vincent Pouliot, 'Methodology: Putting Practice Theory into Practice', in *Bourdieu in International Relations: Rethinking Key Concepts in IR*, ed. Rebecca Adler-Nissen (London: Routledge, 2012), 51.

pink hair, like a bad American film character chasing the meaning of life by backpacking across the exoticized backdrop that is India in so much of the West's cultural repertoire. Even as the pink wore off, the larger point stuck: habitus matters for the interlocutor, too.

This meant, on the one hand, some pejorative assumptions about how much I knew or understood—occasioning several protracted, unprompted elaborations on topics like Indian diplomatic history. These usually continued despite my perhaps overly diplomatic attempts at signalling through vigorous nodding and ostentatious name-dropping just how intimately familiar I was with the subject. On the other hand, it also meant that diplomats felt at ease to expound on sensitive topics in ways they may not have with interviewers of another gender, ethnicity, or cultural background.

Being European, while also perhaps associated with a certain safe ignorance, also brought its own baggage. Officers may have been mindful, for example, of presenting themselves in a manner that accorded with their own imageries of European international society, which I might have been expected to share, or making arguments a European could stereotypically be presumed to want to hear, perhaps about India's commitment to diversity or equality. This was especially the case for those few officers who picked up not on my Europeanness in general but my Northern Europeanness in particular. After such recognitions of my geographical origin, comments about gender and class equality tended to be more pronounced than in other interviews, and the conversation veered towards the interviewee's personal commitment to egalitarian principles, their purported perfection in the High North, and the travesty of their weakness in India. Of course, these comments, too, often came only a few moments before an imaginative attempt at explaining away the interviewee's disdain for lower-class, lower-caste colleagues as a functional necessity of diplomatic representation. Such are the perils of an 'outsider-oriented discourse'. Yet to insist that such commitments can only be performative or insincere would be both deeply cynical and, in assuming that most things orient themselves around Europe and Europeans, reproduce the very hierarchies this book seeks to query.

Sometimes, interviewees also seemed to operate from an assumption of closeness rather than distance. Some diplomats—liberal arts graduates, Oxbridge alumni, culturally mobile millennials, women—drew me into their fold, assuming mutual understanding on a range of issues and speaking presumptively of 'people like us'. How various interviewees situated me in their narratives of the world spoke to where they saw themselves in it. Those emphasizing a shared kind of elite education, for example, usually spoke from a dominant habitus they compared to less polished colleagues, while many female diplomats sensed that they were sharing experiences of womanhood that would be intuitively familiar to their interviewer. These assumptions were sometimes accurate, sometimes mistaken. What they always underscored was the impossibility of extracting myself out of the equation. Insofar as the over 80 interviewees with their diverse backgrounds would have approached the encounter in very different ways, we can at least be assured that no one big, single bias skewed all conversations in equal measure—rather, they were delightfully partial and deeply socially situated in a multitude of ways.

What might not come through in the analysis ahead is the overwhelming magnanimity and warmth which accompanied many interviews. People gave generously of their time—one particularly loquacious diplomat spoke with me for about five hours in total—and went out of their way to secure access to further interviewees and resources. I was regularly offered chai or invited to stay for home-cooked dinners, provided chauffeur rides to and from the interview, and gifted books penned by the interviewees. Once, after a heartfelt conversation about life beyond diplomacy, a retired officer extended a standing invitation for me to come and stay at her holiday home in the Southern state of Tamil Nadu. Having mentioned in passing that our interview would be taking place on my birthday, one old-school gentleman and his thoughtful wife produced an emerald shawl, along with a cake, when I arrived for our interview at their home in the IFS Apartments complex in Mayur Vihar. I am aware that this hospitality may often have been extended to me precisely because of the Oxford pedigree that marked my own habitus, the subliminal exchanges of social capital that this affiliation may have signified to the interviewees, perhaps even the expectation of professional favours one might cash in later. I also know that I was afforded levels of generosity that my Indian colleagues at Indian universities may often not receive when they set about chasing high-ranking officials in their own country. I was nonetheless struck by the care and seriousness with which many interviewees approached complex themes, and the candour that they brought into their conversations with a virtual stranger.

Conclusion

Diplomacy, as a somewhat arcane profession built on social codes, seems intuitively Bourdieusian in its subtlety and elitism. Yet it is in fact Bourdieu's persistent grounding of manners and habits in unequal social orders that allows us to untangle the theoretical backdrop against which this book is written. Situating myself in theoretical debates on global order and international society, I suggested that both the self-professed neutrality of liberal internationalism and the binary reading of power in postcolonial scholarship have rendered many expressions of hierarchy in international life difficult to articulate. Instead, I sought to emphasize the classed and racialized codes of elite belonging in international society that have marked the socialization of international elites since the colonial standard of civilization. I suggested that we think of membership in international society not as a one-off process of formal entry, but as a continuously reproduced and socially articulated performance of belonging, tied to domestic hierarchies of representation. To conceptualize the practices that structure the social world of Indian diplomats, I placed the Indian Foreign Service into a sociological scaffolding of habitus, capital, and fields, even if often in ways that deviate from Bourdieu's original work or the Bourdieusian theorizing done in IR. The chapter then sketched out the contours of the Indian diplomatic cleft habitus and developed caste as a concept of reflexive sociology. Finally, it discussed why social hierarchies also matter in a methodological context, laying out what self-reflexivity demands of the researcher and her research subjects.

If diplomacy is the 'representation and governing among recognized polities',[200] we must ask what kinds of performances this representation calls forth and what its social codes of recognition are. The coming chapters examine how the Indian diplomatic cleft habitus came into being through colonial encounters, how its behavioural and ideational demands have underlain India's engagement with the world, what the changing nature of diplomatic cadres has done to its performance, how these cadres have been trained into imbibing it, and the ways in which the traditions of this habitus are fraying under the weight of internal and external pressures at the dawn of a post-Western world.

---

[200] Ole Jacob Sending, Vincent Pouliot, and Iver B. Neumann, 'The Future of Diplomacy: Changing Practices, Evolving Relationships', *International Journal* 66, no. 3 (2011): 530.

2

Genealogy

Balliol and Bandung

On 10 July 1835, Lord Macaulay presented his *Minute on Indian Education* in the British Parliament, sketching out the anatomy of a future colonized elite, 'Indian in blood and colour, but English in taste, opinions, morals and intellect'.[1] Some rendition of this elite came into being in the Indian members of the ICS—the colonial-era elite administrative corps of around a thousand men that once governed over a quarter of the world's population.[2] In 1920, the British committed themselves to having Indians hold half the posts in the ICS.[3] A cadre of Indian elites was socialized into the British administrative system and its ideologies of the world. Yet by the time a group of former Indian members of this institution was summoned to establish the Indian Foreign Service in the run-up to Independence in 1947, the colonial project had produced an elite adrift—not Macaulay's band of British loyalists but a group marked by its deep ambivalence towards both their imperial masters and Indian compatriots. Emblematic of the condition of local elites in European colonies, this bureaucratic elite, too, was 'cast between two worlds' but, in leading 'a sort of double inner life', was in the end effectively 'rejected by both'.[4] What Bourdieu and Abdelmalek Sayad called the *cultural sabir*,[5] in India was ridiculed as the *brown sahib*—a nationalist tag for Indians willing to 'act the sedulous ape to his white bosses', as Ambassador Vijaya Lakshmi Pandit once mocked.[6] The brown sahib was the caricatured consummation of Macaulay's vision: he had been schooled to 'think British, feel British, act British, and buy British',[7] and yet was never truly part of the fraternity of gentlemen he was expected to mimic.

---

[1] Lord Thomas Babington Macaulay, 'Minute on Indian Education (1835)', in *Archives of Empire, Volume I: From the East India Company to the Suez Canal*, ed. Mia Carter and Barbara Harlow (Duke University Press, 2003), 237.

[2] Arthur S. Lall, *The Emergence of Modern India* (New York: Columbia University Press, 1981), 18.

[3] Lall, 49.

[4] Pierre Bourdieu, *The Algerians* (Boston: Beacon Press, 1962), 144.

[5] Bourdieu and Sayad, 'Colonial Rule and Cultural Sabir'.

[6] Pandit, *The Scope of Happiness*, 7–8.

[7] Tarzie Vittachi, *The Brown Sahib* (London: Andre Deutsch, 1962), 54.

Cosmopolitan Elites. Kira Huju, Oxford University Press. © Kira Huju (2023). DOI: 10.1093/oso/9780198874928.003.0003

The fraught battle over the ideals of being a worldly officer, once waged in the minds of Indian officers under the British Raj, did not cease at Independence. Instead, it became institutionalized into postcolonial structures. As India transitioned into postcoloniality, the cleft habitus settled itself from a deeply personal dilemma of Indian colonial officers into a collective archetype for postcolonial diplomats. What once was a tortured individual balancing act became a shared guiding ideal: a diplomatic cleft habitus for the postcolonial Foreign Service. Under colonialism, the cleft had been suspended between a very real empire and a hypothetical world of decolonization. Now, it straddled the phantom existence of empire and a very real postcolonial world struggling to abide by its radical promise. For the British Raj had given its chosen Indian elites not only employment or status but also a worldview: an image of international society narrated from the perspective of European power. Closely hued to the English School image of the aristocratic international and Elias' notions of the civilizing process, this old world had called forth a set of beliefs, dispositions, and manners that the colonial Indian bureaucratic elite had been trained to imbibe. Even in a formally postcolonial order, this vision of the world persisted, often rather awkwardly, alongside the radical vision of the Indian freedom struggle that had promised not just a postcolonial India but an anti-imperial international society.

This chapter traces the metamorphosis of a personal dilemma of Indian colonial officers into an institutionalized ideal for the postcolonial Indian Foreign Service. The ideal built itself around the dual demands of the diplomatic cleft habitus: an officer comfortable in the old conventions of classic, European international society and yet also attuned to the political and cultural demands of postcoloniality. I locate the origins of the cleft habitus in the elite educational and bureaucratic conditions of empire. It is here that we encounter young Indian ICS officers as they make their way through training at Oxbridge out into India, seeking to adjudicate their place in a complex maze of class and race. I argue that the original cleft was created as Anglophone Indian elites sought to imbibe the idealized image of a sophisticated, supposedly cosmopolitan colonial officer, all the while seeking to prove their allegiance to a radical anti-imperial project of Indian Independence.

The cleft habitus once expressed in the everyday lives of ICS officers is neither a colonial relic nor a historical anecdote. Rather, it is a first cultural sketch for the hybridity of the diplomatic cleft habitus that emerges following Independence. On the one hand, there was a conviction that Indian diplomacy should reflect European notions of diplomatic tradecraft, alongside British—but supposedly universal—bureaucratic traditions. On the other, there was an

80 GENEALOGY: BALLIOL AND BANDUNG

emancipatory project of decolonial restructuring, which spoke for a Service reflective of the radical potential of the decolonial moment, the vast diversity of India once suppressed under the Raj, and the promise of Third World solidarity. The tenor of Bourdieu's arguments suggests that, for him, a cleft habitus was always a problem to be solved one way or the other, a transition to be made, an inconvenient duality to be restored to a state of homogenous normalcy. And yet the cleft habitus of Indian diplomats evolved to speak to two international societies simultaneously, becoming something akin to a governing ideal, always in tension between the two imageries but capable of living with this hybridity as its own sense of normalcy.

Both imageries were telling the diplomats of a new independent nation where and how to belong in the world. While the famous Nehruvian internationalism spoke of Third World solidarity, racial equality, and global economic justice, it was, from its very beginnings, intertwined with elite impressions of a thin cosmopolitanism born out of colonialism, the aristocratic conventions of European international society, and the forms of class consciousness that went with it.

The genealogy of a cleft

The founders

Although Hugh Weightman, the last British Foreign Secretary of India, announced the creation of 'an entirely new Service from scratch' in 1946,[8] the Indian Foreign Service he was describing was not a fully postcolonial creature, neither in organizational structure nor ideational origin. Over two centuries, the Secret and Political Department of the Government of India, founded by Warren Hastings in 1784, had developed considerable freedom in its dealings with fellow members of the Commonwealth.[9] By the end of the First World War, India had achieved quasi-international status as the only non-self-governing country in the League of Nations,[10] its delegates drawn from among perceived British sympathizers, colonial officials, and ruling princes.[11] Juxtaposed at the 1945 founding conference of the UN in San Francisco were

---

[8] Hugh Weightman, 'Communique', 30 November 1946, 'Establishment of a Separate Indian Foreign Service', FSP/47-2(7), NAI.

[9] Benner, *Structure of Decision*, 29.

[10] Charles Herman Heimsath and Surjit Mansingh, *A Diplomatic History of Modern India* (Bombay: Allied Publishers, 1971), 24; Parameswaran N. Nair, *The Administration of Foreign Affairs in India with Comparative Reference to Britain* (New Delhi: School of International Studies, 1963), 37.

[11] Thakur, 'The Colonial Origins of Indian Foreign Policy-Making', 61–62.

India's official delegation—India's future first Foreign Secretary K.P.S. Menon included—and the Congress Party's observer mission, led by India's future first Ambassador to the Soviet Union Vijaya Lakshmi Pandit. In an ironic turn of history, Independence would push these representatives of empire and anti-imperial organizing together in the Foreign Service. The tensions in San Francisco presaged the uncomfortable coexistence of the two visions of international society which would come to characterize the Service.

What is most extraordinary about the supposed postcoloniality of the new Indian Foreign Service is the number of former colonial officials entrusted with its establishment. Along with the nationalist Prime Minister and Foreign Minister Jawaharlal Nehru (himself a product of Harrow and Cambridge), it was a select group of Indian ICS officers employed by the Political Department and other arms of colonial bureaucracy—upper-class, upper-caste Oxbridge graduates serving the empire—who were called upon to inaugurate the Service.[12] Among these officers were future stalwarts of Indian diplomacy such as G.S. Bajpai (first Secretary-General of the MEA), K.P.S. Menon (first Foreign Secretary), N.R. Pillai (second Secretary-General), Badr-ud-Din Tyabji (Ambassador to Belgium and Iran, among others), M.J. Desai (fourth Foreign Secretary), and R.N. Banerjee (later Home Secretary).[13] Another 26 ICS officers were appointed in line with their rank in the colonial cadre,[14] with ties forged under the Raj elevating officers like Subimal Dutt, Bajpai's former subordinate, into the role of Commonwealth Relations Secretary, and later Foreign Secretary.[15] A further dozen ICS veterans who never officially joined the Service, Ambassadors to Washington B.R Sen, L.K. Jha, and B.K. Nehru among them, assumed senior positions.[16] Colonial officers inducted into Home Services also served in Missions abroad, further tightening the grip of the old ICS on the new IFS.[17] The history of Indian diplomacy, therefore, began with an 'ICS generation of men'[18]—very literally, in fact, for women were never allowed to serve in colonial bureaucracy.[19]

ICS officers were joined by about 50 colleagues: eminent recruits from public life, participants in the Congress-led freedom struggle, half a dozen Indian royals, as well as some officials from the British Indian Armed Forces and

---

[12] 'A Note on Organisation of the Ministry of External Affairs', 26 April 1963, 'Questionnaire of the Institute of Public Administration Regarding the Indian Foreign Service', Q (GA)/191/6/63, NAI.

[13] Jayantanuja Bandyopadhyaya, *The Making of India's Foreign Policy: Determinants, Institutions, Processes, and Personalities* (Bombay: Allied Publishers, 1970), 78; Tharoor, Reasons of State, 169.

[14] Rasgotra, *A Life in Diplomacy*, 16.

[15] Rasgotra, 16.

[16] Rasgotra, 17.

[17] Interview 43.

[18] M.O. Mathai, *Reminiscences of the Nehru Age* (New Delhi: Vikas Publishing, 1978), 193.

[19] Dixit, *Indian Foreign Service*, 32.

82 GENEALOGY: BALLIOL AND BANDUNG

four members of Subhas Chandra Bose's dispersed Indian National Army that Bajpai reluctantly accepted at Nehru's insistence.[20] Only the MEA's first Secretary-General G.S. Bajpai and the first Foreign Secretary K.P.S. Menon, having represented India as Agent-Generals in the United States and Kuomintang China, respectively, had diplomatic experience.[21] And yet the self-assured veterans of the ICS envisioned themselves as working above, more so than alongside, the bureaucratically inexperienced emergency recruits.[22] The latter often found themselves marginalized in the everyday decision-making of a Foreign Service dominated by ICS officers who 'did not quite accept them as part of their elite group', as Foreign Secretary J.N. Dixit (1991–1994) would later describe.[23] As Agent-General in Washington, Bajpai had been expected to brief against the freedom struggle and in support of the British response to Gandhi's Quit India Movement in 1942—'in short, to tell a lot of lies about India to unsuspecting Americans on behalf of its wily British masters', as Foreign Secretary M.K. Rasgotra (1982–1985) frames it in his memoir, chastising his former superior.[24] At the same time, ICS officers had more experience running India than those who had most impatiently campaigned for the right to do so. Nehru's handpicked cadre of celebrities, royalty, and personal connections was easily satirized—one journalistic rendition would later describe a Service of 'dispossessed princelings, illiterate cavalrymen, and well-connected nitwits'.[25] Against the steady hands of the former ICS, it was hard for them to leave an imprint on the culture of a Service just coming into its own.

Neither diplomatic histories about a new Foreign Service founded in 1946 nor political theories on Indian nationalist thought capture just how torn such Indians, however nationalistic, were about the brand-new world of postcolonial culture. It was, after all, telling them that all the ideals and behaviours they had painstakingly assumed under colonial rule were now to be illegitimate. Their political support for a postcolonial India coexisted with an embodied, habitual reverence for many of the manners, skills, and professional habits of the Raj. For these elites, seemingly small acts like learning to eat with a fork were performative requests for recognition in a Western-dominated world—a ritual the British Raj introduced for ICS training, which is perpetuated in the training of IFS officers to this day.

---

[20] Dixit, 89; Rasgotra, *A Life in Diplomacy*, 18.
[21] 'Oral History Transcript: K.P.S. Menon', 1976, 3, Oral Histories, NMML.
[22] Guyot-Réchard, 'Stirring Africa towards India', 904.
[23] Dixit, *Indian Foreign Service*, 159.
[24] Rasgotra, *A Life in Diplomacy*, 12.
[25] A description of Indian Foreign Service officers from an article in Seminar magazine in the 1980s, recounted in Interview 43.

Bourdieu reminds us that understanding a habitus requires considering 'possibilities which did not occur'.[26] The Indian Foreign Service would have come to look very different had it been set up by, say, freedom fighters alone. Asked in a private meeting in 1964, the year of his death, about his greatest failure as Prime Minister, the same Nehru who had invited ICS veterans to establish the Foreign Service replied: 'I could not change the administration; it is still a colonial administration.'[27] In fact, ICS veterans outlived Nehru himself. The ICS furnished India's first nine Foreign Secretaries,[28] and for decades, 'the entire superstructure was of ICS officers', with nobody else rising above the Joint-Secretary rank.[29] When the Pillai Committee convened in 1966 to prepare their famous report on re-imagining the Foreign Service, both Houses of Parliament expressed their 'resentment' at the Committee overwhelmingly consisting of retired ICS officials.[30] It was only in 1976 with the appointment as Foreign Secretary of Jagat Mehta, son of ICS-trained Ambassador M.S. Mehta, that the Foreign Service ceased being led by former colonial officers.[31] Even then, Mehta had only missed service in the ICS because an interim independent government was put in place soon after his admission into it.[32] It was perhaps natural then that, upon his appointment, he turned to the family friend K.P.S. Menon 'to seek your guidance and claim your blessings'.[33] One diplomat dated the end of the ICS's reign as late as the 1980s, which is when the last ICS officer finally retired.[34] In fact, many veterans of colonial bureaucracy went on to sit on Foreign Service Interview Boards after retirement, projecting their conception of the ideal diplomat onto future generations, members of which still work in the Foreign Service to this day.[35]

---

[26] Bourdieu quoted in Gisèle Sapiro, 'Field Theory from a Transnational Perspective', in *The Oxford Handbook of Pierre Bourdieu*, ed. Thomas Medvetz and Jeffrey J. Sallaz (New York: Oxford University Press, 2018), 166.

[27] Tarzie Vittachi, 'Bureaucrats Who Won't Lie Down', *The Guardian*, 10 April 1978, 17.

[28] Rasgotra, *A Life in Diplomacy*, 16.

[29] Interview 43.

[30] Lakshmi N. Menon, 'Response to Follow-up Questions on Q 382 by Mulka Govinda Reddy, Rajya Sabha', 23 November 1965, 'Starred question No. II in the Rajya Sabha by Shri M.P. Bhargava regarding Pillai Committee on IFS', Q/GA/125/51/65, NAI.

[31] Rasgotra, *A Life in Diplomacy*, 16.

[32] Jagat S. Mehta, *The Tryst Betrayed: Reflections on Diplomacy and Development* (Gurgaon: Penguin Random House India, 2015), 28.

[33] Jagat Mehta, 'Letter to K.P.S. Menon', 24 February 1976, Individual correspondence, K.P.S. Menon papers, NMML.

[34] Interview 24.

[35] C. Ganesa Aiyar (Secretary, UPSC), 'Letter to M.S. Mehta', 24 December 1958, '1958–59: Appointment as one of the examiners for personality for the IAS examination—connected papers and correspondence with the Secretary, UPSC', SF/45, Mohan Sinha Mehta papers, NMML.

84 GENEALOGY: BALLIOL AND BANDUNG

Of course, it was not the former ICS cadre that held political sway, as diplomats who joined the Service in the first two decades were always careful to emphasize during our conversations. Executive control over foreign policy was a long-held Viceroyal convention, but Nehru's intimate involvement with the diplomatic cadres was unparalleled.[36] Until 1956, he met each probationer individually[37] and from then on addressed them annually as a batch.[38] He would convene even with junior Deputy-Secretaries, and with Joint-Secretaries 'as a matter of course'—an impossible thought in the post-Nehruvian Foreign Service.[39] In the early 1950s, one of the earliest recruits boasted, Nehru knew the names of even the junior-most officers and would strike up a conversation with them at random in the corridors of South Block to keep abreast of their briefs.[40]

However, the popular narratives that paint Nehru as a postcolonial counterbalance to the conservative impulses of the ICS are too comfortably dualistic, too invested in endowing Nehru with a singular egalitarian vision. ICS elites and Nehru did not represent two ends of a cultural pole, each clamouring after mutually exclusive, ideologically opposed ideals of what an Indian diplomat ought to look like. An inherent ambivalence of social position and political performativity defined both ICS cadres and Nehru himself. Nehru, too, had bought into the old-time charms of European aristocratic convention, which he—at least on paper—was in charge of banishing from the bureaucratic culture. It is this ambivalence that we must understand to grasp the inherited complexities of world-making in postcolonial India.

The education of an (anti)imperial elite

The Indians who joined the ICS occupied a very particular kind of place in the hierarchies of empire: an occupational and socioeconomic elite in many ways, and yet always marginalized in the racial hierarchies that structured a European-dominated world. They had come into being as colonization put in unequal circulation the cultural capital that came with knowing the world in the colonizer's language, ushering in a 'rise of an elite of cultural producers in the colonized countries.'[41] As products of a shared socioeconomic milieu, they

---

[36] Benner, *Structure of Decision*, 177–180.
[37] Interview 79, May 2019.
[38] Interview 9; Interview 20.
[39] Rana, *Inside Diplomacy*, 252.
[40] Interview 16.
[41] Sapiro, 'Field Theory', 166.

shared a set of ideational dispositions and manners that spoke to their elite nature.[42] They were, in the words of a diplomat who once worked under them, 'a very privileged, exceptionally small, compact elite.'[43] In fact, a 1919 Home Department document on ICS recruitment notes that Indian officers tended to be of higher socioeconomic standing than their British counterparts.[44] An established background and British education were practically criteria for even appearing in front of the ICS selection committee.[45] B.K. Nehru—1934 ICS batch officer, cousin to Jawaharlal Nehru, and Indian Ambassador in the 1950s and 1960s—concluded that the examination curriculum 'was such that Indians had little chance of competing successfully unless they were rich and had studied at a school in England', especially before 1922, when a parallel examination to the one in London was launched in India.[46] The ICS was a 'high-prestige elite bureaucracy from which large segments of the underprivileged class were excluded',[47] and which by the end of the colonial era had developed into a 'symbol of inequality, casteism' in India.[48] Known as the best-paid governmental career worldwide, with status and glamour aplenty, the ICS solidified the already domestically dominant standing of a local elite.[49]

Colonial administration in India was also brahminical. Out of the 18 Hindus that entered the Service in 1928, for example, all but four (themselves upper-caste) were Brahmins,[50] while only one Dalit, known then as a member of the 'depressed classes', ever entered the ICS, in 1940.[51] In academic language that obfuscated the unequal power relations of both colonialism and caste, anthropologists of colonial India began arguing that Brahmins fit the imperial project because of the normative congruence of brahminical culture and British bureaucratic ideals, both of which supposedly valued self-discipline,

---

[42] Bourdieu, 'What Makes a Social Class?', 6.

[43] Interview 4, March 2019.

[44] David C. Potter, *India's Political Administrators: From ICS to IAS* (Delhi: Oxford University Press, 1996), 116.

[45] Dixit, *Indian Foreign Service*, 89.

[46] B.K. Nehru, 'The Civil Service in Transition', 15 October 1999, Article based on a lecture delivered at the India International Centre, New Delhi—'Speeches/Writings by him', SN/50, B.K. Nehru papers, NMML.

[47] D.S. Chauhan, 'India's Underprivileged Classes and the Higher Public Service: Towards Developing a Representative Bureaucracy', *International Review of Administrative Sciences* 42, no. 1 (1976): 39.

[48] H.K. Paranjape, 'A Trojan Inheritance', 1966, 32.

[49] R.C. Dutt, 'The Civil Service before and after Independence', in *Memoirs of Old Mandarins of India*, ed. Raj Kumar Nigam (New Delhi: Documentation Centre for Corporate & Business Policy Research, 1965), 58–74; V. Isvaran, 'The Indian Civil Servant', in *The Civil Servant in India, by Ex-Indian Civil Servants*, ed. Kewalram Laichand Panjabi (Bombay: Bharatiya Vidya Bhavan, 1965), 247–259; Lall, *The Emergence of Modern India*, 19.

[50] Tim Holmes Beaglehole, 'From Rulers to Servants: The ICS and the British Demission of Power in India', *Modern Asian Studies* 11, no. 2 (1977): 246.

[51] Potter, *India's Political Administrators*, 118.

86 GENEALOGY: BALLIOL AND BANDUNG

duty, academic achievement, and individual excellence.[52] As Western education in district capitals came to be associated with high remuneration and
prestigious occupational standing within the colonial apparatus,[53] 'modern'
Brahmins also came to see the ICS as a way of marking their status in colonial Indian society.[54] If the ICS, 'growing out of the womb of a rotting social
structure, decimated by the caste-system', could not 'escape the hierarchical
compulsions' of its members, as diplomat and Indira Gandhi's confidante P.N.
Haksar would later complain, this was not only because of imperial attitudes
but also because 'the ICS constituted themselves as the Brahmans [sic]', both
literally and figuratively.[55] International and domestic hierarchies were intertwined from the very beginning, as the upper-caste elite sought to leverage its
dominant position in India to ameliorate the subordinate standing of Indians
in the colonial hierarchies of race and class.

In other words, the production of the cleft habitus was only made possible
by the social and cultural capital that members of the brahminical bureaucratic elite possessed. It allowed them to join the imperial project and witness
the world of European international society, even if rarely to challenge it.[56]
Their ambivalent position in the transnational hierarchies of power produced
a contradiction: on the one hand, there was a real sense of prestige that came
with imbibing the colonizer's language and habits, and on the other, a deep
alienation that came with realizing that there would never be an equal place
for even the most elite Indian in a world of empire.

The Indian ICS officer was a product of Anglicized elite education. The ICS
was deeply intertwined with the universities of Oxford and Cambridge,[57] who
were responsible for the (dis)orientation programme that produced the colonial Indian bureaucrat. Future officers were sent to these universities for official

[52] Potter, 119; Ravindra S. Khare, *The Changing Brahmans: Associations and Elites among the
Kanya-Kubjas of North India* (Chicago: Chicago University Press, 1970); Milton B. Singer, *Traditional
India: Structure and Change* (Philadelphia: American Folklore Society, 1959).

[53] Pamela Price, 'Ideology and Ethnicity under British Imperial Rule: "Brahmans", Lawyers and Kin-
Caste Rules in Madras Presidency', *Modern Asian Studies* 23, no. 1 (1989): 162.

[54] Adrian C. Mayer, 'Public Service and Individual Merit in a Town of Central India', in *Culture and
Morality: Essays in Honour of Christoph von Fürer-Haimendorf*, 1981, 153.

[55] P.N. Haksar, 'Commitment: A Dirty Word', August 1973, Article in Seminar Magazine, 'Articles by
him', SN/5, P.N. Haksar papers, NMML.

[56] This is not to endorse the historiography of the 'Cambridge School', captured e.g. in Anil Seal,
*The Emergence of Indian Nationalism: Competition and Collaboration in the Later Nineteenth Cen-
tury*, vol. 1 (Cambridge: Cambridge University Press, 1971). Indeed, it must be possible to consider
Indians as fallible historical agents rather than as objects having history done onto them, without
somehow suggesting that the self-seeking Indian elites were responsible for the perpetuation of British
colonialism.

[57] While some officers were sent to London or Dublin, the (auto)biographical record almost
exclusively discusses Oxbridge.

training, for a year if they had studied in Britain and for two if not.[58] College Masters sat on ICS examination boards and conducted the oral examinations known as *viva voces*.[59] By the early 1920s, the ICS syllabus fit the Oxbridge syllabi so closely that 'if a man got a First at Oxford or Cambridge, the ICS was child's play to him', as K.P.S. Menon once boasted.[60] The Oxford Colleges of Balliol and Christ Church, and at Cambridge Corpus, King's, and St John's, educated a disproportionate number of Indian officers.[61] At Oxford, almost half of Indian students studied at Balliol College. Its Master Benjamin Jowett (1870–1893), an early patron of Oxford's India Institute, envisioned Balliol as a breeding ground for elites irrespective of colour or creed, and offered every candidate who passed the ICS examination a place at the college in the imperial hope that he might 'govern the world through my pupils'.[62] So etched into the Indian imagination has Balliol become that a Delhiite diplomat in Arundhati Roy's novel *The Ministry of Utmost Happiness* could be adequately captured with the dry observation that he 'never lost an opportunity to let people know that he was a Balliol man'.[63]

At Oxbridge, Indians occupied a peculiar space between the disciplining impulses of the British Government and the intellectual fancies of university dons, whose liberal canon from Mill's *On Liberty* to Milton's *Areopagitica* read like a dissident's manual.[64] 'It speaks a lot for the British tradition of freedom and confidence in their society', one officer reminisced, 'that they exposed us, the civil servants of an Empire, to the free and academic atmosphere of a great University, rather than a Government institution'[65]—although one wonders whether the compliment was offered as a palliative to smooth over the disciplinary character of the imperial project. This liberal syllabus did, after all, anticipate a career in service of the decidedly illiberal governing principles of empire. If, as Viceroy Lord Curzon intoned in 1901 at an educational conference at the Indian hill station of Shimla, Oxford offered its students a 'cosmopolitan field of interest and emulation', this was a cosmopolitanism

---

[58] E.N. Mangat Rai, *Commitment, My Style: Career in the Indian Civil Service* (Delhi: Vikas Publishing, 1973), 39.

[59] K.P.S. Menon, 'My Life and Work in the ICS', in *The Civil Servant in India, by Ex-Indian Civil Servants*, ed. Kewalram Laichand Panjabi (Bombay: Bharatiya Vidya Bhavan, 1965), 29.

[60] Menon, 29.

[61] Potter, *India's Political Administrators*, 71.

[62] Richard Symonds, *Oxford and Empire: The Last Lost Cause?* (Oxford: Clarendon Press, 1986), 24, 27, 187.

[63] Arundhati Roy, *The Ministry of Utmost Happiness* (London: Hamish Hamilton, 2017), 186.

[64] Richard Symonds, 'Indians at Oxford before Independence', Synopsis of a Lecture Delivered at the Oxford Majlis, Trinity Term 1985. Majlis Magazine, Oxford, 1986, 8.

[65] Symonds, 10.

88   GENEALOGY: BALLIOL AND BANDUNG

deeply implicated in the hierarchies of empire.[66] In an imperial appeal to the Classics and their universal truths, the British saw their bureaucratic ethos as characterized by the Platonian ideals of loyalty, truthfulness, courage[67]—so much so that Philipp Woodruff, an unreconstructed historian of the ICS, was inspired to give the first two volumes of *The Men Who Ruled India* the Platonian subtitle 'The Guardians'.[68] Yet the supposedly universal but distinctly British renditions of the values of 'chivalry and ceremony, monarchy and majesty' are in fact best thought of as the imperial 'means by which this vast world was brought together, interconnected, unified and sacralized'.[69] The supposedly timeless and universal ideals of worldly governing elites were bound to the temporalities and localities of empire, propagated to advance an individual work ethic but also to legitimate the imperial project.

The attempts at glamourizing imperial bureaucracy came with an almost mythical belief in the intellectual acumen of colonial administrators. This often expressed itself in an emphasis on the kind of academic superiority that anthropologists of colonial India have so readily identified as a common preoccupation of brahminical and British elites. In diplomatic memoirs that have ostensibly set themselves the task of outlining grand developments in world affairs, a discussion of one's university grades seems almost a rite of passage. A First Class degree classification from Oxbridge was 'the most coveted of all distinctions', explained a proud K.P.S. Menon, the first ever Indian admitted into the Foreign and Political Department, who judged his standing first in the ICS examinations of 1921 a lesser feat than his First from Christ Church.[70] In his memoir, K.S. Kirpalani[71]—a 1922 history graduate from Oxford's New College who would go on to represent India at the UN—lingers on the indignities of obtaining merely a Second Class degree, the prospect of which was daunting enough to warrant consideration of dropping one's course altogether.[72] Academic excellence was integral to the mythos of the ICS; G.V. Bedekar, of ICS batch 1933, was drawn to the Service because it attracted 'First Class Honours

---

[66] George Nathaniel Curzon Curzon of Kedleston, *Speeches by Lord Curzon of Kedleston, Viceroy and Governor General of India (Vol. 3)* (Calcutta: Office of the Superintendent of Government Printing, India, 1899), 123.

[67] Symonds, *Oxford and Empire: The Last Lost Cause?*, 32.

[68] Philip Woodruff, *The Men Who Ruled India: The Guardians (Vols I and II)* (New York: St Martin's Press, 1954).

[69] David Cannadine, *Ornamentalism: How the British Saw Their Empire* (Oxford: Oxford University Press, 2001), 122.

[70] Menon, *Many Worlds*, 29, 61.

[71] Not to be confused with a contemporary colleague, High Commissioner S.K. Kripalani.

[72] S.K. Kirpalani, *Fifty Years with the British: Memoirs of an Indian Civil Servant* (Hyderabad: Sangam Books, 1993), 77.

THE GENEALOGY OF A CLEFT   89

Graduates of universities such as Oxford and Cambridge.[73] In fact, Indians regularly outperformed British candidates in the English History and Literature papers of the ICS examination—'somewhat to the chagrin of the India Office and Government of India.[74] Shamaldharee Lall, an ICS officer who studied history at Exeter College in the 1910s, even projected memories of Oxford dons onto his District Officer in Bihar, who displayed an attitude 'exactly the same as that of any tutor at Oxford, always watchful of what I was doing, but interfering as little as possible.[75]

Elite education and the habits that came with it also allowed upper-class, upper-caste Indians to nurture ties of social capital in British high society. M.C. Chagla—a Lincoln College history graduate who served as Ambassador to the US and UK before becoming External Affairs Minister in 1966—unapologetically celebrated Oxford's 'Old Boys ties.[76] B.K. Nehru, son of an Oxford-educated ICS officer and cousin of Jawaharlal Nehru, had his rejection letter from the London School of Economics overturned by Sir Clive Wigram, Private Secretary to the King, who was sufficiently mortified at the prospect of a Nehru joining the University of Nottingham to arrange him a place through personal connections—'a rather early education in the truth that whom you know is more important than what you know', as Nehru put it.[77] In a perfect encapsulation of the cleft habitus—wrapping up semi-aristocratic conventions and progressive radicalism all in one—Nehru unironically follows this tale of social capital with one of the dearest lessons that his liberal university education gave him: 'my total opposition to hereditary privilege.[78]

While Indian elites in the British bureaucratic machinery were learning the importance of whom you know, their bond with Indian compatriots was strained. N.R. Pillai, the ICS-trained second Secretary-General of the MEA, conceded that by the time his colleagues took up their posts, they had 'developed habits of thought and speech unfamiliar to the great mass of their countrymen.[79] In their bid to 'outdo their British masters' in their Britishness,

---

[73] G.V. Bedekar, 'Not Many but Much', in *The Civil Servant in India, by Ex-Indian Civil Servants*, ed. Kewalram Laichand Panjabi (Bombay: Bharatiya Vidya Bhavan, 1965), 271.

[74] Symonds, 'Indians at Oxford', 11.

[75] Shamaldharee Lall, 'An Indian Civil Servant', in *The Civil Servant in India, by Ex-Indian Civil Servants*, ed. Kewalram Laichand Panjabi (Bombay: Bharatiya Vidya Bhavan, 1965), 8.

[76] M.C. Chagla, *Roses in December: An Autobiography*, 9th edn (Bombay: Bharatiya Vidya Bhavan, 1990), 39.

[77] B.K. Nehru, 'My London School of Economics', 1977, Article, 'Speeches/Writings by Him', SN/17, B.K. Nehru papers, NMML.

[78] Nehru.

[79] N. Raghavan Pillai, 'The Civil Service as a Profession', in *The Civil Servant in India, by Ex-Indian Civil Servants*, ed. Kewalram Laichand Panjabi (Bombay: Bharatiya Vidya Bhavan, 1965), 24.

90 GENEALOGY: BALLIOL AND BANDUNG

as one career diplomat of post-Independence India later derided,[80] Indian officers became involved in the most minute rules of etiquette. They applied themselves to polo, hunting, and tennis.[81] Meanwhile, the officers' imagery of an 'Indian people' was shrouded in homebred exoticism, with future ambassadors describing their alienation from 'the poverty-stricken, emaciated, ignorant populace of the villages.'[82] In a 1923 letter to M.C. Chagla about his posting as Assistant Collector in India, K.P.S. Menon—offspring of an aristocratic family in Travancore—found it 'amusing to watch the honest-village-folk looking up to us as a kind of Deux Ex Machina.'[83] Officers' 'patronising, paternalistic' temper revealed an unbridgeable distance, an ICS veteran described.[84] There was a trade-off involved between professional dispassion and closeness to 'the people'—the ability to 'mix freely' with other Indians.[85] Serving Indians, it seems, required removing oneself from them. Indeed, even the concept of 'a people' that transgressed the class boundaries of one's immediate social circles was, to some, a revelation. 'Till I had left India', B. K. Nehru concedes, 'the word "people" meant "people like us".'[86] It did not encompass 'the vast masses of the Indian people who were very different from "us"', and so when Nehru and his peers declared that 'the people of India wanted' something—freedom from foreign rule, a certain kind of India, a particular type of Foreign Service—the word 'people' stood as a placeholder for themselves.[87]

Any dominant habitus will always signal its Other, but it must do so subtly. Indeed, one of the basic intentions of distinction is 'to suggest with the fewest "effects" possible the greatest expenditure of time, money, and ingenuity', so as to display 'the "natural" self-confidence, ease and authority of someone who feels authorized.'[88] Elitism must look effortless, if it is to be elitism at all. Indians in British elite institutions were working from Bourdieu's theoretical claims as though they were stage directions. Oxford, Chagla said of his peers, could 'stamp them as having imbibed the culture which makes them stand out as different from and superior to those less fortunate persons who did not have the same advantage as themselves.'[89] But a word of advice: 'There

[80] Bandyopadhyaya, *The Making of India's Foreign Policy*, 78.
[81] Lall, *The Emergence of Modern India*, 19.
[82] Nehru, *Nice Guys Finish Second: Memoirs*, 92.
[83] K.P.S. Menon, 'Letter to M.C. Chagla', 21 February 1923, Individual Correspondence, M.C. Chagla papers, NMML.
[84] H.V.R. Iengar, 'My Life in the ICS', in *The Civil Servant in India, by Ex-Indian Civil Servants*, ed. Kewalram Laichand Panjabi (Bombay: Bharatiya Vidya Bhavan, 1965), 120.
[85] Isvaran, 'The Indian Civil Servant', 248.
[86] Nehru, *Nice Guys Finish Second: Memoirs*, 90.
[87] Nehru, 90.
[88] Bourdieu, *Distinction*, 380, 250.
[89] Chagla, *Roses in December*, 28.

is an air of superiority about Oxford men which non-Oxford men resent, but this superiority must be effortless if it is to be truly in the Oxford style.[90] The prime characteristic of an ICS man, K.P.S. Menon announced, was 'leisurely perfectionism.'[91]

Of course, the appearance of effortlessness can require considerable effort. The rules for attaining a dominant habitus, and the mere fact of their existence, are always more obvious to outsiders. K.P.S. Menon's attempts at 'acquiring the superficial airs and graces of an Oxford man' required dropping his habit of regularly visiting lectures, since formal tuition was preserved for 'the weaker brethren' unlikely to achieve a First.[92] Christ Church—'the House', after its Latin name *Aedes Christi*—became a training ground for the effortful striving after the effortless habitus: 'Merely to live in the House and breathe its atmosphere was an education', Menon explains.[93] Left unspoken is whether the exercise felt like a privilege well-deserved, an agonized satirization of upper-class belonging, or an imposter's quiet admission of alienation.

Race and belonging in European international society

The efforts at effortlessness also bring into focus the tensions that underlay Indian officers' project of belonging in a Western-dominated world of empire. By the early 1920s, British elite universities were harbouring a band of aristocratically articulate, suit-clad Indians, denouncing the very empire they were hoping to serve in the refined lexicon of its academic heartland. For Bourdieu, local elites in colonized societies were not only 'cast between two worlds' but effectively 'rejected by both', leading 'a sort of double inner life' that encouraged 'either an attitude of uneasy overidentification or one of rebellious negativism.'[94] Future ICS elites often attempted both. One Nehru-era diplomat described his ICS superiors as living through a perpetual 'struggle of contradicting ethics',[95] although it was not just morality but one's entire sense of Self that was on trial. B.K. Nehru describes how

> The Indian student in England in the 'thirties was between two worlds. A generation earlier, he had accepted British rule in India as a law of nature. He had

---

[90] Chagla, 27.
[91] 'Oral History Transcript: K.P.S. Menon', 3.
[92] Menon, *Many Worlds*, 51.
[93] Menon, 52.
[94] Bourdieu, *The Algerians*, 144.
[95] Interview 43.

been thoroughly brain-washed into believing that English civilization was the supreme culmination of the long development of the human race; his salvation lay in achieving as nearly as he could the manners and the graces and the modes of thought and behaviour of his masters. [...] By the 'thirties the British claim to superiority had been shattered [...] We all resented intensely its continuation against the repeated demonstrated will of the people.[96]

Colonial mimicry awoke a certain frustrated hostility among colonized elites, since colonialism set a dominant habitus but 'made it actually impossible to imitate or equal the European'.[97] This hierarchy decreed excessive attention on the part of the colonized to the colonizer's 'words or gestures' which 'seem to us most conventional—greeting, shaking hands, smile' but which in the moment become 'signs of recognition'.[98] A consequence of the inherent inequality that defined the relationship between colonizer and colonized,[99] this status sensitivity was a survival instinct of sorts. This is where the typecast of the formerly colonized as somehow oversensitive—perpetuated in Western writing on Indian diplomats to this date[100]—first appeared.

Future ICS officers were first stranded, in the language of both B.K. Nehru and Bourdieu, 'between two worlds' during their time at Oxbridge. For if cultural capital under colonialism had all the trappings of upper-class Britain, it also bore its racial marks: Macaulay's elite was still 'Indian in blood and colour'. The British Government's Lytton Committee, studying Indians at British universities in 1921, found racial prejudice to be most pronounced at Oxford and Cambridge and lay blame for this with 'public school men', 'among whom there existed a certain pride of class which tended to keep them aloof from men of different race as well as a different class'.[101] For Rajeshwar Dayal, one of the first ICS officers chosen for the IFS after training at Oxford's New College in the early 1930s, this 'snobbishness about "colonials"' was designed to foster 'among the subjects of the British empire, a consciousness of their subject status'.[102] 'Between them and the real Oxford there was a barred door', S.W.R.D. Bandaranaike, future Prime Minister of Ceylon, meditated on his

---

[96] Nehru, 'My London School of Economics'.
[97] Bourdieu, *The Algerians*, 161.
[98] Bourdieu quoted in Go, 'Decolonizing Bourdieu', 58.
[99] Pierre Bourdieu, Derek Robbins, and Rachel Gomme, 'Colonialism and Ethnography: Foreword to Pierre Bourdieu's "Travail et Travailleurs En Algérie"', *Anthropology Today* 19, no. 2 (2003): 18, note 20.
[100] See e.g. Cohen, *India*, 21–23.
[101] Symonds, 'Indians at Oxford', 9.
[102] Dayal, *A Life of Our Times*, 26.

Indian peers who 'lived a life of their own, an Indian Oxford within Oxford'.[103] Elite spaces can be segregated, too—indeed, it seems that elite spaces are particularly susceptible to having their hierarchies set not according to personal merit or academic attainment but the collective parameters of racialized and class-based belonging.

ICS-bound compatriots were never really at home among Indians either. Indian social and political life at Oxbridge centred around the Majlis Society, a club for South Asian students that imitated the respective University Unions of Oxford and Cambridge.[104] 'Anti-government' and 'highly seditious', Majlis members invited officials like the Earl of Lytton, Under-Secretary of State for India, to speak on the future of the Commonwealth,[105] adjudicated members' moral duties after Gandhi's first campaign of non-cooperation in February 1920,[106] and in the mid-1930s received Jawaharlal Nehru himself.[107] Future diplomats of independent India, among them M.C. Chagla (Minister of External Affairs), K.M. Panikkar (Ambassador to China and France), S.K. Kirpalani (Indian delegate at the UN), and K.P.S. Menon (first Foreign Secretary), thought it best to join—and better yet to serve as President, so as to avoid speculation on one's patriotic credentials.[108] Nonetheless, Chagla faced opposition to his Presidency, occasioned by his insufficient 'revolutionary rhetoric and bent'.[109] 'We made vehement speeches which we thought patriotic and which the British thought seditious', a proud Menon announced, before yielding that '[a]t the same time, we went on studiously preparing for the ICS'.[110] 'Some of us did not quite distrust the Britisher as much as some others did', Kirpalani confessed.[111]

The problem of the two worlds then followed Indians into the ICS. Some revolutionaries were caught at the *viva voce*. Showing the distinctly narrow confines of the liberalism Oxbridge paraded in front of future colonial officers, one otherwise promising candidate was promptly awarded 0/300 points

---

[103] S.W.R.D. Bandaranaike, 'The Majlis in the Mid-Twenties', *Hilary Term 1986, The Majlis Magazine, Oxford*, 1986, 23.

[104] Symonds, 'Indians at Oxford', 8.

[105] M.C. Chagla, 'Papers and Correspondence Relating to His Academic Career at School, College and Oxford, 1908–1922', n.d., SN/99, M.C. Chagla papers, NMML.

[106] Kirpalani, *Fifty Years with the British: Memoirs of an Indian Civil Servant*, 55.

[107] 'Oral History Transcript: Apa B. Pant', 1973, 1, Oral Histories, NMML.

[108] Chagla, *Roses in December*, 41–42; Kirpalani, *Fifty Years with the British: Memoirs of an Indian Civil Servant*, 53; Menon, *Many Worlds*, 63; The Oxford Majlis Term Card for Michaelmas Term 1921 suggests that Ambassador M.A. Hussain as well as Foreign Secretaries R.K. Nehru and Subimal Dutt were also members: Chagla, 'Papers and Correspondence Relating to His Academic Career at School, College and Oxford, 1908–1922'.

[109] Chagla, *Roses in December*, 34.

[110] Menon, *Many Worlds*, 54.

[111] Kirpalani, *Fifty Years with the British: Memoirs of an Indian Civil Servant*, 53.

for answering a question on British administration and Indian famines by suggesting that the former tended to cause the latter.[112] No amount of academic theorizing on liberalism, no attempt at imbibing the desirable habitus to its finest detail could disguise the fundamental power asymmetry that underlay the project of imperial governance. For while the language of 'two worlds' might suggest some sort of equilibrium between the two, it was not for Indians to travel freely between them without sanction. Even successful entrants into the ICS were permanent suspects, on whom confidential reports on 'extremist' tendencies were regularly drafted.[113] Kirpalani, for one, was obliged to sign a covenant denouncing his nationalism before beginning service, having argued against British rule in a mock parliamentary debate as part of his official training.[114]

Reconciling mutually contradicting social codes required drawing up some terms and conditions with one's conscience. One former ICS officer, recalled his disciple from a mid-1960s IFS batch, had sworn to resign if Gandhi was allowed to die during a fast.[115] When B.K. Nehru, half his family in British-administered jails, was queried about this moral dilemma during the *viva voce*, he secured 277/300 marks after clarifying that he 'wanted to see for myself whether my being in the ICS would help my people' more than fighting for Independence would, as though loyalties were decided by Benthamite utilitarian arithmetic.[116] K.P.S. Menon reasoned that he would 'become better qualified to serve independent India than those who, carried off their feet by the noble call of patriotism, forsook their studies and entered the serious business of life without adequate preparation'.[117] Menon admired N.R. Pillai for his 'British' Civil Service consciousness, which, faithfully reproducing colonial bureaucratic tropes, accepted that 'it was the duty of a civil servant to serve the government of the day regardless of its political complexion'.[118] And yet, was there not some moral distinction between an Englishman serving a government alien to his politics and an Indian serving a government alien to his people?

This reconciliation was made all the more difficult by the impossibility of escaping the racial divide, even once back in India. Dayal despaired at college

---

[112] Kirpalani, 75.
[113] C.D. Deshmukh, 'Looking Back on My Service Days', in *The Civil Servant in India, by Ex-Indian Civil Servants*, ed. Kewalram Laichand Panjabi (Bombay: Bharatiya Vidya Bhavan, 1965), 4.
[114] Kirpalani, *Fifty Years with the British: Memoirs of an Indian Civil Servant*, 79.
[115] Interview 43.
[116] Nehru, 'The Civil Service in Transition'.
[117] Menon, *Many Worlds*, 54.
[118] Menon quoted in Benner, *Structure of Decision*, 44.

colleagues who, after the passage through Suez, 'metamorphosed into arrogant stand-offish colonials who imagined that their manifest destiny was to rule over the "lesser" races'.[119] In a pointed metaphor about entry, membership, and belonging, K.P.S. Menon found upon his arrival at the North-West Frontier in Peshawar as Under-Secretary to the Chief Commissioner that although his rank should have made him Secretary to the district's Nathiagali Club, as an Indian he was barred from full membership.[120] Of course, capital under colonialism took racialized forms beyond the ICS. The upper-class upset at Gandhi being thrown out of a first-class train compartment in South Africa reflected an analogous betrayal: his English attire and education could never buy him first-class belonging.[121] Yet in the ICS, this racialization of belonging evoked not a denunciation of imperial mores but an attempt to embody them more perfectly: Foreign Secretary Subimal Dutt later explained the arrogance of Indian ICS officers as an anxious attempt at levelling with white colleagues.[122]

The ICS thus produced Indians who were both overconfident and uncomfortable in the hierarchies that punctuated life under colonial rule. Predictably, diplomats remembering their ICS superiors during interviews spoke of a 'superiority complex',[123] but the projection of superiority masked a deeply felt sense of its very opposite, too. Since the status of British ICS officers was 'equivalent of medieval barons or princelings',[124] the 'appearance of partnership' with Britons afforded Indian officers a certain status in the eyes of the world, as they 'revelled in the prestige, comparative affluence, and power that went with the positions they held'—and yet the 'reality was very different from the appearance', Ambassador Arthur Lall, a Balliol history graduate of the 1934 ICS batch, cautions any reader tempted to imagine Indian officers as equal members of some transnational elite.[125] As one diplomat from an early-1960s batch lamented, his seniors had been 'trained in the wrong values',[126] internalizing the racism which was foundational to the colonial project. One infamous confidential report observed of an Indian bureaucrat that he was 'much too

---

[119] Dayal, *A Life of Our Times*, 32.
[120] Menon, *Many Worlds*, 89–90.
[121] Ramnarayan S. Rawat and K. Satyanarayana, 'Dalit Studies: New Perspectives on Indian History and Society', in *Dalit Studies*, ed. Ramnarayan S. Rawat and K. Satyanarayana (Durham: Duke University Press, 2016), 2.
[122] Dutt, *With Nehru in the Foreign Office*, 285.
[123] Interview 43.
[124] Lall, *The Emergence of Modern India*, 18.
[125] Lall, 49.
[126] Interview 30.

96 GENEALOGY: BALLIOL AND BANDUNG

anti-Indian' to the liking of his British superior officer.[127] K.P.S. Menon could never quite diagnose this condition:

> Perhaps the real handicap from which I and most Indian students suffered was that we had a certain complex, resulting from the unnatural relationship between Great Britain and India, the ruler and the ruled. Whether it was an inferiority complex or a superiority complex I do not know; perhaps it was an inferiority complex which, as it often does, took the form of a superiority complex.[128]

It is telling that even the more nationalistically minded autobiographical narrations of Oxbridge invest a great deal of persuasive power and descriptive detail on grades, gowns, and social graces into convincing the reader of the writer's capacity to meet the colonial standard of civilization. Those who did not match the exacting specifications of an English gentleman must have translated their failed attempts at mimicry into world-weary cynicism in an entirely more obvious way. In Kiran Desai's quietly devastating novel *The Inheritance of Loss,* a retired judge of the ICS, Jemubhai, now in reclusive retirement in the remote West Bengali hill station of Kalimpong in the 1980s, is still beset by the trauma of his imperial education. In a decaying bungalow left behind by the British, Jemubhai's quietly carried resentments and laboured Anglophilia make for a misanthropic reading of the world. He 'hangs on to his Anglophilia although every moment of his actual life in England was torture', since 'his English back then was incomprehensible, and his rural and lower-middle class origins rendered him a comical outsider'.[129] Decades after his humiliating education in the social expressions of colonial power, 'Jemubhai constantly lives and relives the insults of his brief stint in England while preparing for exams to enter the ICS': 'Although his written performance had been stellar, the inadequacies of his class origins caught up with him during the interviews' when his Gujarati-inflected recital of Scott's poem *Lochinvar* left his British interlocutors mortifyingly amused.[130] I suggest that we keep the solitary figure of Jemubhai at the back of our minds whenever we encounter the altogether smoother descriptions of Oxbridge and the ICS in the memoirs

---

[127] Haksar, 'Commitment: A Dirty Word'.

[128] Menon, *Many Worlds*, 53.

[129] Sankaran Krishna, 'IR and the Postcolonial Novel: Nation and Subjectivity in India', in *Postcolonial Theory and International Relations: A Critical Introduction*, ed. Sanjay Seth (London: Routledge, 2013), 137.

[130] Krishna, 137.

of Indian bureaucrats: those who dedicated their early lives to the service of empire have an incentive to write shame and stigma out of their story in order to prove their effortless belonging among the globally mobile administrative elite.

As a social process, Macaulay's project of creating an Indian elite 'English in taste, opinions, morals and intellect' was not dissimilar to the diplomatic expressions of an 'expansion of international society' envisioned by the English School, with the mores and principles of colonial powers brought to the colonies to facilitate the process of imperial governing. And just as the original English School narrative failed to consider the space into which international society 'expanded', so too the Macaulayan project neglected to consider what might happen in the uneven encounter 'between two worlds'. What is notable in the autobiographical record of Indian ICS veterans is the curious absence, beyond repeated commitments to Indian Independence presumably intended for postcolonial audiences, of any descriptions of the 'Indian' world that existed alongside the colonial, British, foreign one. The British Home Department estimated that nine out of ten Indians in the ICS exhibited 'distinctly Indian religious practices and beliefs, reflecting values and life-styles very different from their European colleagues',[131] and yet such inflections have not found their way into the autobiographical record. The silences in the sources speak loudly of the imbalances of power and worth that Indian officers sensed. They tell of the constant self-policing that bureaucrats engaged in, curating themselves to appear as insiders in the eyes of the intended readers of their autobiographies. The anxieties of trying to exist in the spaces between would come to shape the postcolonial production of the diplomatic cleft habitus.

The postcolonial metamorphosis

The radical potential of postcolonial reordering

After Independence, India's diplomatic project was to differentiate the newly postcolonial nation from the former colonizer, if not in taste then certainly in opinions and morals. Realizing a new vision of international society meant a rehearsed rejection of old habits. As Jayantanuja Bandyopadhyaya, a one-time

---

[131] Potter, *India's Political Administrators*, 117.

98 GENEALOGY: BALLIOL AND BANDUNG

diplomat who left the Foreign Service in 1960 to become its fiercest critic in academia, forewarned:

> If India was to play a new and important role in world affairs, if her foreign policy was to have a certain romanticist and idealist vision, if her vibrant nationalism and her powerful intellectual and cultural tradition were to be projected into the international sphere, and if her diplomats were expected to represent such a foreign policy abroad, it was imperative for the political leadership to enthuse and galvanise the administration into modes of thought and action radically different from those which it had been attuned during British rule.[132]

As if to affirm the legacy of the freedom struggle and to legitimate its own role as an authentic representative of postcolonial India, the Foreign Service developed a diplomatic idiom reflective of the emotive anticolonial binaries that had animated nationalist campaigning, moulded to revolve around Third World solidarity, anti-imperialism, and the expression of Indian difference. Whatever the outward expressions of cultural assimilation into an old cosmopolitan world of diplomacy, one former Cambridge-educated Foreign Secretary insisted, India had always wanted to 'strike a different path for ourselves.'[133]

As both Prime Minister and Foreign Minister, it was Jawaharlal Nehru's political responsibility to bring about this postcolonial diplomatic era. In a broadcast from Delhi on 7 September 1947, he put the world on notice that India claimed 'equal and honourable treatment for our people' as a prerequisite for international cooperation.[134] At the famous 1955 Conference of Afro-Asian Nations in Bandung, he decreed with an eye towards the West that '[w]e value the friendship of the great countries, but we can only sit with them as brothers.'[135] This was to be a radical break from the colonial order, demanding more than formal sovereign equality. Nehru was asking for social recognition of Indian difference and Third World identities—not as aberrations from a Western norm but as worthy reflections of the diversity of a new postcolonial world in the making.

---

[132] Bandyopadhyaya, *The Making of India's Foreign Policy*, 261–262.

[133] Interview 9.

[134] Jawaharlal Nehru, *Selected Works of Jawaharlal Nehru, Volume 19: 16th July–18th October 1952*, ed. Sarvepalli Gopal (New Delhi: Jawaharlal Nehru Memorial Fund, 1966), 21.

[135] Jawaharlal Nehru, *Jawaharlal Nehru: Thoughts* (New Delhi: Jawaharlal Nehru Memorial Fund, 1985), 7.

During our conversations, diplomats of successive generations presented Nehru as the antonym of the ICS, thwarting its pro-Western sympathies and chastening its elitism.[136] Nehru had already decided in the 1930s that 'no new order can be built in India so long as the spirit of the Indian Civil Service pervades our administration and our public services', it being 'essential that the ICS and similar services must disappear completely.'[137] He took pains to impart his vision for a postcolonial world to diplomatic youngsters, addressing the imperatives of development and democracy, and—in a nation divided into castes, a subcontinent ripped by Partition, and a world recovering from the indignities of colonialism—an understanding of 'the life of a diplomat as a continuous process of self-education in which pre-conceived notions and prejudices had no place.'[138] He spoke against 'slavishly' following Western diplomatic protocol when representing 'a poor country where millions live on the verge of starvation' and cautioned that 'care should be taken that we do not become an appendage or a junior partner' of British embassies in countries to which freshly minted Indian diplomats were accredited.[139] Diplomats were to 'function as Indians and not as imitations of Englishmen' and to curb—in Nehru's exalted English parlance—'[a]ny attempt on the part of any member of the staff to behave pompously as if he is very much Anglicized.'[140] Nehru protested that 'the old officer complex [...] does not fit in today; nor is it desirable.'[141] While '[a]ll over the world there is a strong tendency towards equality', '[i]n India we are backward in this, in spite of our professions', he ruminated—'[t]his is partly due to our old customs, partly to our social set-up, and partly to the traditions of British days which we have inherited'. There was no place in a new world for habits of the old. They were an embarrassing tell, especially when they revealed the shared reservoir of cultural capital that had made upper-class, upper-caste expressions of India's 'social set-up' so compatible with British class society under the Raj.

Nehru sought to signal the dawn of indigenous diplomacy with symbolically significant but concrete changes. The introduction of Nehru jackets and black *sherwanis* at formal functions, to one Oxford-educated liberal arts graduate

---

[136] Interview 16; Interview 17, March 2019; Interview 45.

[137] Jawaharlal Nehru, *An Autobiography* (Bombay: Allied Publishers, 1962), 445.

[138] A.S. Chib, 'The Making of an Indian Diplomat', 27 August 1982, Article, 'Individual correspondence between R.K. Nehru and A.S. Chib', R.K. Nehru papers, NMML.

[139] Jawaharlal Nehru, 'Note for Asaf Ali and K.P.S. Menon', 22 January 1947, Individual correspondence, K.P.S. Menon papers, NMML.

[140] Nehru.

[141] Jawaharlal Nehru, 'Prime Minister's Note for the Guidance of Members of the Foreign Service and More Especially, for Those Serving in Our Missions Abroad', 20 October 1950, FSP/50-11(88), NAI.

who served under Nehru, was 'an indication of how the political leadership wanted the diplomats to develop an identity of their own', a gradual replacement of suits signifying closure for the colonial aesthetic.[142] In a letter from 1950 supposedly about serving alcohol in Indian Missions, complete with Nehru's well-acquainted etiquette advise of going with sherry before and port after dinner, the Prime Minister ruminated:

> It was not merely a question of prohibition, but rather a feeling I had that some of our officers abroad live in a mental climate, which is far removed from that of India. I can well understand that they have to follow, to a large extent, the customs of the countries they are in and old established diplomatic conventions; also that they are affected by their environment [...] But we have always to remain Indians and to remember that an Indian embassy is a bit of India. No individual and no country is respected if he or it tries to ape others [...]
>
> I am not, what might be called, a traditionalist or a person trying to revive the ways of life of a past that is over. I look to the future and I think that we have a great deal to learn from the present-day civilization of the West. I think I have myself learnt much from it and I hope to learn more. But I see no reason to be swept away by any custom or practice of the West, simply because it is popular there, or because it might make me popular there [...][143]

The choice between whisky and wine may not have sounded like a classical diplomatic dilemma to a European diplomat, nor might the question of prohibition naturally seem like an occasion for Ministry-wide soul-searching. And yet K.P.S. Menon thought the letter important enough to circulate to all diplomats at Headquarters, too.[144] For what was on the line were the principles by which the Indian diplomatic habitus was to be ordered, the customs it would be bound by, and the dispositions it would legitimate and stigmatize. Indeed, the symbolism of sobriety was deemed more important than the practicalities of diplomatic sociability. Alcohol could lubricate ties of social capital in a diplomatic world which was quite fond of its drink. One polite letter of protest against prohibition from an Indian Consul in Saigon in 1948 sought to convey, in particular, 'the difficulty of conducting negotiations with French

---

[142] Interview 40, April 2019.
[143] Nehru, 'Prime Minister's Note for the Guidance of Members of the Foreign Service and More Especially, for Those Serving in Our Missions Abroad'.
[144] K.P.S. Menon, 'Note', 7 January 1950, 'Prime Minister's Note for the Guidance of Members of the Foreign Service and More Especially, for Those Serving in Our Missions Abroad', FSP/50-11(88), NAI.

officials without alcohol.'[145] And yet Nehru knew that his was a project of re-education: if the Indian diplomatic habitus was to be moulded into a carrier of Indian postcoloniality, it needed to shed old signs of colonial conditioning and signal an indigenous identity founded on new ideals.

Even the most status-conscious ICS officers vied to exhibit the progressive practices of the new world—at least on paper. In letters, they reminded each other not to treat themselves 'as a separate class but as members of the society at large,'[146] in the words of T.N. Kaul, and performatively declared, like R.K. Nehru, that the 'upper class approach should now be given up', since it 'does not fit in with the new order that we are trying to create.'[147] Such declarations sought to conform to what Jawaharlal Nehru repeatedly reminded them was 'our ideal for India, where we want no class distinctions to subsist.'[148] R.K. Nehru, in a conscientious letter to the Prime Minister (and his cousin) in September 1955, admitted that Indian bureaucracy needed changing 'as it is the product of conditions which are very different from those existing today.'[149]

The calls for a new egalitarian spirit were indicative of the normative appeal of postcolonial principles, but their frequency also suggests a recognition of how difficult such a spirit would be to practise. Indeed, it often seems as though such calls became a collective mantra repeated in the hope that the message would slowly sink into the old hierarchical psyche of the caller, too. In 1949, a frustrated ICS-trained Ambassador-designate to the Netherlands, M.S. Mehta, dryly noted the 'strange irony that allegations should emanate from interested quarters about my loyalty towards our National Government, while in the regime of the old Political Department I was consistently accused of being a supporter of the Congress and its radical ideology.'[150] These are the kinds of quotidian balancing acts, the kinds of performative shows of solidarity that were required for old colonial officers to prove their commitment to the new project of postcolonial world-making. ICS veterans knew that colonial habits

[145] H.V.R. Iengar, 'Letter to Vijaya Lakshmi Pandit', 22 March 1948, 'August 1947–61: Correspondence exchanged by Mrs Pandit with G.S. Bajpai (Secretary-General, MEA, and Commonwealth Relations) in Her Capacity as India's Ambassador to Moscow and Later USA' SF/56, Vijaya Lakshmi Pandit papers, NMML.

[146] T.N. Kaul, 'Letter to the Foreign Secretary', 2 September 1955, 'Official Notes', SF/84, Subimal Dutt papers, NMML.

[147] R.K. Nehru, 'Letter to Jawaharlal Nehru', 4 September 1955, 'Official Notes', SF/84, Subimal Dutt papers, NMML.

[148] Jawaharlal Nehru, '(Circular) Letter to Y.D. Gundevia (Indian Ambassador to Switzerland)', 22 November 1953, 'Correspondence between Y.D. Gundevia and Jawaharlal Nehru', Y.D. Gundevia papers, NMML.

[149] Nehru, 'Letter to Jawaharlal Nehru'.

[150] Mohan Sinha Mehta, 'Letter to G.S. Bajpai', 13 January 1949, '1948–49: Correspondence with K.P.S. Menon, G.S. Bajpai Regarding His Appointment as Ambassador to Holland and Clarification of His Views vis-à-vis Jaya Prakash Narayan', SF/7, Mohan Sinha Mehta papers, NMML.

102 GENEALOGY: BALLIOL AND BANDUNG

went against everything the postcolonial project represented, as Subimal Dutt's note on administrative reform in the autumn of 1955 demonstrates:

> What we are trying to create is a welfare state based on a pattern of society which will be free from our traditional weaknesses, e.g., privilege, caste, discrimination and inequality. The administrative system that we are using is, by origin, of the colonial type. It was designed to uphold our weaknesses and to help in preserving the established order. In keeping with this order, a class structure was developed among the services [...] I think our approach has been influenced, to some extent, though perhaps unconsciously, by the class structure of the administration.[151]

If the overemphasis on British mores was once a performance, so too was the attempt at embodying India's newfound egalitarian, solidarist postcoloniality. In one article draft on the modern diplomat, T.N. Kaul, catching himself, has struck out an unfashionably condescending 'our common folk' and dutifully replaced it with a politically correct 'many people'.[152] In a note from the Indian Embassy in Moscow in August 1965, he instructed that although '[w]e were, in the beginning, apt to copy the British and adopt their methods and manners', now '[w]e should, as far as possible, speak to each other in an Indian language'—note the audience—'especially before foreigners'.[153] It was in the eyes of the world that India was to be remade in the image of its newfound 'authenticity'. The popular tropes about India's pompous ICS officers, perpetuated by much of the historical record and diplomatic juniors alike, fail to acknowledge the arduous attempts by the most status-conscious ICS veterans to align themselves with what often must have felt like a rather unintuitive process of re-education. This was an elite seeking to refashion itself to survive a global transition into a new kind of world, run by a new kind of elite.

Brave old world

And yet, for all the fanfare on clean slates and new beginnings, the emerging Indian diplomatic habitus echoed the manners and ideals not only of the

---

[151] Subimal Dutt, 'Response to Ministry of Home Affairs, Appleby Report', September 1955, 9–10, 'Official notes', SF/84, Subimal Dutt papers, NMML.

[152] T.N. Kaul, 'Diplomacy and Diplomats', n.d., Incomplete article, 'Speeches/Writings by Him', SN/111, T.N. Kaul papers, NMML.

[153] T.N. Kaul, 'Note', 11 August 1965, 'Circular Letters Issued by N.R. Pillai Chairman, IFS Committee, B.K. Nehru, Foreign Secretary and Other Papers Relating to ICS/IFS Services Matters', SF/14, T.N. Kaul papers, NMML.

'Bandung spirit' but of the 'Balliol man'. Writing with Sayad about the cultural logics of decolonization, Bourdieu abandoned his former notions of romantic revolutionary postcoloniality, arguing that the structuring power of the habitus would ensure that colonial-era 'manners of behaving and thinking' would survive decolonization.[154] And so it was in India, where the Foreign Service had no bureaucratic precedent to fall back on—'except', as one early-1960s recruit noted with some defensiveness, 'to borrow whatever we could from the British'.[155]

While formally severing the bonds to an old imagery of European international society, Indian diplomats once employed in the ICS continued to nurture an assemblage of its practices and ideals. T.N. Kaul, 1939 batch ICS officer and Foreign Secretary, knew his kind:

> The 'old hands' [...] tried to lay down certain conventions and codes of conduct, borrowed mainly from the British. What was lacking was the enthusiasm and elan that a newly independent nation feels on achieving freedom. Old habits die hard and the senior people brought along with them some of their old prejudices and bureaucratic procedures.[156]

The 'obsession with the British model' among senior Indian diplomats became an often-heard complaint within Indian progressive circles.[157] Doing onto others as the British had done onto them, ICS veterans brought austere bureaucratic hierarchies into the Foreign Service.[158] They continued to draw higher salaries and operate under ICS Rules,[159] and signed their letters with colonial queues of 'Esq., CIE., ICS', signifying the various titles and Orders of Chivalry bestowed upon them by the British crown.[160] These status sensitivities erupted into an 'Excellency boom' in Indian Missions, which Nehru was forced to

---

[154] Bourdieu and Sayad, 'Colonial Rule and Cultural Sabir', 471–472.

[155] Interview 30.

[156] Triloki Nath Kaul, 'New World Economic Order', n.d., Miscellaneous articles, 'Speeches/Writings by Him', SN/141, T.N. Kaul papers, NMML.

[157] Sankar N. Maitra, 'Ills of the Indian Foreign Service: A Comment', *Economic and Political Weekly* 1, no. 13 (1966): 551.

[158] Interview 43; Head of Mission of India, Cairo, 'Note Responding to Jawaharlal Nehru's Letter on Prohibition', 6 December 1950, 'Prohibition of Alcoholic Drink in Official Parties by Our Missions Abroad', 21(5)—G II/51, NAI.

[159] Interview 18; Interview 74; Interview 79; Jawaharlal Nehru, 'Letter to the MEA', 9 September 1955, 'Official notes', SF/84, Subimal Dutt papers, NMML.

[160] Many letters from G.S. Bajpai and K.P.S. Menon carried such abbreviations; see also Mohan Sinha Mehta, 'Letter to K.P.S. Menon', 14 December 1948, '1948–49: Correspondence with K.P.S. Menon, G.S. Bajpai Regarding His Appointment as Ambassador to Holland and Clarification of His Views vis-à-vis Jaya Prakash Narayan', SF/7, Mohan Sinha Mehta papers, NMML.

104 GENEALOGY: BALLIOL AND BANDUNG

manage by officially regulating use of the title in 1948.[161] Complaining about the opposition from ICS officers to more cooperative working methods at the Embassy in Moscow in 1950, Ambassador Pandit singled out Prem Krishen, First Secretary, who epitomized 'the worst kind of ICS complex', leading him to assume an 'offensive attitude' towards 'all those who did not belong to the ICS'.[162]

The 'tyranny of the ICS', imaginatively derided in a 21-page deposition by Ambassador Dhamija to the 1966 Pillai Committee on IFS reform,[163] was not strictly a question of official posts. Rather, it was a matter of embodied culture. IFS officers who eventually advanced to replace their ICS-trained predecessors 'acquired many of the same attitudes to their profession'.[164] Under the influence of their colonially educated superiors, they came to consider themselves 'a class apart, as the elite', 'so cut off from their roots that they sometimes lost their original moorings', a rueful Kaul observed.[165] As one diplomat confided about his colleagues who joined under Nehru, they became 'more attuned to the ways of functioning of the ICS' than they might have cared to admit.[166] A Cambridge-educated recruit of the early 1960s extended a mischievous apology for the inherited elitism: filling the shoes of ICS officers required 'being a bit of a toff'.[167]

Former colonial officers and anti-colonial campaigners, now joined together in the postcolonial Foreign Service, sustained lifelong connections with British luminaries of the Raj. K.P.S. Menon was still exchanging affectionate letters replete with news about his family life with Sir Olaf Caroe, former Foreign Secretary to the Government of India, at least into the late 1970s, only a few years before each of their passing,[168] while Vijaya Lakshmi Pandit was the only non-relation present at Lord Mountbatten's burial in 1979, having come in a personal capacity, 'simply as "Nan" to say her last goodbye to Dickie'.[169] Nehru would call Churchill whenever he was passing through London, and

[161] N. V. Raman, *Indian Diplomatic Service: The First Thirty-Four Years* (Delhi: Chanakya Publications, 1986), 12.

[162] Vijaya Lakshmi Pandit, 'Letter to G.S. Bajpai', 9 October 1947, '1947–1951: Correspondence of V. L. Pandit (as Indian Ambassador to USSR) with G.S. Bajpai—Secretary General, MEA, regarding official matters', SF/55, Vijaya Lakshmi Pandit papers, NMML.

[163] Dhamija quoted in Tharoor, *Reasons of State*, 171.

[164] Tharoor, 171.

[165] Kaul, 'New World Economic Order'.

[166] Interview 35.

[167] Interview 9.

[168] Olaf Caroe, 'Letter to K.P.S. Menon', 15 February 1979, Individual Correspondence, K.P.S. Menon Papers, NMML.

[169] Sastri Brata, 'Article on Vijaya Lakshmi Pandit', n.d., 'Speeches/Writings by Others', SN/27a, T.N. Kaul papers, NMML.

Jagat Mehta was convinced that 'had Churchill revisited India, Nehru would have presided over a great public welcome to an old imperialist signifying how both could rise above former animosities'.[170]

The social capital that once tied the Indian elite to British high society now complicated any radical departures from the colonial imagination. Amidst the organizational preparations for Independence, British officials once involved in the diplomatic affairs of colonial India pressed their Indian colleagues to 'build on experience in the foreign field gained in the British Commonwealth generally and in India in particular, and to avoid too drastic a change in any direction', as Sir Olaf insisted.[171] Leveraging an unflattering comparison to American diplomats, who were unable to 'compete on level terms with what were regarded as their trained and subtle colleagues' in Britain, he encouraged Indians to forego this sorry fate by 'making use of the traditions and the *esprit de corps*' of British bureaucracy.[172] In a personal letter to Sir Olaf, N.R. Pillai repeated his 'fullest concurrence in all your proposals'.[173] Although objections were raised to the suggestion of seconding British diplomats into the Indian Foreign Service,[174] the conversations we might think of as concerning the ideal diplomatic habitus were considerably more amiable. Major A.S.N. Shah, involved in crafting the Foreign Service after a career in the colonial army, suggested that even an Indian Foreign Service 'nationalist in its outlook' would 'need the Foreign Office tradition and high standard of diplomacy', proposing that Indian diplomats be recruited in London and trained at the British Foreign Office.[175] R.N. Banerjee stressed that 'every effort' should be made to retain ICS officials—a curious method for realizing his vision for a 'self-contained', 'entirely new' Service.[176]

ICS fingerprints were all over the emerging notions of how the ideal postcolonial Indian diplomat should be. The IFS Conduct Rules, governing diplomats' behaviour and duties, were modelled on their ICS equivalent.[177] Internal policies were justified with reference to British Foreign Office precedent

---

[170] Mehta, *The Tryst Betrayed: Reflections on Diplomacy and Development*, 47.

[171] Olaf Caroe, 'Note: "Indian Representation Abroad"', 1945, 'Establishment of a Separate Indian Foreign Service', FSP/47-2(7), NAI.

[172] Caroe.

[173] N. Raghavan Pillai, 'Letter to Olaf Caroe', 27 July 1945, 'Establishment of a Separate Indian Foreign Service', FSP/47-2(7), NAI.

[174] H. Dayal, 'Response to Olaf Caroe', 24 November 1945, 'Establishment of a Separate Indian Foreign Service', FSP/47-2(7), NAI.

[175] Major A.S.N. Shah, 'Secret Appendix to Notes: "An Indian Diplomatic Service"', n.d., 'Establishment of a Separate Indian Foreign Service', FSP/47-2(7), NAI.

[176] R.N. Banerjee, 'Confidential Note to Olaf Caroe', 16 February 1946, 'Establishment of a Separate Indian Foreign Service', FSP/47-2(7), NAI.

[177] Interview 16; Interview 48.

on everything from diplomats publishing on foreign affairs[178] to the role of diplomatic spouses.[179] The ICS officers' 'social graces, manner of conducting themselves' set a social standard of elite comportment for the Foreign Service, a diplomat who worked under them for two decades explained.[180] The ideal diplomat, T.N. Kaul explained in an article draft replete with allusions to the aristocratic charms of old-world diplomacy, showed 'sophistication in the manner of his [sic] presentation'.[181] One junior's highest praise for R.K. Nehru was to paint him as a 'suave, meticulously dressed man with an aristocratic bearing', who 'tended to be rather strict and severe as he believed in maintaining a high standard of discipline and efficiency'.[182] A description of a Head of Mission in Afghanistan in 1948 spoke of a man who 'possessed certain essential qualities that contributed to the success of an envoy': a person 'with refined manners', 'invariably clad in immaculate' clothing, who 'carried himself like a benevolent feudal lord'.[183] Or, as was Foreign Secretary Jagat Mehta's (1976–1979) assessment of Asaf Ali, India's first Ambassador to the United States: 'He was one of those early-generation Congressmen who, like Nehru, was elegant, well-educated, with Anglicized style and taste, yet with unquestionable commitment to Independence', who 'had some lingering nostalgia for what he felt was Western diplomacy' and 'enjoyed an old friendship with Nehru as both shared occidental refinements'.[184] G.S. Bajpai, in Mehta's appreciative rendition, 'had balanced cadences, like Gibbon or Macaulay, which showed he had imbibed the classics'.[185] This was the 'aristocratic international', domesticated.

What had once seemed decidedly colonial was beginning to be presented as amorphously cosmopolitan. Indian ICS officers had tamed their personal dilemma into a governing standard: colonial conventions on diplomatic decorum and practice were being repurposed as self-evident, universal ideals for a worldly elite. For all our theoretical efforts at 'provincializing Europe' and 'decolonizing IR', we must also investigate the self-styled universalizations of former colonial subjects. In their crafting of an ideal habitus for the Indian

---

[178] 'Extracts of Noting from File No. 117(71)FSP/58 Relating to Publication of a Novel by Shri B. Rajan of the Embassy of India, Vienna', n.d., 'IFS Rules—Question whether Foreign Service Officers Can Be Permitted to Write and Publish Books of Literary, Artistic or Scientific Character', 21(1) GA/59, NAI.

[179] GA Section (MEA), 'Note', 15 March 1968, 'IFS (PLCA) Rules 1961—Amendments to—Proposal to Allow Single Women Officers to Take Either of Their Dependent Parents to Their Station of Posting Abroad', Q/GA/791,468 (Pt. I), NAI.

[180] Interview 39.

[181] Kaul, 'Diplomacy and Diplomats'.

[182] Chib, 'The Making of an Indian Diplomat'.

[183] Raman, *Indian Diplomatic Service*, 11–12.

[184] Mehta, *The Tryst Betrayed: Reflections on Diplomacy and Development*, 79–80.

[185] Mehta, 42.

diplomat, old-school hands perpetuated much of the cultural repertoire of colonialism that they had formally liberated themselves from in 1947. They presented as universal that which once was colonial. It will not do, therefore, to think of the provincialization project of postcolonial scholarship simply as forsaking our focus on Europe or unleashing some sort of 'authentic' or 'native' essence. Rather, we must investigate the ways in which imageries of a white, colonial, upper-class European international society came to be reproduced inside the formally postcolonial apparatuses of power across the decolonized world.

The dual imageries of international society were endowed to future diplomatic generations not only through stated missions and explicit rules but through the inheritance of quotidian behaviour and taste. In interviews, diplomats who joined the Service after Independence to work under ICS veterans volunteered that they made a 'conscious attempt to emulate them'[186] and that 'the *esprit de corps* began with them embracing us as youngsters to be brought up.'[187] 'There was a code of conduct that the British Civil Service had established', to which newcomers were 'moulded', described a diplomat who joined the Service only a few years into Independence.[188] For ICS grandees, diplomacy 'was not just work, it was a lifestyle', as one critical member of an early-1960s batch explained with a mockingly raised eyebrow—and 'the lifestyle was already defined; it's not like diplomats entering the Service after 1947 could change it.'[189] 'Thomas Babington Macaulay's spirit continued to dominate the [...] work in the Ministry', Dixit, too, wrote, rather bluntly.[190] Socialization into the postcolonial Foreign Service was, in some ways, socialization into a bygone world of upper-class imperial notions of 'worldliness'.

Postcolonial recruits considered their ICS seniors with a combination of begrudging admiration and practised disdain. The seniors were applauded for knowing 'how to keep up a conversation at the dinner table'[191] and being 'well-read', 'able to take a wider view of things'[192]—and 'they had dash, they had confidence'[193] and 'swagger in their gait'[194] to show for it. One of the first juniors to work under them, serving up a series of colonial British upper-class

---

[186] Interview 28, April 2019.
[187] Interview 16; The same interpretation was offered in Interview 23; Interview 18; Interview 35.
[188] Interview 18.
[189] Interview 45.
[190] Dixit, *Indian Foreign Service*, 84.
[191] Interview 43.
[192] Interview 25.
[193] Interview 29, April 2019.
[194] Rasgotra, *A Life in Diplomacy*, 16.

108 GENEALOGY: BALLIOL AND BANDUNG

ideals, complimented Pillai as a 'thorough gentleman', Bajpai as an 'excellent speaker' with 'thorough control of his pen', and Menon, with biting understatement, as a 'very polite man'.[195] One might be tempted to second-guess the sincerity of such compliments, verging as they often seemed to on satire. And yet they were usually offered in a tone which suggested that admitting that there was something admirable about ICS officers at all signified a personal failure to imbibe an appropriately emancipatory spirit. '90% were British stooges', a diplomat of one of the earliest batches added for effect after some approving comments—it took them time to fully appreciate after Independence that 'they didn't have to go and do *salaams* to the whites'.[196]

The standard narrative of postcolonial change, espoused not only in written accounts of Indian diplomatic history but by diplomats who witnessed the beginnings of the Service, presents a clean cultural battle. This battle pitted the old ICS hands against the anti-imperial, egalitarian impulses of Nehru. And yet what made it possible for the cleft habitus to become institutionalized and normalized following Independence was precisely the fact that the reverence for an old conception of international society was not an unfashionable obsession of old colonial officers alone. Nehru himself often seemed more comfortable in its conventions than those of the new world he was arduously creating. Just as his father Motilal, at the age of 60, had 'turned from flamboyant epicure to ascetic nationalist overnight', surrendering Anand House, the family mansion, for nationalist campaigning and burning the family's Western attire,[197] so too there was something rehearsed about Nehru's pursuit of a radical postcoloniality. An interview question in the Civil Service exams in the late 1970s still asked one candidate to reckon with the statement '*voh toh Angrezi hai*', intimating that Nehru had for all intents and purposes been an Englishman.[198] Living 'in the lap of luxury and Western-style comfort', the 'Nehrus' Brahmin pride, bolstered by their affluence and education, meant they considered themselves (and were considered) the social equals of the ruling British elite in the country', as an article on Vijaya Lakshmi Pandit once described.[199] One diplomatic admirer who worked under him for a decade laconically agreed with Nehru's own description of himself as 'the last Englishman to rule India'.[200] A less enamoured colleague who joined just before Nehru's passing in 1964 scoffed

[195] Interview 16.
[196] Interview 79.
[197] Brata, 'Article on Vijaya Lakshmi Pandit'.
[198] Interview 41.
[199] Brata, 'Article on Vijaya Lakshmi Pandit'.
[200] Interview 79.

that the title of his 1946 opus *The Discovery of India* simply betrayed Nehru's need to discover the country for himself upon returning from Cambridge.[201]

Nehru's politics jarred with those of upper-class imperial Britain but many of his cultural preferences did not. Unwittingly echoing Sir Olaf, he demanded—in the paraphrasing of a senior diplomat—that his diplomats 'stand up to the best minds around the world'.[202] His hand-picked envoys, recruited before standardized entry examinations began in 1949, 'circulated within the closed circle of the Indian community', lingering in the organizational structures of postcolonial diplomacy as 'symbols of a decadent past'.[203] One officer who served under him suggested it was 'Nehru's bias' that drove him to pick diplomats from among 'people with a social presence' and 'social sophistication'—'people who felt comfortable abroad', as the gracious euphemism went.[204] K.P.S. Menon recalled his 'partiality for people who had been at college with him' at Cambridge.[205] In fact, most Indians fighting the Raj belonged to the same social circles, often even the same families, as those serving it, as an apologetic R.K. Nehru once offered in self-defence.[206] Their political resumes diverged at crucial junctions but their personal biographies—and thus their dispositions, education, language, comportment—did not. It is perhaps for this reason that Nehru's personal relations with ICS veterans never seemed to suffer from the political disconnect.[207]

The appreciation for colonially tainted, European upper-class markers of status is also what made Nehru—who purportedly once pronounced Indian royalty a 'nuisance in the whole freedom struggle' best 'finished with'[208]—to make diplomats of half a dozen royals.[209] Despite their diplomatic colleagues' dim view of their professional and moral virtues,[210] Nehru pursued the offspring of India's princely states because they exhibited what one senior

---

[201] Interview 45.

[202] Interview 14, March 2019.

[203] Raman, *Indian Diplomatic Service*, 17.

[204] Interview 9.

[205] 'Oral History Transcript: K.P.S. Menon', 2.

[206] 'Oral History Transcript: K.P.S. Menon', 3.

[207] 'Oral History Transcript: R.K. Nehru', 1971, 7, Oral Histories, NMML.

[208] 'Oral History Transcript: Apa B. Pant', 2.

[209] For a reading of how the representational ideals of princely decorum coexisted with a practice of Gandhian asceticism for India's pioneering, aristocratic Ambassador to East Africa, Apa Pant, see Guyot-Réchard, 'Stirring Africa towards India'.

[210] Vijaya Lakshmi Pandit, 'Letter to N.R. Pillai (Secretary-General, MEA)', 18 March 1957, '1955–60: Correspondence of Vijaya Lakshmi Pandit as Indian High Commissioner to London with P.N. Haksar, N.R. Pillai, R.K. Nehru, M.J. Desai and S. Dutt', SF/17, Vijaya Lakshmi Pandit papers, NMML; G.S. Bajpai, 'Letter to Vijaya Lakshmi Pandit', 25 July 1951, '1947–1951: Correspondence of V.L. Pandit (as Indian Ambassador to USSR) with G.S. Bajpai—Secretary General, MEA, Regarding Official Matters', SF/55, Vijaya Lakshmi Pandit papers, NMML.

diplomat, who once worked with them, called 'social confidence'.[211] They were 'people with sophistication', who truly knew the task of 'representation',[212] another explained—not, of course, in any egalitarian sense of representing 'the people' but in the sense of being representable in the once aristocratic world of diplomacy.

For all the talk of making the Service reflective of India, Nehru not only picked among royalty and cultural elites but also almost exclusively from among the upper castes. To Nehru, the staunch secularist, the fact of most of his handpicked confidantes being Brahmins—Kashmiri Pandits in particular— might have seemed irrelevant.[213] However, his comfort around them spoke to a certain elitist insularity and an unproductive pretence of caste blindness[214] which did nothing to dislodge the brahminical dominance that had once characterized the ICS. The dominance of upper castes both reflected itself in and was reinforced by a predisposition towards dynasties, of which the Nehrus were famously no strangers themselves. While political control over the Indian National Congress Party rests with descendants of the Nehru family line to this day, Jawaharlal Nehru also kept early diplomatic appointments in the family: the Prime Minister's sister Vijaya Lakshmi Pandit was one of India's most prominent diplomats, with ambassadorial postings to the US, Soviet Union, Britain, and the UN; his cousin B.K. Nehru served in many of the same positions from the 1960s onwards; R.K. Nehru, another cousin, became Foreign Secretary in 1952.[215] And while Nehru condemned all manner of elites in his speeches and writing, his very presence only encouraged young recruits to think of themselves as one—knowing that the MEA was essentially Nehru's 'pet, not a normal ministry'[216] legitimated a sense of being, in the words of one of Nehru's many ardent admirers among the early batches, 'a chosen cadre'.[217]

Instead of championing a sweeping transition to an egalitarian postcoloniality, both former ICS officers and Nehru—as well as the juniors who joined the Service under them—normalized the ambivalence between two very different

---

[211] Interview 9.

[212] Interview 7.

[213] Benner, *Structure of Decision*, 186.

[214] Referring to learned Brahmins, he even casually addressed his senior diplomats as the 'pandits of the Ministry'. 'Oral History Transcript: K.P.S. Menon', 33.

[215] Anne Guthrie, *Madame Ambassador: The Life of Vijaya Lakshmi Pandit* (New York: Harcourt, 1962); Sarvepalli Gopal, *Jawaharlal Nehru: A Biography, Volume 3 (1956–1964)* (New Delhi: Oxford University Press, 1975), 207; 'MEA Press Release', 22 July 1961, 'Appointment of Shri B.K. Nehru as Ambassador to the USA', F/73(74)–AMS/1961, NAI.

[216] Rana, *Inside Diplomacy*, 252.

[217] Interview 9; The twin motives of admiration and sense of special status among those who served under Nehru was also a topic in Interview 1; Interview 16; Interview 18; Interview 25; Interview 30; Interview 31; Interview 40; Interview 43; Interview 79.

imageries of international society. What came to animate the Foreign Service was a kind of parochial postcoloniality: passionately devoted to representing a decolonized, egalitarian, and diverse world but wary of allowing that diversity to be represented within the exclusive Foreign Service itself.

Conclusion

All high ideals have deep social roots. The genealogy of the diplomatic habitus that would come to be idealized by the Indian Foreign Service can only be understood by considering the social position and lived experience of Indian bureaucratic elites under the British Raj. It was during the Raj that Indian officers of the ICS first developed a kind of cleft habitus, suspended between the conventions of European international society and the imperatives of anti-imperial agitation and Indian difference. At Independence, this cleft was not 'solved', as Bourdieu might have expected, but rather took on a new form and became institutionalized. No longer suspended between an existing empire and the promise of a decolonized world, the postcolonial rendition of the cleft habitus spanned the divide between the lingering memory of European international society and a very real postcolonial world. Having been born as a felt tension in the minds of colonial officials, the cleft habitus now became institutionalized as a socially shared ideal for the postcolonial diplomat. The strange twin imperatives of being comfortable in the old elite conventions of a white European world while also being a fierce advocate for an anti-imperial, solidarist international society became the new 'duality of social regulations'[218] that an ideal Indian diplomat had to master. Instead of dividing the Service into British sympathizers and anti-colonial firebrands, I argue that this twin imperative was honoured both by former ICS officials and Prime Minister Nehru, who passed it down to the first generations of career diplomats.

These twin beginnings also meant an awkward intermingling of two visions of internationalism. Both the colonial and postcolonial imageries of the world enacted their own politics: one of elite domination and the other of subaltern representation. While the former entrusted an enlightened elite with governing an inherited world, the latter sought to reshape the world in the image of its former margins. While the egalitarianism of the postcolonial vision might seem more intuitively cosmopolitan, there is also an elite cosmopolitanism that has always existed inside the Foreign Service. In fact, as I will argue, it

---

[218] Bourdieu's French expression translated in Go, 'Decolonizing Bourdieu', 59.

112 GENEALOGY: BALLIOL AND BANDUNG

is this kind of cosmopolitanism that has been dominant. The compliment offered to ICS elites of being able to 'take a wider view of things'[219] had, in many ways, become 'a possibility only because of the existence of empire, that cosmopolitanism could have been inspired or authorized only by the imperial scale'.[220] Or, as Timothy Brennan polemically describes cosmopolitanism: '[i]t is a discourse of the universal that is inherently local—a locality that is always surreptitiously imperial'.[221] We need not define our terms as uncompromisingly as Brennan to appreciate the colonial undertones in the early descriptions of 'worldliness' among India's effortlessly superior diplomatic elites. These different readings of internationalism, cosmopolitanism, and worldliness will matter greatly, in various guises, in the chapters to come. For one, the tensions between colonial convention and postcolonial invention came to define the world-making of Indian diplomats after Independence.

---

[219] Interview 25.

[220] Bruce Robbins and Paulo Lemos Horta, 'Introduction', in *Cosmopolitanisms*, ed. Bruce Robbins and Paulo Lemos Horta (New York: New York University Press, 2017), 4.

[221] Timothy J. Brennan, *At Home in the World: Cosmopolitanism Now* (Cambridge, Mass.: Harvard University Press, 1997), 81.

3

World-making

Protest and protocol

Writing in a letter in 1950, an Indian Head of Mission in Cairo laid out the many worlds that Indian diplomats should learn to navigate.[1] Firstly, he wrote, their attitude ought to be based on 'respect for and adherence to the principles laid down by our Prime Minister', which should be unmoved by 'European ridicule'—an anti-colonial world of Third World difference. Seemingly unfazed by the orientalist contradiction, he continued, secondly: 'we must learn the iron discipline of the British Foreign Service', because '[s]ometimes we put on the garb of independence and display our lack of breeding'. This was a world of the well-born and the fine-mannered, one which, the Head of Mission seemed to believe, called for imitation of the former colonizer. Indian diplomats have been presented with an impossible trade-off: they must conform to the elitist practices of old European international society while rejecting them as decadent and outdated. Finally, he declared, 'we must also be true citizens of the world'—cosmopolitans, if you will. In the form of a diplomatic dispatch, this is the set of tensions that Indian diplomats have embodied as they engage with the world around them.

A provincialized account of global order asks how it has always been produced by, against, and with (once) colonized spaces. In so many ways, the 'theory and practice of the "international" was forged in colonized worlds': the 'international' was not a space that decolonized states like India entered at Independence, but one which 'they themselves had shaped and within which they had staked claims, fought battles, forged alliances, and envisaged end-states for decades'.[2] Crucially, however, it is not only the idiom of decolonial protest in which India has made its mark. Recall that the provincialization of global order, in parallel with Dipesh Chakrabarty's provincialization of Europe, must mean not only studying moments in which non-European actors break away from Westernized practices. It must also involve comprehending

[1] Head of Mission of India, Cairo, 'Note Responding to Jawaharlal Nehru's Letter on Prohibition'.
[2] Pallavi Raghavan et al., 'The Limits of Decolonisation in India's International Thought and Practice: An Introduction', *The International History Review* 44 (2022): 813.

Cosmopolitan Elites. Kira Huju, Oxford University Press. © Kira Huju (2023). DOI: 10.1093/oso/9780198874928.003.0004

114 WORLD-MAKING: PROTEST AND PROTOCOL

the entangled parallel processes of Othering and joint imagining that made India's colonized elites indispensable to the once dominant imagery of a Europeanized international society, too.

The ambiguities of world-making have dovetailed with ambiguities about social status. Indian diplomats exist as members of a domestic elite, with ties to a transnational elite club of diplomats. At the same time, they have represented a nation that has thought of itself as a victim of a hierarchical, Western-dominated order. These competing registers each reflect a very different sense of Indian diplomats' place in the world. In the old, fading imagery of European international society, Indians have represented something akin to what Iver Neumann has called the 'constitutive outside of international society'[3]—a late-comer trying to fit in, by its very presence demarcating its boundary conditions for belonging. In the imagery of a postcolonial international society, India was a founding member, not only because it won independence early, but because of its pioneering Third Worldist diplomacy, Non-Aligned advocacy, and pow-erful diplomatic rejections of imperialism, colonialism, inequality, and racism. While belonging in the cultural universe of European international society implies continuous permission-seeking, belonging in postcolonial interna-tional society is an act of assuming one's rightful place. This straddling of worlds has produced forms of social status that have distinguished India both *within* and *from* the old-school European conceptions of international society—the former implying distinction in the sense of accomplishment according to established parameters (the 'worldly' diplomat), the latter under-standing distinction as a diversion them (the 'Third Worldist' diplomat).

This chapter explores the world-making of Indian diplomats: what kind of world they have sought to bring about and where they have placed them-selves within in, whose struggles they have waged or evaded, and how they have come to think of the world-embracing but ultimately broken promises of cosmopolitanism. Policy-wise, India has long existed in a liminal space where its foreign policy towards the contemporary rule-makers of global order oscillates 'between compliance and resistance'[4] This chapter queries what this ambivalence looks like not in policy papers or as diplomatic doctrine, but as a deeper underlying social ambivalence expressed in the lived experience of everyday diplomatic life. It proceeds in three phases. It first considers the

---

[3] Iver B. Neumann, 'Entry into International Society Reconceptualised: The Case of Russia', *Review of International Studies* 37, no. 2 (2011): 472.

[4] Kate Sullivan, 'India's Ambivalent Projection of Self as a Global Power: Between Compliance and Resistance', in *Competing Visions of India in World Politics: India's Rise Beyond the West*, ed. Kate Sullivan (London: Palgrave Macmillan UK, 2015), 15–33.

ways in which Indian diplomats have pioneered and sought to bring about a postcolonial international society. Officers of the Indian Foreign Service are renowned—in the West, notorious—for a very particular diplomatic register: diplomacy as postcolonial protest. Yet, secondly, the chapter studies the parallel conviction among India's representatives that it is not yet safe to stop imagining the world as an extension of white European international society, living in cultural overtime, making demands on Indian officers from the imperial graveyard. Diplomats have, therefore, also sought to seek membership in the elite club of diplomats as they believe themselves to have found it: Western-dominated, quasi-aristocratic, sustained on protocol and worldly charm. Finally, the chapter asks what cosmopolitanism looks like in this messy world. It considers cosmopolitanism not in a theoretical framework of assumed equality but through the lived experience of political, material, racial, and cultural inequality. The chapter also demarcates the limits of the officers' own commitments to global solidarity, as it queries the intersections of race and caste in Indian world-making.

A revolution unfinished

Third World difference

After 1947, Indian diplomats became founding members of postcolonial international society, borrowing from the cultural grammar of the freedom struggle a conception of diplomacy as protest. This was postcoloniality in the making, reflective of the newfound 'authenticity' that colonial order had once suppressed. In India, it was Nehruvian in nature: secular, Third Worldist, internationalist, solidarist, and fiercely invested in democratizing international society. In the Nehruvian vision, the domestic and the international were inextricably intertwined, and therefore required, in the words of T.N. Kaul, 'look[ing] upon India in the world perspective and India's struggle for independence as part of the struggle of all colonial peoples and territories'.[5] Nehru had endowed the Service with an 'internationalist, globalist culture', a proud Stephanian elucidated; it was 'like fish swimming in water' for officers to think of themselves as part of a larger project of remaking the world in the image of its former margins.[6]

---

[5] T.N. Kaul, 'Draft of an Introduction to a Manuscript of Autobiographical Nature', n.d., 6, 'Miscellaneous Articles by T. N. Kaul'. Speeches/Writings by Him, S. No. 141, T.N. Kaul papers, NMML.

[6] Interview 23.

116   WORLD-MAKING: PROTEST AND PROTOCOL

The postcolonial expression of difference represented what Itty Abraham calls a 'boundary-making technology': the deliberate establishment of an ideational, cultural, and political boundary between the Western and the non-Western, the European and the Third World, the colonizer and the Indian.[7] As a former Ambassador—who lectures diplomatic probationers on the need to abandon lingering colonial ideals—argued, diplomatic dignity could never be achieved by engaging in 'derivative mimicry'.[8] Postcolonial pride demanded a world made anew, its principal architects the formerly oppressed. Diplomatic social capital became a matter of articulating solidarity: 'Care should be taken to avoid the semblance of membership of that group', Nehru wrote about the British Commonwealth in his letter to Ambassadors Asaf Ali and K.P.S. Menon on 22 January 1947—noting elsewhere in the letter that '[o]ur Ambassadors should meet, whenever they have the chance, prominent African leaders'.[9] In this slim three-page letter, formulated as concise, numbered points on how to represent India abroad, the tenth point raised the question of American racism and how Indian representatives should position themselves in Washington, DC: 'Our sympathies are entirely with the Negroes. There is no reason to hide this because that is our basic policy'. Even when serving in the heart of American power, an Indian diplomat's sympathies were to lie not with the newly crowned hegemon but with the oppressed people it presided over.

Developing a postcolonial vision meant propagating a political division of the world that bowed not to power-political distinctions but to the acuteness of postcolonial disparities. India would force Western diplomatic counterparts out of any polite liberal illusion of compatible interests. As Foreign Secretary R.K. Nehru (1952–1955) noted in an article on the international system:

> The conventional method of looking at the international system is by way of uni-polar, bi-polar and multi-polar worlds. Underlying these perceptions is the perception that only the military and industrial power of the nations count in international relations. Looking at it from the developing world, the international system would appear to consist of two strata [the developed and the developing]. Therefore, the international system will have to be considered as a two compartmental system and not as a single system of

---

[7] Itty Abraham, *How India Became Territorial: Foreign Policy, Diaspora, Geopolitics* (Palo Alto: Stanford University Press, 2014), 1; see also Manu Bhagavan, *India and the Quest for One World: The Peacemakers* (Basingstoke: Palgrave Macmillan, 2013); Andrew B. Kennedy, 'Nehru's Foreign Policy: Realism and Idealism Conjoined', in *The Oxford Handbook of Indian Foreign Policy*, ed. David M. Malone, C. Raja Mohan, and Srinath Raghavan (Oxford: Oxford University Press, 2015), 92–103.

[8] Interview 4.

[9] Nehru, 'Note for Asaf Ali and K.P.S. Menon'.

over 130 actors. [...] There is also a conflict of interest between the developed and the developing worlds as was evident in the three UNCTADS.[10]

Articulated in the radical imagery of postcoloniality, points of diplomatic principle folded into a broader Third Worldist agenda. This agenda may have assigned India a leading role, but always consciously apart from the insiders and incumbents of global order. Diplomats made a point of standing out: they did not seek to obfuscate but to accentuate what they considered an unbridgeable divide between North and South, developed and developing. Moving towards a postcolonial world required rejecting some neo-imperial diplomatic vocabulary, too. In 1955, Nehru ordered India's Mission in Washington, DC to avoid expressions like 'The Free World', 'bamboo curtain', and 'peace-loving nations'—'which mean something more than they say', legitimating a Western-centric reading that assented to the persistent supremacy of Western forms of world-ordering.[11] One former Foreign Secretary believed that India engaged in 'inverse snobbery': it took great pride in believing itself to have rejected the petty status games of Western counterparts.[12] This serves a purpose not unlike the traditional purposes of Bourdieusian signalling: as a former senior Ambassador from the early 1980s batches explained, Nehruvian thinking 'distinguished us' from the diplomats of other countries.[13] A postcolonial moral high can be a form of distinction—and a deliberate outsider status, too, is a kind of status to be cherished.

India's role as *primus inter pares* among the formerly colonized required a distinct language of diplomacy. Its engagement with the world constituted 'a self-reflective ethico-political project of identity construction that emerged in reaction to the colonial encounter',[14] as Priya Chacko has described. As such, it has always been deeply invested in a language of rights and wrongs. 'Coloured by left-wing ideals', as one member of the 1970s batches put it,[15] India's diplomatic vocabulary has traditionally been characterized by anti-imperial moralism. In interviews, arguments were often couched not in assessments of capability or capacity, but in lexical binaries of fair/unfair, equal/unequal.[16] What defined the institutional architecture of diplomacy,

---

[10] R.K. Nehru, 'Current International System and Indian Approach to It', n.d., Article draft, 'Writings/speeches by him', SN/7, R.K. Nehru papers, NMML.

[11] Jawaharlal Nehru, 'Letter to the Indian Ambassador in the US Washington, DC', 22 April 1955, 'Avoidance of offensive terminology—Instructions regarding', F/18(120)-G/55, NAI.

[12] Interview 6.

[13] Interview 3.

[14] Priya Chacko, *Indian Foreign Policy: The Politics of Postcolonial Identity from 1947 to 2004* (London: Routledge, 2013), 3.

[15] Interview 33.

[16] Interview 15, March 2019; Interview 19.

from the UN Security Council to the Nuclear Non-Proliferation Treaty, was that the 'system is not fair': India's diplomatic stance, therefore, was one of permanent protest against international 'inequity', as one prominent senior Ambassador explained.[17] A former Cabinet Minister who had worked with high-ranking IFS officials derided their 'sense of victimhood': 'there is a white man and a black man, and the white man screwed the world'.[18] The argument may have been offered as a criticism, but as a point of principle, it was not something diplomats were interested in refuting: 'The lexicon of our parlance could not but echo our experience of [...] suffering under foreign rule', as Foreign Secretary M.K. Rasgotra (1982–1985) argues in his autobiography.[19]

This postcolonial moral universe elevated difference into an ethical good. Instead of suppressing the vast diversity of the world for the sake of imperial governability or homogenizing it in the name of liberal internationalism, postcolonial diplomacy propagated a discourse of diversity. This discourse brought together world-making and nation-building. It reflected India's hopes for the emerging world order but was also deeply rooted in a domestic project of managing India's own internal diversity.[20] India was a 'multi-racial, multi-linguistic, multi-cultural society', as Nehru's handpicked US Ambassador and ICS veteran M.C. Chagla, born to Muslim parents, never ceased to emphasize—and Nehruvian secularism was not only a 'great philosophical and political ideal' for India, but one 'which one day might be accepted by the whole world'.[21] Foreign Secretary T.N. Kaul believed that 'India represents in a way a mini-world, a multi-religious, multi-lingual and multi-racial society different parts of which are at different stages of development—like the world at large'.[22] India's first female career diplomat saw India's internal diversity as a blueprint for recasting the world after empire: 'India's acceptance of diversity, often called its "tolerance", is a better model for a future world society than the existing models of uniformity and intolerance whether of race, religion, political ideology or other factors', Ambassador C.B. Muthamma outlined.[23]

---

[17] Interview 19.

[18] Interview 8, March 2019.

[19] Rasgotra, *A Life in Diplomacy*, 367.

[20] Internal diversity along religious lines can also be a tangible diplomatic asset: there seems to be a recurring pattern whereby the Service's few Muslims are posted in Muslim-majority countries, presumably on the assumption that the intimacy of a religious bond strengthens diplomatic ties.

[21] M.C. Chagla, '"Nehru and Secularism"', 1966, 2, Article in a booklet entitled 'A Rose Never Withers, It Lives in Remembrance—Nehru's 2nd Death Anniversary', 'Speeches/Writings by Him', F/16, M.C. Chagla papers, NMML.

[22] T.N. Kaul, '"Some Thoughts on the Concept and Relevance of Revolution in India"', n.d., Miscellaneous articles, 'Speeches/Writings by Him', SN/141, T.N. Kaul papers, NMML.

[23] C. B. Muthamma, *Slain by the System: India's Real Crisis* (New Delhi: Viveka Foundation, 2003), 100.

The postcolonial compromise on 'Indianness', purposefully amorphous and civic rather than religious or ethnic in nature, was reflective of India's world-making. Indeed, India's emphasis on diversity in its diplomacy represented an internationalization of the domestic 'diversity talk' of liberal postcolonial elites,[24] which celebrated a composite culture that, unlike European nations, rejected the construct of 'one people, one language, one religion'.[25] Visions of home and the world were intertwined: India's diversity was a living embodiment of the newfound diversity of postcolonial international society. India did not seek for signs of sameness across the world, in line with liberal internationalism's ideals of neutrality and universality. Rather, India celebrated its inherent diversity as proof that a postcolonial re-ordering of the world was afoot.

The practice of postcoloniality

In diplomatic practice, the postcolonial enactment of difference was purposefully emotive and animated. To fight Apartheid and imperialism at Bandung and the UN, India adopted 'a theatrical and aggressive manner'.[26] For this, it often bore the brunt of white orientalizing, as its diplomatic counterparts revelled in declaring India's diplomacy 'irrational', sentimental, and ungentlemanly.[27] What this willingness to be ridiculed shows is just how sincerely Indian officers believed in the postcolonial world they were creating. It also goes to show that, despite the prevalent language of 'diplomatic etiquette' propagated by Indian diplomats themselves, diplomatic performances have never cohered around a singular European conception of appropriate behaviour. This does not make postcolonial diplomacy any more 'authentic', however, or indeed any more intuitive for Indian diplomats to practise.

All diplomacy must be learned, rehearsed, or unlearned—this is how practices and performances function, as sociologists tell us. Postcolonial world-making was about learning to embody ideals of equality and anti-imperialism in practice. However principled, such world-making has required some discipline on the part of diplomats. For all the professed allegiances

---

[24] Srirupa Roy, 'Instituting Diversity: Official Nationalism in Post-independence India', *South Asia: Journal of South Asian Studies* 22, no. 1 (1999): 81.

[25] Lion König, *Cultural Citizenship in India: Politics, Power, and Media* (Oxford: Oxford University Press, 2016), 15.

[26] Alexander E. Davis and Vineet Thakur, '"An Act of Faith" or a New "Brown Empire"? The Dismissal of India's International Anti-Racism, 1945–1961', *Commonwealth & Comparative Politics* 56, no. 1 (2018): 25.

[27] Davis and Thakur, 27.

120 WORLD-MAKING: PROTEST AND PROTOCOL

to the postcolonial Third World, some retired diplomats candidly admitted that India, even today, is 'over-concerned with the West in the implementation of diplomacy'—a preoccupation not lost on frustrated Asian and African partners expecting India to live up to its role as a 'natural leader' of the Third World.[28] The ideational insistence on Third Worldism came with its own learning curve. The earliest members of the Service, especially those who had served under the Raj, did not, Foreign Secretary Dixit believed, find a meaningful way of imbibing the Non-Aligned Movement's solidarist emphasis on developing countries.[29] Having spent much of the interview evaluating Indian diplomatic behaviour against European convention, a mid-1950s recruit exclaimed that his superiors 'felt at home with English-speaking foreign diplomats' but 'didn't have the foggiest idea where Africa was'[30]—an accusation that brings to mind Ambassador Apa Pant's first reaction upon hearing that he would be India's first Commissioner to East Africa: 'Where is East Africa?'[31] Today, postings to Africa sometimes even serve a disciplinary function: repeat postings in particular are interpreted as signalling displeasure on the part of senior officials at something an officer did in a previous post.[32] In ideal theory, Third World solidarity is fundamental to Indian diplomacy, but in diplomatic practice, serving in the formerly colonized world is a professional punishment.

There has always been an underlying sense of a trade-off involved: postcoloniality had to come at the expense of something else, weighted against competing priorities. Any trade-offs had to be carefully curated. In a letter to his newly appointed diplomats Asaf Ali and K.P.S. Menon on 22 January 1947, Nehru sought to establish an unsteady equilibrium between standing out and fitting in:

> Our Ambassadors will represent a great country and it is right that they should make others feel that they do so. But they should also represent a poor country where millions live on the verge of starvation. They cannot forget this nor indeed should they do anything which seems in violent conflict with it. [...] To some extent we shall be guided of course by the usual rules and procedures which obtain in other embassies. But there is no reason why we should

---

[28] Rana, *Inside Diplomacy*, 48.
[29] Dixit, *My South Block Years*, 38.
[30] Interview 79.
[31] 'Oral History Transcript: Apa B. Pant', 22.
[32] Interview 2, February 2019; Interview 43; Interview 45; Interview 49.

consider ourselves bound by them completely. Where considered necessary we can strike out a new line, provided this is not unbecoming or indecorous.[33]

Although many academic careers have been built on marketing India's post-colonial project as a thing of the past to foreign audiences, its basic tenets regularly resurface in diplomatic reasoning. The debates on recognition and moralism have most recently found expression in Indian responses to the normalizing discourse about whether India is becoming a 'responsible power'.[34] Senior and retired officers—as ever, fully read up on and ready to debate academic work done on themselves—rejected the notion that 'responsibility' was a neutral descriptor,[35] remaining wary of just how suspiciously similar it tended to be to whatever Western powers happened to expect of India at the time.[36] Three different Foreign Secretaries made a point of rejecting the responsibility rhetoric as an expression of the Western-centrism of the discourse on global order. Cutting through the abstractions that supposedly strip academic terms of their politics, one former Foreign Secretary defined the everyday responsibilities of a 'responsible power' as 'doing what other countries expect it to do'.[37] If India was an 'inflexible' negotiator, another former Foreign Secretary phrased it, it was only because it was up against an unfair world (while Balkan countries, for example, 'don't have any qualms about being supplicants, this is not the case with India').[38] 'I don't need a certificate' from the West, a more recent Foreign Secretary clarified—the responsibility of an Indian diplomat was owed to the people of India.[39] World-making is a project, process, and aspiration all in one: postcoloniality, too, must be enacted and defended, day to day.

The recognition that a truly postcolonial world is still only in the making is also what feeds India's struggle against deep-seated Western dominance in global governance. Outlining India's case for a permanent seat on the UN Security Council, a former Permanent Representative to the UN declared that while 'we are doing our bit for the world', the P-5 'doesn't want anybody else to enter their elite club', as though it was 'their proprietary right'

---

[33] Nehru, 'Note for Asaf Ali and K.P.S. Menon'.
[34] Dormandy, 'Is India, or Will It Be, a Responsible International Stakeholder?'; C. Raja Mohan, 'India and the Balance of Power', *Foreign Affairs*, August 2006, 17–32; Narlikar, 'Is India a Responsible Great Power?'
[35] Malone, *Does the Elephant Dance?*, 270.
[36] Interview 6; Interview 9.
[37] Interview 9.
[38] Interview 39.
[39] Interview 6.

122 WORLD-MAKING: PROTEST AND PROTOCOL

to govern the inner circles of international society.[40] On climate diplomacy, Indian discourse is predicated on bifurcating the world into developed and developing nations, rather than accepting what a former chief climate negotiator considered the false 'shared global responsibility' discourse of 'glossy magazines' produced for Western audiences.[41] In making their arguments about differentiated responsibilities, what these diplomats are doing is contesting the universalizing language of the common good, equally shared and similarly understood across the world.[42] The notion of a liberal, rules-based international order is foreign to India's diplomatic vocabulary not because its diplomats are somehow incapable of understanding it, but because India sees very little that is genuinely liberal, rules-based, or particularly orderly about it.

Reversing the moral gaze

The Indian penchant for postcolonial protest has evoked hostile reactions not only from Western diplomatic counterparts but among the academics who make it their work to understand India's diplomacy. In less than flattering phraseology, Indian diplomacy has been described as 'self-congratulatory'[43] and delivered 'from a moral high horse'.[44] Diplomatic counterparts have sometimes found their Indian colleagues 'arrogant' and 'confrontational', to a point where 'India's long position as a moralistic and contrarian loner in the international community has not excited others about working with India at the apex of the UN system'.[45] India's postcolonial practices have been read as gratuitously antagonistic, its protest as counterproductive.

Yet Indian moralism is an almost ironic response to the hypocrisies of Western-dominated global order. Listening to Foreign Secretary Dixit's team make the case for India's right to nuclear capabilities amidst the Indo-US negotiations in August 1993, an agitated US Assistant Secretary of State Lyn Davis objected to India constantly 'raising questions of philosophy and theory'.[46] Yet these questions of philosophy and theory were there for the benefit of the powerful: they betrayed that the emperor—the only one to ever have dropped a

---

[40] Interview 67.

[41] Interview 15, March 2019.

[42] On India's approach to climate negotiations, see e.g. Navroz K. Dubash, 'Copenhagen: Climate of Mistrust', *Economic and Political Weekly* 44, no. 52 (2009): 8–11; Lavanya Rajamani, 'Differentiation in the Emerging Climate Regime', *Theoretical Inquiries in Law* 14, no. 1 (1 January 2013): 164.

[43] Bhagavan, 'India and the United Nations, or Things Fall Apart', 605.

[44] Narlikar and Narlikar, *Bargaining with a Rising India*, 73.

[45] George Perkovich, 'Is India a Major Power?', *Washington Quarterly* 27, no. 1 (2003): 142.

[46] Dixit, *My South Block Years*, 201.

nuclear bomb in war—had no clothes. They were the expression of an urge not just to stand apart from the moral consensus presided over by the US, but to dismantle the rickety moral legitimacy of continued Western dominance which ought to have ceased at decolonization.[47] The American insistence on its own intrinsic moral virtue rendered American diplomats 'mostly insufferable', complained one self-avowed internationalist officer, who deduced from the American position a general tendency towards moralizing 'hypocrisy' among Western counterparts.[48] An arch-liberal former Foreign Secretary concurred: 'India has kicked against' the notion that European and American interests can transcend into universal concerns from the very beginning—'and long may that unpopularity continue!'[49] It is curious, then, that it is so often Indian moral positions that attract cynical ridicule. It is a curiosity that speaks to the asymmetries of moral power in the world: some nations are assigned an endowed right to speak in the language of universal ideals, while others are chastised as moralistic for speaking back.

In the conventional critique of India's postcolonial vision, the insistence on conscientious protest also betrays a certain naivete. If, for example, 'very few people in India think of the UN as a theatre of power play', as one Nehru-sceptic charged, this was because 'slightly woolly thinking' was 'imbibed in us' through Nehruvian influences on the Foreign Service.[50] In a demonstration of the tenacity of Nehruvian world-making, it was also a favourite rhetorical device of a distinctly anti-Nehruvian former Foreign Secretary to denounce viewpoints he disliked simply by labelling them 'power-political arguments', and to assume as a primary motive for Western intransigence in the face of a variety of Indian diplomatic demands the 'cynical power play in the West'.[51] Balance-of-power politics was not some unalterable logic of diplomacy but a self-afflicted habit of the imperial West: 'Europe and America are far too much used to thinking in terms of military or economic power', Nehru lamented.[52] Later, Kissinger became a favourite villain of Delhi's diplomatic cadres, pityingly diagnosed by Foreign Secretary Rasgotra with an 'obsession with the doctrines of linkage and global balance of power'.[53]

---

[47] For an analysis of the Indo-US 'clash of exceptionalisms', see Priya Chacko, 'New "Special Relationship"? Power Transitions, Ontological Security, and India–Us Relations', *International Studies Perspectives* 15, no. 3 (August 2014): 337–338.

[48] Interview 41.

[49] Interview 9.

[50] Interview 22, April 2019.

[51] Interview 39.

[52] Jawaharlal Nehru, *Letters for a Nation: From Jawaharlal Nehru to His Chief Ministers, 1947–1963*, ed. Madhav Khosla (Gurgaon: Allen Lane, 2014), 277.

[53] Rasgotra, *A Life in Diplomacy*, 260.

124 WORLD-MAKING: PROTEST AND PROTOCOL

The conventional critique of India's postcolonial world-making has taken it literally, but not seriously: it believes that Nehruvians are literally incapable of thinking in terms of hard power and ridicules this failure as a form of diplomatic immaturity.[54] We should do the opposite, however: to take the postcolonial project very seriously, but not always literally. Nehru was a strategic thinker and the postcolonial vision of Indian diplomacy founded upon his thinking was very much alive to the power imbalances India faced.[55] What the ceremonial rejection of power politics offers is not a policy doctrine but a social identity: a way of constructing a distinct, status-affirming, and culturally separate sense of Self. It allowed Indian diplomats to move through an unequal world with their head held high, the stigma of geostrategic inferiority and colonial dependency overcome by a sense of world-healing righteousness. The Nehruvian 'projection of a superior moral standing'[56] spoke not only to the anti-imperial, democratic actor India believed itself to be, but to what it hoped to symbolize in the postcolonial world. It was also a method for excising the lingering influences of the Raj by consciously acting upon a new diplomatic predisposition. Postcolonial protest was supposed to counteract the deeply entrenched colonial instinct of falling in line in order to belong.

The cosmopolitan standard of civilization

For all the valour of reimagining the world in the wake of decolonization, there was no clean break, no cut-and-run transition from one kind of world to another. Upon Independence in 1947, India entered an international system long in the making before its own recognition as a sovereign member, leading Ambassador and ICS veteran Badr-ud-Din Tyabji to caution those with a romantic postcolonial vision that diplomacy had been 'well-set in its traditional ways since the dawn of modern history' and could not be refashioned for 'the Indian way of life' overnight.[57] This meant that to exist in the world and to engage with one's diplomatic counterparts necessitated a set of behaviours reflective of these supposedly fixed ways of European diplomacy. And so, alongside a project of building a bold new postcolonial world, Indian

---

[54] See e.g. Ganguly, 'India's Foreign Policy Grows up'; Malone, *Does the Elephant Dance?*; Mohan, *Crossing the Rubicon*.

[55] See e.g. Srinath Raghavan, *War and Peace in Modern India* (Basingstoke: Palgrave Macmillan, 2010).

[56] Tripurdaman Singh and Adeel Hussain, *Nehru: The Debates that Defined India* (London: William Collins, 2021), 130.

[57] Badr-ud-Din Tyabji, *Indian Policies and Practice* (Delhi: Oriental Publishers, 1972), 17.

diplomats also envisioned themselves as still enmeshed in an older world, whose rules had to be mastered as a price of admission into the club.

Sisir Gupta's paradox

In their status ambivalence, Indian diplomats have been exemplary illustrations of what the theoretician of Indian diplomacy Sisir Gupta meant when he spoke of India as 'a Third World country with a First World attitude'.[58] Their ability to navigate both the colonial and postcolonial is born out of necessity, but many take great pride in proving their belonging among a global elite, which was always assumed to model itself around the dispositions of the 'First World', not the 'Third'.

In the lingering European, white imagery of international society, hierarchies both domestic and international looked very different from those professed by Third World internationalism. Taking it upon himself to capture the expectations that his Western colleagues had of subcontinental diplomats—with an unthinking confidence only available to a man of the Global North talking to representatives of the Global South—former Canadian High Commissioner Robert J. Moore once outlined how '[i]n Western Europe and North America, the new diplomats were expected to regard themselves as heirs to those traditions; they might be black or brown or something in between, but the old practises would remain intact'.[59] Or, as a member of one of the very first diplomatic batches of independent India explained: the Foreign Service 'had to fall in line with the world practice' of diplomacy, with its own etiquette, meanings, and practices.[60]

It may be tempting to consider the lingering valorization of Westernized protocol an exercise in vanity, particularly on the part of diplomats with a reservoir of Westernized cultural capital. The insistence on European etiquette did, after all, legitimate the continued dominance of a cadre whose elite status in Indian society was premised on the belief that this cadre was uniquely suited to navigate a still Western-dominated world. In the words of R.C. Dutt of the 1937 batch, the project of old ICS officers in particular was 'to secure in independent India their own position and that of the class from which they came'.[61] Those with poetic English, foreign elite degrees, and

---

[58] Sisir Gupta, *India and the International System* (New Delhi: Vikas Publishing, 1981), 47.
[59] Moore, *Third World Diplomats*, 18.
[60] Interview 16.
[61] Dutt, 'The Civil Service', 65.

126 WORLD-MAKING: PROTEST AND PROTOCOL

Europeanized cultural references imagined a world in which precisely these qualities mattered—power constellations and cultural imaginations are always intertwined.

Yet the anxieties about etiquette and eloquence also spoke to a still unequal international society. In it, deviance from an old European script could be costly for those in an already subordinate position, much as there had been social sanctions for deviance from British prescriptions under the Raj. Indeed, reminiscent of some of the performative excesses of Britishness under the ICS, diplomats seem to have felt they needed to overperform what they thought defined the once-European club. The 'elegance of presentation' became paramount in diplomatic dispatches—so much so that Dixit, as Under-Secretary on the Bhutan, Tibet and Sikkim Desk, would habitually present six drafts before the Deputy-Secretary approved a regular letter.[62] 'Random Thoughts on Office Routine', a circular letter penned by Deputy-Secretary N.C. Banerjee on 18 December 1970, was in fact a methodical instruction manual of considerable breadth, covering, among other details, the philosophy and practice of 'paragraphing of notes and drafts, etc', admonitions against 'redundant phrases and cliches' in diplomatic dispatches, as well as meticulous directions on how to handle the metallic tag-ends of paper files.[63] What to outsiders may have seemed, in Dixit's antique vocabulary, 'antediluvian' and 'foppish' was intended to ensure that Indian representatives lived up to the 'tact, politeness and social grace' they believed to define the old world of a not quite bygone European international society.[64]

Since international societies are regimes of recognition, presenting a carefully curated diplomatic habitus was about defending the status of the nation and the worthiness of its representatives amongst the global elite of diplomats. As Shashi Tharoor has it, Indian envoys have 'long tried (with uneven success) to maintain standards of style and hospitality on limited resources while avoiding the appearance of either miserliness or vulgarity'.[65] Vijaya Lakshmi Pandit, as Ambassador to Russia, relayed back to G.S. Bajpai on 10 June 1949:

It is not so much the frequency of one's parties but their quality that counts and, rightly or wrongly, one is judged by them as you know. It is important, therefore, that whatever one does should be of a standard consistent with

[62] Dixit, *Indian Foreign Service*, 83–84.
[63] N.C. Banerjee (Deputy Secretary, ADP), '"Random Thoughts on Office Routine"', 18 September 1970, F/Q/O&M/552/1/71, NAI.
[64] Dixit, *Indian Foreign Service*, 95.
[65] Tharoor, *Reasons of State*, 174.

one's national prestige. It is a pity that one's prestige should be judged by such standards but that is the Western code.[66]

This anxiety percolated down to practical questions of budgeting and pay scales. In a ministerial note from March 1946, H. Dayal pleaded for salaries and representation allowances to reflect a standard which would 'ensure that India's representatives abroad are able to uphold her dignity and not merely reflect the poverty and squalor in which so many of her citizens live, and their emoluments do not differ markedly from those of their opposite numbers in posts under the British Foreign Office or the Depts. Of External Affairs of the Dominions.'[67] One respondent to the note captured how seemingly trivial practices ultimately divulged a desire for equal standing in the world:

> To present a credible appearance; to be housed and equipped well; and to entertain well; these are nearly as essential to successful representation of one's country as purely professional efficiency. Quite a lot of a diplomat's work is done in the course of his social contacts and the American crack 'don't laugh at that guy there in the striped pants eating cake—he is working' has a lot of truth in it. Even so democratic a country as Soviet Russia which scorned the trimmings of diplomacy in the post-revolution period has recognized this. Members of the Soviet Foreign Service, however hairy about the heel in private life, have now returned to the full paraphernalia of uniform, evening dress etc. And their entertainments and general diplomatic set-up are on a lavish scale. It follows that India's future Foreign Service should be more than just adequately paid [...].[68]

Indeed, the project of belonging among a global cosmopolitan elite began with Indian diplomats feeling able to level with counterparts in former colonial metropolises—intellectually, culturally, educationally. The elaborations on First Class Oxbridge degrees and Society Presidencies in diplomatic autobiographies, outlined in the previous chapter, are easily pathologized as self-seeking subplots. Yet the Oxbridge stamp endowed the first generation of Indian diplomats with a self-confidence—'effortless superiority'—that proved

---

[66] Vijaya Lakshmi Pandit, 'Letter to G.S. Bajpai', 10 June 1949, '1947–1951: Correspondence of V. L. Pandit (as Indian Ambassador to USSR) with G.S. Bajpai—Secretary General, MEA, regarding official matters', SF/55, Vijaya Lakshmi Pandit papers, NMML.

[67] H. Dayal, 'Note', 17 June 1946, 'Establishment of a Separate Indian Foreign Service', FSP/47-2(7), NAI.

[68] (Indecipherable signature), 'Response to Dayal', 29 April 1946, 'Establishment of a Separate Indian Foreign Service', FSP/47-2(7), NAI.

'one of the qualities most needed in the establishment of new States'.[69] ICS mentors, one of the very first examination-recruits explained, taught their IFS juniors 'the psychology of diplomacy', which involved believing 'they could stand up to any king' and remembering that 'you treat yourself as equal'[70]—a lesson Indian ICS officers had fought to memorize under profoundly unequal circumstances. In the uncertain international hierarchies of the postcolonial world, one prominent member of the early 1960s batches argued, an Indian diplomat with a 'superiority complex' was 'better than one with a damaged ego'[71]—although K.P.S. Menon's soul-searching would remind us of how often these were, in fact, one and the same. This is where the paradoxical justification for domestic elite perpetuation was born: the continued dominance of a small Anglophile club in India is legitimized by a desire to establish equality abroad, which only this elite claims for itself the ability to achieve.

Seeking to excel according to the principles it believed a Western-dominated world to operate by, the Indian Foreign Service cultivated performances that would win its diplomats recognition as worthy members of the diplomatic club. The Service was 'forced to adapt' to alien mores like knives, forks, or wines, because 'you should be like the best from the rest of the world', as one former Foreign Secretary declared in a self-evident tone.[72] A once colonially enforced familiarity with the customs and conventions of old Europe allowed Indian diplomats to leverage this 'cultural exposure in both directions' after Independence, as a former senior diplomat and Cambridge graduate recalled of his time in the Indian High Commission in London.[73] Many diplomats in the older generations explained to me that diplomatic culture had been shaped by European aristocrats, 'and we continued that', as one member of the mid-1970s batches offered, almost proudly.[74] One veteran who joined the Service in the early 1960s even suggested that the reason liberal arts graduates made the best diplomats was because 'we know what is suitable for a life abroad', having studied nineteenth-century European diplomacy at university.[75]

Having set itself what it imagined to be a global standard—a refashioned cosmopolitan standard of civilization—the Foreign Service functioned on the anxious assumption that it could fail it at any point. Social approval matters,

[69] Symonds, 'Indians at Oxford', 11.
[70] Interview 16.
[71] Interview 43.
[72] Interview 45.
[73] Interview 9.
[74] Interview 69.
[75] Interview 30.

and social approval from Western counterparts seems to have mattered especially acutely for many diplomats. At times, Indian diplomacy has been lured into framing itself not on its own terms but as a meta-reference to its perception in the Western gaze. Practices like etiquette training became a kind of defence mechanism: learning to whirl around wines in their correct glasses mattered, a 1960s recruit intoned bitterly, 'because otherwise your interlocutors will have a poor opinion of you'.[76] For at least about two decades after Independence, the Foreign Service regularly engaged US nationals as Public Relations specialists, with experts such as a Mr Bernayes in the early 1950s under Ambassador Pandit and Mr Moss later in the decade employed to communicate a desirable image of the postcolonial nation to Western audiences.[77] In a meeting between Prime Minister Indira Gandhi and the 1982 IFS batch on 5 May 1983, one daring probationer asked the Prime Minister if the 'hypersensitivity' among Indian elites about Western media coverage of the country was rooted in its colonial heritage, to which Gandhi replied with a defensive retort about the West's distorted obsession with depicting India as a land of backwardness.[78] Disproving the charge of backwardness was not about socioeconomic progress alone. It also required that the country's representatives embody the ideals of a cosmopolitan class whenever in the presence of foreigners. Foreign Secretary Rasgotra conveyed this concern to the heads of Indian Missions on 10 May 1982, lamenting that 'our diplomats did not entertain enough and in the right manner', and lacked a 'sufficiently wide range of interests', reminding his colleagues of the importance of a diplomat being 'a conversationalist, with broad knowledge and interests'.[79]

Those who possessed classically sanctioned markers of cultural capital and embodied the 'correct' worldly habitus were usually called upon to represent India where such status signalling was thought to matter the most: Europe. It was conventional for young officers to first be posted to developing countries, where they would be polished before dispatch to Europe.[80] European postings, not only in the early decades but well into the new millennium, have come with an institutional prestige disproportionate to their geostrategic weight. The senior-most ambassadors tend to cluster in Western capitals, with

---

[76] Interview 35.

[77] B.K. Nehru (Ambassador to the US), 'Letter to B.K. Sanyal (Director—West)', 19 April 1963, Publicity Activities in the USA—i) Note of Shri B.K. Nehru, Indian Ambassador in Washington, regarding difficulties and reasons for failure of Indian—, F/302(7) WWII/63, NAI.

[78] 'PM's Meeting with IFS Probationers (1982 Batch), 5 May 1983—Record of Discussions', 10 May 1983, Training of IFS(P) of 1982, F/580/28/82, NAI.

[79] M.K. Rasgotra (Foreign Secretary), 'Circular Letter to Heads of Missions', 10 May 1982, 'Training of IFS(A) of 1982', F/580/28/82, NAI.

[80] Interview 12.

130   WORLD-MAKING: PROTEST AND PROTOCOL

Bern in Switzerland still the monopoly of Ambassadors in Grade I (equivalent to the highest-ranking civil servant, Secretary to the Government of India), while postings in regional capitals of arguably higher political salience, like Kathmandu, are generally lower in grade.[81]

Complaining about an officer who was about to join the Indian High Commission in London in the mid-1950s, an incensed Vijaya Lakshmi Pandit argued that since 'the personality of the officer, his ability to develop contacts and mix with people, his personal habits etc. are very important considerations', it was unfortunately the case that '[w]hile O.P. Khosla may be suitable as P.R.O. in a place like Dhakarta [sic], he would not be suitable for London'.[82] What might be most immediately striking about this taunt is the haughty rejection of an officer based on seemingly superficial markers. However, Ambassador Pandit's snub also speaks to the duality of the two imageries of international society: there are different prescriptions for correct diplomatic performance in the old colonial heartlands and in the new heart of the 'Bandung spirit' of the Third World born in Indonesia in the 1950s.[83]

Posting prestige was tied to a global colour line of social capital. As an old Europe hand of the Service phrased it, positions in South Block that revolved around 'relations with white people', such as the Joint-Secretary and Secretary posts for Europe–West, were coveted 'because those were positions with power'.[84] One might expect such instincts to have been unlearned long ago, and certainly it would be caricatured hubris to argue that they have not abated. And yet, the tenacity of this dated imagery of white European international society remains a source of sarcastic self-criticism in the Service. 'We Indians are so used to seeing ourselves as these bastards of Macaulay', one self-deprecating Under-Secretary in her forties announced with an apologetic grin, seven decades into independent Indian diplomacy.[85]

Reminiscent of a classic distinction between the 'high' diplomacy of well-spoken gentlemen and the 'low' diplomacy of diplomatic technicians, there was also a conception among senior diplomats that economic, commercial, and technological diplomacy offered little professional prestige.[86] One officer who served until the early 2010s contended offhandedly that during his time,

---

[81] Rana, *Inside Diplomacy*, 48.

[82] Vijaya Lakshmi Pandit, 'Letter to B.F.H.B. Tyabji (Special Secretary, MEA)', n.d., '1955–60: Correspondence of V. L. Pandit as Indian High Commissioner to London with P. N. Haksar, N.R. Pillai, R. K. Nehru, M. J. Desai and S. Dutt', SF/17, Vijaya Lakshmi Pandit papers, NMML.

[83] See e.g. Heloise Weber and Poppy Winanti, 'The "Bandung Spirit" and Solidarist Internationalism', *Australian Journal of International Affairs* 70, no. 4 (2016): 391–406.

[84] Interview 81, May 2019.

[85] Interview 59.

[86] Dixit, *Indian Foreign Service*, 86.

'you thought that there was somebody subordinate to you who would take care of commercial work'.[87] India's elite diplomats 'felt like commercial and economic diplomacy was too exotic, inferior to political affairs', one St Stephen's and Cambridge-educated brahminical officer batted off the question of evolving diplomatic duties.[88] Invoking notions of purity and pollution more at home in India's caste system, an officer of a 1950s batch recalled that commercial diplomacy in particular was seen as so 'dirty' that the clerical branch IFS(B) was tasked with conducting it.[89] A materially weak nation ought perhaps—from the fabled rationalist perspective—have accorded such work the very highest priority. And yet, its diplomats looked down upon 'low' diplomacy with visible disdain. Even as officers spoke persuasively about representing the world's downtrodden in their speeches, concerning oneself with the practical details of material improvement was beneath the dignity of an elite diplomat. Old-world eloquence prevailed over the less glamorous technicalities of postcolonial development.

By contrast, tastes and knowledge which had little direct bearing on defending India's national interest were repeatedly offered up by senior officers as defining features of the best diplomats—'whether they can appreciate a foreign play', for example.[90] The distinction between a brilliant diplomat and a mediocre one, a Cambridge graduate of the late 1960s batches delineated, lay in 'sophistication, refinement, the ability to appreciate the arts, music, paintings, good conversation, good wine'.[91] One particularly poised member of a 1970s batch ascribed a 'typical European style' to herself, thinking back with pride to how she once 'fit in very well into the cosmopolitan world of Paris'.[92] Many diplomats were sure to mention, quite unprompted, if they were 'fanatic about jazz'[93] or enjoyed classics of French literature in the original language.[94] They quoted Francis Bacon and 'Yes, Minister'.[95] Such small rituals of recognition can matter greatly in diplomacy. One former Foreign Secretary suggested that mastery of Westernized 'social graces' could 'help in timing your gestures correctly', and that the rapport between Margaret Thatcher and M.K. Rasgotra (who in his own telling resented all Tories) during his 1988–1990 term as High Commissioner in the UK, despite significant political differences, was 'purely

---

[87] Interview 69.
[88] Interview 43.
[89] Interview 40.
[90] Interview 18.
[91] Interview 37, April 2019.
[92] Interview 81.
[93] Interview 18.
[94] Interview 41.
[95] Interview 25; Interview 56; Interview 65, May 2019.

132 WORLD-MAKING: PROTEST AND PROTOCOL

on this basis'.[96] Knowing the customs and tastes of Europeanized international diplomacy was an act of displaying cultural capital—an act, ultimately, of belonging.

The cultural capital of constructive ambiguity

The British Raj left in its wake a form of cultural capital that postcolonial elites have skilfully traded for recognition in the diplomatic club: English. The English language bequeathed the formerly colonized a shared means of communicating throughout much of the world, most notably with former British colonies and Commonwealth nations but also, especially with the rise of American power, with the wider world. Deprived of material power as a currency of persuasion, English established itself as one of the sharpest assets of eloquent Indian diplomats, known abroad for marshalling their arguments in expressive turns of phrase, a gift which diplomats believed held them in good stead in international negotiations.[97] A form of cultural capital, English was also—as one ardent Anglophile calling it 'the link language' alluded[98]—a precondition for social capital in the diplomatic club. Investigating the politics of language inside the Indian Foreign Service, then, also means considering the hierarchies of capital that underpin the dominant language of the cosmopolitan elite.

English made India a 'natural' choice for committee work and drafting at the United Nations,[99] granting the country significantly more diplomatic sway than its rank in the world's material distribution of power would have suggested—for, as an Anglophile retiree of the Foreign Service strategized, 'the person who presents the first draft has the advantage'.[100] With the quiet force of the pen, India could shape diplomatic language in a manner that benefitted developing countries, as one proponent of the drafting theory of Indian power explained.[101] The fluency made possible all the work that Indian diplomats have pioneered at and around the UN, as their conflict mediation, human rights, development, and anti-racist efforts have placed many an officer

---

[96] Interview 39.
[97] Interview 12; Interview 17; Interview 25; Interview 43.
[98] Interview 25.
[99] Interview 4; Interview 20; Interview 26; Interview 28; Interview 29.
[100] Interview 28.
[101] Interview 17.

in a prominent position in multilateral diplomacy.[102] A deep familiarity with English that could only have been born out of lifelong use allowed Indian diplomats to practise the kind of 'constructively ambiguous' phraseology that made for successful diplomacy and widened India's room for diplomatic manoeuvre, believed one retired multilateralist.[103]

This linguistic leverage has convinced officers that India has 'punched above its weight' in a Western-dominated global order because of the quality of its Anglophone diplomats.[104] Sisir Gupta's paradox is on display as an Additional-Secretary describes 'the sense you have that we are meant for bigger things'.[105] This everyday act of cultural levelling made multilateral drafting a considerable source of professional pride. In the middle of describing the broadest strokes of Indian philosophies of diplomacy, a former lead climate negotiator paused to emphasize that India had been the first country to put a full draft declaration on the table, later disrupting a train of thought to remark: 'I remember that wording because I drafted that.'[106] It was therefore with some despair that many diplomats viewed the relaxation of English requirements, after the Kothari Commission's findings led to reforms in the entry examination into the Civil Services in the early 1980s.[107] 'You will see less and less of an imprint on drafting' from India and the 'ability for India to articulate' its policies and priorities, one former multilateralist chided,[108] lamenting India's loosening grip on the cultural grammar of a colonially constituted practice of diplomatic communication.

English, then, is another expression of the curious justification pattern whereby the need to establish parity abroad is used to rationalize long-standing hierarchies at home. If Indian diplomacy has traditionally been 'a preserve of the English-speaking elite' and it has been 'hugely difficult [to] break into the English-speaking club', as one serving diplomat involved in translating works of Indian foreign policy into vernacular languages complained,[109] it is not only because of the traditional dominance of Anglophone elites in Indian society and bureaucracy. Rather, it is because this dominance is, in the eyes

---

[102] Malone, *Does the Elephant Dance?*, 254; Stanley A. Kochanek, 'India's Changing Role in the United Nations', *Pacific Affairs* 53, no. 1 (1980): 50; Shyam Saran, 'India and Multilateralism: A Practitioner's Perspective', in *Shaping the Emerging World: India and the Multilateral Order*, ed. Waheguru Pal Singh Sidhu, Pratap Bhanu Mehta, and Bruce D. Jones (Washington, D.C.: Brookings Institution Press, 2013), 43.
[103] Interview 15, March 2019.
[104] Interview 33; Interview 39; Interview 58, May 2019; Interview 67.
[105] Interview 70.
[106] Interview 15, March 2019.
[107] Interview 3; Interview 12; Interview 17; Interview 25; Interview 43; UPSC, 'Kothari Report', 53.
[108] Interview 27, April 2019.
[109] Interview 61, May 2019.

134 WORLD-MAKING: PROTEST AND PROTOCOL

of Anglophile diplomats, entirely legitimated by the extrinsic demands of an Anglophone international society, impressing its fixed cultural codes on Indian officers who are merely abiding by them.

The significance of English is not only a technical question about diplomatic efficiency. It is, rather, a cultural story of belonging and exclusion among the cosmopolitan class. Indeed, the prevalent argument of senior diplomats that how an issue was expressed was just as significant as the issue itself[110] is a conviction that has long frustrated the vernacular speakers of the Service. The heavy emphasis on English cannot be exhaustively explained by the mechanical requirements of drafting and committee work. An impossibly erudite former Foreign Secretary believed that English had been especially crucial because Indian diplomacy traditionally prioritized 'getting the perspective out' and was 'not so action-oriented'.[111] Yet perhaps Indian diplomacy had become so centred around performative eloquence precisely because Indian diplomats took such pride in their English. Perhaps, as one former Cabinet Minister complained, India's articulate diplomats had been 'helped by their English too well'.[112] Various expressions of this same frustration are common in Indian autobiographical writing on diplomacy. There could be an 'excessive emphasis on form rather than substance', as Foreign Secretary Dixit once despaired.[113] Clear outcomes on 'tangible, well-defined national objectives' often became an afterthought, Ambassador Tyabji, too, lamented, with ambassadors returning to Delhi from international negotiations content that they had fulfilled their duty 'to project the Indian point of view'.[114] The former Cabinet Minister, who had toured the climate summit circuits in 2009, found that little had changed, at least in the diplomatic community's perceptions of India: one saying suggested that it was difficult to get Japanese officers talking and equally difficult to get Indian representatives to stop talking.[115] English is not a self-evident good of purely instrumental value. It is also a reflection of personally felt and socially expressed fault lines within the Service, which themselves reflect what officers believe about the entry rules into the cosmopolitan club.

By contrast, only 'Hindi fanatics' used to advocate for Hindi typewriters and translators at every Embassy, one of the Service's oldest living members recalled in a dismissive tone.[116] This is not to say that Hindi was entirely

---

[110] Interview 27; Interview 31.
[111] Interview 9.
[112] Interview 8.
[113] Dixit, *Indian Foreign Service*, 84.
[114] Tyabji, *Indian Policies and Practice*, 10.
[115] Interview 8.
[116] Interview 16.

inconsequential; in fact, the question of Hindi skills among diplomats has animated parliamentarians and bureaucrats alike since Nehru's time.[117] Nehru appointed the famous Hindi poet and Cambridge PhD H.R. Bachchan to teach Hindi to probationers, and Ministry officials summoned to Parliament ensured their audience that those few Ambassadors who spoke no Hindi were 'being equipped with credentials in Hindi for presentation', so that minimum standards could be obtained across the Service.[118] A simple departmental language test, though falling below the threshold of Hindi 'proficiency', has been compulsory for officers before official confirmation into the Service since 1951.[119] And yet the question of linguistic diversity is fraught. The replacement of English with Hindi would not have been a straightforwardly democratizing move, as the closeness of English with elite circles would suggest. Rather, it would sacralize one major language as the only authentically Indian idiom of diplomacy in a country of striking linguistic diversity. Another paradox of the proxy wars on representation emerges: English embodies both an exclusionary project that perpetuates the dominance of a small Anglophone elite and an anti-majoritarian project that seeks to preserve Indian diversity in the face of a narrow linguistic 'authenticity'. This balance has only truly begun to shift in favour of Hindi since the arrival of a Hindu nationalist government in Delhi in 2014.

While the two modes of world-making may seem permanently at odds with one another, they can, in fact, overlap on occasion. This is especially so when it comes to multilateral diplomacy that presents India with an opportunity to present its drafting skills to the world. It should not have come as any surprise to dismayed Western commentators, then, when Indian negotiators made a decisive last-minute intervention at the COP26 climate summit in Glasgow in November 2021, pushing through an amendment by which fossil fuels would not be 'phased *out*' but rather 'phased *down*'. This domestically celebrated move was lauded by Union Environment Minister Bhupender Yadav as 'a success from India's standpoint because we articulated and put across the concerns and ideas of the developing world quite succinctly and unequivocally'.[120] The ideals of the two worlds coalesced: India had presented itself

---

[117] "'Lok Sabha Starred Questions No. 19634 and 19639 Regarding Passing of Hindi Examination before Confirmation of IFS Officers'", 1968, FSI/1968—F/125(6), NAI; Kaul, 'Note'.

[118] Jawaharlal Nehru, 'Note', 17 September 1955, 'Additional posts in Hindi Section of the Ministry of External Affairs: Appointment of Dr. HR Bachchan', F/13(76)–CP/1955(Part II), NAI.

[119] MEA, 'Written Reply', 17 April 1968, 'Lok Sabha starred questions No. 19634 and 19639 regarding passing of Hindi Examination before confirmation of IFS officers', FSI/1968—F/125(6), NAI.

[120] 'India Calls COP26 Climate Summit in Glasgow a "Success"', *The Economic Times*, 14 November 2021, https://economictimes.indiatimes.com/news/india/india-calls-cop26-climate-summit-in-glasgow-a-success/articleshow/87699968.cms.

WORLD-MAKING: PROTEST AND PROTOCOL

both as a moral defender of the developing world and as a drafter of fine-tuned diplomatic distinctions predicated on an elegantly simple swap between two cognate phrasal verbs.

Provincializing European international society

In Western-centric narrations of the history of international society, one must be alive to the unspoken definitions which dictate that '[j]ust as "society" is restricted to certain well-mannered classes, "international" also means Europe and not the colonies'.[121] And so it was with Indian diplomats, seventy years on from Independence, who in interviews repeatedly equated the world of diplomacy with a world of soft-spoken gentlemen and recycled 'international' and 'Western' as interchangeable descriptors.[122] How are we to make sense of these lexical slip-ups and the power imbalances that they speak to?

'To provincialize' Europe is not pretend as though Europe does not matter at all, but to do what Dipesh Chakrabarty originally articulated as the intellectual task of provincialization: 'to find out how and in what sense European ideas that were universal were also, at one and the same time, drawn from very particular intellectual and historical traditions that could not claim any universal validity', and in so doing, ask about the continued 'silent and everyday presence of European thought in Indian life and practices'.[123] An Additional-Secretary of an early 1990s batch concluded that internationally resonant 'cultural references' were an indispensable currency wherever in the world one was serving,[124] but did not touch upon the narrowly European frame of reference that most of the cultural repertoire of his colleagues drew on. An imagined Europe joined every interview, quietly sitting in the background. We must interrogate which kind of political imaginations structure interpretations of Europe, who is allowed to imagine this Europe, and how these imageries meet the postcolonial revolt designed, often, as its antithesis.

The imagery of Europeanized international society, ostensibly making demands on reticent diplomats who would personally have preferred to behave otherwise, was always partly a fiction perpetuated by Indian diplomats themselves. The most traditional Western diplomats may have expected 'the right mix of drinks, flowers, cheese', but nobody in Moscow seemed to care

---

[121] Callahan, 'Nationalising International Theory', 318.
[122] Interview 25; Interview 26; Interview 28; Interview 42, April 2019; Interview 48.
[123] Chakrabarty, *Provincializing Europe*, xiii.
[124] Interview 70.

much for such conventions, an officer wary of his Service's cultural convictions recalled.[125] While suits may have worked in Geneva, in Kathmandu wearing kurtas 'made it easier to talk to the Nepalis, who were not part of the elite' of international society, one former Ambassador to both believed.[126] Indeed, as T.N. Kaul's social report from the Indian Embassy in Beijing from June 1952 acknowledges, 'the diplomatic community' was rather more heterogeneous than Indian officers sometimes made it out to be: while the 'Asian group has succeeded in more or less sticking together and parties where the Chinese and Asian representatives only are present are very successful' and the 'Western Europeans and Scandinavians are very sociable (partly because they have little else to do) and welcome entertainment by the Asian group', the latter have 'to be invited separately from the Chinese and the Eastern Europeans if the party is to be a success'.[127] It would be ontologically bold to claim some absolute existence for a culturally fixed diplomatic club of cosmopolitan elites. It can, however, be brought into being in the shared subconsciousness of a Foreign Service making sense of the legacies, practices, and status conventions of the world around it. The notion of a singular diplomatic club, which features so prominently in the autoethnographies of Indian diplomats, is in many ways a cultural projection.

The imagery of Europe itself was, to some extent, a figment of the Indian diplomatic imagination. It fixed and eternalized a partial vision of Europe, exaggerated its features, and drew a caricature-like image of an aristocratic club which never really existed in such stark terms on the continent itself. As the character of Saleem Sinai offers in Salman Rushdie's novel *Midnight's Children:* 'Perhaps it would be fair to say that Europe repeats itself, in India, as farce.'[128]

In much of the world, the supposedly worldly enactments of effortless cosmopolitanism were outright detrimental. There were considerable audience costs to reproducing this imagery especially in the Soviet Union, China, and different corners of the Third World. 'We were, in the beginning, apt to copy the British and adopt their methods and manners for want of any other experience', T.N. Kaul noted in a letter from the Indian Embassy in Moscow in August 1965—which was 'useful in some countries but a handicap in others'.[129] In a letter from 26 January 1948, Vijaya Lakshmi Pandit relayed to G.S. Bajpai at

---

[125] Interview 12.
[126] Interview 24.
[127] T.N. Kaul, 'Report (Social), Indian Embassy in Beijing, for June, 1952', 3 July 1952, Embassy of India in China, Peking—utilization of frais—Social Reports, F/14(6)—FSP/52, NAI.
[128] Salman Rushdie, *Midnight's Children* (London: Penguin Vintage Edition, 2008), 256.
[129] Kaul, 'Note'.

138   WORLD-MAKING: PROTEST AND PROTOCOL

the Headquarters in Delhi that there was 'a good deal of criticism' from some
countries, especially Russia, about the Foreign Service's continued reliance on
English, instead of Hindi.[130] In another letter, she admonished:

> Russia is not Washington or London. What would be right and proper in
> either of these capitals does not fit into the framework of Moscow where
> human beings and policies are judged from different angles. It is not enough
> to choose your representative to this capital on Satow's principles of 'good
> temper, good looks and good health' with an 'average intelligence' thrown in
> for good measure. The first question here is 'what have you done to deserve
> the honour of representing your country?' And because our reply to this
> could not, in the nature of things, be the right one, we have had to be spe-
> cially [sic] careful of our actions and behaviour generally—our unfortunate
> background has also been responsible for a good deal of suspicion regarding
> us.[131]

Faced with a similar charge in the 1960s, Ambassador Jayantanuja Bandyopadhyaya was witness to a lapse in cordiality by a Russian diplomat following a
game of chess: 'Your High Commissioner and many of the other Indian diplomats I have met do not represent India or the Indian people in any way.'[132]
The ideologies and political systems of the West may have appalled the Soviet
Union but at least British and American diplomats embodied them well, he
decreed, while 'most Indian diplomats do not represent their culture, their
country, or their people.'[133] India's enactments of effortless worldliness were
not received as proof of elite belonging but as a sign of a domestic elite adrift.
Bandyopadhyaya recalls protesting out of duty, not conviction.

In much of the world born out of decolonization and wedded to the binaries of the Cold War, the keenness of Indian representatives to embody
old-time graces was read as a colonial lag. Their insufficient expressions of
postcoloniality were held against them as a sign of their separateness from the
group of anti-imperialists they believed themselves to be leading. 'We made
too much of this being-at-ease-with-the-rest-of-the-world', a recently retired

---

[130] Vijaya Lakshmi Pandit, 'Letter to G.S. Bajpai', 26 January 1948, 'August 1947–61: Correspondence
exchanged by Mrs Pandit with G.S. Bajpai (Secretary-General, MEA, and Commonwealth Relations)
in her capacity as India's ambassador to Moscow and later USA', SF/56.

[131] Vijaya Lakshmi Pandit, 'Letter to G.S. Bajpai', 5 February 1948, '1947–1951: Correspondence
of V.L. Pandit (as Indian Ambassador to USS) with G.S. Bajpai—Secretary General, MEA, regarding
official matters'. SF/55, Vijaya Lakshmi Pandit papers, NMML.

[132] Bandyopadhyaya, The Making of India's Foreign Policy, 185.

[133] Bandyopadhyaya, 185.

Stephanian concluded,[134] in language reminiscent of Bourdieu's thinking on the 'the "natural" self-confidence, ease and authority of someone who feels authorized'.[135] Imagining oneself among the chosen few of the cosmopolitan club was not an act of world-embracing solidarity. Instead, it was an act of alienating oneself from much of the non-Western world. The Indian diplomat could cut a lonely figure. 'An Indian diplomat is quite alone', a retired multilateralist concluded; for while American and European diplomats had their 'reference group' among themselves, and Africans and Arabs often forged intuitive diplomatic groupings, India straddled the spaces between—a Third World country with its First World attitude.[136]

The everyday forms of cultural self-policing inside the Indian Foreign Service act as constant reminders that India's membership in international society was not, as Buzan has argued about postcolonial nations, a question settled once and for all with the formal end of empire. In fact, one is reminded of what Deepak Nair has argued in his astute Bourdieusian reading of everyday diplomacy in Southeast Asia: expressions of cultural hierarchy, such as inequalities in language or accents, academic degrees or 'embodied ease' 'profoundly complicate the performances of sovereign equality'.[137] Instead of a closed case of formal admission, Indian diplomacy constitutes an ongoing performance of belonging, reproduced in the everyday practices of representation. The body of the 'cosmopolitan diplomat' carries a lingering, self-perpetuating standard of civilization: to belong is to live up to ideals associated with a semi-aristocratic, white, worldly—and often almost fictional—elite.

Non-universal cosmopolitanism

The realities of cosmopolitanism at the margins of Western-dominated order are messy. The ideal theory and social lives of cosmopolitanism are very different things. The ideals of liberal internationalism assume a cosmopolitanism that has been intuitively 'understood to have a positive valence and progressive implications'.[138] In line with such impressions, Indian diplomats, too, sometimes began their elaborations on the term by briefly tying it to a set of abstract

---

[134] Interview 19.

[135] Bourdieu, *Distinction*, 250.

[136] Interview 33.

[137] Nair, 'Saving Face in Diplomacy: A Political Sociology of Face-to-Face Interactions in the Association of Southeast Asian Nations', 10.

[138] Thomas Bender, 'The Cosmopolitan Experience and Its Uses', in Cosmopolitanisms, ed. Bruce Robbins and Paulo Lemos Horta (New York: University Press, 2017), 116.

140 WORLD-MAKING: PROTEST AND PROTOCOL

ideals, rooted in coexistence with an Other,[139] the universality of human rights, or a belief in multilateralism.[140] At home, it dovetailed with a commitment to oppose various forms of discrimination, be they along lines of religion, gender, or caste.[141] What tended to follow this declaratory phase of the conversation, however, was a far more ambivalent moment of soul-searching on the meaning of cosmopolitanism in the everyday life of global order—an order defined not by its inherent tolerance but its underlying hierarchies.

'Actually existing cosmopolitanism' always exists *somewhere*. It has a context, a world in which it develops its meaning. What defines cosmopolitanism in the Indian diplomatic imagination is the kind of world-making that it has been tied to. Curiously, in the parlance of diplomats, cosmopolitanism is more instinctively related to the imagery of the old, white club of worldly elites than to the radical potential of the postcolonial world. Not a single diplomat, among over 80 interviewees, tied their reading of cosmopolitanism to Third Worldist solidarity or Nehru's highly suggestive discourse on 'One World'.[142] There was no impulse to think about postcoloniality and cosmopolitanism together; rather, cosmopolitanism was placed in the context of lingering hierarchies of an old regime of power in the world. Cosmopolitanism had come to signify exclusivity, not emancipation.

Cosmopolitanism and power

For all the universalistic language of cosmopolitanism as ideal theory, officers of the Indian Foreign Service know it is not an ethic propagated from a place of equal standing. Even those who most wished to embrace it did not feel recognized as equal shapers of a globally developed cosmopolitan praxis. A former diplomat who has published widely on the question of Indian identity felt that the 'huge cultural asymmetry' that governed international society meant that India was always being coaxed to 'co-opt' into a global 'mainstream',[143] rather than shaping it. Breaking the third wall and commenting on the academic literature that Indian diplomats were themselves part of, one disillusioned member of the early 1960s batches complained about some of the IR literature he had studied, whose atmospherics of an international 'brotherhood' of

---

[139] Interview 27; Interview 37; Interview 41; Interview 49; Interview 56; Interview 57; Interview 74; Interview 76, May 2019.
[140] Interview 23; Interview 27; Interview 28; Interview 52, May 2019; Interview 74.
[141] Interview 7; Interview 42; Interview 46; Interview 85.
[142] Nehru, *Selected Works of Jawaharlal Nehru, Volume 19: 16th July–18th October 1952*, 42.
[143] Interview 4.

diplomats was 'a piece of nonsense'—'they want all of us in the Global South [...] to conform to standards' developed elsewhere, while 'nobody asks African diplomats whether they can contribute to this shared culture'.[144] The fiction of the global common good, a nationalistically minded former Foreign Secretary argued, was perpetuated by a slanted literary canon: 'So much is written on international affairs [...] from the viewpoint of Western interest'.[145] 'The standards have been set by the West', concluded a wry former Foreign Secretary in an indirect response to a question about the cosmopolitan character of international diplomacy.[146] Gupta's 'Third World country with a First World attitude' was caught up in a lexical deception: a vision of 'one world' under cosmopolitanism was 'a sometimes unconscious, sometimes unconscionable, euphemism for "First World" culture'.[147]

This sense of cosmopolitanism as an exclusive realm for the powerful has deep historical roots. India's experience has always been that of an aspiring cosmopolitan disappointed. Speaking at the League of Nations Assembly on 12 September 1921, India's colonial envoy V.S. Srinivasa Sastri sought to impress upon his diplomatic colleagues 'that we are cosmopolitan reality, that we are citizens of the world'.[148] This cosmopolitan reality adamantly claimed by Sastri was so deeply entangled in colonial hierarchies that it could not even envision an independent India at the time of Sastri's speech. India was speaking of 'citizens of the world' at a time when its people could not even claim citizenship at home. It was advocating for a cosmopolitan utopia from a place of colonial reality. It is this potent disjuncture between an India willing to engage with principles of cosmopolitanism and a world unwilling to grant India the same favour that underlay the frustration of many diplomats during our conversations, nearly a century after Sastri's speech.

Far from embodying a set of political principles, then, a belief in cosmopolitanism at the margins of global order requires *apoliticization*. In order to swear by equality and tolerance in a world of deep racial, class, and national hierarchies, cosmopolitanism in places like India has to continuously enact a double elusion: 'a downplaying of the present importance of past atrocities (including those perpetrated by colonialism), and a relative disregard for the

---

[144] Interview 1.
[145] Interview 39.
[146] Interview 45.
[147] Ackbar Abbas, 'Cosmopolitan De-Scriptions: Shanghai and Hong Kong', in *Cosmopolitanism*, ed. Carol A. Breckenridge et al. (Durham, NC: Duke University Press, 2002), 210.
[148] Thakur, *India's First Diplomat: V.S. Srinivasa Sastri and the Making of Liberal Internationalism*, 81.

142 WORLD-MAKING: PROTEST AND PROTOCOL

economic structures that produce inequality.[149] A former Foreign Secretary with a pronounced nationalistic streak was, in a way, referring to such evasions when he complained of colleagues who 'try to advocate building bridges by skirting big issues'—they were 'so taken up by their linguistic affinities' that they failed, or perhaps refused, to see the fundamental power asymmetry that lay underneath.[150] This made him the only diplomat to reject the cosmopolitan moniker outright. In a world of unequal power, cosmopolitanism was a luxury Indians could not afford—'you have to stand your ground'.[151]

There is no cosmopolitanism under liberal order that is innocent of power. As Rahul Rao has argued, the unequal power relations between the Global South and the Global North mean that 'the praxis of liberal cosmopolitanism today assists in the consolidation of Western hegemony'.[152] Cosmopolitan commitments, in an unequal world, place 'an ethical mask' on hegemonic power,[153] precisely by refusing to acknowledge that power operates at all. There is also a practised innocence to the way that the history of cosmopolitanism is narrated in the West. When the English School theorist Hedley Bull spoke of 'cosmopolitan civilization' and 'cosmopolitan awareness', he dated the emergence of cosmopolitanism as a feature of international society right after the Second World War, 'at least in the advanced countries'.[154] This ahistoricized account gives cosmopolitanism a standard-of-civilization logic, audaciously claiming to speak for humanity while pleading ignorance to the recent realities of empire and elevating the West as a carrier of a higher moral consciousness. The cosmopolitan imperative, in this respect, resembled Ranajit Guha's analysis of English education in colonial India, which 'stood not only for enlightenment but also authority', and which in its everyday garb elided the fundamental asymmetry of colonial pedagogy so that it was possible to 'look upon it as a purely cultural transaction, and ignore that aspect which related it directly to power'.[155]

---

[149] Bruce Robbins and Paulo Lemos Horta, 'Introduction', in *Cosmopolitanisms*, ed. Bruce Robbins and Paulo Lemos Horta (New York: University Press, 2017), 8.

[150] Interview 39.

[151] Interview 39.

[152] Rao, *Third World Protest*, 36; See also Craig Calhoun, 'The Class Consciousness of Frequent Travelers: Toward a Critique of Actually Existing Cosmopolitanism', *The South Atlantic Quarterly* 101, no. 4 (2002): 869–897.

[153] David Harvey, *Cosmopolitanism and the Geographies of Freedom* (New York: Columbia University Press, 2009), 84.

[154] Hedley Bull, *Hedley Bull on International Society*, ed. Kai Alderson and Andrew Hurrell (Basingstoke: Macmillan, 2000), 137, 221.

[155] Ranajit Guha, *Dominance without Hegemony: History and Power in Colonial India* (Cambridge, Mass.: Harvard University Press, 1997), 166.

These unequal rules of cosmopolitanism are carried in the Indian diplomatic habitus. 'Our identity is partly shaped by recognition or its absence, often by the misrecognition of others', as the political philosopher Charles Taylor tells us, 'and so a person or a group of people can suffer real damage, real distortion, if the people or the society around them mirror back to them a confining or demeaning or contemptible picture of themselves'.[156] The felt inferior position was expressed in the body of the Indian diplomat, as officers spoke of a latent uneasiness when serving in Western postings, the emotional toll of European condescension, and the need to imbibe Western etiquette in order to manage the alienation.[157] 'No matter how good your accent is, it's still a foreign accent', one recently retired Stephanian noted sardonically about his colleagues' attempts at belonging among a hallowed Anglophone international elite setting the rules of belonging for the rest of the world.[158] Writing of his professional challenges as High Commissioner in London (1973–1977) in tellingly casteist terms, B.K. Nehru once complained that in the British diplomatic imagination, 'the Indian High Commission had quite definitely been relegated to the Shudra category of Third World missions who did not matter and whose views were not worth bothering about'.[159]

How, then, to make the world bother about India's views? Recognition for one's cosmopolitanism, in the minds of Indian diplomats, required a performance of elite assimilation into European imageries of international society. This is not a practice of equals, but a scheme in which some play catch-up with a world theoretically long past. Through the performance of 'cosmopolitan' discourse and its elite markers, upper-class diplomats seek to transcend their grievous misrepresentation as the lower castes of the world. Cosmopolitanism atrophies: it retreats from attempting to be an international ethic and settles itself into an individualized marker of elite distinction. This process has also coloured the social dynamics inside the Indian Foreign Service, to which the next chapter attends.

Caste and race in international society

The hypocrisies of actually existing cosmopolitanism do not run along the divide between West and non-West, former colonizer and former colonized,

---

[156] Charles Taylor, *Multiculturalism and the Politics of Recognition* (Princeton: Princeton University Press, 1992), 25.
[157] Interview 14; Interview 33, 33; Interview 35; Interview 41; Interview 82.
[158] Interview 19.
[159] Nehru, *Nice Guys Finish Second: Memoirs*, 552.

alone. Its exclusionary character is more complex, and the culprits for this exclusion more numerous. Indian diplomats have long been alive to the ways in which hegemonic forms of cosmopolitanism fail to affirm equal standing for individuals irrespective of nationality and race. However, their own attempts at cosmopolitanism have failed to affirm such equality for individuals irrespective of caste. Their visions drag the ideal theory of cosmopolitanism to the everyday ground on which battles for status, inclusion, and dignity are fought in India. They show that the broken promises of cosmopolitan inclusion depend not only on international hierarchies of worth but also on domestic lines of difference. In conversations, some diplomats were quick to claim that being a cosmopolitan also meant rejecting discrimination based on caste, but were incensed when the conversation turned to diplomatic initiatives to alleviate caste oppression. The lines of cosmopolitan solidarity are drawn selectively in Western circles, as the diplomats were right to emphasize. Yet they are drawn selectively among India's diplomatic elite, too.

With domestic and international hierarchies deeply entangled, Indian world-making has necessitated difficult balancing acts, questions of voice and authority, and debates behind closed doors on, who, precisely, is allowed to represent the symbolic subaltern that Indian diplomats have sought to give voice to. On questions of caste, this voice has not belonged to Dalit campaigners, politicians, or even diplomats. The ambivalent status of Indian diplomats in the various hierarchies that govern their work has long underpinned their beliefs about which hierarchies are worth resisting. Racial and caste hierarchies are particularly ambivalent in this regard.

In India's postcolonial reading of the world, international relations were read as race relations early on.[160] At a time when post-imperial Britain and the segregationist US were only beginning to develop a vocabulary in which to talk about race as part of a diplomatic human rights agenda, India was assiduously championing the notion that anti-racist advocacy could not afford to respect sovereign boundaries.[161] Fights for global racial equality were not considered accessory to India's interests, as a Ministerial review of India's foreign policy noted in 1970, but instead, '[i]t is also part of the conception of India's national interests to eliminate colonialism, imperialism and racialism', and to lend support to the 'oppressed races and nations of the world'.[162] This meant providing material assistance to African liberation movements in the form of medical equipment and clothing, and, in a more traditional

---

[160] Nehru, 'Note for Asaf Ali and K.P.S. Menon'.

[161] Cohen, *India*, 87; Pandit, *The Scope of Happiness*, 222–223.

[162] 'A Review of India's Foreign Policy—Document No. 4977', 1970, 'A Review of India's Foreign Policy', FS/70–F/ WII 101(45)/70, NAI.

diplomatic mode, pressing for decolonization, anti-discrimination measures, and economic sanctions against Apartheid at the United Nations and other international bodies.[163] India's first Commissioner to East Africa, Apa Pant, was deeply involved with Kenyan nationalists and implicated in their quest for decolonization in the late 1940s and early 1950s;[164] in Ghana in the late 1950s and early 1960s, India's Foreign Service Research Bureau and the Special Branch effectively built Accra's security service in an act of Afro-Asian decolonial cooperation.[165]

Yet while anti-racism has been a prominent—albeit understudied[166]—facet of Indian diplomacy, Indian diplomats have fought with conviction against anti-casteism making it onto the diplomatic agenda. While the two systems of oppression have their distinct genealogies, social logics, and political contexts, activists and academics have been developing elaborate comparisons and solidarities between the two struggles[167] at least since the anti-caste reformer Jyotirao Phule dedicated his 1873 book on the fight against Brahminism under the British Raj to those fighting racial discrimination in the US.[168] The contemporary struggles against caste and racial oppression run parallel organizationally, too: The Dalit Panthers of India, having adopted their name in solidarity with the Black Panthers of the US in the 1970s, held a historic meeting with Black Panther organisers in Maharashtra in May 2022.[169] In October 2022, in testimony to the global resonance of a caste-race nexus, the Indian human rights campaigner and researcher Ashwini KP made diplomatic

---

[163] 'Note from C.D. Chaudhri (Under-Secretary, UN-I)', 22 April 1966, 'International Convention on the Elimination of All Forms of Racial Discrimination, 1965—Ratification of India', F/ UI/106/7/66, NAI; 'Oral History Transcript: Apa B. Pant', 22; MEA/UN and Conference Division, 'India's Country Report to the Second World Conference to Combat Racism and Racial Discrimination', 1981, 'Second World Conference to Combat Racism and Racial Discrimination, Genova August 1983', F/ UI/352/60/81, NAI.

[164] Guyot-Réchard, 'Stirring Africa towards India'.

[165] Avinash Paliwal, 'Colonial Sinews of Postcolonial Espionage—India and the Making of Ghana's External Intelligence Agency, 1958–61', *The International History Review* 44, no. 4 (2022): 914–934.

[166] Davis and Thakur, '"An Act of Faith" or a New "Brown Empire"?', 23.

[167] See e.g. Suraj Yengde, 'Race, Caste and What It Will Take to Make Dalit Lives Matter', The Caravan, 3 July 2020, https://caravanmagazine.in/essay/race-caste-and-what-it-will-take-to-make-dalit-lives-matter; Anand Teltumbde, 'Race or Caste, Discrimination Is a Universal Concern', *Economic and Political Weekly* 44, no. 34 (2009): 16–18; Gyanendra Pandey, *A History of Prejudice: Race, Caste, and Difference in India and the United States* (Cambridge University Press, 2013); Ambrose Pinto, 'UN Conference against Racism: Is Caste Race?', *Economic and Political Weekly* 36, no. 30 (28 July 2001): 2817–2820; Deepa S. Reddy, 'The Ethnicity of Caste', *Anthropological Quarterly* 78, no. 3 (2005): 543–584; Nico Slate, 'Translating Race and Caste', *Journal of Historical Sociology* 24, no. 1 (2011): 62–79; Shobana Shankar, *An Uneasy Embrace: Africa, India and the Spectre of Race* (London: Hurst & Company, 2021).

[168] Jyotirao Phule, *Slavery in the Civilised British Government under the Cloak of Brahmanism (1873)*, trans. P.G. Patil (Bombay: Education Department of the Government of Maharashtra, 1991).

[169] Suraj Yengde, 'Dalit Panthers Was an Ideology and a Sight of the Dalit Response to Injustice', *The Indian Express* (blog), 29 May 2022, https://indianexpress.com/article/opinion/columns/dalit-panthers-black-panthers-maharashtra-br-ambedkar-7941737/.

146 WORLD-MAKING: PROTEST AND PROTOCOL

history by becoming the first Dalit woman to be appointed Special Rapporteur on contemporary forms of racism, racial discrimination, xenophobia, and related intolerance by the UN.[170] Nonetheless, the MEA and members of the IFS have vigorously opposed the proposition of protecting Dalits under the banner of descendance-based discrimination. They have used their outsized influence on drafting at the UN to block discussion and inclusion of Scheduled Castes in international conventions or monitoring mechanisms at least since the mid-1970s.[171]

On caste, India's famous drafting power, which it had pledged to dedicate to defending the global subaltern, allowed its delegates to exclude struggles for caste equality from the written record of global anti-discrimination diplomacy. In a letter to J.S. Teja, Additional Secretary (UN), from 14 August 1983, India's Permanent Representative to the UN, M. Dubey, reports on the drafting triumph of India having 'succeeded in having references to disadvantaged groups deleted', ensuring that minorities were repeatedly prefixed with the qualifier of being 'racial and ethnic' in nature, so as to carefully expunge caste-based minorities from the text and 'to make it clear that we are talking of minority groups only in the context of racial discrimination', as well as having 'the title of the chapter on minority rights [...] amended to reflect our concern'.[172]

The imperfect parallels between race and caste were forced out into the open at the UN World Conference Against Racism in Durban in 2001. Dealing with race, racial xenophobia and 'related intolerance', the Conference sparked a spirited debate in India about whether caste ought to be tabled for discussion in Durban, as UN officials had done and Dalit campaigners had long insisted upon.[173] The official Indian line suggested that the UN was mistaken to consider caste a form of descendance-based discrimination, that India had

---

[170] Balakrishna Ganeshan, 'Interview: Dalit Woman Appointed UN Special Rapporteur Says Caste a Global Phenomenon', *The News Minute*, 10 October 2022, https://www.thenewsminute.com/article/interview-dalit-woman-appointed-un-special-rapporteur-says-caste-global-phenomenon–168746.

[171] Srivivasan (First Secretary, PMI New York, 'Letter to A.K. Gupta (Director, UN.I/MEA)', 9 April 1975, 'International Convention on the Elimination of all Forms of Racial Discrimination. Fourth Periodic Report as required under Article 9', F/UI/151/18/75, NAI; Muchkund Dubey (Permanent Representative, UN), 'Letter to J.S. Teja (Additional-Secretary, UN)', 14 August 1983, 'Second World Conference to Combat Racism and Racial Discrimination, Genova August 1983', F/UI/352/60/81, NAI.

[172] M. Dubey, 'Letter to J.S. Teja (Additional Secretary (UN))', 14 August 1983, Second World Conference to Combat Racism and Racial Discrimination, Genova August 1983, F/UI/352/60/81, NAI.

[173] Human Rights Campaign, 'Press Release: "Campaign of Untouchables and Buddhists of India—Mass Demonstration of Indian Untouchables in London"', 26 January 1975, '1975–78: Press release and press clippings regarding violation of human rights, also includes problems on human rights on untouchables', SF/60, Gopal Singh papers, NMML; Ambedkar International Mission (on behalf of eight Dalit organizations), 'Letter to General Kurt Waldeim (UN Secretary-General)', 17 September 1978, '1975–78: Press release and press clippings regarding violation of human rights, also includes problems on human rights on untouchables', SF/60, Gopal Singh papers, NMML.

developed sufficient procedures to ameliorate caste discrepancies—and, in a long-running argument which the Ministry has upheld for decades, that unlike anti-racist advocacy, which did justify interference in the domestic affairs of sovereign nations, it would be an affront to Indian legal sovereignty to discuss anti-casteist advocacy at the UN.[174] Emotions ran high across the MEA. Former Foreign Minister Yashwant Sinha, interviewed by political theorist Luis Cabrera about Dalit activists reaching out to UN human rights bodies, was particularly intemperate in his verdict: 'They should have been sent to Guantanamo. Anyone who does not believe in the sovereignty of India doesn't deserve to live here.'[175] In their quest for transnational justice, Dalits became terrorists undermining the nation, not fellow Indians engaged in the laborious mission of delivering the promise of India's postcolonial project of equality. They were not cosmopolitans but criminals. In the end, caste was dropped as a category of descendance-based discrimination, but only after Indian representatives threatened to boycott the entire UN Conference.[176]

India's decades-long insistence on excluding Dalits from the descendance-based framework, under various government coalitions, is not upheld by Government or political parties but by a diplomatic consensus generated by career diplomats.[177] By illustrative contrast, the Ministry of Law gave its blessing to the ratification of the International Convention on the Elimination of all Forms of Racial Discrimination adopted by the UN General Assembly at its 20th session held in 1965, drawing an implied parallel between race and caste by answering a question on racial discrimination by pointing to Article 17 of the Indian Constitution which banned caste discrimination, as well as to the Untouchability (Offences) Act of 1965 aimed at eradicating the practice of untouchability, and arguing from these legal premises that the Convention on racial discrimination would be in alignment with existing legal norms in India.[178] There is no unified front in Indian government and bureaucracy against comparisons between race and caste, however vehemently many diplomats insisted so. It is therefore worth investigating the social context in which race and caste have been made sense of in India's world-making.

---

[174] Shepherd, *Buffalo Nationalism*, 73; K.B. Srinivastava (SRO (UN—Indian Permanent Representation in New York)), 'Memorandum', n.d., Volume I. Second World Conference to Combat Racism and Racial Discrimination, Geneva August 1983, F/WI/352/60/81 (sic), NAI.

[175] Cabrera, *The Humble Cosmopolitan*, 1.

[176] Shiv Visvanathan, 'The Race for Caste: Prolegomena to the Durban Conference', *Economic and Political Weekly* 36, no. 27 (July 2001): 2512.

[177] Dag Erik Berg, 'Sovereignties, the World Conference against Racism 2001 and the Formation of a Dalit Human Rights Campaign' (Ceri Sciences Po, 2007), 13, Research in question—No. 20—April 2007.

[178] K.S. Pandalai (Ministry of Law), 'Memorandum to the MEA', 29 August 1966, International Convention on the Elimination of All Forms of Racial Discrimination, 1965—Participation of India, F/UI/106/7/66, NAI.

148   WORLD-MAKING: PROTEST AND PROTOCOL

The diplomatic intersections between race and caste have long been read differently depending on one's caste position. The influential Committee on Untouchability and Economic & Educational Development of Scheduled Castes sensed a parallel struggle: 'I may venture to say this problem is akin to the "negro problem" with the exceptional stress that it is more acute, inhuman and intolerable in the present day when the emphasis is to abolish the differences between various races, religions and nationalities', wrote the Committee Chairman L. Ellayaperumal in a direct letter to the UN Secretary-General U. Thant on 30 November 1967, arguing about the Dalit community that a 'recognition of their problem by the UN will give a fillip to the advancement of these communities'.[179] The letter, which the MEA tersely suggested the UN Secretary-General 'may be advised to ignore',[180] went so far as to propose the appointment of Maragatham Chandrasekar, a prominent Dalit politician of the Congress Party who had served in Indian delegations to the UN in the early 1960s, for a high-level posting at the UN as 'an encouragement to the 11 crores[181] of the population of India who are striving constantly to emerge with the society both national and international'. Dalit campaigners have understood the struggle against caste oppression as inherently international, as inseparable from transnational struggles against all other descendance-based forms of oppression that the Foreign Service has insisted must be addressed on the global stage.

Ambedkar also saw an urgent parallel. In 1946, he wrote to W.E.B du Bois, the pioneering African-American sociologist and founder of the National Association for the Advancement of Colored People, comparing Dalit and African American liberation struggles and raising the possibility of action through the UN:

There is so much similarity between the position of the Untouchables in India and of the position of Negroes in America that the study of the latter is not only natural but necessary. I was very much interested to read that the Negroes of America have filed a petition to the U.N.O. [United Nations

---

[179] L. Ellayaperumal (Chairman of the Committee on Untouchability and Economic & Educational Development of Scheduled Castes), 'Letter to U. Thant (Secretary-General of the UN)', 30 November 1967, Indians at the UN—Appointments, F/UI/151/1/68, NAI.
[180] S. Shahabuddin (Deputy Secretary (UN), 'Letter to G. Parthasarathi (Permanent Representative of India at the UN in New York)', 16 January 1968, Indians at the UN—Appointments, F/UI/151/1/68, NAI.
[181] 'Crore' is an Indian unit of measurement indicating ten million.

Organisation]. The Untouchables of India are also thinking of following suit.[182]

Martin Luther King, a self-avowed Gandhian, drew a connection between struggles for racial and caste equality, too, at one point planning to travel to India and while there, to visit 'Harijan centres' set up for the advancement of Dalits. This prompted Subimal Dutt, wary of the proposal that the Indian Ambassador in Washington formally extend an invitation to Dr King in 1958, to suggest that the invitation be delegated to some Indian social organization to avoid the MEA provoking US authorities.[183] One suspects that the itinerary of the visit had provoked many inside the MEA, too.

Parallels were sometimes drawn between the experience of Dalits and African Americans in the broader conversation that unfolded over the course of my interviews with diplomats, too.[184] Yet as the discussion turned to more official diplomatic acknowledgements of the relevance of a comparison, the mood often soured, the tone turning combative and defensive about the various ways in which diverging biological, sociological, and historical experiences rendered the comparison unviable, or how a focus on caste would distract from the more pressing concerns over race.

What comes out in anonymized interviews, however, is a stark caste divide in how questions of caste, cosmopolitanism, solidarity, and diplomacy are thought of among India's career diplomats. These disagreements lay bare the importance of caste hierarchies inside the Indian Foreign Service to the diplomatic work India does outside. It also reminds us of why it matters whose perspective is rendered commonsensical or makes it into international headlines. In my conversations with diplomats, different renditions of India's national interest ran along caste lines. Every non-Dalit officer interviewed on the topic presented the official line with considerable conviction: race was genetic while caste was sociological,[185] the fight against caste discrimination was an internal matter while the fight against race discrimination was international.[186] Not so among Dalit officers. 'All the Dalits within the Service were rooting for it', sighed a millennial Dalit officer about the proposed

---

[182] Ambedkar cited in Eleanor Zelliot, 'India's Dalits: Racism and Contemporary Change', *Global Dialogue* 12, no. 2 (Summer 2010): 4.

[183] Subimal Dutt, 'Letter to R.R. Diwakar (President of Gandhi Smarak Nidhi)', 29 November 1958, SF/56—'Individual Correspondence', Subimal Dutt papers, NMML.

[184] Interview 28; Interview 33; Interview 67; Interview 71; Interview 75.

[185] This, in itself, is a highly contentious claim. See e.g. Lauren Davenport, 'The Fluidity of Racial Classifications', *Annual Review of Political Science* 23, no. 1 (2020): 221–240; Sharjeel Sabir, 'Chimerical Categories: Caste, Race, and Genetics', *Developing World Bioethics* 3, no. 2 (2003): 170–177.

[186] Interview 11, March 2019; Interview 26.

inclusion of caste into the anti-discrimination framework.[187] 'I will tell you, as an SC officer, what is denied to me—and you are telling the world that there is no discrimination?' a retired Dalit diplomat recalled his plea to the colleague in charge of UN Affairs ahead of the Durban Conference.[188] Reservations meant that Dalits had a place in the Service, but it did not guarantee them a voice. There had been no consultation to draw on the lived experiences or professional opinions of Dalit diplomats, few decision-making positions for the UN ever fell to Dalits to begin with, and even then, Dalit officers doubted whether any of them would have felt at liberty to express a dissenting view on the upper-caste rendition of India's multilateral anti-discrimination stance.[189] As a consequence, representing India as a Dalit sometimes meant that 'you get into tricky situations' in which, in order to perform your diplomatic duties, you have to 'tell untruths' about India's respect for equality and diversity, one multilateralist admitted—noting with a subtly raised eyebrow that it was important to remain 'diplomatic' at all times, including when asked about the topic during an interview with a foreigner.[190]

The rejection of Dalit claims as legitimate diplomatic demands betrays not only the taboo character of caste in Indian political life but the implicit upper-caste standpoint of 'actually existing cosmopolitanism'. In interviews, liberal upper-caste diplomats who spoke about the need to redress racial inequalities head on repeatedly explained that, as progressives, they 'did not see caste'.[191] Kancha Ilaiah Shepherd has suggested that India's 'ultra-nationalist theoreticians' suppress international debate on caste because of a concern for India's global prestige.[192] Yet the imperatives of prestige have also occupied the liberal upper castes for whom caste is a philosophical embarrassment and a marker of political regression. This has turned caste into a taboo form of social stratification—one of the very few forms of hierarchy that Indian diplomats have not sought to fight in their diplomatic work. The upper-caste diplomacy on descendance-based discrimination has shown, as Bourdieu would have it, that '[w]hat is at stake in the struggles about the meaning of the social world is power over the classificatory schemes and systems which are the basis of the representations of the groups and therefore of their mobilization and demobilization'.[193]

---

[187] Interview 71.
[188] Interview 54.
[189] Interview 75.
[190] Interview 67.
[191] Interview 11; Interview 26; Interview 31; Interview 52; Interview 85.
[192] Shepherd, *Buffalo Nationalism*, 74.
[193] Bourdieu, *Distinction*, 481.

NON-UNIVERSAL COSMOPOLITANISM   151

The selectively anti-hierarchical nature of Indian diplomacy ties back to the ways in which race, class, and caste have played themselves out in the history of India's engagement with the world. The brahminical elites of the ICS were marked by the unequal race relations of the British Raj, when even high-ranking Indian civil servants could not hope to achieve the same standing as the British occupying the land.[194] Thus, the ignominy of racial discrimination was a vivid lived experience for the pioneering Indian elite championing anti-racist causes abroad. In fact, it bears mentioning that the crowning jewel of India's anti-racist diplomacy—its early pioneering of the global fight against Apartheid South-Africa, admirably begun at the very first session of the UN General-Assembly in 1946—was originally motivated by the plight of Indians, not black South-Africans, in the country.[195] 'Gandhiji got thrown out of a train in South-Africa', was the impassioned reply of a recently retired officer, visibly irritated at the notion of caste discrimination being an international issue, to a question about why race was one.[196]

In fact, as Sankaran Krishna shows in his searing comparison between Gandhi's and Ambedkar's visions of global order, the struggle for higher racial status in the world for India's upper castes came at the expense of its lower castes.[197] By the second half of the nineteenth century, upper-caste intellectuals had begun to propagate not only their cultural and racial equality with the West, but a shared genetic lineage with it.[198] Du Bois commented in 1938 on India's desire to 'stand apart from the darker peoples and seek her affinities among whites', having 'long wished to regard herself as "Aryan", rather than "colored" and to think of herself as much nearer physically and spiritually to Germany and England than to Africa, China or the South Seas'.[199] While anchoring itself to an 'Aryan' Caucasian heritage, this colonial intelligentsia distanced itself not only from 'foreign others' such as Sub-Saharan Africans but from 'domestic Others'—Dalits, Muslims, tribals—never acknowledged as equals to the upper-caste standard-bearers of Indian culture. In its quest to negate 'any straightforward notion of European racial superiority', the elite 'happily appropriated the idea of civilizational hierarchy' to stake its claim to

---

[194] Shepherd, *Buffalo Nationalism*, 73.
[195] Davis and Thakur, '"An Act of Faith" or a New "Brown Empire"?', 23.
[196] Interview 26.
[197] Krishna, 'A Postcolonial Racial/Spatial Order: Gandhi, Ambedkar, and the Construction of the International'.
[198] Peter Robb, *The Concept of Race in South Asia* (New Delhi: Oxford University Press, 1995).
[199] Du Bois quoted in Vijay Prashad, *The Karma of Brown Folk* (University of Minnesota Press, 2000), vii–ix.

152 WORLD-MAKING: PROTEST AND PROTOCOL

equal standing with Europeans.[200] Upper-caste elites sought to re-negotiate a more dominant position for themselves within a global racial hierarchy by distancing themselves from many fellow Indians. This is a history of seeking to address the global colour line not by championing its abolition but by insisting that India's upper-caste elite has been incorrectly ranked along it.

While the need to achieve racial parity was paramount on their minds, the need to fight caste discrimination had no roots in the lived experience of most of India's colonially educated postcolonial elite. 'But race is written on my face' was the frustrated objection of an upper-caste multilateralist to the notion that caste and race might operate in similar ways in everyday life.[201] That is: racial hierarchies bore their brunt on him, too, but caste inequities did not. Vineet Thakur observes that India's League of Nations delegate could play respectability politics in the racial hierarchies of colonial diplomacy because of his caste: 'As a Tamil Brahmin, Sastri was more than aware of the social mobility that his caste status allowed him, even internationally.'[202] Only Ambedkar, as a rare Dalit voice in the global anti-colonial struggle, had suffered the double indignity of caste discrimination among Indians and racial discrimination across empire.[203] The anti-racist idiom championed by India's historically uppercaste diplomatic elites had no place for caste, because while this elite could relate to the humiliation of a well-spoken, suit-wearing, elite-educated Gandhi being thrown off a train in South-Africa, they had no social reference point to empathize with Ambedkar's struggle.

Just as upper-caste freedom fighters had once considered Dalit struggles against untouchability a sectarian concern detracting from a national effort,[204] so too the upper castes of the Foreign Service now consider the fight against casteism a distraction from India's global fight against descendance-based discrimination. This stance brings together the domestic and the international in how India has imagined the world. Exploring the connections between a domestic struggle against social backwardness and an international battle against geopolitical backwardness, Rahul Rao locates the caste taboo among India's elites at the junction between two interlocking anxieties:

Caste conflict must be hidden from international scrutiny, not least because its persistence is an embarrassing reminder of the endurance of atavistic

---

[200] Subho Basu, 'The Dialectics of Resistance: Colonial Geography, Bengali Literati and the Racial Mapping of Indian Identity', *Modern Asian Studies* 44, no. 1 (2010): 79.
[201] Interview 11.
[202] Thakur, *India's First Diplomat: V.S. Srinivasa Sastri and the Making of Liberal Internationalism*, 14.
[203] Shepherd, *Buffalo Nationalism*, 73.
[204] Rawat and Satyanarayana, 'Dalit Studies: New Perspectives on Indian History and Society', 8.

social attitudes and the incompleteness of the postcolonial state's developmental mission, both of which undermine its bid for great power status. But the concealment of caste in the international image that India projects also reflects a growing impatience with, perhaps even a repudiation of, its historic commitment to the amelioration of backwardness in the imaginary of the middle-class, dominant-caste elites who play a disproportionate role in the crafting of that image.[205]

Although the Foreign Service's opposition to Durban-like projects seems incongruent with its broader fight in the symbolic name of a global subaltern, its resistance is in many ways congruent with the performative demands of both expressions of the cleft habitus. The quasi-aristocratic mores of European international society are premised on performing elite belonging, which an elevation of Dalit experience sits uncomfortably with. The cosmopolitanism of white international society is conversant with upper-caste cosmopolitanism. At the same time, the postcolonial performance of diplomacy elevates the professed commitment to egalitarianism into a founding doctrine of Indian diplomacy, in light of which international scrutiny of the realities of caste discrimination at home would mean losing diplomatic face. Little space is left in this dual reading of the world for Dalit cosmopolitan projects. Little legitimacy remains for contesting naturalized upper-caste dominance in Indian world-making.

Conclusion

Two very different readings of the world have long animated how India navigates it. Embedded in inherited imageries of colonial bureaucracy and wedded to classical markers of European diplomacy, India's diplomats have traditionally embraced much of what they perceived to be Westernized cosmopolitan culture with a singular vehemence and skill. At the same time, Indian diplomacy has reflected its imperial past in a tone of defiance against a Westerncentric world order, in a bid to distinguish an 'authentic', postcolonial India from an unequal diplomatic club. What has ensued is a seemingly paradoxical diplomatic performance: colonially tinted practices and anti-colonial grandstanding, elite-signalling and allegiances with the powerless, all intensely

---

[205] Rahul Rao, *Out of Time: The Queer Politics of Postcoloniality, Out of Time* (Oxford University Press, 2020), 200.

focused on distinguishing India both *within* and *from* inherited conceptions of a Western-dominated order.

India's engagement with the world has also been defined by the status ambivalence of its representatives. Because of the formative experience under the Raj and the cultural capital that has accrued to the Anglophone liberal arts graduates of the Foreign Service, India's subordinate position in the global balance of power has been mitigated by its diplomats' intimate familiarity with Western culture. The world is not foreign to India, not even when it is imagined as a Westernized system, because Indian diplomats have been conversant with Western culture, history, and convention with a fluency that puts many in the West to shame. As Blaney and Inayatullah have said of the powerless in international politics, 'those who envision themselves as living "below" have, by necessity, a [...] complex critical vision'.[206] However, this vision is complicated further by the fact that some who envision themselves as living 'below'—as representatives of the Third World—also represent a powerful elite at home and wish to join a transnational elite abroad.

Growing out of this ambivalence is India's fraught relationship towards cosmopolitanism. There is a sense among Indian diplomats that, even if its abstract ideals are noble, much of what counts as cosmopolitanism in the real world is Western parochialism masquerading as universalism—a less-than-categorical imperative that demands world-embracing inclusion from India but never returns the favour. At the same time, the upper-caste resistance to anti-casteist diplomacy alongside India's long-standing commitment to anti-racist diplomacy has shown the limits to India's own commitment to global equality and solidarity. The worldviews of Western liberal internationalists are not innocent of power, but neither are those of India's upper-caste elites.

The historical significance of performing according to a 'standard of civilization' shows why seemingly trivial diplomatic practices around etiquette and manners are in fact intensely political, infused with the colonial legacies, racial hierarchies, and class distinctions of traditional diplomacy. A deep drive for recognition in this kind of world among India's liberal-arts educated, upper-class, upper-caste diplomatic elites has complicated a more systematic critique of Western-centric world-making. It has also complicated the task of 'democratizing' the officer corps of the Foreign Service, because it has made the Service's traditional elites wary of entrants from 'non-traditional' backgrounds, unable to appreciate the finer points of this white, upper-class world—a topic for the chapter to come.

---

[206] Blaney and Inayatullah, 'International Relations from Below', 663.

4

Representation

Cosmopolitan elites, domestic Others

The Indian Foreign Service decreed at its founding that it was to be a Service reflective of the country it represented, in a world remade. For a young postcolonial nation, democratization of the Civil Services was an end in itself.[1] India's secular, socialist Constitution of 1950 was an aspirational document; if it was to be translated into principles of governance, its mandate for an equal society needed to rest with a representative body of bureaucrats.[2] In a nation weighed down by both ancient and modern imbalances of power, democratizing the elite Services in particular would affirm that 'we not only preach equality and diversity but practise it.'[3] A representative body of diplomats would mean an embrace of postcolonial international society and a rejection of the bureaucratic elitism that had characterized the Raj.

Yet this has often been a commitment more honoured in the breach than the observance. For if the diversification of diplomatic cadres was a 'natural corollary of a country coming into its own' and 'expanding [its] definition of representation' in the wake of decolonization, as one recently retired Ambassador of Grade I so eloquently chronicled,[4] this process of becoming has proven fraught. Who makes it into the Civil Services each year is a topic of intense public debate in India, where successful applicants are listed in order of exam performance in newspapers across the country. The question of who becomes a diplomat has not only held deep political significance—politics and society have also reflected themselves in diplomatic recruitment and promotion patterns. As Bourdieu noted, '[a] group's presence or absence in the official classification depends on its capacity to get itself recognized, to get itself noticed and admitted, and so to win a place in the social order.'[5] In these battles for recognition, what matters for an institution like the Foreign Service are

---

[1] Interview 1; Interview 19; Interview 48; Interview 49.
[2] Interview 43.
[3] Interview 11; The same claim was made in Interview 1; Interview 21, April 2019.
[4] Interview 3.
[5] Bourdieu, *Distinction*, 483.

Cosmopolitan Elites. Kira Huju, Oxford University Press. © Kira Huju (2023). DOI: 10.1093/oso/9780198874928.003.0005

156 REPRESENTATION: COSMOPOLITAN ELITES, DOMESTIC OTHERS

[t]hose secondary characteristics which are often the basis of their social value (prestige or discredit) and which, though absent from the official job description, function as tacit requirements, such as age, sex, social or ethnic origin, overtly or implicitly guiding co-optation choices, from entry into the profession and right through a career, so that members of the corps who lack these traits are excluded or marginalized.[6]

Understanding the social composition of the Foreign Service requires thinking carefully about what we mean in IR when we use instinctively appealing terms like 'democratization', 'representation', or 'diversity'. The 'democratization' of the Service is a parable for why democratization in numbers cannot be equated with democratization in culture, worth, or voice—of why a diversity which proves itself by pointing to the presence of a diverse collection of people is a shallow kind of diversity. Access does not equal adaptation. For example, when it came to reservation recruits, one upper-caste officer explained, 'their presence' was important for the Service[7]—but presence alone is a distinctly passive form of inclusion.

Democratization, too, can mean many different things to different constituencies up and down a hierarchy. What the officers themselves call 'democratization', but we might more accurately consider a demographic de-elitification, is a process whereby the annual intake of new diplomatic probationers becomes more representative of India at large. This slow demographic transition is captured in the first part of the chapter, as the exclusive character of the early cadres erodes under regulatory changes in entry criteria in the early 1980s, the shifting meanings of class in the wake of the liberalization of the Indian economy in the early 1990s, and the concurrent 'Mandal amendments' to reservations. Yet the chapter also captures an absence of deeper change, detailing the social processes and cultural hierarchies that have shielded the dominant habitus from meaningful challenge. A democratization of institutional culture has not followed demographic democratization, nor has equal access to dominant positions or the networks of social capital that maintain caste, class, gender, religious, and educational hierarchies inside the Foreign Service.

If diplomacy is about representation, then the question of who represents the nation also arises—as do questions about whether 'representation' is better thought of as semantically tied to *representativeness* or *representability*.

[6] Bourdieu, 96–97.
[7] Interview 24.

'Democratization' can be read either as a belated realization of a postcolonial Service that reflects all of India in a representative manner, or as a crisis of representability that creates a de-elitified cadre that will struggle to find recognition among the suave club of global cosmopolitans.

In fact, appeals to the diplomatic ideal of a representable cosmopolitan have stood in the way of democratizing the Foreign Service. Following on from the ethical disappointments and political shortcomings of cosmopolitanism found in the previous chapter on Indian world-making, this chapter looks at the domestic fallout of cosmopolitanism being reduced to a marker of elite distinction. Tying cosmopolitanism to hierarchies of caste, class, religion, and educational background, I consider who gets to be a cosmopolitan in the Foreign Service. The practice of 'actually existing cosmopolitanism' among Indian diplomats is about policing the social boundaries of elite belonging in international society and at home.

Elite reproduction, disrupted

The India that reflected itself outward from the young Foreign Service had little to do with the vast diversity that the postcolonial project had pledged to give voice to both at home and in the world. A self-reflective Foreign Secretary Kaul once regretted that 'British rule in India created an artificial sense of administrative unity without taking into consideration the economic, social and cultural variety and richness of the country'.[8] Whatever the postcolonial, solidarist commitments of many of its members, something similar can be said of the conspicuously uninterrupted rule of the elite-educated upper-caste, upper-class men of the early Foreign Service. In a Service marked by the strikingly similar backgrounds of its members, no precedent was set for practising the much-preached diversity of India and the postcolonial world. The world could be governed in the name of the subaltern, but not by them.

Corps d'élite

With its small and selective ranks, the Foreign Service began life as an elite club. Into the 1960s, only three to ten probationers gained entry each year.[9]

---

[8] T.N. Kaul, 'Nationalism and Communalism', n.d., Speech draft—Miscellaneous articles, 'Speeches/Writings by Him', SN/141, T.N. Kaul papers, NMML.

[9] P.N. Haksar, 'Memo', 6 January 1961, '1960-61: Official papers relating to Shri P.N. Haksar's appointment as High Commissioner for India, Nigeria', SF/6, P.N. Haksar papers, NMML; 'Union

158   REPRESENTATION: COSMOPOLITAN ELITES, DOMESTIC OTHERS

The entire Service could fit inside a conference room—as it once did for a meeting in the 1950s.[10] Nehru had decreed that nobody below the 15th place in the all-India Civil Service entry examinations was to enter his favoured Service,[11] giving a privileged elite the legitimating cover of officially certified meritocracy. In fact, Service elders fought to supress cadre numbers out of fear of losing this elitist edge, even as existing positions stood vacant and the Ministry of Finance had sanctioned funds for cadre expansion.[12] Under these conditions, the Service grew into a strikingly homogenous whole, dominated by upper-caste, upper-class men with elite degrees from a handful of universities and families. As one self-ascribed outsider who had witnessed this clique since the early 1960s abbreviated: the Service was 'pretty feudal'.[13]

In fact, in the words of two Oxford graduates who joined in the early 1960s, early IFS recruits and ICS veterans 'were pretty much in the same mould—you couldn't tell the difference',[14] since they 'had almost similar backgrounds'.[15] The ICS and IFS recruited overwhelmingly from the same five cities—Delhi, Bombay (Mumbai), Calcutta, Madras (Chennai), and Allahabad.[16] Joining Government was a 'very standard aspiration' for Delhiites in particular,[17] lending the Service its reputation as a dominion of metropolitan elites.[18] Its state-wise composition has been so skewed as to spawn Parliamentary Questions in the Lok Sabha, the Lower House of Parliament, where the urban clustering of diplomats was debated as a question national concern in a session in April 1972.[19]

While the batches of the 1950s and 1960s were 'heavily Oxbridge',[20] the legacy bearers of elite education in postcolonial India soon became the graduates of Indian missionary colleges like Delhi's St Stephen's, Mumbai's St Xavier's, and the Presidency College in Calcutta.[21] With their dominance came

---

Public Service Commission Notice No. F5/28/57-E.I', 22 February 1958, '1958–59: Appointment as one of the examiners for Personality for the IAS examination—connected papers and correspondence with the Secretary, UPSC', SF/45, Mohan Sinha Mehta papers, NMML.

[10] Interview 79.

[11] 'Oral History Transcript: J.N. Dixit', 2000, 28, Oral Histories, NMML.

[12] Prem Krishen (Joint-Secretary, MEA), 'Memo', 10 August 1955, 'Cadre—Indian Foreign Service—Refixation of cadre on the basis of anticipated requirements for five years', FSP/55- F/1(2), NAI.

[13] Interview 45.

[14] Interview 37.

[15] Interview 31.

[16] 'Synopses of IFS Officers', 1952, 'Statement of Services of IFS Officers', FSP/52- F/4(1), NAI; Dixit, *Indian Foreign Service*, 90.

[17] Interview 31.

[18] Interview 15, March 2019; Interview 41; Interview 69; Interview 77, May 2019.

[19] Surendra Pal Singh (Deputy Minister, MEA), 'Response', 27 April 1972, 'Lok Sabha unstarred question No 8723 for 27.4.72 by Shri Bibhuti Mishra regarding recruitment to Foreign Service', F/Q/GA/125-(II)/72, NAI.

[20] Interview 43.

[21] Dixit, *Indian Foreign Service*, 90.

the dominance of the liberal arts: batches through to the mid-1980s were almost exclusively made up of history, economics, literature, and political science graduates.[22] Delhi University contributed the largest number of candidates for the all-India Services[23]—St Stephen's, its most iconic college, became a veritable metonym for the meritorious.[24] The nine-strong 1960 batch boasted seven Stephenians.[25] With the vast numbers of Stephenians applying to or already in the Foreign Service, Civil Service aspirants at the college essentially had a 'coaching camp in-house'.[26] For a senior diplomat who joined the Service in the early 1980s, his Stephanian social circles meant that diplomacy was a 'default made without too much choice'.[27]

Diplomacy was also a family affair. The political scientist Stanley Hoffman spoke of the 'largely hereditary castes of diplomats' who once ran diplomacy in Europe,[28] but India's upper-caste 'Civil Service families' were made up of hereditary castes in an altogether more literal sense. G.S. Bajpai's sons Uma Shankar Bajpai and K.S. Bajpai became prominent members of the Foreign Service.[29] In his memoir, K.P.S. Menon—whose son Shankaran passed the entrance exam when Menon relinquished his post as Foreign Secretary in 1952 and whose daughters and granddaughter would be married off to IFS officers—repeatedly speaks of diplomacy as a 'family tradition'.[30] Little could he have known at the time just how entrenched this tradition would become: when Shivshankar Menon, arguably the most well-known Indian Foreign Secretary of the twenty-first century, assumed his role in 2006, he followed in the footsteps of his Foreign Secretary uncle, also called K.P.S., and diplomat father, P.N. Menon, securing the Menons three consecutive generations of Foreign Secretaries to their name.[31] As fellow Foreign Secretary Jagat Mehta declared: 'There is probably no comparable pedigreed diplomatic family anywhere.'[32] Yet the Menons were not alone: a 1966 statistic showed 47% of IFS officials having parents in government positions.[33] The Menons were not even the only ones

[22] Interview 3; Interview 6; Interview 12; Interview 14; Interview 25; Interview 28; Interview 29.
[23] UPSC, 'Kothari Report', 21.
[24] Interview 9; Interview 10, March 2019; Interview 40; Interview 43; Interview 66, May 2019; Interview 67.
[25] Interview 1.
[26] Interview 27; Also Interview 36.
[27] Interview 19.
[28] Stanley Hoffmann, 'An American Social Science: International Relations (1977)', Daedalus 106, no. 3 (1977): 42.
[29] 'Sir Girija Bajpai: Architect of Indian Diplomacy', The Times, 6 December 1954.
[30] Menon 1981, 276.
[31] Economic Times, 'The IFS Kid Keeps Family Flag Flying', 16 September 2006, https://economictimes.indiatimes.com/news/politics-and-nation/the-ifs-kid-keeps-family-flag-flying.
[32] Mehta, The Tryst Betrayed: Reflections on Diplomacy and Development, 40.
[33] Benner, Structure of Decision, 54.

160 REPRESENTATION: COSMOPOLITAN ELITES, DOMESTIC OTHERS

whose family tradition could be traced back to the ICS.[34] One interviewee had held the exact same Ambassadorship as his father before him.

These diplomats knew that Indian bureaucracy was for 'our kind of families'[35]—that is, the kind of 'typical middle-class family where everyone is in the civil services'.[36] Officers from batches between the late 1940s and early 1980s habitually commented upon (or accidentally revealed with depictions of their own experience) just how easily 'children of known Delhi figures' obtained stellar marks in entry interviews conducted by family friends.[37] Some parents received unofficial assessments from the Interview Board about their child's performance, while K.P.S. Menon ensured the successful entry of an interviewee at the request of his well-connected father.[38] One exceptionally blunt example of nepotism is known among older generations as the 'Jagat Mehta batches': under Foreign Secretary Mehta's instructions, IFS batch sizes were increased for a number of years in the second half of the 1970s, as Mehta unsuccessfully sought to make a diplomat of his own son, who was allowed to sit the exam in London, unsupervised, more times than national guidelines allowed, with the inflated batch sizes intended to improve his chances.[39]

The tight circles of social capital in postcolonial India produced a distinctive sense of *esprit de corps:* 'We come from the same kind of families' was the unhesitating explication of a retired Delhiite officer to a question about where her Service's once-famous collegiality originated.[40] So well-established were these familial trajectories that one reluctant diplomat was strong-armed by his father into applying in the late 1960s, because unless one appeared towards the top of the all-India merit list that ranked all the candidates throughout the country, 'people in our circles' would assume one had taken the entry exam and failed.[41] Familial social capital underpinned the reproduction of the Indian diplomatic elite.

Anyone who seriously sought to democratize the Foreign Service had to do more than take a hard look at the class hierarchies entrenched under the British Raj, however. Democratization was also about mending millennia of caste injustice, with brahminical elites monopolizing the sphere of intellectual pursuits and Dalits and Shudras excluded from upper-caste society altogether. And yet even the constitutionally guaranteed reservations system could do

---

[34] Interview 4; Interview 6; Interview 23; Interview 70.
[35] Interview 28; Also Interview 21.
[36] Interview 42.
[37] Interview 1; also Interview 6; Interview 12; Interview 35.
[38] Interview 23; Interview 34, April 2019.
[39] Interview 24; Interview 27; Interview 41; Interview 70.
[40] Interview 81.
[41] Interview 10.

ELITE REPRODUCTION, DISRUPTED   161

little to moderate the upper-caste character of the early Foreign Service.[42] Only one Dalit entered the Service throughout the 1950s and the first Scheduled Tribe officers joined in 1959.[43] Archival records from the 1960s indicate years in which no Dalits were included in diplomatic batches at all.[44] Unused reserved seats were often brought forward from previous years, although they also lapsed after a while.[45] Faced with external scrutiny, the Service sought to balance its books by inducting ST/SC probationers originally designated for a Home Service,[46] sometimes even providing estimates that counted the MEA's overwhelmingly lower-caste peons and chauffeurs as diplomats.[47]

The power differential has been tremendous. Lower-caste officers are painfully aware of the cultural expectations that their upper-caste colleagues have of them, while those at the top of the caste hierarchy have the luxury of not seeing caste. 'I had no idea what a Scheduled Caste was!', explained one urban upper-caste officer about his social awakening upon entering the Service in the 1970s—the term was 'almost a passing reference or detail'.[48]

For most of its existence, the Foreign Service has also employed fewer women than male officers with the surnames Mehta or Menon. The trail-blazing C.B. Muthamma joined the Service in 1949 after standing first in the IFS merit list[49]—to the dismay of her examiners, who had sought in vain to persuade her to pick another Service and awarded her suspiciously low interview marks.[50] Yet while an internal document listing female officers and probationers for 1965 shows that 15 women had entered the Service

---

[42] There are also different entry regulations for different categories. While the general number of attempts allowed at the annual exam is six, this limit has been pushed upward to nine for OBC candidates and suspended altogether for SC/ST applicants. Similarly, although the age limit as of 2019 was 32, it was 35 for OBC communities and 37 for SC/ST aspirants. See UPSC, 'Examination Notice No. 04/2019-CSP', 19 February 2019, https://upsc.gov.in/sites/default/files/Final_Notice_CSPE_2019_N. pdf.

[43] 'Lists of SC/ST Officers with Their Batch Affiliation', n.d., 'Lok Sabha provisional starred question No. 5493: Criteria for posting officers of Scheduled Castes/Tribes in offices of Trade Commissioners and Trade Representatives abroad', Q/PA II/125/10/78, NAI.

[44] 'Statement Showing Recruitment to the Indian Foreign Service during the Years 1962 to 1967 and Percentage of Scheduled Castes and Scheduled Tribes among Them', n.d., 'Lok Sabha Starred Question No. 23428 from Shri Kameshwar Singh—regarding Scheduled Caste and Scheduled Tribe Candidates in the Indian Foreign Service', Q/FSI/125/7/68, NAI.

[45] '"Annual Returns Showing Representation of Scheduled Castes and Scheduled Tribes in Services under the Central Government (1964)", F/Q/GA/551/10/65', n.d., 65, NAI.

[46] Interview 45.

[47] '"Unstarred Question—Lok Sabha—No. 2321 for 15.03.1965 by Shri Naval Prabhakar Regarding Scheduled Castes Employees in Indian Missions Abroad", F/Q(GA)-125/4/65', July 1968, NAI.

[48] Interview 41.

[49] Dixit, *Indian Foreign Service*, 50; Nivedita Jayakumar, 'C B Muthamma: India's First Woman IFS Officer', Feminism in India, 16 December 2019, https://feminisminindia.com/2019/12/16/c-b-muthamma-indias-women-ifs-officer/.

[50] Nupur Basu, 'Chonira Muthamma, India's First Woman Career Diplomat', NewsBlaze, 8 December 2009, https://newsblaze.com/world/south-asia/chonira-muthamma-indias-first-woman-career-diplomat_11341/.

162 REPRESENTATION: COSMOPOLITAN ELITES, DOMESTIC OTHERS

since 1948, it marks a third of them as 'resigned'[51]—a consequence of regulations asking women to leave diplomacy upon marriage.[52] Serving one's country abroad thus required women to defy deep social convention. Many promising candidates consequently forsook a diplomatic life altogether, joining a Home Service despite having qualified for the prestigious IFS.[53] By ironic contrast, the wives of male diplomats were seen as a diplomatic resource:[54] until the early 1970s, officer reports featured sections on the suitability of respective wives, complete with separate columns for personality and 'standard and style of entertainment'.[55] Of course, a female diplomats' spouse could conceivably have been of similar use—except that 'in the male chauvinist real world, that does not happen often', as Ambassador Kishan Rana soberly notes.[56]

When the Pillai Committee undertook its famous review of IFS practices in 1966, it concluded that since it was objectively true that marriage intervened in women's professional duties, the rules were 'non-discriminatory'.[57] While certainly regressive, these restrictions cannot be read as signs of uniquely retrograde gendered attitudes in Indian diplomacy—for example, Sweden only permitted women into its diplomatic service in 1948,[58] while the US State Department lifted identical rules requiring married female diplomats to resign in 1971.[59] While they differ in their specifics from those of female colleagues across the globe, the experiences of Indian female diplomats speak to broader patterns of how gendered performances play themselves out in the historically male-dominated diplomatic club, 'one of the most male-dominated spheres of the state'.[60]

However secular in conviction, the Service has also reflected the stark demographic reality which defines the religious divide of the Indian polity: an

---

[51] 'Lists of Female Diplomats of Different Batches', n.d., 'Employment of Women in various Services of the Government—Statistics regarding', F/Q/PA II/551/6/74, NAI.

[52] Avtar Singh, 'Proposal', 28 August 1968, 'IFS (PLCA) Rules 1961—Amendments to—Proposal to allow single women officers to take either of their dependent parents to their station of posting abroad', F/Q/GA/791468 (Part I), NAI.

[53] Rasgotra, *A Life in Diplomacy*, 128.

[54] By way of contrast, the British Foreign Office only did away with the Annual Confidential Report's section on diplomatic wives' entertaining abilities in the 1980s, after considerable lobbying from the Diplomatic Service Wives Association, and the Report still speaks of their health and language skills. See Cynthia H. Enloe, *Bananas, Beaches and Bases: Making Feminist Sense of International Politics* (Berkeley: University of California Press, 2014), 192.

[55] Dixit 2005, 292.

[56] Rana 2000, 305.

[57] Rana, *Inside Diplomacy*, 304.

[58] Karin Aggestam and Ann Towns, 'The Gender Turn in Diplomacy: A New Research Agenda', *International Feminist Journal of Politics* 21, no. 1 (2019): 15.

[59] Enloe, *Bananas, Beaches and Bases*, 198.

[60] Ann Towns and Birgitta Niklasson, 'Gender, International Status, and Ambassador Appointments', *Foreign Policy Analysis* 13, no. 3 (2017): 522.

overwhelming majority of officers are Hindu. The question of religious representation has accompanied Indian administrative history ever since the imperial policy objective of 'Indianizing' the ICS in the early 1870s threw up an awkward question: which religions represent India? Muslim leaders demanded that admission rules ensure adequate representation for Muslims, who would struggle to match more socioeconomically advanced Hindu constituencies in open competition.[61] Partition came between Hindus and Muslims in the young Foreign Service, too.[62] When the Indian Independence Act received royal assent on 18 July 1947, Lord Mountbatten split each Indian Government department in two, staffed by ICS officers chosen by the Congress and the Muslim League, respectively. Subimal Dutt speaks of 'strained relations' as most Muslims opted to serve Pakistan.[63] The minority that stayed 'rightly or wrongly felt themselves neglected'.[64] To Badr-ud-Din Tyabji, sole Muslim founder of the Foreign Service, South Block was, 'out of ignorance and prejudice', 'apt to dismiss all Islamic movements and parties [...] as somehow anti-Indian', suspecting even Muslims who chose to serve in Delhi of insufficient patriotism.[65]

A subtle form of socio-administrative sorting took place through the fact of the Central Civil Services (Conduct) Rules requiring men in polygamous marriages to obtain governmental approval for their marital arrangements; diplomatic probationers accepting their place in the Foreign Service had to sign a declaration confirming they were not polygamous.[66] This would have had the effect of excluding Muslim men with multiple wives, living according to conservative interpretations of The Muslim Personal Law (Shariat) Application Act of 1937, from becoming Indian diplomats. Muslims who did join, therefore, tended to be of a more liberal persuasion.

At least once, an entire decade lapsed without a single Muslim joining India's diplomatic community.[67] The absence of Muslim diplomats cannot be exhaustively explained by reference to the demographic minority status of Muslims, who make up about 15% of India today. Sikh officers offer a stark contrast since, at less than 2% of the Indian population, they are by statistical compulsion overrepresented in any of the small IFS batches which have them. It is

---

[61] Srivastava 1965, 185.
[62] Dayal 1998, 504.
[63] Dutt 1977, 4.
[64] Dutt 1977, 42.
[65] Tyabji 1972, 49.
[66] 'Copies of Filled and Unfilled Declarations on Marital Status from Incoming Probationer', n.d., Recruitment of Candidates for the Indian Foreign Service on the results of the Competitive Examination held by the UPSC in 1954, F/2(3)—FSP/55, Part I, NAI.
[67] Interview 7.

164 REPRESENTATION: COSMOPOLITAN ELITES, DOMESTIC OTHERS

therefore notable how many batches have, from the earliest years, included at least one member of the Sikh community—one mid-1970s batch had five, pushing their proportion of the overall batch to 25%.[68] While the Service's Sikhs and its few Christians—mostly from India's South and the Northeast—took great pains to downplay the significance of religious affiliation during interviews,[69] the strikingly disproportionate underrepresentation of Muslims in the Foreign Service stands out.

Of course, the Indian Muslim community, too, is internally socially stratified—though we have fewer official data on these hierarchies than we did under the British Empire, when the imperial census recorded both a religious sect (Shia, Sunni, Fararis, and so on), 'ethnic category' (Syed, Sheikh, Pathan, for example) and, crucially, a caste for Muslim respondents, too.[70] While the Indian Muslim population may be socioeconomically weaker than the Hindu majority statistically speaking, the original lack of reserved seats in the 1950 Constitution for the Muslim minority seems to have rendered the Service's small Muslim constituency relatively more privileged in terms of class than the average Hindu diplomat.[71]

By national standards, then, one was dealing with a strikingly unrepresentative body of diplomatic representatives. At the same time, the old guard's elaborations on their family histories during our conversations suggest that there was also an element of *parvenu* to this elite: many had only just arrived in the upper echelons as relative newcomers to the world of a higher-ranking socioeconomic class. Instead of being scions of feudal or aristocratic families, many represented the thin upper layers of the Indian *petit bourgeoisie*. They could adjust their pallet to discern types of wine during their time at St Stephen's, but their effortless cosmopolitanism may have taken some more effort to perform. These performances would most likely have been accepted as signs of elite status at home—and it is fascinating how many chose to confidently portray themselves as the offspring of a privileged elite when asked to think about their place in Indian society. In postings to Western capitals and multilateral institutions from New York to Geneva, however, one imagines a series of cultural *faux pas* and a latent anxiety about being 'found out'—some of

---

[68] Interview 26.

[69] Interview 3; Interview 7; Interview 9; Interview 20; Interview 25; Interview 26; Interview 53, May 2019; Interview 72; Interview 74.

[70] Bhagat, 'Census and Caste Enumeration'.

[71] The new reservations for OBC communities under the Mandal reforms did designate some isolated Muslim communities as backward, thus allowing them entry into Government Services through affirmative action—even if the scarcity of Muslim officers suggests few have availed themselves of these seats. See Seik Rahim Mondal, 'Social Structure, OBCs and Muslims', *Economic and Political Weekly* 38, no. 46 (2003): 4892–4897.

which the previous chapter chronicled. And yet in the self-narrations of diplomats up and down the social hierarchies of the Service, there was a duality: a *savarna* fraternity of the upper-class cosmopolitan elite at the top and a culturally out-of-place contingency of perpetual outsiders at the bottom of the class/caste/gender scales of the Service. Those who could pass as members of the former in the eyes of the latter seem to have made the most of it.

Selection as exclusion

If the Foreign Service resembled 'a cosy club',[72] as one prominent veteran of the Service admitted, many diplomats interpreted this as an inevitable consequence of the social inequities of India itself.[73] In the words of the ICS-educated offspring of a princely state Ambassador Apa B. Pant in 1977: 'Perhaps it is inevitable that the present structure of our society, and the methods of our education and selection make it inevitable that the middle and upper-middle class elements are more represented in the Indian Foreign Service than other ones.'[74] Yet there was also a regulatory framework that preserved the Service's privileged elite character for decades, judiciously curating entry and exclusion in the name of merit.

At Independence, two schools of thought clashed on the question of diplomatic recruitment, revealing the duality of international societies that the Service was seeking to belong in. While the elite-internationalist tendencies of IFS founders supported the notion of an exclusive Service that would recruit only among India's socioeconomic elites, the egalitarian commitments of postcolonial Nehruvianism necessitated an inclusive Service that would keep the promise of inclusion and empowerment.

Many ICS veterans pined after a cadre of classy cosmopolitans fluent in languages, world history, and international etiquette.[75] 'Foreign education would be an advantage', one communique noted.[76] Recruitment guidelines for the ICS[77] and British Foreign Office[78] were closely consulted for inspiration. A joint note from 1947 explained that, all applicants holding First-Class

---

[72] Interview 4.

[73] Interview 30.

[74] Apa B. Pant, 'Indian Diplomatic Missions Abroad and Their Problems', 11 October 1977, Article, 'Speeches/Writings by Him', SN/37, Apa B. Pant papers, NMML.

[75] Dixit, *Indian Foreign Service*, 26.

[76] H. Dayal, 'Qualifications to Be Prescribed for New Entrants into the Service', 27 March 1946, 'Establishment of a Separate Indian Foreign Service', FSP/47-2(7), NAI.

[77] Dayal, 'Note'.

[78] Hugh Weightman, 'Communique to H. Dayal', n.d., 'Establishment of a Separate Indian Foreign Service', FSP/47-2(7), NAI.

degrees having already been selected for interview, the next step was to expand the pool to all candidates with a British or American degree.[79] That same year, Secretary-General G.S. Bajpai protested against holding the entry examinations in June on the grounds that it clashed with the Tripos and Schools examinations at Cambridge and Oxford, which would lose the Service 'some good material'.[80] Out of the 400 candidates initially recommended to the Service, he accepted only around 60, and attracted charges of nepotistic elitism from Parliament and press by establishing his own interview committee which operated without official criteria or external scrutiny.[81] Pillai and Bajpai both pushed for entry regulations favouring candidates from upper-middle class backgrounds and urban centres, suggesting they would adjust best to diplomatic life.[82] The ideal candidate of former ICS officers, in other words, looked an awful lot like 'a result of their respective social background and value systems of colonial India'.[83]

Women, too, were considered a cultural hazard. Proposing a full ban on women entering the postcolonial Foreign Service, the last British Foreign Secretary of India, Hugh Weightman, found support among Indian ICS veterans who were, to borrow Dixit's euphemism, 'not enthusiastic' at the prospect of female colleagues.[84] Unspecified Indian values, women's poorer education, the inevitabilities of motherhood, and difficult working conditions abroad were interchangeably cited to make the case against women's entry into diplomacy.[85] Imageries of international society legitimate not only hierarchies of class or caste but also of gender.

In the end, Nehru's insistence on a cadre reflective of the postcolonial commitment to equality and diversity won the day.[86] As a matter of principle, he wanted to welcome all of India into the Service—'[e]very member of the staff, whether he [sic] is a Hindu, a Muslim, a Sikh, Christian, Brahmin, non-Brahmin, Harijan or any other, or whatever State he [sic] comes from, must

---

[79] 'Joint Note from IFS Officers', n.d., Question of holding Combined Examination for the Indian Foreign Service and All India Administrative Service in November–December Every Year. Prescription of high minimum mark at the interview for recruitment to the Indian Foreign Service, F/22 (11)—FSP/47, NAI.

[80] G.S. Bajpai, 'Note', 7 June 1947, 'Question of holding combined examination for the Indian Foreign Service and All India Administrative Service in November-December Every Year. Prescription of high minimum mark at the interview for recruitment to the Indian Foreign Service', FSP/47–22(11), NAI.

[81] Rasgotra, *A Life in Diplomacy*, 16–18.

[82] Benner, *Structure of Decision*, 54; Dixit, *Indian Foreign Service*, 31.

[83] Dixit, *Indian Foreign Service*, 31.

[84] Dixit, 32.

[85] Dixit, 32.

[86] Benner, *Structure of Decision*, 54; Dixit, *Indian Foreign Service*, 20,31.

be treated alike', Nehru emphasized in a circular letter in October 1950.[87] True to his convictions, he struck out the clause excluding women from the final version of the Foreign Service Rules.[88] Nehru not only held the 'right of first refusal' in staffing the Service[89] but interviewed the earliest batches himself,[90] and it was on his orders that the most outlandish suggestions for maintaining the Service's elitist character were rejected. The Service settled on an austere list of requirements for potential candidates: a 'good University degree', an 'aptitude' for languages, and 'good character'.[91]

The introduction of standardized entry examinations in 1948 was meant to facilitate this democratization process by allowing for a broader constituency of candidates,[92] at least in theory. Unlike most foreign ministries worldwide who recruit their diplomats in a dedicated procedure, in India, those hoping to become a government bureaucrat apply through a joint all-India examination—organized by the Union Public Service Commission (UPSC)[93]—and are allowed to choose from among the many branches of the country's Civil Service according to their ranking in the all-India merit list. As a wary G.S. Bajpai lamented in 1951:

We have tied our hands in the matter of selection by depending upon the Union Public Service Commission which, as you know, choose people on the strength of their achievements in a written examination. How many misfits we get into the IFS every year in this manner will become manifest only as time goes on.[94]

And yet Bajpai's misfits were nowhere to be seen. Although the UPSC system was supposed to imprint a 'stronger Indian stamp' on the entry process,[95]

[87] File 11 (88)—FSP/50. Prime Minister's note for the guidance of members of the Foreign Service and more especially, for those serving in our missions abroad. Note dated 20 October 1950. NAI.

[88] Jawaharlal Nehru, 'Response to a Supplementary Question by Begum Aizaz Rasul', 21 November 1947, 'Question in the Constituent Assembly of India (Legislative) by the Hon'ble Sethi Govinddas in regard to recruitment to the Indian Foreign Service by the F.P.S and the number of persons appointed with Indian Embassies—Nehru's reply, 21st November 1947', FSP/47- F/18(11), NAI.

[89] Interview 30.

[90] Interview 9; 'Oral History Transcript: J.N. Dixit', 28.

[91] 'Statement Attached to the Summary: "The Creation of an Indian Foreign Service"', n.d., 'Establishment of a separate Indian Foreign Service', FSP/47-2(7), NAI.

[92] 'Foreign Service Probationers—Confidential Reports', 18 March 1949, '1948–49: Correspondence with K.P.S. Menon, Secretary, Ministry of External Affairs and Commonwealth Relations, carried out as Indian Ambassador to the USSR', SF/9, Vijaya Lakshmi Pandit papers, NMML.

[93] UPSC, 'Kothari Report', 31.

[94] G.S. Bajpai, 'Letter to Vijaya Lakshmi Pandit', 11 May 1951, '1947–1961: Correspondence exchanged by Mrs Pandit with G.S. Bajpai (Secretary-General, MEA, and Commonwealth Relations) in her capacity as India's Ambassador to Moscow and later USA', SF/56, Vijaya Lakshmi Pandit papers, NMML.

[95] Interview 9.

168 REPRESENTATION: COSMOPOLITAN ELITES, DOMESTIC OTHERS

its original procedures, examination subjects, and elective essays were 'pretty much a copy' of the ICS template,[96] veterans of the Service recalled. One could sit the examinations in London until the early 1980s.[97] The papers were 'almost identical' to those taught at Oxbridge.[98] Long after the British had amended their own recruitment methods, India's were, in the wording of a critical Government-commissioned report, 'essentially little different from what was introduced more than a hundred years ago by the British following the recommendations of the Northcote–Trevelyan Report for the British Civil Service and the Macaulay Report for the Indian Civil Service.'[99] A Stephenian from a Civil Service family called the UPSC system a 'totally merit-based', 'very democratic examination'[100]—raising the question: is merit democratically distributed across society? The levers of inclusion and exclusion are often subtler than the narratives of democratization propagated by India's diplomatic elite suggest.

In fact, the entry regulations implicitly excluded most of India from even applying. Speaking to the early Indian conceptions of diplomacy as intimately tied to colonial imageries of international society, English became the only language of examination.[101] The compulsory papers on English Essay, General English, and General Knowledge[102] presumed mastery of a language that few in India spoke at all.[103] In some ways, English became a condition of entry because it was perceived as a condition of entry into the cosmopolitan world of diplomacy itself. Yet, since English was also a marker of socioeconomic status,[104] one presumes that omitting the Indian vernacular was also a politically permissible mechanism for perpetuating the elite nature of Indian bureaucracy.

The imperative of eloquence was expressed in the significance of the entry interview, which for decades carried higher points and minimum thresholds

---

[96] Interview 23.
[97] UPSC, 'Kothari Report', 51.
[98] Interview 40.
[99] UPSC, 'Kothari Report', 8.
[100] Interview 39.
[101] Nehru, 'The Civil Service in Transition'.
[102] 'Union Public Service Commission Notice No. F/5/49/540EI', 12 February 1955, 'Recruitment of candidates for the Indian Foreign Service on the results of the competitive examination held by the UPSC in 1954', Appendix II. F/2(3)–FSP/55, Part I., NAI.
[103] Today, only about 5–10% of Indians speak English—a figure that faithfully reflects class and educational divides, and would have been lower still when the UPSC guidelines were introduced. Rukmini S, 'In India, Who Speaks in English, and Where?', Livemint, 14 May 2019, https://www.livemint.com/news/india/in-india-who-speaks-in-english-and-where-1557814101428.html.
[104] See e.g. Vaidehi Ramanathan, *The English-Vernacular Divide: Postcolonial Language Politics and Practice* (Clevedon: Multilingual Matters LTD, 2005).

for the Foreign Service than any of its cousin bureaucracies.[105] That the interview was 'like the *viva* at Oxford', as one Oxford history graduate from the early 1960s appreciatively reminisced,[106] was no collective Freudian slip—K.P.S. Menon, as Head of the Board of Interviews 'always kept in mind, as a model, my own interview for the ICS in 1921'.[107] This meant that it favoured articulate generalists with the cultural confidence to argue their way through an impossible range of topics in front of an eminent panel of senior bureaucrats, academics, and public figures [108]—Menon's own interview, after all, had stretched from the political standing of the Maharaja of Travancore to how he might 'solve the Irish problem'.[109] After Independence, probationers would field questions on Immanuel Kant's categorical imperative, Pakistani elections, the Cuban Missile Crisis, and hydropower development in the state of Karnataka.[110] As one recently retired diplomat politely alluded, this 'gave a certain advantage to certain people from certain colleges'.[111] In a reflection of the diverging depositories of social capital and familiarity with dominant culture, only a few diplomats from outside the Delhiite Civil Service circles thought the interview tested academic knowledge.[112] Others understood that 'they weren't really interested in testing your knowledge, but rather how you conduct yourself, your poise'.[113] With the ethereal emphasis on 'having a kind of manner',[114] aspirants from elite backgrounds were at an advantage not academically but because they fit the dominant habitus.[115]

Deregulated ambitions

In the span of seven decades, the Indian Foreign Service has grown to a little shy of a thousand IFS(A) officers—a desperately modest number

---

[105] 'Union Public Service Commission Notice No. F/5/49/540EI'; UPSC, 'Kothari Report', 33; M.K. Narayan (Home Department), 'Response to Suggestions from the Foreign Service', n.d., 'Question of holding combined Examination for the Indian Foreign Service and All India Administrative Service in November–December Every Year. Prescription of high minimum mark at the interview for recruitment to the Indian Foreign Service', FSP/47-F/22(11).
[106] Interview 37.
[107] Menon, *Many Worlds*, 62.
[108] Interview 6; Interview 24.
[109] Menon, *Many Worlds*, 62.
[110] Interview 12; Interview 25; Interview 31; Interview 54.
[111] Interview 11.
[112] Interview 38, April 2019; Interview 54; Interview 58.
[113] Interview 12.
[114] Interview 9.
[115] Interview 19; Also Interview 75.

by international comparison, but unprecedented in the Service's history.[116] Although it is now possible in some years—to the perpetual dismay of seniors—to make it into the Service from around the 200th place on the all-India merit list (or below the 900th place for reservation recruits),[117] the Foreign Service has become more competitive statistically speaking: a vanishing 0.01% of UPSC candidates join the IFS.[118] Through this metamorphosis, the Service has gone from ICS veteran Subimal Dutt arguing in 1955 that 'we should get away from the class structure by taking positive steps to develop initiative and other qualities by anyone who shows promise'[119] to democratization fatigue—'maybe we have democratized too much', one guarded Joint-Secretary ventured.[120] A retired officer who had followed her parents and grandparents into government service spoke at length about the incoming 'hoi polloi', her almost anthropological language suggesting both morbid fascination and social distance.[121] Who, to borrow her revealing phrase, are the hoi polloi and how should we make sense of their presence in a once exclusive space?

Demographic change has come to the Indian Foreign Service through regulatory compulsion, constitutional amendment, and societal change. Arguably the two most significant forces in shaping the changing nature of diplomatic cadres began to exert their influence in the last two decades of the twentieth century. Long-debated amendments to UPSC regulations agreed before the 1980 examinations lifted several procedural barriers to entry, as recommendations set out in the 1976 Kothari Committee Report were implemented, and the existing structure—the Civil Service Examination (CSE)—came into being.[122] Noting that '[t]here should be a deliberate effort to attract meritorious candidates from weaker sections of the community, and also from areas other than big metropolitan cities', so as to 'make the services truly representative of the country', the Report introduced changes such as the addition of technical subjects like management and engineering as optional papers, the move from essays to multiple-choice questions and 'general knowledge', and the introduction of preliminary exams which would screen candidates for the main

---

[116] V.K. Singh, 'Reply by Minister of State in the Ministry of External Affairs', 3 January 2018, 'Strength of diplomats', unstarred question No. 2625 in the Lok Sabha, https://www.mea.gov.in/lok-sabha.htm?dtl/29300/QUESTION+NO2625+STRENGTH+OF+DIPLOMATS.

[117] Minimum rank by category, 2008–2018, 'All You Need to Know about the Indian Foreign Service (IFS)', Byju's, 2018, https://byjus.com/free-ias-prep/all-you-need-to-know-about-ifs/.

[118] Sudha Ramachandran, 'The Indian Foreign Service: Worthy of an Emerging Power?', The Diplomat, 12 July 2013, https://thediplomat.com/2013/07/the-indian-foreign-service-worthy-of-an-emerging-power/.

[119] Dutt, 'Response to Ministry of Home Affairs, Appleby Report'.

[120] Interview 61.

[121] Interview 52.

[122] UPSC, 'Kothari Report', 27.

examination at new testing centres, more evenly distributed across India.[123] The additional papers for applicants into the 'superior Civil Services', the IAS and IFS, which used to 'permit recruitment to these services of candidates with better intellectual and other capabilities', were abolished.[124]

The place of English in governing entry into government service also continued to evolve. The formerly elevated maximum grade for interviews—to which it was thought nearly a fourth of diplomats owed their place in the Foreign Service[125]—was lowered to the standard 300 marks for all Services, while the qualifying minimum was eliminated.[126] This contributed to the gradual equalization of language regulations and the loosening monopoly of Anglophone elites, begun through a 1967 Parliamentary resolution ordering that some segments of the examination be made available in all 22 of India's recognized languages.[127] However, although many products of Hindi Medium Schools now work alongside officers from English Medium Schools,[128] more permissive regulations hide a still narrow language landscape. The first round of the CSE is only set in English and Hindi, educational inequities and the dearth of preparatory material and coaching classes in regional languages perpetuate the language imbalance, and serving officers struggled to name a single colleague who had cleared the exam in anything but English or sometimes Hindi.[129] Regulatory amendments can remove technical barriers to entry, but they cannot erase socioeconomic difference.

A socioeconomic shift did, however, begin a decade later. The liberalization of the Indian economy in the early 1990s restructured economic opportunity, recast the cultural landscape of middle-class aspiration, and reformed the class connotations of government service.[130] As Leela Fernandes has argued, while the 'old middle class' associated cultural and economic status with government service, the 'new middle class', reshaped by globalization, began pursuing careers in multinational corporations, global finance, and international organizations.[131] This rendered government service a primary aspiration for classes

---

[123] UPSC, 24,28.

[124] UPSC, 50.

[125] UPSC, 70.

[126] UPSC, 63.

[127] Dixit, *Indian Foreign Service*, 216; UPSC, 'Kothari Report', iv.

[128] Maruthi Tangirala, 'Language Choice and Life Chances: Evidence from the Civil Services Examination', *Economic and Political Weekly* 44, no. 39 (2009): 16–20.

[129] UPSC, 'Examination Notice No. 04/2019-CSP'; Interview 78, May 2019; Interview 63.

[130] See e.g. Akhil Gupta and Kalyanakrishnan Sivaramakrishnan, eds, *The State in India after Liberalization: Interdisciplinary Perspectives* (London: Routledge, 2010); M.N. Panini, 'The Social Logic of Liberalization', *Sociological Bulletin* 44, no. 1 (1995): 33–62.

[131] Leela Fernandes, 'Restructuring the New Middle Class in Liberalizing India', *Comparative Studies of South Asia, Africa and the Middle East* 20, no. 1 (2000): 92; Also Interview 1; Interview 2; Interview 16; Interview 27; Interview 33; Interview 44, April 2019; Interview 50, May 2019.

172 REPRESENTATION: COSMOPOLITAN ELITES, DOMESTIC OTHERS

falling below the new 'middle'. In India's new class imagination, government service is not so much for the already privileged, but for less dominant sections of society aspiring to new heights of class status. One wealthy upper-caste IFS aspirant, educated in International Relations, was advised by family friends to reconsider her career plans, since the IFS was no longer known in their circles for having 'people from our kind of families'.[132]

As liberalization lured socioeconomic elites out of government employment, constitutional amendments to the reservations system instituted more seats for the lower castes. Despite the SC/ST reservations guaranteed in the 1950 Indian Constitution, it was not until the 1970s—when the UPSC was looking to commission sociologists to explain the lingering caste gap in exam performance[133]—that the records indicate a regularization of the reservations system.[134] A jolt to the system were the Mandal reforms of 1990. These reforms inducted 'Other Backward Castes' (OBCs, or Shudras) into the reservations system, raising the proportion of reserved seats from 22.5% to 50%. The amendments angered some of the Service's general-category officers, for whom deprivation among OBCs was not dire enough to warrant the further damage that would be exacted upon 'pure merit' and the Service's 'prestige'.[135] They also incensed some Dalits, who saw OBCs as accomplices in enforcing caste hierarchies against them, especially in the villages.[136] At the same time, reservations have yet to take full effect in the IFS. Since it is possible for reservation-designated lower-caste aspirants to make it onto the general-merit list, too, lower-caste officers should in fact constitute more than the prescribed minimum half of officers. A tally of officers posted to Indian Missions abroad in 2018, however, showed upper-caste diplomats still comprising 62% of the cadre.[137] Even in pure demographic terms, then, the Service is yet to fulfil its constitutional obligations on caste representation.

Regulatory changes to examination procedures, economic liberalization, and the doubling of reserved seats under the Mandal amendments have

---

[132] Interview 84, June 2019.

[133] UPSC, 'Kothari Report', 26.

[134] 'Annual Returns Showing the Total Number of Govt. Servants and Number of Scheduled Castes/Tribes amongst Them as on 1-1-67', n.d., F/Q/FSI/558/5/68, NAI; N.C. Banerjee (MEA), 'Letter on Enforcement of Reservations to P.L. Gupta (Ministry of Home Affairs)', 27 December 1969, 'Instructions and orders regarding requirements of and reservations orders etc for Scheduled Castes and Scheduled Tribes in Services', F/Q/GA/551/27/68, NAI.

[135] Interview 3.

[136] Interview 9; Interview 43; Interview 58; Interview 56; Interview 61; Interview 75.

[137] 'Rajya Sabha Unstarred Question No. 3053 on IFS Officers Belonging to SC/ST and OBC Categories, by Pratap Singh Bajwa, Answered by V.K. Singh (Minister of State, MEA)', 22 March 2018, https://mea.gov.in/rajya-sabha.htm?dtl/29716/QUESTION+NO3062+FUNDING+FOR+SOUTH+ASIAN+UNIVERSITY.

ushered in a new demographic balance. The UPSC acronym has become an emblem of aspiration for the half a million applicants who appear for the preliminary exams each year. In his colourful travelogue of small-town India, Pankaj Mishra conveyed that '[i]t was said that the first letters of the English alphabet for young middle-class children in Bihar were not A, B, and C but UPSC'.[138] In interviews, the products of this new alphabet told of dedicating over half a decade to the exams, resigning their jobs to study full time, and moving halfway across the country to the Delhi colony of Old Rajinder Nagar, taken over by one of the many clusters of coaching centres that epitomize the enterprising industry of UPSC aspiration.[139] Increasing rural representation in government service has often been a story of the uneven rewards of liberalization: the majority of rural recruits are from a few economically disadvantaged states like Uttar Pradesh and Bihar, where the lack of a thriving private sector has preserved the status of the Civil Services as 'the mother of all jobs'.[140] These applicants are hungrier than their seniors, one of whom declared it undignified for youngsters to be sitting the exam up to the allotted six-time maximum, when he himself would never have graced the Interview Board with his presence a second time.[141]

With the introduction of technical papers and multiple-choice questions in the examination, the once triumphant liberal arts graduates began finding themselves in the minority of batches dominated by engineers, scientists, and management graduates from the Indian Institutes of Technology (IITs) and Management (IIMs).[142] By the 1990s, Civil Service intake from engineering and technical backgrounds hit an average of 60% of incoming cadres,[143] and by the new millennium, the IITs at Kanpur and Delhi were producing the largest number of civil servants.[144] If the Service is filling with engineers, this, too, is because when 'you try and be socially mobile', it is engineering that Indian parents choose for you, as one rising star from the millennial batches—an engineer himself—explained.[145]

---

[138] Pankaj Mishra, *Butter Chicken in Ludhiana: Travels in Small-Town India* (Pan Macmillan, 2006), 245.

[139] Interview 66; Interview 72; Interview 77; Interview 83, May 2019.

[140] Vijay Jung Thapa, 'Enter the New Babu', *India Today*, 1 January 2001, https://www.indiatoday.in/magazine/nation/story/20010101-new-civil-service-recruits-undergo-serious-phase-of-transition-role-definition-776063-2001-01-01.

[141] Interview 28.

[142] Interview 44; Interview 56; Interview 57; Interview 58; Interview 60, May 2019; Interview 71; Interview 72; Interview 80, May 2019.

[143] R.K. Barik, 'Social Background of Civil Service: Some Depressing Trends', *Economic and Political Weekly* 39, no. 7 (February 2004): 626.

[144] Rana, *Inside Diplomacy*, 280.

[145] Interview 60.

174 REPRESENTATION: COSMOPOLITAN ELITES, DOMESTIC OTHERS

As a result, the Service's demographic complexion has come to stand at odds with its cultural self-perception. The new examination format, one sceptic of the changes complained, attracts individuals who 'want to *do* things, not *contemplate* things.'[146] If the old format rewarded eloquent essayists, the new one bows to the Indian penchant for rote-learning vast quantities of information by heart. The offspring of diplomats, once prime candidates for the Foreign Service, are now at a disadvantage: their International Baccalaureate certificates and unfamiliarity with Indian pedagogical ideals makes it hard for them to pass even the first round of exams.[147] The regulatory mechanisms of elite reproduction have, in many ways, been disrupted.

Because of the peculiarities of India's ranking system for entry exams and the changing face of the UPSC aspirant, many candidates now land in the Foreign Service almost by accident, because their rank does not afford them their first preference in the Home Services.[148] These reluctant diplomats point to a curious paradox: domestic interest in shaping Indian diplomacy is declining in reverse proportion to India's rise up the ranks of international politics. Yet their presence is an occasion for social schism inside the Service, too, as dominant officers project a set of cultural anxieties onto them. These accidental diplomats are less likely to carry the kind of familial or educational markers that have conventionally predicted a preference for the Foreign Service. The Indian Administrative Service (IAS) or the Indian Police Service (IPS) hold an immediate kind of authority outside India's metropolitan heartlands, where exposure to the Government is primarily through District Collectors or police officers wielding power over districts and development blocks—while the IFS confers an intangible status, signalling belonging in an imagined international community uprooted from the local context.[149] A common accusation levelled against these bureaucratic upstarts by the old guard is that their original preference for the entrapments of power in the Home Services reflects a new, materialistic generation; an unbecoming sign of a post-Gandhian era.[150] Yet what it also reflects is a different class position—one in which societal power has not been inherited but needs to be earned.

---

[146] Interview 22.

[147] Interview 10; Interview 22; Interview 44; Interview 45; Interview 84.

[148] Interview 7; Interview 24; Interview 33; Interview 36; Interview 38; Interview 58; Interview 59; Interview 63; Interview 68, May 2019; Interview 72; Interview 73, May 2019; Interview 77; Interview 83.

[149] Interview 5, March 2019; Interview 7; Interview 29; Interview 44; Interview 49; Interview 58; Interview 72.

[150] Interview 1; Interview 10; Interview 16; Interview 20; Interview 29; Interview 52; Interview 63; Interview 70.

ELITE REPRODUCTION, DISRUPTED   175

Women entering diplomacy in greater number has been a result of evolving gender roles in society at large as well as reforms to Foreign Service Rules. As Additional-Secretary Avtar Singh outlined in 1968, 'in the context of the existing social structure, it is difficult to expect young Indian women, who are brought up in the traditional Indian way, to come forward enthusiastically without apprehension for some time to come to join the Indian Foreign Service with its liability to serve anywhere in the world'.[151] Many female diplomats from the 1960s and 1970s batches testified to conservative social pressures against a nomadic, wine-drinking career in diplomacy—consequently, female diplomats were even more frequently products of liberal-minded, upper-middle class households than their male counterparts (making it incongruous to talk of their inclusion as 'democratization' per se).[152] Even as these pressures gradually dissipate, the march towards gender parity has been meandering: the 1977 and the 1990 batches had no women at all.[153] Women have been hovering just below the 20% mark for almost a decade now, having begun the new millennium at 13% of the overall Service.[154] In the decade since 2009, the number of female officers jumped from 94 to 176, according to internal documents cited by a diplomat who had recently reviewed them.[155] One milestone was the perfectly gender-balanced 2008 batch,[156] which has been followed by batches whose female intake has stayed between one-third to half of probationers.[157]

Making it into the Service has only been the first hurdle for female diplomats seeking to establish themselves. In a scolding Supreme Court ruling following Muthamma's ultimately unsuccessful suing of the MEA in 1979 after she failed to make Foreign Secretary, Judge Krishna Iyer confirmed that 'sex prejudice against Indian womanhood pervades the service rules' and ordered the Service 'to remove the stain of sex discrimination, without waiting for ad hoc inspiration from writ petitions or gender charity' by striking down Articles 8(2) and 18(4) of the 1961 Indian Foreign Service Rules on marriage, which had made career progress all but impossible for women.[158] Since future Foreign Secretary Jagat Mehta's wife had been forced to resign, the Service had in fact been

---

[151] Singh, 'Proposal'.

[152] Interview 15, March 2019; Interview 46.

[153] Interview 26; Interview 36; Interview 42; Interview 49; Interview 51, May 2019; Interview 54; Interview 57; Interview 58; Interview 61; Interview 70.

[154] Kishan S. Rana, *The Contemporary Embassy: Paths to Diplomatic Excellence* (Basingstoke: Palgrave Macmillan, 2013), 124–125; V. Sudarshan, 'Mama MEA', *Outlook Magazine*, 1 March 2004, http://magazine.outlookindia.com/story/mama-mea/223122; Interview 82.

[155] Interview 82.

[156] Interview 59.

[157] Interview 63; Interview 80; Interview 82.

[158] Supreme Court of India, 'C. B. Muthamma v. Union of India and Others (AIR 1868)', 17 September 1979, http://www.judis.nic.in/supremecourt/qrydisp.aspx?filename=4724.

176 REPRESENTATION: COSMOPOLITAN ELITES, DOMESTIC OTHERS

making exceptions to its own rules.[159] Yet women still required permission to marry until the early 1980s, needing to submit a draft resignation letter that the Service held onto in case the weight of domestic life rendered women, as this logic would have it, bad diplomats.[160] 'Looking back', a retired Muthamma tallied in 2008, 'I cannot help but conclude that my tenure with the External Affairs Ministry was one long tussle with the anti-women bias'.[161]

Even as caste and gender often become topics of heated—if usually private— discussion among diplomats, the sacralization of secularism has kept meaningful debate about religious representation at bay and archival records practically non-existent. While the small minorities of Christians and Sikhs tend to be, if anything, overrepresented in government service,[162] Muslim representation remains distinctly sparse. The 2006 Sachar Committee Report found that, even as Muslims made up around 13% of India's population, they were only 1.8% of the Foreign Service—a strikingly low figure, even by comparison to those for the IAS (3%) and the IPS (4%).[163] An undifferentiated figure for all Services in 2018 was 5%, presumably once again hiding a much lower percentage for the Foreign Service. Intersecting identities made some kinds of officers rarer still: circumstantial commentary suggests that only a few Muslim women have ever joined the Service, for example.[164] When diplomats spoke of female empowerment or gender inclusion, then, there seemed to be an unannounced assumption that the female officer was Hindu—perhaps even upper-caste and upper-class.

The democratization process is ongoing. It has even acquired an explicit outreach component: since 2019, the MEA Public Diplomacy Division's *Sameep* programme (Hindi for 'near' or 'close') has been sending diplomats to their hometowns and alma maters to deliver talks on a diplomatic career in the hopes of encouraging youngsters to apply—thereby also boosting the Service's momentarily ailing popularity.[165] Demographic representation matters, and it is the register in which most of the conversation on the democratization of the IFS seems to take place. Yet entry figures alone tell us little about how,

---

[159] Interview 5.

[160] Interview 5; Interview 15, March 2019; 'Article 8(2). The Indian Foreign Service (Conduct and Discipline) Rules, 1961', 1965, 'Tendency among All-Indian Service Officers to approach Ministers, MPs and other prominent public personalities regarding Service matters', Q(GA)/793(5)/65, NAI.

[161] Kurane 2008.

[162] Syed Najiullah, 'Representation of Minorities in Civil Services', *Economic and Political Weekly* 41, no. 8 (2006): 688.

[163] Sanya Dhingra, '5% Muslims among New Civil Services Recruits, Only One in Top 100', ThePrint, 4 August 2020, https://theprint.in/india/governance/5-muslims-among-new-civil-services-recruits-only-one-in-top-100/474488/.

[164] Interview 57.

[165] Interview 2; Interview 32, April 2019; Interview 51.

when, or whether those once excluded from the Service make their presence felt upon their arrival.

The standard bearers

'Democratization' can mean many things, or it can mean little. In the rigorous public debate on the Civil Services, the 'cause of democratization' is usually a question of 'how to make it more representative in the context of regions, caste, and class'.[166] It unfolds to the extent that a Service once made up of a narrow elite of upper-caste, upper-class, liberal-arts educated urban men has expanded to include wider demographics. In many ways, India's attempts at conceiving of its Foreign Service as a nationally representative body in a deeply unequal country is a project of considerable achievement. Its efforts at democratization have been extraordinary by international comparison, too: as diplomats pointed out about their foreign counterparts, diplomatic services in places like Pakistan (which only has reservations for regional representation) are far more elitist in their social makeup.[167] And yet seniority rankings, cultural imagery, and old networks of social capital have preserved many old hierarchies inside the Indian Foreign Service. Its demographic democratization must be evaluated against a context of cultural and social elite reproduction.

Presence and presentation

Merely being present does not make one seen. This incongruence has a long history inside the Foreign Service. As Ambassador Apa B. Pant—princely offspring turned Gandhian revolutionary—noted on IFS culture back in 1977, 'the so-called "salt-of-the-earth" Indian may feel quite out of place in the West-oriented Foreign Service of ours'.[168]

The most tangible sign of a democratization incomplete is that more 'representative' officers have not reached high postings in proportional measure to their numbers at entry. As the new decade began in 2020 upon my return from Delhi, the previous, current, and incoming Foreign Secretaries were all Stephanian men.[169] The lower castes and Adivasis have not seized an equivalent share

---

[166] Barik, 'Social Background of Civil Service', 626.
[167] Interview 66; Interview 75.
[168] Pant, 'Indian Diplomatic Missions Abroad and Their Problems'.
[169] 'Some Distinguished Alumni', St Stephen's College, accessed 20 August 2020, https://www.ststephens.edu/notable-alumni/.

178 REPRESENTATION: COSMOPOLITAN ELITES, DOMESTIC OTHERS

of prestigious postings or finance-controlling positions—a grievance thrown in the Ministry's face by Parliament and various Committees every few years.[170] A 2015 inquiry found that although SC/ST/OBC officers made up almost a third of diplomats, they were fewer than a fifth among Ambassadors, High Commissioners, or Permanent Representatives.[171] Even many of these ambassadorships, one retired Dalit diplomat claimed, are repeat appointments to 'inconsequential postings', while Missions to P-5 countries[172] and the neighbourhood are run by 'the ruling elite of the Foreign Service'.[173] The senior-most Secretary ranks are still inhabited by 'blue-blooded Brahmins', a serving Dalit diplomat contended.[174] As one retired senior Ambassador explained on the topic of reservations, as though offering assurance to a concerned interlocutor, 'democratization' is mostly a question of entry figures—over the first few years, unsuitable officers are 'sifted' out.[175]

After decades of having their careers cancelled for marrying, women's ascent in the hierarchies of the Foreign Service has been uneven. Three groundbreaking appointments marked a shift in the twenty-first century, as Chokila Iyer (2001–2002), Nirupama Menon Rao (2009–2011), and Sujatha Singh (2013–2015) made Foreign Secretaries—and Iyer, an ST officer who upon marrying her Brahmin husband abandoned her Adivasi surname Tshering, became the first Foreign Secretary from a reserved-category background.[176] Breaking important ground on strategic postings, Meera Shankar (2009–2011)

---

[170] '"Unstarred Question—Lok Sabha—No. 2321 for 15.03.1965 by Shri Naval Prabhakar Regarding Scheduled Castes Employees in Indian Missions Abroad"', F/Q(GA)-125/4/65'; '"Parliament Questions: Information Regarding Members of Scheduled Castes and Tribes in the IFS"', F/Q/FSI/125/2/68, Part II', February 1968, NAI; '"Lok Sabha Starred Question No. 23428 from Shri Kameshwar Singh—Regarding Scheduled Caste and Scheduled Tribe Candidates in the Indian Foreign Service"', F/Q/FSI/125/7/68', July 1968, NAI; '"Representation of Scheduled Castes in IFS—IFI Section"', F/Q/FSI/551/10/68', October 1968, NAI; '"Lok Sabha Starred Question No. 5382 by Shri D.R. Parmar Regarding Indian Diplomats Belonging to Scheduled Castes and Scheduled Tribes, Due for Answer on 31.7.1968"', F/Q/FSI/125/11/68', July 1968, NAI; '"Lok Sabha Unstarred Question No. 8723 for 27.04.1972 by Shri Bibhuti Mishra Regarding Recruitment to Foreign Service"', F/Q/GA/125(II)/72', 1972, NAI; '"Lok Sabha Provisional Starred Question No. 5493 Regarding Criteria for Posting Officers of Scheduled Castes/Tribes in Offices of Trade Commissioners and Trade Representatives Abroad"', F/Q/PA II/125/10/78', October 1978, NAI.

[171] 'Top IFS Posts Still out of Bounds for SCs, STs', The Hindu, 5 December 2015, https://www.thehindu.com/news/national/top-ifs-posts-still-out-of-bounds-for-scs-sts/article7950262.ece.

[172] P-5 refers to the permanent members of the UN Security Council: the US, China, the UK, France, and Russia.

[173] Interview 54.

[174] Interview 75.

[175] Interview 3.

[176] Sagarika Ghose, 'At Home on Foreign Affairs', Outlook Magazine, 15 January 2001, https://www.outlookindia.com/magazine/story/at-home-on-foreign-affairs/210681; 'Lists of SC/ST Officers with Their Batch Affiliation'; HT Foreign Bureau, 'Nirupama Is New Foreign Secretary', Hindustan Times, 1 July 2009, https://www.hindustantimes.com/delhi/nirupama-is-new-foreign-secretary; Ashok Tuteja, 'Seniority Prevails, Sujatha Singh Is New Foreign Secy', The Tribune, 2 July 2013, https://www.tribuneindia.com/2013/20130703/main6.htm.

and Nirupama Menon Rao (2011–2013) became Ambassadors to the US in succession.[177] However, the ensuing complaints about 'feminist domination in the Indian Mission in Washington', echoing official complaints to Foreign Secretary Muchkund Dubey by men of the Foreign Service Association in the 1980s,[178] bore testimony to the creative reinterpretations of gender parity that develop when women ascend historically male hierarchies.

The types of postings women receive matter for how far they progress. Only Muthamma's 1970 ambassadorial appointment to Hungary ended a rule barring a woman from ambassadorial ranks 'in case she leaked the state secrets' to an unsuspecting husband.[179] Women are overrepresented in lower-ranking 'cultural diplomacy' positions and other sites considered to belong on the softer edges of diplomacy—an imbalance sustained by gendered readings of diplomacy which most female officers abhorred, and which many had sought to escape by avoiding cultural diplomacy altogether.[180] As Khushi Singh Rathore cautions, there is no single glass ceiling for women in the IFS to shatter, but rather a succession of interconnected barriers sustained by patriarchal attitudes and conventions, which are no less deserving of systemic redress because individual women have made it to the very top.[181]

An yet the most common male response to questions about gender equality among Indian diplomats was to do with 'soft postings': women moving 'from A post to plus-A post', that is, from one comfortable posting to another.[182] One of the more notable office intrigues of the late 1970s was the infamous circular letter from Foreign Secretary Jagat Mehta (whose wife resigned the Service upon marrying him), reprimanding women officers for unfairly exploiting their womanhood to gain easy postings by appealing to their family arrangements—an intrigue followed by the circular's quiet retraction after an outcry over its selective evidence base.[183] Confronted with the debate, female interviewees noted that posting favours had always been an art perfected by well-connected men.[184] They also offered anecdotal counterexamples, from women posted in Tripoli during the evacuations of Indian nationals around 2011 to three

---

[177] 'Nirupama Rao Named India's next Ambassador to U.S.', *The Hindu*, 16 July 2011, https://www.thehindu.com/news/national/Nirupama-Rao-named-Indiarsquos-next-ambassador-to-U.S./article13745784.ece.

[178] Dixit, *Indian Foreign Service*, 217; Interview 49.

[179] Basu, 'Chonira Muthamma, India's First Woman Career Diplomat'.

[180] Interview 34; Interview 42; Interview 57; Interview 63; Interview 80; Interview 81; Interview 82.

[181] Khushi Singh Rathore, 'Where Are the Women in Indian Diplomacy?', *The Diplomat*, 12 November 2020, https://thediplomat.com/2020/11/where-are-the-women-in-indian-diplomacy/.

[182] Interview 49; The same complaint was made in Interview 1; Interview 12; Interview 29; Interview 31; Interview 49.

[183] Dixit, *Indian Foreign Service*, 217.

[184] Interview 5; Interview 15, March 2019; Interview 34; Interview 42.

180 REPRESENTATION: COSMOPOLITAN ELITES, DOMESTIC OTHERS

consecutive women serving in Cote D'Ivoire during the civil wars of the new millennium.[185]

At the same time, to this day, those who volunteer for difficult, dangerous placements, desiring acknowledgement as 'serious officers'[186] in the career-defining first decade,[187] are often rejected—as one Under-Secretary exclaimed—for 'the most ridiculous reasons'.[188] Without such prestigious 'hard postings', obtaining senior-most positions becomes hard, too. This pattern is not an Indian idiosyncrasy, but rather reflects the gendered nature of the diplomatic club more broadly. As Ann Towns writes on gendered posting practices across diplomatic services worldwide, 'power and positions of influence are often associated with alleged traits of masculinity, whereas femininity is instead often linked with positions of subordination and lesser status'; this involves men being overrepresented in posts requiring allegedly 'masculine' traits such as military and political affairs, and women being posted to serve in 'feminized' positions such as cultural diplomacy.[189] In India, the debate about soft postings represents the logical conclusion of the long-standing male conviction that 'lady officers' were unsuited for tough posts—a charge previously used to exclude them from the Service altogether.

Official rank is one way of querying the true impact of 'democratization'. Yet there are cultural imbalances that no official recognition can paper over. One retired diplomat who reached the very highest levels of seniority in the Service after ranking at the top of his batch could never shake the sense of being an outsider, because the all-India merit rankings only conferred status on those who entered with the correct habitus: 'frankly, one felt disadvantaged, even if one had taken the same elite exam', and excelled at it.[190] As Bourdieu would have it, initial cultural capital still matters after a supposed process of equalization, 'as one finds whenever social origin distinguishes individuals whose qualifications are identical'.[191] Subliminal hierarchies can reflect themselves not only in the distribution of capital but in how the same forms of capital are interpreted differently depending on their carrier. One tribal officer from outside Delhi's elite circles—with flowery, impeccable English—was bewildered that anybody considered him worth interviewing, especially by comparison to his Stephanian superior who had nominated him for the interview, because 'the people

---

[185] Interview 15, March 2019; Interview 57; Interview 80; Interview 81.
[186] Interview 57.
[187] Interview 63; Interview 80; Interview 82.
[188] Interview 59.
[189] Towns and Niklasson, 'Gender, International Status, and Ambassador Appointments', 526.
[190] Interview 74; The same argument was made by another high-ranking official: Interview 45.
[191] Bourdieu, *Distinction*, 99.

that you have talked to, they are all so polished', whereas he was 'rougher'.[192] Those who are not perceived as embodying the dominant habitus are often consigned to situating themselves in relation to it.[193]

How, then, do we make sense of big concepts like 'democratization' or 'inclusion' in a space which has been constitutionally mandated to rectify caste imbalances, has for decades recruited Indians from non-traditional backgrounds, and yet seems to wear its official diversity so lightly? Presence does not, of its own accord, afford either position or power. Access on the part of non-dominant actors does not guarantee adaptation on the part of the dominant. Arguing against the prevalent narrative that liberal, post-industrial societies had guaranteed equality of opportunity through education and democracy, Bourdieu contended that elites in formally equal societies perpetuate their dominant position by putting their cultural and social capital to use.[194] Since rare forms of capital are valued most, capital is a primary force in the reproduction and entrenchment of status hierarchies over time. Indeed, it is precisely the inequalities of capital that guarantee its worth. In 2015, one young anonymous OBC diplomat spoke to *The Hindu* about the difficulties of advancing in the Service without the social connections that 'those from elite families have' and an awareness of the 'etiquette' they all seemed to know.[195] Against demographic change, inherited legacies of cultural and social capital distinguish between formally equal members of the Foreign Service.

Even as other Ministries were moving 'down to earth', a 1970s batcher recalled partly laughing, partly scoffing, the Foreign Service was for a very long time stacked with Secretaries in 'three-piece suits with cigars'.[196] An 'elitist style, based on the initial circumstances of the very early profile of the Service' was still predominant, as Ambassador Rana observed in the new millennium.[197] Even with the changing nature of incoming cadres and the world transforming around them, few diplomats gave any indication in our conversations that much had changed about the ideal Indian diplomat.[198] Although he 'brings in a different perspective', an OBC recruit of a late-2000s batch from a village weighed in, he was not convinced that perspectives like his mattered to those socialized into not considering them.[199] Even the doubling of reserved

---

[192] Interview 77.
[193] Bourdieu, *Distinction*, 98.
[194] Bourdieu, 'The Forms of Capital (1986)', 81,83.
[195] 'Top IFS Posts Still out of Bounds for SCs, STs'.
[196] Interview 49.
[197] Rana, *Inside Diplomacy*, 37.
[198] Interview 7; Interview 12; Interview 19; Interview 41; Interview 59.
[199] Interview 78; The same argument was made from the perspective of a 1960s batcher: Interview 46.

seats in the 1990s had, in the words of a general-category colleague, produced 'very little of a sense of overhaul'.[200]

In other words, the standard bearers of the dominant habitus have remained largely the same. The image of an Anglophone, upper-caste, presentable, well-dressed, eloquent male liberal arts graduate was an often-subconscious benchmark.[201] Even as their actual numbers in the Service began dwindling towards the new millennium, Stephenians have defined the 'St Stephen's type' that colours conversations on the internal hierarchies of the Service to this day.[202] Stephenians were described as 'the cultural reference group'[203]—one Stephanian of a 1960s batch went as far as to suggest that the IFS 'represents the ethos of St Stephen's'.[204] As a Dalit officer with a science background noted when describing the superficiality of change in the Service: 'I think subconsciously many still want to be like them'.[205] Indeed, even those who explicitly declared the elitist reverence for Stephenians passé sometimes then went on to exclusively name individual Stephenians as examples of the ideal diplomat.[206] Being from St Stephen was not about having mastered a specific body of academic knowledge which had prepared you for the world of diplomacy. Instead, as one proud alumnus proclaimed, 'it had been imbued in us that we were superior culturally, socially, and intellectually'.[207] This effortless superiority lent the Stephanian elite a sense of having a birth right to the Foreign Service; it supplied them the raw material to inhabit the dominant habitus.

Who has merit?

Reservations guarantee the Indian Foreign Service a unique social complexion. The Service is dominated by historically homogenous elites, but a significant proportion of its membership is made up of historically marginalized Indians who may embark on their careers entirely unfamiliar with the elite conventions of diplomacy. A Bourdieusian reading of caste relations in the Foreign Service makes sense of these asymmetries of cultural power and the ways in which they feed into constructions of habitus and imageries of international society.

---

[200] Interview 66.
[201] Interview 59; Interview 57; Interview 75.
[202] Interview 4; Interview 19; Interview 24; Interview 31; Interview 36; Interview 38; Interview 54.
[203] Interview 43.
[204] Interview 23.
[205] Interview 75.
[206] Interview 27; Interview 80; Interview 83; Interview 85.
[207] Interview 43.

In Indian public debate, 'merit' is a signifier pregnant with so much political baggage that one is rarely, in fact, discussing the question of academic excellence or professional suitability. Its centrality nevertheless reflects itself in the striking rank consciousness officers exhibit, not only in terms of their seniority but also their performance in entry examinations for the Service, which are invested with much meaning. Elderly officers in particular would mention their exact all-India rank or interview marks in conversation, recall their batch mates in rank order of their examination results, and refer to colleagues who had performed best over half a century ago as 'toppers' when speaking of them in a seemingly unrelated context.[208] One Additional-Secretary complained of the 'obsession' with examination rank which still defined so much of one's career from language choice to promotions, noting that 'in our interaction we don't notice it, but when a decision goes against us, we invoke our rank'.[209] A high-achiever of the late-1990s batches mentioned that seating arrangements during ministerial meetings are still organized by examination rank.[210]

This hierarchization has an institutionalized caste element which follows new entrants into the Foreign Service. A millennial Dalit officer spoke of his embarrassment during training, as probationers were seated for lectures and ordered to stand in line in accordance with their all-India rank—thus repeatedly 'outing' the tail end of reservation recruits in a profoundly embodied manner.[211] Caste, therefore, conditions the very way in which an Indian diplomat occupies physical space. These imbalances are partly an administrative consequence of the separate merit lists around which many of the Service's practices cohere. Batch-toppers have tended to make Foreign Secretaries, and one's rank at entry matters throughout one's entire career.[212] The higher maximum age afforded to reservation recruits matters, since joining the Service late also means progressing less far by retirement.[213] Languages are allotted according to rank, so that batch toppers from the general merit list can pick career-promoting UN languages like Chinese or French to study during training.[214] In this way, seemingly neutral practices like language allocation institutionalize caste discrepancies.

The sociologist Satish Deshpande conceives of the exam ranking system as 'a moral-ethical ordering' that legitimates lingering caste differences by

---

[208] Interview 31; Interview 35; Interview 37; Interview 40.
[209] Interview 70.
[210] Interview 83.
[211] Interview 71.
[212] Interview 43; Interview 45.
[213] Interview 7; Interview 77.
[214] Interview 75; Interview 77.

184 REPRESENTATION: COSMOPOLITAN ELITES, DOMESTIC OTHERS

associating them with seemingly neutral markers of academic achievement.[215] Ajantha Subramanian picks up on the same theme of an Indian 'obsession with ranking', as she details the quotidian meaning-making around rankings among engineering students at IITs, as part of which 'the miniscule differences in scores acquire far more weight when they are translated into neatly distinguished ranks as the objective truth of relative intelligence'. The rank not only codifies and quantifies academic achievement in a particular examination, but becomes a token of general intelligence and a talismanic explanation of future successes and failures. In India's aspirational imagination, it acquires a life of its own. In any open competition between members of highly unequal communities, what standardized examination measures is often socioeconomic privilege. The focus on rank naturalizes socioeconomic inequality into a neat referencing guide—a socially acceptable hierarchy of pure talent and hard work.

Caste and meritocracy may seem to represent two irreconcilable prescriptions for how to organize society: the former is emblematic of prescribed, collectivized hierarchy while the latter plays off themes of democratization, fair competition, and individual striving. Caste is parochial and fixed; merit is abstract and universally attainable. The language of caste is presented as unenlightened, the language of merit as modern. Indeed, meritocracy gestures towards an ideal-type social order which Bourdieu described as an 'imaginary universe of perfect competition or perfect equality of opportunity, a world without inertia, without accumulation, without heredity or acquired properties'.

Yet the relationship between caste and merit is, in fact, intimate. As Subramanian argues 'Indian meritocracy is part of a much longer history of modern political thought and its reconciliation of universal equality and naturalized social hierarchy'.[216] Reservations give caste a modern life, an institutionalized jargon in which to express caste difference. Subramanian writes about the social categories that reservations created: 'Merit came to be mapped onto an emergent form of upper-caste identity where what mattered was not caste affiliation based in understandings of endogamy and history but the governmental distinction between the "general" and the "reserve"'.[217]

---

[215] Satish Deshpande, 'Pass, Fail, Distinction: The Examination as a Social Institution', in *Marjorie Sykes Memorial Lecture* (Regional Institute of Education, Ajmer: National Council for Educational Research and Training, 2010), 19.

[216] Subramanian, *The Caste of Merit: Engineering Education in India*, 17.

[217] Subramanian, 236.

In India, merit talk has a distinctly liberal slant and purpose to it. Insofar as proponents of the liberal project see themselves as doing the work of modernity, it is of great consequence that reservations allow the upper castes to seemingly divorce themselves from their caste identity while continuing to benefit from it. The ostensibly technocratic and neutral logics of merit have allowed for 'the reconstitution of upper castes as casteless, meritocratic moderns'.[218] Merit talk is a kind of sociological sleight of hand, whereby 'upper-caste urban professionals are thought to have transcended caste to adopt more modern forms of identification; thus, they are assumed to be casteless by virtue of their modernity'.[219] Only the lower castes, who avail themselves of reservations, are marked by their caste: 'It was only the reserved who came to be marked by history and identity, while the non-reserved stood in simply for casteless, ahistorical excellence'.[220]

There is, therefore, a deeper cultural grammar to caste relations inside the Foreign Service. Concepts produce groups—for as Bourdieu would have it: 'What is at stake in the struggles about the meaning of the social world is power over the classificatory schemes and systems which are the basis of the representations of the groups and therefore of their mobilization and demobilization'.[221] As such, even seemingly sterile words like 'merit' have social baggage and cultural consequences.[222] With the division of candidates into the 'general merit list' of mostly upper-caste candidates and a stigmatized 'reservations list' of lower castes and tribal groups, the selection system has called forth a parallel class of diplomats, whose ranking in one examination marks them out as 'reserved types' for the rest of their diplomatic careers.[223] For brahminical senior officers in particular, the very concept of reservations has traditionally been an affront to the prestige of government service, with Dalit officers 'chosen from competition among themselves', not against better-qualified upper-caste rivals.[224] When, after almost two decades of unclaimed reservation seats, three SC/ST candidates joined the IFS batch of 1966, an incensed article in the left-leaning journal *Economic and Political Weekly*

---

[218] Subramanian, 21.

[219] Subramanian, 3.

[220] Subramanian, 217.

[221] Bourdieu, *Distinction*, 481.

[222] This loaded term has animated debate in the Service from the earliest years: Haksar, 'Memo'; Eric Gonsalves, 'Memo', 23 January 1961, 'Review of the Indian Foreign Service', FSP(I)/MC/3/61, NAI.

[223] Interview 54; Interview 75; Interview 71.

[224] J.M. Lobo Prabhu, 'My Work in the ICS', in *The Civil Servant in India, by Ex-Indian Civil Servants*, ed. Kewalram Laichand Panjabi (Bombay: Bharatiya Vidya Bhavan, 1968), 223; T.N. Kaul feared that reservations would trigger upper-caste brain-drain: T.N. Kaul, 'President's Letter: Reservations—Where Do We Go from Here?', n.d., Miscellaneous articles, 'Speeches/writings by him', SN/141, T.N. Kaul papers, NMML.

186 REPRESENTATION: COSMOPOLITAN ELITES, DOMESTIC OTHERS

announced that reservations meant that 'there cannot be an insistence on quality in these recruitments for some time'.[225] Dalits and Adivasis, it was implied, could not be meritorious. M.S.S. Pandian's work decodes such discursive moves, which the upper castes perform to talk about caste without ever uttering the word. In them, 'caste masquerades as something else and makes its muted modern appearance'.[226] Merit is the socially acceptable way of talking about caste without ever appearing to do so.

I argue that the language of 'merit' inside the Foreign Service works this way, too: it allows for a conversation that is fundamentally about caste but takes place in the safety of a liberal lexicon of technocracy and individual achievement. Given the narrow margins by which candidates outdo each other in the entry exams and the inescapable element of luck that diplomats admitted was involved in the process[227]—as well as the valuable reminder from one Dalit officer that 'you can have academic merit and be a mediocre diplomat'[228]—the faith in this strict bifurcation of merit seems empirically fragile. Yet there is a purpose to it. The seemingly apolitical language of merit divorces the diplomat from society, with little regard to the inequities of social, economic, and cultural capital that make the meritorious thus.[229] It obscures the cultural capital endowed on certain diplomats through elite schooling or the social capital inherited through birth into a 'Civil Service family'. It depoliticizes inequality. The inference that those on the general list have merit while those on a reserved list do not produces a culture within which the largely upper-caste general-category diplomats can naturalize their dominance in South Block as an impartial reflection of their intrinsic capabilities. The seemingly cultural conversations around reservations and 'reserved types' rationalize a caste order that liberal upper-caste officers would otherwise struggle to justify. They allow caste inequalities in career trajectories to be divorced from conversations about persistent stereotypes, implicit bias, cultural expectations, or an unequal distribution of social capital which segregates reservation recruits from overwhelmingly upper-caste diplomatic networks.

Despite continued upper-caste dominance, the injustice that most reliably animated upper-caste officers was the deservingness of the 'creamy layer':[230]

---

[225] G.S. Bhargava, 'The Ills of the Indian Foreign Service', *Economic and Political Weekly* 1, no. 10 (October 1966): 410.

[226] Pandian, 'One Step Outside Modernity', 1735.

[227] Interview 22; Interview 44; Interview 60; Interview 66; Interview 71.

[228] Interview 38.

[229] Shamus Khan and Colin Jerolmack, 'Saying Meritocracy and Doing Privilege', *The Sociological Quarterly* 54, no. 1 (February 2013): 9–19.

[230] An Indian Supreme Court judgement in 1992 directed the government to exclude the 'creamy layer' from incoming OBC reservations. Based on the criteria recommended by the Justice Prasad

members of historically marginalized communities who have lived through a generation or two of relative privilege and whose entry into the Services on reservations, so the indictment, distorts their very purpose.[231] Those branded by colleagues as members of this upper crust of the marginalized, primarily Dalits, insisted on the necessity of elite exposure, since otherwise 'people of my background don't even know that there exists this creature called the Foreign Service officer.'[232] Reservations were never about social or economic deprivation, they argue. Especially so in the Foreign Service, which represents India out into the world, 'reservations are about representation.'[233] The ambivalent status of 'creamy layer' diplomats is emblematic of the social hierarchies and cultural expectations that go into producing the diplomatic habitus. It is also reflective of broader social arguments in India, which have sought to portray reservations as inherently unfair. 'Through the prism of anti-reservation rhetoric', Subramanian writes, 'we see an upside-down world where stigmatization and exclusion are the plight of upper castes and reservation is a corruption of pre-existing norms of equality, fairness, and justice.'[234]

Many women in the Service also sensed that the male officer remained an unacknowledged archetype of the technically gender-neutral diplomatic habitus. One female Joint-Secretary thought back with visible irritation to occasions on which female officers had been tasked with taking foreign dignitaries' wives' shopping or handing over the flower bouquet while men conducted the official work.[235] Bourdieu noted that most social orders owed their persistent male bias to gendered readings that had been rendered commonsensical: 'the androcentric vision imposes itself as neutral and has no need to spell itself out in discourses aimed at legitimating it.'[236] This was also the case with the Indian Foreign Service, where the pervasive if subconscious use of 'he', 'men', and 'good guys' in reference to the generic diplomat in archival texts and interviews with men of all generations suggested an unintentional but chronic masculinization of the diplomatic habitus.

Commission, the government defined this group as the offspring of Class I and II bureaucrats in federal and provincial services, military personnel of colonel rank or above, officers in public sector organizations, as well as industrialists, traders and individuals with annual incomes above Rs. 100 000. No such exclusions existed when the SC/ST reservations were created in the 1950 Indian Constitution. See Suri, 'Competing Interests', 245.

[231] Interview 1; Interview 2; Interview 3; Interview 5; Interview 12; Interview 18; Interview 19; Interview 20; Interview 25; Interview 27; Interview 28; Interview 36; Interview 43; Interview 46; Interview 49; Interview 52; Interview 58; Interview 70; Interview 85.

[232] Interview 75; Also Interview 67.

[233] Interview 75.

[234] Subramanian, *The Caste of Merit: Engineering Education in India*, 241.

[235] Interview 75.

[236] Bourdieu, *Masculine Domination*, 9.

188 REPRESENTATION: COSMOPOLITAN ELITES, DOMESTIC OTHERS

Yet when female diplomats performed some of the traits traditionally associated with the unofficially masculinized habitus of a diplomat, social punishment followed. Men seemed uncomfortable with authoritative women as their superiors,[237] and gendered 'double-standards' in annual evaluations and daily work penalized women for the 'bossiness' applauded in men as 'decisive'.[238] Men who had worked with C.B. Muthamma, India's first female career diplomat, insisted that she 'was her own worst enemy' and 'could have been a little less brazen'.[239] A diplomat of 'high intellectual capacities' possessing a 'profound awareness of India's national interests', Dixit admits that her failing to make Foreign Secretary—a post she 'from every logical point of view' deserved—betrayed a discomfort among her superiors with the notion of an outspoken woman elevated to Grade I.[240] One male Additional-Secretary gave voice to what young female officers had named 'the stereotype of the cranky single lady',[241] lamenting that his ambitious female colleagues tended to become 'anti-personal', incapable of using 'the entire range of their capabilities' over the decades.[242] This, to the extent that it had any meaning at all, reflected female officers' attempts at abiding by an unofficially masculinized habitus, downplaying overt displays of emotion or light-heartedness in the hope of being taken seriously as diplomats.

Therefore, although women have now formally scaled the official ranks of the Foreign Service, they are curiously absent in its cultural imageries of merit. Seeking acknowledgement for one's merit as a female diplomat often means thinking three impossible things before breakfast: she should fit a gender-neutral habitus, she should seek to abide by the male-signified markers of the not-really-gender-neutral habitus, but at the same time, she ought to keep some stereotypically feminine traits lest she be perceived as anti-personal and hence, coming full circle, as a lesser diplomat. The ideal of a meritorious officer was implicitly gendered. 'If you ask people to name three officers they admire', one female Under-Secretary challenged me, 'see how many of them name a single woman'.[243] I did. None were named. And while only men were mentioned as individual examples of the ideal diplomat, only female officers were singled out by name as bad ones. It once even happened that a male interviewee observed a female colleague walking past our table at the India

---

[237] Interview 15, March 2019; Interview 34.
[238] Interview 5; Interview 15, March 2019; Interview 34; Interview 42.
[239] Interview 1; Also Interview 31.
[240] Dixit, *Indian Foreign Service*, 50.
[241] Interview 59; Interview 63.
[242] Interview 70.
[243] Interview 59.

International Centre and made a point of telling me what a terrible diplomat she was and what an awful interviewee she would make.[244] Many of the dominant conceptions of merit have a caste, but they also have a gender.

The segregation of social capital

In his 2013 autobiography, Ambassador P.L. Bhandari rejoiced in the conveniences of Indian diplomacy several decades into Independence and across Missions around the world: 'wherever you went, you met people who knew the people you knew.'[245] Or, in Bourdieu's lexicon: you had social capital. This was not, however, a universal condition. Rather, it was another reflection of the Service's power imbalances.

In the words of one world-weary Ambassador, this was the 'you-know-whom's logic'[246] which, despite the ritualized appeals to merit, still defined so much of a diplomat's career. For the offspring of the well-connected, a 'closed-door network' nurtured those who 'went to the Gymkhana Club to meet their fathers' friends', receiving generational wisdom on bureaucratic life and position openings, remembered one disillusioned 1970s-batcher.[247] A colleague who joined later into the decade observed his better-connected peers navigate processes like language allotments by befriending 'the right people in the Ministry', after their Delhiite Civil Service families had 'fed them with background information'.[248] Since Stephenians were seen as practically ruling Indian bureaucracy,[249] it was also common for them to talk to me about the diplomats, politicians, academics, and celebrities they counted among their friends, many of whom they already knew from the Shakespeare Society or debating classes at 'the College'.[250] Even as the hold of the 'Oxford–Cambridge–St Stephen's–Doon School clique'[251] has waned, along with the social capital that comes from familial ties, it will take decades before the generational churn lessens their power in the Service's culture-defining senior layers. For now, inherited social capital shapes much of the social fabric of the

---

[244] This, of course, occasioned me to ensure that I could conduct an interview with the female diplomat thus targeted.

[245] P. L. Bhandari, *How Not to Be a Diplomat: Adventures in the Indian Foreign Service Post-Independence* (London: The Quince Tree, 2013), 1.

[246] Interview 24.

[247] Interview 14.

[248] Interview 41.

[249] Interview 79.

[250] Interview 27; Interview 33; Interview 69; Interview 81; Interview 85.

[251] Interview 43.

190   REPRESENTATION: COSMOPOLITAN ELITES, DOMESTIC OTHERS

Service: as one contract agent of the Ministry phrased it, he had never 'seen anybody whose father was in the IFS who got posted to Malawi'.[252]

Social capital in the Foreign Service has also always had a caste. In a rare written anecdote, former officer J. Bandyopadhyaya recalled of his time in an unspecified posting that his High Commissioner shunned the senior Deputy High Commissioner 'who belonged to a Scheduled Caste and had no family connections worth the name'.[253] Yet with all the liberal taboos surrounding caste in a space like the Foreign Service, one does not query the caste underpinnings of social capital by asking diplomats to describe outright networks—although one retired Christian diplomat did redefine some key diplomatic terms by explaining that the '*esprit de corps* means Brahmins want to help each other'[254] and a Dalit diplomat spoke at length about discreet but 'socially segregated' networks along caste lines.[255] Indeed, many Dalits explicitly contrasted their experience with the more overt expressions of caste in the Home Services: some celebrated the fact that the Foreign Service, unlike the IAS, had no openly-paraded 'caste constituencies',[256] while others admired the IAS for having staff to support ST/SC officers and lauded those state cadres with organized caste associations that fend against discrimination in Government employment.[257]

Instead, to gauge the caste of social capital, one allows diplomats to freely describe their batches, colleagues, friends, and favourite diplomats. One striking feature that emerged from this exercise was the practice among some diplomats from the 1950s–1970s batches to entirely exclude reserved-category entrants from their own batch. Diplomats who only moments before had eloquently outlined the moral case for reservations would sometimes give a peculiarly small number for their own batch size and, upon a suggestion that the size seemed smaller than the respective ministerial documents indicated, only then add reserved-category colleagues to their tally.[258] It was as if these lower-caste diplomats were not really there, at least not in the social imagination of some upper-caste peers. One diplomat who joined in the 1960s batted off a question about officers' caste identities with the visibly offended retort that 'I didn't look at it from that perspective', only to then turn pensive: 'It's funny ... I never had any colleagues [from reserved categories] ... I

---

[252] Interview 2.
[253] Bandyopadhyaya 1970, 184.
[254] Interview 25.
[255] Interview 54.
[256] Interview 54.
[257] Interview 75.
[258] Interview 7; Interview 31; Interview 35; Interview 39.

had very little to do with them.'[259] A member of an adjacent batch spoke at length about batch solidarity even beyond retirement, before clarifying that he had no contact with colleagues from outside the general merit list.[260] Those who insisted that they were well-acquainted with lower-caste diplomats would, across different batches, usually mention the one and same individual diplomat[261]—and, as a fellow Dalit officer pointed out, the same officers would also 'crack jokes' about his lack of erudition behind his back.[262] Social capital in the Foreign Service was less blind to caste than the principles its officers pledged allegiance to.

Finally, even if Bourdieu might not have thought of social capital as gendered, Indian female diplomats certainly have. In the early years of Independence, inherited diplomatic protocol effectively institutionalized a gender disparity in social capital. When a female ambassador showed up at a diplomatic dinner party, how did protocol suggest that she be seated at the table—as a spouse, invitee, or ambassador? 'Surely she should join the ladies?' Foreign Secretary Rasgotra ventured a guarded guess, reliving his troubles making sense of Vijaya Lakshmi Pandit's role in the early post-Independence years.[263] 'Joining the ladies' precluded one from being seated with the ambassadors, for by and large, ambassadors were men. And while female diplomats were expected to join the wives at diplomatic dinners, their male colleagues would talk politics and grow closer with their superiors[264]—a convention that already infuriated Ambassador Pandit in the 1940s[265] but seems to have taken the better part of the twentieth century for the Service to abandon.[266] Many more contemporary diplomatic bonding practices still exclude women by social convention, be it hot baths in Japan or drinks at the Gymkhana Club in Delhi.[267] 'It's the class example of an Old Boy's Club', declared one woman from the millennial batches who had spent a decade navigating the intricacies of a system where many vacancies at Headquarters are never openly advertised and even men from rural backgrounds had begun finding their way around the hierarchies by 'help[ing] each other out' amongst themselves.[268] Implicitly,

---

[259] Interview 31.
[260] Interview 43.
[261] Interview 7; Interview 35; Interview 36; Interview 43.
[262] Interview 54.
[263] Rasgotra 2015, 24.
[264] Interview 15, March 2019; Interview 21.
[265] Pandit, *The Scope of Happiness*, 251.
[266] Interview 15, March 2019.
[267] Interview 15; Interview 42.
[268] Interview 59; Also Interview 15, March 2019; Interview 21; Interview 42; Interview 63; Interview 82.

192 REPRESENTATION: COSMOPOLITAN ELITES, DOMESTIC OTHERS

both imageries of merit and conventions of social capital continue reproducing formally discarded conventions, quietly perpetuating old hierarchies.

Cosmopolitanism as an elite aesthetic

Interviews are complex processes, in which much is revealed, concealed, and creatively reinterpreted. It is particularly challenging to get self-identifying liberals—among whom many elite diplomats explicitly counted themselves—to talk about the ways in which hierarchical thinking informs how they inhabit their social world. And yet there was one consistently revealing way—almost a sociological shortcut of sorts; one I stumbled upon by accident—to tease out an underlying sociocultural hierarchy to the internal operations of the Indian Foreign Service. No moment drew out as many beaming eyes, poised smiles, and declarations of conviction as the question: 'Would you describe yourself as a cosmopolitan?' Most diplomats, otherwise careful to weigh up their responses to the most casual of questions, enlisted themselves as committed cosmopolitans with hasty self-evidence.[269] When explicitly pushed to think of the term as a moral principle of international relations, many officers showed themselves to be dedicated but disillusioned, as the previous chapter showed. Yet when they were at liberty to understand the term as it most intuitively appeared to them and applied to themselves, what tended to follow were not discussions that conceived of cosmopolitanism as an *egalitarian ethic* at all. Rather, cosmopolitanism behaved like an *elite aesthetic*. How diplomats proceeded to divide their Service into those who were and were not classed as cosmopolitan opened up an entire rule book on the social codes of elite belonging. For, as it turns out, cosmopolitanism signalled much more—or less—than an internationalist commitment.

The cosmopolitan club

In the everyday performance of diplomatic life, one might perhaps think of cosmopolitanism as a matter of tradecraft: a diplomat is cosmopolitan by profession. Some Indian officers, however, discerned a global comparative scale: 'The Japanese are less cosmopolitan than the Indian diplomats', one Additional-Secretary evaluated, expressing a recurrent subtext of social

---

[269] Interview 7; Interview 27; Interview 37; Interview 57; Interview 59; Interview 63; Interview 42; Interview 48; Interview 55; Interview 69; Interview 70; Interview 82.

distance from other Afro-Asian diplomatic services that in theory were comrades in a struggle against Western impositions but were never, in fact, considered on par with India's worldly diplomats.[270] Drawing a similar parallel that instinctively measured another Asian nation against a cosmopolitan standard of civilization that Indian diplomats seemed to clear with greater ease, a recruit from a late 2000s batch hesitated: 'I would love to say "yes, you have to be a cosmopolitan to do well"', but then, 'you have these boorish Chinese people'—diplomats who 'drink their wine with ice'.[271] The argument about the boorish Chinese with their iced beverages is not trivial. It lays bare a deeper tension in the very notion of cosmopolitanism, as it is actually used and understood around South Block. It was a term of distinction which carried undeclared baggage: class, caste, educational privilege, family background. Cosmopolitanism, for all its world-embracing language, was not available to just anybody.

In fact, the notion that cosmopolitanism was an expression of one's place in a social hierarchy was one of its most prominent features. In these narrations, uses, and abuses of cosmopolitanism, the notion of being a cosmopolitan becomes a socially grounded 'badge of privilege'.[272] Instead of an ethic or political commitment, it presents itself, as Craig Calhoun has it, as 'a term of self-congratulation' and 'a compliment for the suave and debonair'.[273]

Cosmopolitanism had its own social code: it required knowledge of Anglophone cultural references and 'an understanding of where people are coming from when they say things', one millennial recruit felt, after half a decade deciphering this code among his more privileged colleagues.[274] Some even began the account of their cosmopolitanism by describing their lifestyles.[275] The class script for cosmopolitanism was so deeply engrained in the collective consciousness of the Foreign Service that one Hindi-speaking Joint-Secretary from rural India felt the need to qualify that he may not *look* like a cosmopolitan to me, but identified as one nonetheless, 'opinion-wise'.[276] Cosmopolitanism was aspirational—more established officers adjudicated on who qualified as cosmopolitan, while many who were still adjusting to the elite lifestyle of diplomacy worried about whether their colleagues would call them thus.[277] Even cosmopolitans' professed values—inclusion, tolerance,

---

[270] Interview 70.
[271] Interview 59.
[272] Robbins and Horta, 'Introduction', 2017, 3.
[273] Craig Calhoun, 'A Cosmopolitanism of Connections', in *Cosmopolitanisms*, ed. Bruce Robbins and Paulo Lemos Horta (New York: NYU Press, 2017), 192.
[274] Interview 65.
[275] Interview 37; Interview 73.
[276] Interview 58.
[277] Interview 55; Interview 46; Interview 52; Interview 72; Interview 76; Interview 78.

194 REPRESENTATION: COSMOPOLITAN ELITES, DOMESTIC OTHERS

respect for difference—had a class edge to them: 'Yes, I am a cosmopolitan because I don't want to live like middle-class Indians with their prejudices!', an upper-class Mumbaikar of the 1970s batches exclaimed.[278]

To the extent that these readings of cosmopolitanism had an international dimension, they signalled an internationalization of cultural class. For example, in classic Bourdieusian fashion, cosmopolitanism was a matter of taste: 'Culturally, your tastes were international, probably because the English language led you there', an instinctive outsider from the mid-1970s batches appraised.[279] 'I like foie gras better than chicken curry' was the explanation of one Francophile officer to what made her a cosmopolitan,[280] while a contemporary tied it to the importance of knowing one's wines.[281] One retired diplomat subscribed to the *Financial Times* Weekend edition— 'that's my reading, the word cosmopolitanism comes up [...] so I'm very comfortable when you ask me about cosmopolitanism'.[282] Cosmopolitanism was something to consume.

This transnational uniformity of cultural class was often presented as a move beyond the narrow-minded constraints of the nation state: 'Irrespective of a person's nationality, I get along with people who have a certain educational background and the same social references', was one Under-Secretary's explanation of her cosmopolitanism.[283] Indeed, the cosmopolitanism of the Indian Foreign Service was rooted in complex myths about the rooted and the rootless. Bourdieu himself indulged in this language, describing elite schools as breeding grounds for 'a group cut off from its local ties'.[284] However, in my interviews, an urban background and thus a very specific sociogeography was repeatedly raised as a quintessential qualifier for a pure-bred cosmopolitan.[285] At the same time, many seemed to define cosmopolitanism as a portable effortlessness of sorts, suggesting that a true cosmopolitan is 'comfortable' or 'at ease' anywhere,[286] or speaking of themselves as 'at home in the world'.[287] One is

---

[278] Interview 41.
[279] Interview 74.
[280] Interview 81.
[281] Interview 42.
[282] Interview 7.
[283] Interview 59.
[284] Bourdieu in Cohen, 'Pierre Bourdieu and International Relations', 229; Pierre Bourdieu, *The State Nobility: Elite Schools in the Field of Power* (Palo Alto: Stanford University Press, 1996).
[285] Interview 7; Interview 28; Interview 33; Interview 37; Interview 42; Interview 49; Interview 55; Interview 57; Interview 61; Interview 65; Interview 66; Interview 68; Interview 72; Interview 73; Interview 77; Interview 80; Interview 83.
[286] Interview 37; Interview 40; Interview 48; Interview 52.
[287] Interview 57.

yet again reminded of Bourdieu's remarks about 'the "natural" self-confidence, ease and authority of someone who feels authorized'.[288]

The gravitational force of the cosmopolitan aesthetic was such that it could rearrange conventional domestic hierarchies to match its own social demands. The ideal of the worldly diplomat made surprising insiders of some communities otherwise marginalized in Indian society. The highest praise from upper-caste Hindu diplomats was preserved for the tribal communities of Northeast India, who have traditionally dominated the Service's ST quota, and many of whom had attended the prestigious St Paul's Boarding School in Darjeeling and St Stephen's College in Delhi.[289] With their Anglophone education and 'beautiful English',[290] upper-caste Hindu officers celebrated their tribal colleagues as 'well-groomed'[291] and 'very presentable'[292]—and the crowning compliment: they were often 'more cosmopolitan in their outlook than many others'.[293] These Adivasi communities, many older diplomats approvingly explained, were 'not the archetype tribal you think about'[294]—evoking exoticized images of destitute communities cut off from the conventional flows of capital that defined Delhiite elite circles. No such welcome was extended to the tribal communities from states like Jharkhand or Odisha, who were less likely to have been subjected to Western missionary pedagogies, were of darker complexion than the Adivasis of the Northeast, and who, in the frank obviousness of one Hindu officer were 'not so readily suitable to the outside world'.[295] Unlike the 'creamy layer' of Dalits who were held responsible for degrading the very principle of affirmative action, 'the elite of the Northeast'[296] were never singled out for a similar charge. At the same time, even many critics of the much-maligned community of 'creamy layer' Dalits admitted that it was better, for outward diplomatic representation, to have lower-caste diplomats who had 'already been socialized into the cosmopolitan, urban world' upon entering the Service.[297]

A similar appreciation traditionally extended to the Service's few Muslim officers. Although Nehru was famously particular about ensuring appropriately senior rank to the Muslims who entered as emergency

---

[288] Bourdieu, *Distinction*, 250.
[289] Interview 7; Interview 18; Interview 20; Interview 22; Interview 27; Interview 31; Interview 43.
[290] TA/7. Also EG/18; MA/71; MSA/43.
[291] Interview 35.
[292] Interview 22.
[293] Interview 27.
[294] Interview 27.
[295] Interview 22.
[296] Interview 7.
[297] Interview 22; Also Interview 41; Interview 75.

196 REPRESENTATION: COSMOPOLITAN ELITES, DOMESTIC OTHERS

recruits,[298] he had lamented the scarcity of 'suitable Muslims' after entry regulations were formalized,[299] not least because much of the Muslim elite, which he probably would have most intuitively recognized as fitting the desired habitus, had departed for Pakistan during Partition.[300] In the absence of religious reservations or inclusion of Muslims in the original affirmative action around caste, the Service mostly attracted the '*crème de la crème* of Muslims', who were 'very warmly accepted' because 'they came from very good pedigree', one retired Muslim diplomat chronicled, almost proudly.[301] The Service may have been 'casteist and classist [...] but not communal', he continued, so 'a person like me would be easily accepted because of my class'. Social imageries are hard to shake, however. Eschewing a negative typecast of Indian Muslims as somehow less refined than their Hindu peers, these Muslim officers took great pains in our conversations to emphasize their elite education and upbringing.[302]

There was a subtext of erasure to this way of inhabiting the dominant habitus. An upper-caste diplomat from the mid-1970s batches offered her admiration of the Service's Muslims in a strange kind of compliment: 'if you met them, you would never know they are Muslim!'[303] The Muslim diplomat represents a deviation from a supposedly universal ideal, which nonetheless excludes the possibility of religious and cultural difference.[304] The way for a Muslim to perform cosmopolitanism 'correctly' involved a vanishing act of sorts: erudite, elite-educated Muslims were cherished precisely because their Otherness in Indian society was not discernible in their dominant habitus.

The cosmopolitan aesthetic also invites a conditional form of gender equality for a particular kind of female diplomat. As Iver Neumann writes of classed and gendered foreign ministries, 'in any sizeable organization, where more than one class is represented, performance of gender will meld with questions of class'.[305] Products of upper-class, upper-caste households and Anglophone education have recourse to the cultural capital provided by their primary socialization, facilitating their approximation of the cosmopolitan habitus. That is: while diplomatic practice is always gendered,[306] female officers of a

---

[298] Dutt, *With Nehru in the Foreign Office*, 18, 42.
[299] 'Oral History Transcript: Lakshmi N. Menon', 1971, 8, Oral Histories, NMML.
[300] Interview 30.
[301] Interview 7.
[302] Interview 9; Interview 53; Interview 57.
[303] Interview 52.
[304] For a discussion on the epistemic and ethical consequences of imposing a secular conception on Indian Muslims and seeing all observable difference as an unwanted expression of communalism, see Faisal Devji, 'Hindu/Muslim/Indian', *Public Culture* 5, no. 1 (1992): 2.
[305] Neumann, *At Home with the Diplomats*, 135.
[306] Aggestam and Towns, 'The Gender Turn in Diplomacy: A New Research Agenda'.

certain class and caste can secure recognition for their cosmopolitan performance in ways unavailable to female officers from disadvantaged backgrounds. 'Actually existing cosmopolitanism', then, acts as a leveller of gendered difference for privileged women, while providing a cultural rationale for the further marginalization of lower-caste, lower-class female diplomats. Understood as an elite aesthetic, cosmopolitanism accentuates processes whereby gender intersects with hierarchies of class and caste in producing diplomatic practice.

By contrast, the cultural cache of cosmopolitanism in the mythologies of Indian diplomacy also created a category of internal Others. Those without elite education or urban backgrounds were 'hemmed in' by life in foreign capitals, a Stephanian from the early 1990s batches expounded.[307] Officers who had originally pined after a position in a Home Service, and thus a domestic career in India, were often the most maladjusted: 'those who were put in the IFS were very unhappy people—in terms of lifestyle, it was even more difficult to integrate than for me', one senior diplomat from outside Delhi's Civil Service circles commiserated.[308] Some thought that the Home Services would have better suited those from rural India[309]—mirroring the logic of an indignant Ambassador Vijaya Lakshmi Pandit who in 1949 tried to transfer an addition to her staff at the India's Moscow Embassy: '[t]here must be plenty of work for her in her home Province where she will not be such a complete misfit as she is here'.[310] Those who did not speak the 'poetic' English of the Service with its 'flowery' dispatches,[311] or those with 'a heavy Indian accent',[312] were never truly part of the circle of elite cosmopolitans either.

If cosmopolitanism was supposed to transcend parochial classifications, it ought to have transcended caste—a qualifier that some liberal diplomats attached to their description of cosmopolitanism as a commitment to anti-discrimination, even if sometimes only moments before beginning their descriptions of all the various ways in which lower-caste officers failed to be sufficiently worldly.[313] A Joint-Secretary complained that OBC communities were 'by nature less cosmopolitan'[314] and a retired diplomat, in response to

---

[307] Interview 56; Also Interview 51.
[308] Interview 45.
[309] Interview 70; Interview 63.
[310] Vijaya Lakshmi Pandit, 'Letter to G.S. Bajpai', 10 November 1949, '1947–1951: Correspondence of V. L. Pandit (as Indian Ambassador to USSR) with G.S. Bajpai—Secretary General, MEA, regarding official matters', SF/55, Vijaya Lakshmi Pandit papers, NMML.
[311] Interview 49; Also Interview 58; Interview 73; Interview 77.
[312] Interview 45.
[313] Interview 38; Interview 46; Interview 55.
[314] Interview 57.

my incredulous clarification question on whether Dalits could be cosmopolitan, pronounced with a baffled self-evidence: 'of course not'.[315] The problem is the social 'suitability' of reservation recruits for life in international society, one former Foreign Secretary carefully emphasized, in order to make the point that there were no political objections against lower-caste diplomats[316]—only sociological ones. Reserved-category officers, in particular, 'did not have the confidence', as an otherwise sympathetic former Foreign Secretary argued[317]— to which one serving Dalit officer retorted that the much-discussed 'lack of confidence' among reservation recruits was fed by the stigmatization they faced from the very same diplomats telling them to be more at ease with the world.[318] In true Bourdieusian fashion, both renouncers and defenders of reservation recruits believed that they could be identified merely by observing their manner, dress, tastes, speech, and writing.[319] This is 'diagnostic work', whereby officers seek to discern the caste of colleagues through a careful reading of their habitus.[320] One officer of a 1960s batch even suggested that although the Home Services should observe reservations on moral grounds, the outward-facing nature of diplomatic work meant that those of marginalized lower-caste backgrounds ought not to become diplomats at all.[321]

The inherited aristocratic reading of diplomacy as the domain of exalted prose and cultural anecdotes also made many liberal-arts diplomats suspicious of their colleagues from the hard sciences and engineering. In the folklore of the Service's liberal arts graduates, such officers 'see the world in very binary terms',[322] and are not 'able to articulate ideas' or grasp 'broader concepts' like their liberal arts peers.[323] Liberal arts graduates, at every level of seniority, pre-emptively mourned after the Service's hallmark eloquence and breadth of historical and political awareness, threatened by the takeover of top posts by engineers and scientists.[324] Although some of these distinctions appeared overdrawn, it might be noted that the only officer to turn down an interview upon hearing what the research project sought to accomplish was a brash young officer from a top engineering college who struggled to see the

---

[315] Interview 7.
[316] Interview 9.
[317] Interview 45; Also Interview 25; Interview 35; Interview 36; Interview 41; Interview 70; Interview 85.
[318] Interview 75.
[319] Interview 7; Interview 22; Interview 24; Interview 35; Interview 63; Interview 70.
[320] Subramanian, *The Caste of Merit: Engineering Education in India*, 251.
[321] Interview 35.
[322] Interview 33.
[323] Interview 28.
[324] Interview 52; Interview 57.

purpose in something as woolly, confidently advising quantitative methods instead—an uninvited suggestion which perhaps did speak to a rather binary, dry disposition.

Since the social practices of elite sorting are hardly the standard occupation of traditional IR, Sankaran Krishna has reached to the postcolonial novel to talk about the postcolonial nation and its relationship to 'the international'. In his reading of novels by the Indian luminaries Kiran Desai, Arundhati Roy, and Amitav Ghosh, Krishna finds a literary rendition of what I call the cosmopolitan standard of civilization: characters with exposure to elite networks and cultures order the postcolonial nation and its different classes of people 'in terms of their familiarity with, and comfort within, the cultures of imperialism', so that 'their distance from or proximity to this culture becomes a metric by which people are classified as sophisticated, desirable and cosmopolitan versus provincial, unsophisticated, and anachronistic'.[325] In other words, we must ask 'how fellow citizens are graded in terms of their approximation to a desired international culture'.[326] This is precisely the kind of ranking exercise that Indian diplomats are engaged in whenever they assess one another's comportment, sartorial choices, parlance, literary refinement, culinary habits, and familiarity with upper-class mores.

Diversity as decline

The expressions of 'actually existing cosmopolitanism' illuminate why the *world-making* of Indian diplomats, explored in the previous chapter, must also be understood as *nation-making*. Imageries of international society shape and legitimate visions of social order in India, too. In a striking parallel with white anxiety about the cultural chaos that would follow decolonization, the traditional diplomatic elite has often interpreted the newfound diversity of officers inside the Service as a break-down of standards inside a once homogenous elite club. These cultural anxieties explain some of the concern over the Foreign Service's much-debated democratization. In a seemingly self-serving rationale, the traditional elites of the Service have maintained their status amidst demographic flux by leveraging the imperatives of the cosmopolitan aesthetic against less worldly colleagues. Some things you 'cannot sacrifice for the sake of democratization', as one recently retired diplomat emphasized, echoing a

[325] Krishna, 'IR and the Postcolonial Novel: Nation and Subjectivity in India', 124.
[326] Krishna, 127.

much-repeated philosophy which many, perhaps most, senior interviewees professed: democratization is also decline.[327]

In a world which does not truly abide by the egalitarian ideals of cosmopolitanism as ideal theory, cosmopolitanism as an elite aesthetic can secure officers recognition and belonging, measured against a lingering standard of civilization. Diplomacy was an inherently elitist endeavour, poorly suited for the kind of democratization the Service had been pressurized to undergo, a former Foreign Secretary from the early twenty-first century argued in a defensive tone—'in my time, "elite" wasn't a bad word'.[328] For, in the innocuous words of a retired Stephanian multilateralist: 'you cannot be a person who is not presentable' abroad.[329] International diplomacy had its own exclusions and standards, and the Indian Foreign Service was merely abiding by them.

In such a world, cosmopolitanism becomes a personalized coping mechanism or a cultural resource of sorts. We could also think of it as an audition, whereby dominant officers showcase their own compatibility with 'worldly' elite markers of distinction to win a place in the transnational hierarchies of class, race, and caste. Fulfilling the social status markers of a cosmopolitan could push one up a cultural hierarchy in the world, just as it could push less polished officers down the hierarchy back in South Block. Diplomats with the confidence of background could level some of the playing field in diplomatic encounters, the 'natural self-confidence' of an effortless cosmopolitan standing in for the international status that has often eluded India as a developing nation. This sense of entitlement has meant that 'you're not subdued' when negotiating abroad, as one Stephenian argued in his defence,[330] unwittingly echoing the arguments of Nehru and ICS veterans in an earlier time. Indeed, this is an old pattern. On Indian envoy V.S. Srinivasa Sastri's tour of Australia in the summer of 1922, the Australian Prime Minister William Hughes announced that India's bold case for independence had 'gained in weight by the eloquence and reasonableness with which it had been urged'.[331] An elite cosmopolitan aesthetic has been like an embodied social language, in which Indian diplomatic demands have been articulated to find resonance in a Western-dominated world.

---

[327] Interview 3; Also Interview 2; Interview 10; Interview 16; Interview 28; Interview 41; Interview 63; Interview 69; Rana, *Inside Diplomacy*, 284.

[328] Interview 6.

[329] Interview 23.

[330] Interview 19.

[331] Thakur, *India's First Diplomat: V.S. Srinivasa Sastri and the Making of Liberal Internationalism*, 110.

In these narratives of representation, diversity and cosmopolitanism become mutually exclusive. The diversification of the diplomatic cadre constitutes a lowering of standards which has made it harder for Indian officers to be recognized abroad as fellow members of a transnational elite. In these narrations, the inward-facing political project of creating a *representative* Service is interpreted as incompatible with the outward-facing diplomatic project of producing a *representable* one. As Sankaran Krishna writes of the character of Ambassador Rahel in Arundhati Roy's celebrated novel, *The God of Small Things*: 'the postcolonial ambassadorial class is clearly not so much a *representative* of India to the world as it is a sign to the world that some Indians' cosmopolitanism and culture are at least an equal to the best to be found in the West.'[332] Sensing they were losing the battle, ICS elders once even suggested that, in the spirit of the 'increasing tendency in most countries to widen the sector of society from which officers are recruited to the Foreign Service', India might mimic such efforts by establishing a separate branch, known today as IFS(B), so that the lower strata of Indian society could join the Ministry as stenographers and consular assistants, while being kept out of the diplomatic club.[333] In the decades since, these gate-keeping processes have become subtler—but, as conversations with diplomats at the margins of the Service suggest, they have not dissipated.

Cosmopolitanism, therefore, is a powerful metonym: it allows diplomats to approximate opinions they do not wish to express in so many words—or feel the very word 'cosmopolitanism' already encompassed. It was common, for example, to describe the process of democratizing the Service or the expansion of reservations as making the Service less cosmopolitan.[334] 'They wouldn't even know what a cosmopolitan is!', proclaimed an anguished diplomat of a late 1960s batch, decrying entrants from conservative households or provincial schools, who could not 'appreciate a wider world culture.'[335] With a nod to the imperative of effortlessness, a Delhiite Joint-Secretary lamented that owing to amendments in entry procedures, 'a lot of the people from the Delhi-cosmopolitan background are no longer getting in', meaning that 'the level of sophistication, cosmopolitanism, relaxed upper-class background' had suffered.[336]

---

[332] Krishna, 'IR and the Postcolonial Novel: Nation and Subjectivity in India', 135.

[333] T.N. Kaul, 'India's Foreign Service', n.d., Article, 'Speeches/writings by him', SN/16, T.N. Kaul papers, NMML.

[334] Interview 7; Interview 57; Interview 61.

[335] Interview 37.

[336] Interview 57.

202 REPRESENTATION: COSMOPOLITAN ELITES, DOMESTIC OTHERS

If cosmopolitanism was a metonym, it was a metonym of exclusion: it designated boundaries of belonging in international society using class markers and status signals, and then mobilized these boundaries to construct a hierarchy of cultural belonging inside the Service. A declining degree of cosmopolitanism among Indian diplomats did not mean a fading interest in universal rights or liberal tolerance but rather a decline in the social standards of comportment, taste, and lifestyle. These practices of a particular kind of elite cosmopolitanism read questions of diversity and difference very differently from the theoretical interpretations that normative theory might give us. In their quotidian exclusions, to borrow from Pratap Bhanu Mehta, they often came to 'enact the very parochialism they decry'.[337]

There is tragedy in this shrinking vision of cosmopolitanism—a term which could have propagated a practice of liberation. One young Dalit officer had imagined his life abroad as a flight to freedom. He had joined the Foreign Service because 'when you've been marginalized inside, you want to see the world outside'—'there is an escapism that comes from your personal circumstances'.[338] He had envisioned that, because 'the slice of people that you meet would qualify as elite' in his line of work, he would also be 'meeting people who are progressive'. He would encounter international society as a worldly individual, not as a member of a marginalized community. There is therefore particular cruelty in the way that dominant members of the Indian Foreign Service reproduce inaccessible and colonially tainted conceptions of belonging in international society. In marginalized spaces inside the Foreign Service itself, some were seeking to imagine the world as welcoming of difference, only to be told by their colleagues that somebody of their own social identity could never be welcomed in it. *What kind* of cosmopolitanism we envision matters, but it crucially also matters *whose* cosmopolitanism becomes dominant.

Conclusion

Born into a fragile postcoloniality that espoused Third Worldist principles of inclusion even as it measured itself against old colonial ideals of exclusion, the Indian Foreign Service has been seeking to uphold the ideals of the cleft habitus since its founding. While the first four decades were marked by the pronounced un-representativeness of the upper-class, upper-caste, elite-educated

---

[337] Pratap Bhanu Mehta, 'Cosmopolitanism and the Circle of Reason', *Political Theory* 28, no. 5 (2000): 633.
[338] Interview 71.

men who by and large constituted the diplomatic cadre, administrative changes in entry regulations in the early 1980s as well as broader societal changes brought about by the deregulation of the Indian economy and changing reservation provisions in the early 1990s have gradually rendered incoming diplomats more representative of India at large. This, in the narratives of traditional IFS elites, is a process best described as 'democratization'. In these terms, it is also a remarkable process, not least for the range of regulatory and constitutional interventions expended to allow marginalized communities a chance at diplomatic life. The project of inclusion spoke to the postcolonial promise of India's freedom struggle: it celebrated difference and rejected colonially inherited conceptions of what representatives of India ought to look like.

Yet it is also remarkable just how light the footprint of this kind of democratization has been on the cultural hierarchies of the Service. Senior positions rarely reflect the Service's changing demographics, social capital perpetuates existing hierarchies, and the ideal habitus of the Indian diplomat appears not to have yielded to demographic pressures. Conceptions of merit are tangled up with caste and gender. In fact, it seems that there has been no meaningful change in conceptions of the ideal diplomatic habitus, just in the average ability of an incoming officer to inhabit it. Demographic changes have only made the bearers of this correct habitus rarer and thus more culturally powerful.

Instead of transcending private loyalties, as political theory tells us cosmopolitanism does, 'actually existing cosmopolitanism' in the Indian diplomatic imagination is tied to class, caste, habitus, and forms of cultural capital. Self-described cosmopolitans spoke the language of diversity while engaging in practices of social exclusion, in which internal Others were marked by their inability to imbibe the cosmopolitan aesthetic. These interpretations speak to the subtle persistence of a formally by-gone imagery of international society, in which the quasi-aristocratic conventions of a white European world underpin the diplomatic habitus and old ties of social capital among a small elite can be legitimated by appeals to diplomatic convention. Indeed, India's loud postcolonial rejections of the whiteness of the European club of elite men has long enabled an exclusive club of Indian men to denounce unfair power imbalances along a global colour line, while allowing the hierarchies of caste, class, and gender to work in its favour at home. There is an inherent tension between the postcolonial drive for democratization on the one hand and the colonial inheritance of a class-connoted pursuit of elite cosmopolitanism on the other. This tension displays the deep domestic significance of how international society is envisioned at the margins of Western-dominated global order.

5

Pedagogy

Making diplomats in India

The world-making and nation-making of India's diplomacy are both predicated on the creation of the Indian diplomat in the image of these projects. Diplomatic training, therefore, assumes social significance. This training constitutes an ongoing attempt at reproducing the ideal diplomat, wedded to the demands of the cleft habitus. Its pedagogies have institutional and ideational genealogies (Chapter 2), reflect the ideas of the world that Indian diplomats believe themselves to inhabit (Chapter 3), and respond to demographic pressures (Chapter 4). They have sought to reflect the inherited social demands once born under European international society as well as the political ideals that tied the spirit of the freedom struggle to a wider culture of postcoloniality. Over the decades, they evince an evolving ambivalence about what kind of India, precisely, ought to be reflected out into the world, and what kind of world, precisely, Indian diplomats are to be taught to engage with.

As Bourdieu wrote in *The State Nobility*, 'the sociology of education lies at the foundation of a general anthropology of power and legitimacy'.[1] Education is as an instrument of legitimation and hierarchization, distinguishing insiders from outsiders and valourizing certain social features—accents and skills, particular cultural references, ways of relating to the world—over others, 'with the dominant group always having the capacity to make its particular attributes universal ones'.[2] That is, pedagogical processes tend to propagate the cultural capital and ideals of the dominant social class. This is the pedagogical crux of the Service's democratization, too, as probationers from non-traditional backgrounds have been socialized into reflecting the social ideals of the 'St Stephen's type'.

This chapter analyses underlying pedagogical patterns instead of chronicling the empirical minutiae of individual syllabi—indeed, outsiders barely have access to any of the latter. Training structures, organizational

---

[1] Bourdieu, *The State Nobility*, 5.
[2] Sapiro, 'Field Theory', 166.

Cosmopolitan Elites. Kira Huju, Oxford University Press. © Kira Huju (2023). DOI: 10.1093/oso/9780198874928.003.0006

arrangements, and academic contents expressed in the form of syllabi or mission statements are what Bourdieu, writing with Passeron, called *explicit pedagogy*—that, in essence, which is formalized into instructions and vocalized as overt aims.[3] What I focus on, by contrast, is *implicit pedagogy*—the underlying ambitions and unspoken assumptions of training. The chapter first dissects how the implicit pedagogy of IFS training reflects the ideals of the cleft habitus and seeks to reproduce officers in its image. It then asks what the 'democratization' of the Service has done to the accents of the pedagogical balancing act and shows how the relative weight assigned to different training components has shifted in reaction to the Service's changing demographic composition. From an earlier emphasis on making 'real' Indians out of suspiciously worldly elites, Indian diplomatic training now coalesces around anxieties that future diplomats may be excessively 'real' and insufficiently comfortable in the global club of cosmopolitan colleagues. These processes involve both attempts by seniors to instil a certain habitus in their youngsters and autodidactic attempts by self-professed outsiders to imbibe the ideal habitus outside official training hours.

A pedagogy of two worlds

There are some essential features to the pedagogies of Indian diplomacy that have expressed themselves in various guises and institutional arrangements. The sequencing and duration of different elements have changed over time and the training has come under pressure from significant resource and time cuts. At the same time, some elemental building blocks of training have stood in place for five decades, since the Service discontinued the practice of sending probationers to Western universities and training at the British Foreign Office in the late 1950s. A foundation course, jointly attended with probationers of the Home Services, has covered the first principles of Indian governance, economics, and politics. Field-specific academic lectures—transferred from Sapru House to the Jawaharlal Nehru University in the 1960s, and then again to a brand-new Foreign Service Institute (FSI) in 1986—have acquainted probationers with international relations, law, organizations, and diplomacy as well as India's foreign, defence and economic policy.[4] Future diplomats have

---

[3] Pierre Bourdieu and Jean Claude Passeron, *Reproduction in Education, Society and Culture (1977)* (London: Sage, 1990), 50.

[4] 'Statement from the Director of the Indian School of International Studies', 1968, 'Revised training programme for IFS probationers of 1968 batch and subsequent batches', F/Q/FSI/580/10/68, NAI;

206 PEDAGOGY: MAKING DIPLOMATS IN INDIA

also learned a language allotted to them according to their rank in the entry examination and are finally posted as Third Secretaries to Missions in countries where their language is spoken. These efforts have been complemented through learning-by-seeing as well as learning-by-doing. Brief army, navy, and air force attachments, sometimes only for a day, as well as a *Bharat Darshan* ('pilgrimage of India') tour remain part of the curriculum. A protocol attachment can send probationers to, say, an ASEAN summit, and desk attachments take place in various wings and Territorial Divisions of the Ministry at Headquarters.[5] Meanwhile, one unusual pedagogical practice, possibly unique to India, has been entirely removed. 'District training', which for about five decades saw diplomatic probationers spend between three and six months in Indian villages observing local administration, was abridged to one month in the new millennium, and discontinued in 2014[6]—to the universal dismay of older generations.[7] It sought to put in practice the ideals of a postcolonial world by imprinting on the minds of young diplomats the everyday subaltern life of India, tying their sense of representation to the imperatives of development, equality, and voice—and yet, in replicating the 'settlement training' for the ICS under the British Raj, it also reflected colonial ideals of bureaucratic pedagogy.

Whatever their pedagogical merits, however, the standardized reading lists and lectures have not left the kind of lasting imprint on probationers that those doing the training may have presumed or prayed they would. A common thread in the recollections of diplomats across generations was the dismissal of explicit teaching as a near-irrelevance, to which little attention ought to or had been heeded—instead, I was made privy to fond memories of skipping lectures in favour of a round of card games or drinks with one's new peers.[8] For many, training was about social capital: places like Mussoorie were remembered mostly for the social bonding among the future administrative elites of India, as IFS and IAS probationers in particular—always standing at

---

K.P. Misra (Dean, SIS), 'Letter to M.K. Rasgotra (Foreign Secretary)', 28 August 1982, 'Training of IFS Probationers of 1981 batch at the School of International Studies, Jawaharlal Nehru University, New Delhi', F/Q/PA II/580/16/82, NAI; D.K. Jain (Under-Secretary, FSP), 'Memorandum', 10 September 1982, 'Training of IFS probationers of 1981 batch at the School of International Studies, Jawaharlal Nehru University, New Delhi', F/Q/PA II/580/16/82, NAI; 'Reading List for IFS Probationers' Training Course', n.d., 'Training of IFS Probationers of 1981 batch at the School of International Studies, Jawaharlal Nehru University, New Delhi', F/Q/PA II/580/16/82, NAI; Rana, *Inside Diplomacy*, 286.

[5] Interview 32.

[6] Interview 12; Interview 20; Interview 22; Interview 28; Interview 32; Interview 66; Interview 68; Interview 71; Interview 74; Interview 76; Interview 83; 'Chapter on "Organisation and Administration"', (Iii) 8', 1966, 'Annual Report of the Ministry of External Affairs for the Year 1965–1966', F/Q (GA)551/132/65, NAI.

[7] Interview 35; Interview 36; Interview 37; Interview 45; Interview 48; Interview 61.

[8] Interview 25; Interview 35; Interview 38; Interview 57; Interview 61; Interview 73; Interview 74; Interview 78; Interview 80; Interview 83.

some distance from 'lesser' Services—developed ties of social capital between themselves.[9] Handwritten notes from probationers, now sat in the archives, corroborate the notion that there was some academic apathy from both sides, with future diplomats nonplussed by the intricacies of International Relations theory and academics unconvinced that probationers were worth their intellectual investment.[10] One former Dean of the FSI—a position reserved for career diplomats—sighed that he had always sensed a 'lack of faith in the institution', even by successive Deans themselves.[11] Two experts of foreign affairs recently entrusted with lecturing future diplomats reported feeling resigned and unimpressed, claiming to have lacked both resources and a captive audience.[12] Yet there is more to education than the explicit communication of standardized knowledge—indeed, it is through implicit pedagogies that the Indian diplomat is produced.

Education, Bourdieu reminds us, is about appropriation. The pedagogies of the Indian Foreign Service, like those of any institution imparting knowledge, are also about 'imposing cultural practices that it does not teach and does not even explicitly demand, but which belong to the attributes attached by status to the position it assigns [...] and the social positions to which the latter give access'.[13] With juniors 'groomed over a period of time', both during official training and the socialization that ensues within the Service, diplomats are 'moulded',[14] so that 'after a while, your outlook becomes the same'.[15] Officers are supposed to learn to 'project a certain, more or less homogenous identity'.[16] As Ambassador Badr-ud-Din Tyabji impressed on his colleagues in a letter in 1961: 'I am convinced that we shall never be able to function as efficiently as we are capable of doing, unless we have a homogenous service'.[17] Out of many came one: 'when you are abroad [...] diversity welds into one', as one officer, echoing comments from colleagues, poetically phrased it.[18] The question then becomes: who governs this unity—who disciplines diversity into an acceptable whole and defines what its dominant expression looks like?

[9] Interview 22; Interview 23; Interview 39; Interview 43; Interview 52; Interview 54; Interview 72; Interview 73, 7; Interview 74; Interview 76; Interview 80; Interview 83.

[10] Anonymous probationer, 'Handwritten Note on Training', n.d., Training of IFS Probationers of 1981 Batch at the School of International Studies, Jawaharlal Nehru University, New Delhi, F/Q/PA II/580/16/82, NAI; Jain (Under-Secretary, FSP), 'Memorandum'.

[11] Interview 45.

[12] Interview 44; Interview 64, May 2019.

[13] Bourdieu, *Distinction*, 18.

[14] Interview 16; Interview 22; Interview 36; Interview 70.

[15] Interview 22.

[16] Interview 19.

[17] Badr-ud-Din Tyabji, 'Memorandum', 17 January 1961, 'Review of the Indian Foreign Service', FSP(I)/MC/3/61, NAI.

[18] Interview 20; Similar sentiments expressed in: Interview 3; Interview 16; Interview 19.

The shared identity of Indian diplomats was to be produced by having all probationers come to embody the cleft habitus.[19] It was in the name of an imagery of an old-fashioned, European international society that commentary on etiquette training and 'social graces' repeatedly occupied the traditional elites of the Service during interviews, as they fretted over the future fates of their less elegant colleagues in the diplomatic club. Conversely, practices like the *Bharat Darshan* tour and district training were supposed to root probationers in Indian soil and instil an appreciation for the primacy of development and poverty alleviation in their roles as Indian representatives abroad. These latter pedagogical exercises spoke to a different reading of the world: one that saw diplomats as servants of the people, congruent with the stated commitment to the subaltern in whose name the Third World ought to be governed.

The inculcation of the cleft habitus is not a set process, abstracted from time and place. Rather, it reflects particular political moments, power equations, and cultural anxieties. At the founding of the Service, there was a division between those who, like K.P.S. Menon, wanted to immediately dispatch fresh recruits into British universities for 18 months, as the British Foreign Office did with its probationers, 'when the cadets' minds will be most receptive and they will be best able to assimilate the extra-curricular advantages of travel', and those who wished to organize an attachment at Headquarters first, 'on the ground that only so will the new recruits be able to acquire a basic knowledge of conditions in their own country', instead of imbibing a foreigners' conception of their own nation.[20] The contestation was about how best to produce a balanced habitus. It spoke to a dual anxiety: how should probationers be trained so that they are both attuned to the still supposedly dominant practices of European diplomacy, while also becoming propagators of a postcolonial world in which diplomatic priorities were formed closer to the ground? In various guises and with varying conceptions of the correct balance, the management of these two tendencies has structured the logic of Indian diplomatic training throughout much of its postcolonial history.

From the Raj to the Taj

The history of Indian diplomatic training began with colonial hangovers, dressed up as sober assessments of the 'realities' of global order. In one of the many administrative ironies of Indian Independence, the ICS generation

---

[19] Tyabji, *Indian Policies and Practice*, 18.
[20] 'Statement Attached to the Summary: "The Creation of an Indian Foreign Service"'.

that India had fought to rid itself of assumed charge of training postcolonial diplomats—'students of British Indian administration but teachers of the new bureaucrats'.[21] Dixit considered it an obvious outcome that IFS training was grounded in 'the conventions and practices of the late 19th century and pre-second-world-war-traditions and practices of the British imperial administration'.[22] Sketches for diplomatic training repeatedly appealed to pedagogical precedent under the British Raj.[23] With a fabricated emphasis on practicality over principle, the British diplomat C.B. Duke impressed on his Indian counterparts in 1947 that

> For training of a new entrant to the Foreign Service the most satisfactory method in practice would clearly be attachment in the earlier years of service both to the Foreign Office in London and to British missions abroad for the Indian cadet to acquire something of the tradition and technique of the Foreign Office [...] There might be at first some political agitation in India against such deputation but I think that practical and responsible Indians charged with the duties of the Government would recognise the advantages to India of this form of training, at least for about 25 to 30 years until the Indian Service and Indian missions abroad were sufficiently established to be able to undertake exclusively the training of their own young men [sic].[24]

Duke got his way, even if imperfectly: for a little over a decade after Independence, diplomatic batches were sent to the Anglophone West for training.[25] Much like ICS-training had involved a period at Oxford or Cambridge, postcolonial probationers, too, spent 18 months at a European or American university—primarily at Oxford and Cambridge in Britain or at the Fletcher School of Diplomacy at Tufts University in the US.[26] The majority of probationers, sent off to the academic epicentre of the British Raj, also attended a course run by the Commonwealth Relations Office in London, intended to familiarize future Indian diplomats with the idioms of British diplomacy and

---

[21] Mathai, *Reminiscences of the Nehru Age*, 193.
[22] Dixit, *Indian Foreign Service*, 95.
[23] H. Dayal (Under-Secretary, MEA), '"The Type of Training Required by New Entrants, Non-Officials and Officers Recruited from Various Sources"', 27 March 1946, 'Establishment of a separate Indian Foreign Service', FSP/47-2(7); Dayal, 'Qualifications to Be Prescribed for New Entrants into the Service'.
[24] Response from C.B. Duke to Shah, 'Secret Appendix to Notes: "An Indian Diplomatic Service"'.
[25] Interview 16.
[26] B.K. Kapur, 'Memorandum', 27 May 1947, 'Question of holding combined Examination for the Indian Foreign Service and All India Administrative Service in November-December Every Year. Prescription of high minimum mark at the interview for recruitment to the Indian Foreign Service', FSP/47-F/22(11), NAI; Dixit, *Indian Foreign Service*, 48.

210 PEDAGOGY: MAKING DIPLOMATS IN INDIA

the workings of the British Foreign Office.[27] One grandee of the Foreign Service, who partook in this training in the 1950s, recalled being lectured by Harold Nicolson himself.[28] The Marxist anti-imperialist in residence, High Commissioner Krishna Menon, had organized this training so as to acquaint his juniors, as Foreign Secretary Rasgotra recalled his experience, with 'the British diplomatic tradition of formal speech, lightened by an occasional touch of typical British humour'.[29]

Ministerial notes suggest that the MEA considered the time probationers spent abroad as 'invaluable for the broadening of their outlook'.[30] And yet just as, according to a 1920 British Home Department document, a primary objective of sending Indian ICS probationers to train in the UK had been 'that they may be, to put it crudely, to some extent Europeanized',[31] so too the 'broadening of outlook' during postcolonial training more accurately constituted a particular form of narrowing. Diplomatic youngsters, who would soon serve a postcolonial India in a world transformed by decolonization, post-war reconstruction, and Third World assertiveness, were socialized into anachronous imageries of an aristocratic European world. To conform to the culture of the Foreign Service in the early decades, a recruit from the late 1960s instructed, it was important to be 'conscious of the old-style grace' of the ICS.[32]

Having lost the battle on only admitting foreign-educated Indians into the Service, ICS veterans saw foreign training as a subtle substitute for a foreign degree, allowing a similar process of socialization to unfold without a comparable political backlash.[33] Notably, Indian probationers were not at these universities to follow a particular syllabus or acquire a specific corpus of knowledge—there were no examinations for them to pass, no actual training in diplomacy.[34] Instead, they would 'absorb as much as possible from the environment of Oxford', in the words of one probationer sent to Brasenose College in the late 1940s, who had spent a lot of time attending debates at the Oxford Union and browsing books at Blackwell's bookshop.[35] The idea was to 'spend a year polishing themselves at Balliol' so that they would 'speak English well, write English well' upon their return, as one Cambridge graduate from

---

[27] 'Oral History Transcript: B.K. Acharya', 1976, 10, Oral Histories, NMML; Chib, 'The Making of an Indian Diplomat'.
[28] Interview 79.
[29] Rasgotra, A Life in Diplomacy, 66.
[30] 'Statement Attached to the Summary: "The Creation of an Indian Foreign Service"'.
[31] A Home Department letter from 26.03.1920 quoted in Potter, India's Political Administrators, 116.
[32] Interview 28.
[33] Dayal, 'Qualifications to Be Prescribed for New Entrants into the Service'.
[34] Interview 16; Interview 18; Interview 31; Interview 40; Interview 79.
[35] Interview 16.

the mid-1960s batches approvingly described.[36] Tellingly, those who already held an Oxbridge degree were not usually sent back, because 'you've got that exposure and background' already, as an Oxford history graduate from the 1950s mentioned like it was the most natural decision.[37] The pedagogy of early Indian diplomatic training, then, had less to do with a body of academic or even practical knowledge than it did with acquiring the old-world graces and bearing of a Balliol man—validating the sociological adage that when it comes to educating the elites, it is often less important to learn *about* the world than to learn 'how to carry oneself *within* the world', for 'the mark of privilege, corporeal ease, is anything but easy to produce'.[38]

After the 1958 batch, the pedagogical umbilical cord was cut, officially on the grounds that it was 'expensive and of little practical value' to send probationers to foreign universities and the British Foreign Office,[39] but also because such training was 'considered unrealistic in the long run from the national point of view', it having become paramount to develop 'a wholly indigenous training programme', as the ICS-trained diplomat A.S. Chib emphasized.[40] And yet this decision did not signal a closure for an old colonial imagery of the world.[41] Recruits were still to be brought up to an internationally recognized standard of demeanour, which bore a cunning resemblance to Western diplomatic practice.[42] Such mannerisms were never an afterthought, Dixit clarified, but crucial for 'the sociological training' of Indian diplomats.[43] Ernest Satow's *Diplomatic Practice* was 'the gospel which one referred to when in doubt about procedures, functions and protocol'.[44] Against the postcolonial imperative of standing apart, diplomats believed that '[w]e must all study the etiquette with the one object of attaining smoothness of contact in the social sphere in which we work', as one Head of Mission in Cairo tutored in 1950.[45] Hoping to impart wisdom on decorum and tact from the ICS onto young diplomats in the early

[36] Interview 23.
[37] Interview 40; Also Interview 43.
[38] Shamus Rahman Khan, *Privilege: The Making of an Adolescent Elite at St. Paul's School* (Princeton and Oxford: Princeton University Press, 2012), 83.
[39] Dixit, *Indian Foreign Service*, 58.
[40] Chib, 'The Making of an Indian Diplomat'.
[41] Training at the Academy in Mussoorie also upholds a further colonial curiosity: horse riding. Preparing officers for life in remote areas, the final ICS examination had involved a riding test. Of course, if horse riding had been a mere practicality, the Academy might have settled for a simple routine to be taught to the Home Services alone. And yet, although only compulsory for the IAS, IFS officers across the decades of postcolonial Indian history have been invited to mount horses on their road to international negotiating table—to this very day, in the words of a millennial officer, 'trot, gallop, canter—all of that is still there'.
[42] Tyabji, *Indian Policies and Practice*, 18.
[43] Dixit, *Indian Foreign Service*, 92–93.
[44] Dixit, 96; Also Interview 30; Interview 48.
[45] Head of Mission of India, Cairo, 'Note Responding to Jawaharlal Nehru's Letter on Prohibition'.

212   PEDAGOGY: MAKING DIPLOMATS IN INDIA

1950s, K.P.S. Menon penned the short monograph *Do's and Don'ts in the Indian Foreign Service.*[46] Delving into the details of appropriate attire, entertainment, and official and private behaviour, the guidelines reproduced British administrative mores for the modern era, virtually untouched by postcolonial demands for Indian difference. Old diplomatic hands knew this tension was politically fraught—a letter from G.S. Bajpai to Vijaya Lakshmi Pandit on 11 May 1951 warned about the 'awkward possibilities that may flow from such a pamphlet falling into the hands of unauthorised and possibly malicious persons.'[47]

Learning the art of diplomacy meant learning to think of oneself as part of the elite. Dixit recalls the daily routines at Metcalfe House in Delhi as 'very Sahib-like', with one *chaprasi* (bearer) assigned to a pair of probationers, so that each future diplomat began their day with tea served by the bedside as though to a master of the house.[48] Saturday evenings were for formal dining, for which probationers wore the Indian equivalent of a formal suit— a black *Bandhgala* with white trousers in winter, a white *Bandhgala* with black trousers in summer. Following the Appleby and A.D. Gorewala Reports' suggestion that the Superior Civil Services train together, IFS trainees were relocated from Metcalfe House, in use since the British Raj, to the new Lal Bahadur Shastri National Academy of Administration in Mussoorie in 1959, where the foundation course has taken place ever since.[49] Here, diplomatic recruits have been initiated into protocol formalities and dining etiquette, premised on 'conventions of the West European type.'[50] Intent on impressing their seniors—eager to make 'brown young Englishmen out of us', as one sharp-tongued attendee caricatured—some youngsters resorted to enjoying their *chapatis* and *sambar* with knife and fork, too.[51] For all the talk of a break with colonial mores after the Service developed its indigenous training programme, one diplomat who trained in the mid-1970s still recalled formal dinners, with 'bearers in the Raj style.'[52]

Since the establishment of the FSI in 1986, social graces have been imparted through exposure to the supposedly luxurious lifestyle of diplomats at Delhi-ite five-star hotels, where probationers have spent anywhere from a few days to a week matching wines, sequencing spoons, memorizing vocabulary on

---

[46] Dixit, *Indian Foreign Service*, 95.
[47] Bajpai, 'Letter to Vijaya Lakshmi Pandit', 11 May 1951.
[48] Dixit, *Indian Foreign Service*, 60.
[49] Interview 40; Dixit, *Indian Foreign Service*, 59.
[50] Dixit, *Indian Foreign Service*, 60.
[51] Bandyopadhyaya, *The Making of India's Foreign Policy*, 216.
[52] Interview 7.

French cookery, and imbibing 'Western manners of behaving ourselves', as one attendee recalled of his training in the early 1990s.[53] Since the world of etiquette is as gendered as the world of diplomacy it is embedded in, some recent batches of female probationers have also undergone 'grooming sessions' at the Taj Hotel, learning, among other things, how to correctly do their eyebrows.[54] One female millennial officer from a late 2000s batch spent a whole week learning with the 'ladies of the External Affairs Spouses Association'[55]—a lesson on how to look one's best while defending India's national interest, which male probationers were not invited to.

The intangible markers of diplomatic practice—unwritten rules of social and professional conduct, a certain slant of speech, a way of carrying oneself—are also learned during Mission attachments and the first few postings, by observing one's Ambassador and seniors.[56] Indeed, the most consistent administrative trend from the 1980s onwards has been a push to shorten training in favour of more 'practice', so as to 'add more emphasis on practical training in the Missions during the probationers' first posting'.[57] Outside official training hours, senior officers are expected to take young recruits under their wings, inviting them to cocktail and dinner parties intended as dress rehearsals for international occasions.[58] One disgruntled disciple recalled his ICS superiors' interest in joining all kinds of exclusive clubs across Delhi.[59] Another remembered how, at least as late as the mid-1970s, probationers were counselled to 'make sure you get Gymkhana membership' at the exclusive Delhi club.[60] A similar imperative of fluency in the idioms of European international society came through in interviews with junior officers, too: 'It's easy to laugh about it, but there's a subtext there—it's foreign etiquette, it's not our own, but that's the global reality,' explained one millennial recruit about the need to study Western diplomatic code.[61] And yet, if this subtext was accepted as an article of diplomatic faith, it has always existed alongside a very different, if equally naturalized, need to make Indian diplomats into servants of a postcolonial subaltern.

---

[53] Interview 58; Also Interview 45; Interview 61; Interview 57.
[54] Interview 80.
[55] Interview 63.
[56] Interview 6; Interview 7; Interview 16; Interview 24; Interview 25; Interview 28; Interview 31; Interview 39; Interview 43.
[57] Jain (Under-Secretary, FSP), 'Memorandum'.
[58] Dixit, *Indian Foreign Service*, 92–93.
[59] Interview 24.
[60] Interview 29.
[61] Interview 63.

214   PEDAGOGY: MAKING DIPLOMATS IN INDIA

The Discovery of India

It is emblematic of the cleft habitus that, even as the Foreign Service was sending its probationers to the British Foreign Office for training, the same probationers would be treated to a 'pep-talk' by Krishna Menon at the Indian High Commission in London on the topic of 'what India stood for', from Non-Alignment to Third World solidarity and socialism, and were advised to join the Oxford Labour Club—for whatever Anglophilia Indians harboured, colonial history compelled that 'we hated the Tories—it was our psychology'.[62] Indeed, the troubled debates on belonging among ICS officers had taught the founders of the IFS a lesson: an independent, postcolonial identity, too, was not something to be assumed but rather to be rehearsed.

The postcolonial political commitments that underlay diplomatic pedagogy dictated that aspects of training were to 'be related to the actual needs and conditions in the country', and 'rural bias and a simpler mode of life should be encouraged', T.N. Kaul, wary of reproducing ICS culture for the postcolonial age, pleaded in 1955.[63] For, as P.N. Haksar implored six years later, a 'Foreign Service officer, unless he [sic] is firmly tethered to his own country, is likely to be a spiritual castaway', and this 'casts a heavy burden and imposes an onerous responsibility on those who are called upon to train' the possible fugitive.[64] Therefore, as Dixit explained about diplomatic training in postcolonial India, the 'new Indian diplomat was to be deeply imbued with a sense of social, economic and cultural realities of India when representing India abroad and when articulating Indian interests to foreign civil societies and foreign chancellors of the world'.[65]

Much as Nehru had written *The Discovery of India* as a kind of late introduction to the country for himself, so one purpose of diplomatic training was to 'acquaint you with India'.[66] And much as Nehru, the early batches too had often, through family and schooling, been 'completely Anglicized—they were a little cut off from India', as a rueful member of the mid-1970s batches argued.[67] 'There was no problem with the West', one such Anglicized officer of the 1960s batches offered on behalf of what he considered to be most of his peers, 'the problem was with the East'.[68] A self-professed Nehruvian, this

[62] Interview 16.
[63] Kaul, 'Letter to the Foreign Secretary'.
[64] Haksar, 'Memo'.
[65] Dixit, *Indian Foreign Service*, 48.
[66] Interview 3.
[67] Interview 69.
[68] Interview 43.

officer had christened himself 'a coconut: brown on the outside, white on the inside'. The postcolonial insistence on acquainting officers with the country they would go on to serve was also an appeal to Indian 'authenticity' and Third World difference, once suppressed under the Raj and the homogenizing imperatives of the colonial standard of civilization.

The lectures at Mussoorie spoke to a very particular reading of postcoloniality, Indian priorities, and its place in the world. Lessons on Indian history, law, economic policy, culture, and public administration were complemented with sessions on 'Gandhian philosophy' and the evolution of modern India 'as a democratic, secular and welfare state'.[69] Thus, even as the language of Indian postcoloniality suggests liberation from imposed standards, it has also itself been a hegemonic discourse with its own truisms and heresies. 'You learn the same things, so you also think the same way' afterwards, as one self-ascribed free-thinker and Additional-Secretary snickered, in a thinly veiled critique of the continued reproduction of socialist vocabulary even as the Government's official economic philosophies were evolving.[70] One particularly disaffected mid-career officer from the late-1990s branded it, more bluntly, a 'brainwash syllabus'.[71] At the same time, for those of a more radical persuasion, Mussoorie was a process of 'de-schooling' which ushered probationers from their youthful rebellion into 'sophisticated mediocracy' by 'restructuring your mindset; that you are a government man', as one retired sociology-major-turned-diplomat with Marxist sympathies explained with a mischievous smile.[72]

The two most cogent elements of the diplomatic Discovery of India were the *Bharat Darshan* tour and district training. While it was 'a common complaint against Civil Service in general [...] that they fail to respond to social and other developments in the country', as the 1966 Pillai Committee Report noted, 'the specific criticism against the Foreign Service is that its officers tend progressively to lose contact with developments in India in the economic, social and cultural fields, spending as they do so much of their working life abroad out of personal contact with our people'.[73]

---

[69] 'Outline of the Syllabus for the Foundational Course', 1968, 'Revised training programme for IFS probationers of 1968 batch and subsequent batches', F/Q/FSI/580/10/68, NAI; Also 'Training of IFS Probationers of 1970 Batch at the National Academy of Administration, Mussoorie', 1970, F/Q/FSI/580/9/70.

[70] Interview 70.

[71] Interview 83.

[72] Interview 54.

[73] 'Summary: "Bharat Darshan Tours"', 1966 Pillai Committee Report', 1967, Paragraph 157, 'Pillai Committee Report—Recommendations regarding Bharat Darshan Tours', F/Q GA)792(27)–67, NAI.

Bharat Darshan pre-empts this alienation.[74] An all-India tour completed in small groups for up to 15 days,[75] it offers probationers 'a bird's eye view of India by taking them to different parts of the country to see a few places of outstanding historical and cultural interest, representative of India's rich heritage, and some of our foremost industrial plants and scientific institutions'.[76] One tour could stretch from the High Altitude Warfare School in Srinagar, Kashmir, to the Meenakshi Temple in Madurai and the Thumba Rocket Launching Centre in Kerala's Trivandrum.[77] The charm of *Bharat Darshan* was built on 'the beauty of the monuments' and the 'great technological achievements'.[78] Undertaken on trains with separate compartments for probationers, it shows future diplomats 'the rich India, not the actual India'—'a very luxurious kind of thing', in the words of one millennial recruit, which 'makes you want to represent the good part of India'.[79]

As though reading off the same script, diplomats of all generations declared that *Bharat Darshan* was about being exposed to and coming to treasure the exceptional diversity of India[80]—even if one was supposed to emerge from the exercise with a concomitant appreciation for the 'great underlying unity which the foreign observer often misses'.[81] 'Psychologically and subconsciously, it encouraged this business of unity in diversity', as one tourer of the 1960s put it.[82] A millennial sceptic conceded it was a 'great narrative: you go around India, you see the diversity, you are of a piece'.[83] As such, a fellow sceptic and Under-Secretary explained, *Bharat Darshan's* notions of unity-in-diversity were 'part of the mythology of the Service you grow up with'.[84]

District training, by sending probationers to administrative districts in villages across the country, showed probationers the 'other' India. For Bourdieu, the goal of education is always a kind of 'cultural appropriation' of the

---

[74] Officers embarking on new foreign assignments are invited on another *Bharat Darshan* tour, which concentrates on sites of pertinence to the bilateral relationship or field of expertise in question, and involves meeting with representatives of state governments, business chambers or scientific centres. Badr-ud-Din Tyabji, 'Note', 2 March 1961, 'Criteria for Bharat Darshan Tours', F/21(3) GA/61, NAI; Rana, *The Contemporary Embassy*, 56.

[75] Interview 1; Interview 3; Interview 20; 'Note', 10 March 1961, 'Criteria for Bharat Darshan Tours', F/21(3) GA/61, NAI.

[76] 'Summary: "Bharat Darshan Tours", 1966 Pillai Committee Report', Paragraph 321.

[77] 'Bharat Darshan Tour Programme of Indian Foreign Service Probationers of 1981 Batch: September–October 1982', 4 October 1982, 'Bharat Darshan of 1981 Batch of IFS Probationers', F/Q/PA II/580/22/82, NAI.

[78] Interview 37.

[79] Interview 80.

[80] Interview 1; Interview 3; Interview 4; Interview 12; Interview 22; Interview 24.

[81] Interview 4.

[82] Interview 35.

[83] Interview 71.

[84] Interview 59.

tastes and habits of the dominant classes by those of non-dominant classes.[85] The philosophy of district training turns Bourdieu on his head, even if only for a few months: district training is a performative attempt at imbibing the habits and ambitions of the subaltern classes by members of more dominant classes. The anticipated process of all-Indian identity formation would solve the representational challenges of the elitist diplomatic corps: the project was one of making future diplomats 'more representative of their nation than they were' in actuality.[86] Authenticity was to be artificially manufactured.[87]

Preparing local authorities for the arrival of diplomatic probationers, the MEA instructed in 1974 that the 'training in the districts is meant to give them an idea of how the country is run at District level, the problems of the rural population and of the varied aspects of development activities in the country to enable them to project a proper image of India abroad', on which probationers were expected to compose fortnightly reports to Headquarters.[88] In the company of a District Collector or an Organizer for Tribal and Dalit Welfare, probationers toured development projects and met with Directors of Agriculture, divisional engineers, district judges, and forest conservators to discuss local projects and development challenges.[89] A *Model Programme for the District Training of IFS Probationers,* released by the MEA in 1967, explains that a probationer was 'encouraged to associate himself [sic] with the local scene [...] become a member of the local club, join cultural institutions, attend functions of organisations such as the Rotary, the Lions International, or the local college', as well as 'be introduced to the leading private citizens and engage in discussions with local MLAs so that his [sic] knowledge goes beyond

---

[85] Bourdieu, *Distinction*, 15.

[86] Tharoor, *Reasons of State*, 175.

[87] In fact, there sometimes is an air of quiet desperation to these pedagogies aimed at imbibing some subaltern spirit that could be recognized by 'the people' if they ever were witness to its diplomatic manifestations. One is reminded of Rosalind O'Hanlon's remark on elites seeking to do popular politics across South Asia: 'this consuming ideological imperative makes it intolerable for us to accept publicly that we cannot appropriate the masses to our projects, that there may be only silence where their own authentic voices should be raised in our support'. Rosalind O'Hanlon, 'Recovering the Subject: Subaltern Studies and Histories of Resistance in Colonial South Asia', *Modern Asian Studies* 22, no. 1 (February 1988): 195.

[88] Surendra Sinh Alirajpur (MEA), 'Letter to V.S. Mathews (Development Commissioner for the Government of Orissa, IAS)', 7 January 1974, 'District Training of IFS Probationers of the 1974 Batch', F/Q/PA II/580/16/74, NAI.

[89] Vinay Shanker (Collector, Jabalpur, IAS), 'Training of Shri J.S. Pande, Indian Foreign Service (Probationer) in Jabalpur District', 10 March 1974, 'District Training of IFS Probationers of the 1974 Batch', F/Q/PA II/580/16/74, NAI; M.D. Ashthana (Deputy Commissioner, Sonepat, IAS), 'Training Programme of Shri V.S. Verma, IFS Probationer, from 3rd March, 1975 to 25th May, 1975', 29 March 1974, 'District Training of IFS Probationers of the 1974 Batch', F/Q/PA II/580/16/74, NAI.

218   PEDAGOGY: MAKING DIPLOMATS IN INDIA

mechanism of administration and he [sic] understands the broad administrative objectives in our new socio-political set-up.'[90] Probationers learned about irrigation methods, co-operative banking, and animal husbandry,[91] and visited minority settlements to 'observe their social, religious and other customs.'[92] One interviewee recalled staying with a tribal community in a Bihari forest for three days.[93]

One element of district training was epistemic: 'If you don't know your own country, you can hardly represent it' was a popular interpretation among diplomats of all generations.[94] Sheer geographical reach made it impossible for one Indian to grasp the full breath of experiences that made up the nation, which is also why the original convention was for probationers to travel as far away from their home state as possible, from Bihar to Tamil Nadu and from West Bengal to Rajasthan.[95] They would discover how rural India looked upon the administration,[96] but also how the administrator looked upon India: district training sought to 'align your thoughts in a manner that [a district bureaucrat] could recognize.'[97] These 'babus' among whom 'structures, status and hierarchy' mattered greatly, were reportedly very different from South Block inhabitants, who in their own telling were disinvested from traditional forms of status.[98] If there is any truth to this claim, it might be because young probationers longed for recognition not from fellow bureaucrats in the districts but diplomatic counterparts abroad.

District training also made implicit ontological claims about 'real' India. Probationers had apparently grown up in an India that only existed in their heads; earnest comments about exposure to 'the Indian reality' were common in interviews.[99] One former Foreign Secretary, when lecturing youngsters during training, used to remind them of a shared origin story: most of them were

---

[90] 'Model Programme for the District Training of IFS Probationers', 1967, Reports of District training by the IFS probationers of 1967 batch, F/Q/FSI/580/5/68, NAI.

[91] Government of Tamil Nadu, 'Memorandum Regarding the Training of Three IFS Probationers in Tamil Nadu', 2 February 1974, 'District Training of IFS Probationers of the 1974 Batch', F/Q/PA II/580/16/74, NAI.

[92] R.N. Vaidya (Collector, Raipur, IAS), 'Training Programme of Shri Deepak Ray, IFS Probationer in Raipur District', 11 March 1975, 'District Training of IFS Probationers of the 1974 Batch', F/Q/PA II/580/16/74, NAI.

[93] Interview 67.

[94] Interview 46; Also Interview 1; Interview 20; Interview 25; Interview 67.

[95] Interview 20; Interview 27; Interview 35; Interview 24.

[96] Interview 12; Interview 14; Interview 24; Interview 26; Interview 27; Interview 41; Interview 62, May 2019; Interview 72; Interview 74.

[97] Interview 72.

[98] Interview 71.

[99] Interview 9; Interview 19; Interview 20; Interview 29, 29; Interview 37; Interview 46; Interview 68.

only a few generations away from the village.[100] It was 'important that you are connected to the roots', one Under-Secretary explained, even if they were not technically one's own.[101] Wherever the probationer was sent should be a 'representative village, which is neither too big or [sic] too small, neither too rich or [sic] poverty-stricken',[102] as one ministerial instruction from 1974 advised, as though the essence of 'real' India could be adjudicated by calculating a perfect median of all different possible Indias. The discovery of this newfound Indian reality had to be supervised, lest it be completed incorrectly: 'On return from Bastar, the Probationer should report to the Development Asst. to Collector. He will then have an opportunity to correct and balance his impressions', read the programme for probationer Deepak Ray, training under the Collector for Raipur in 1974.[103] Real postcolonial India, itself, was a carefully curated construct.

Somewhat ironically, district training was in fact 'a hangover from ICS days',[104] which after Independence was continued according to 'the British pattern',[105] as retired diplomats readily conceded. Even the term 'District Collector', still in use in the IAS, was 'a name that came down to us from the British'.[106] During ICS 'settlement training', the probationer was 'taught what his behaviour should be, how he should acquaint himself with the culture, customs, desires and difficulties of the people in the villages'—in other words, as B.K. Nehru affirmed in his retirement, 'to know the people by living among them'.[107] In fact, the pedagogical irony of postcolonial diplomacy was that, whatever charges of distance were levelled against ICS-trained diplomats, 'the older group of ICS officers had the advantage of having served in the country for a number of years before going into the Foreign Service' following Independence, and so they, unlike many of their equally privileged juniors, 'were able to project India abroad with full knowledge of the internal conditions of the country'.[108] District training was an attempt to make up for this curious chasm, whereby colonially trained officers could claim to grasp the ground realities better than the newly minted representatives of postcolonial India.

---

[100] Interview 6.
[101] Interview 72.
[102] Vaidya (Collector, Raipur, IAS), 'Training Programme of Shri Deepak Ray, IFS Probationer in Raipur District'.
[103] Vaidya (Collector, Raipur, IAS).
[104] Interview 37.
[105] Interview 79.
[106] Interview 36.
[107] Nehru, 'The Civil Service in Transition'.
[108] Kaul, 'Note'.

220   PEDAGOGY: MAKING DIPLOMATS IN INDIA

Yet the philosophy of district training was also not without precedent in Indian nationalist thought. The confidence that geographical proximity and rural living could reshape elite identities had driven Gandhi to order that Indian National Congress annual sessions be held in villages, so the 'rural problems most vital for India would surround the Congress delegates and keep them aware of their purpose'.[109] Inspired by Gandhi's example, Vijaya Lakshmi Pandit in her memoirs repurposed the project for the global stage, musing on the idea of holding UN summits in impoverished Third World villages to recenter diplomatic minds.[110] On this point, the imperialists and anti-imperialists believed the same thing: the Indian elite could merge with 'the people' in whose name it ordered the world by temporarily living among them.

Paying homage to this premise, many officers sought to convince me that their encounters with rural, often poverty-stricken India had shaped how they came to think of their roles as diplomats.[111] One officer with an extended resume of multilateral postings had, he believed, been driven to work on the UN Sustainable Development Goals because of his time in the districts;[112] a former Foreign Secretary had deduced from district training the importance of Third World solidary in the face of poverty—a realization which had 'stood us in good step' around international negotiation tables.[113] Diplomacy was not about 'smoke-filled rooms'; from trade to climate, 'foreign policy has to be relevant to the social problems' of India, 'taking into account the interests of the people'.[114] If Indian diplomats vied to belong among the international elite, they believed themselves to be doing so in the name of a symbolic subaltern.

And yet the postcolonial creation of India was always a backbreaking political project, not a matter of animating some dormant sense of oneness. Sometimes probationers were stranded in a state whose language they did not speak, leaving them to fend for themselves in English (not known for its vernacular reach) or Hindi—which especially in the South could lead to charges of creeping language imperialism, with one particularly awkward stay in Tamil Nadu in the 1960s coinciding with anti-Hindi riots that lasted all throughout the district training period.[115] For all the emotive investment in empathizing with the lived experience of India's downtrodden, there are pedagogical limits

[109] Pandit, *The Scope of Happiness*, 219.
[110] Pandit, 219.
[111] Interview 28; Interview 36; Interview 48.
[112] Interview 27.
[113] Interview 48.
[114] Interview 48.
[115] Alok Prasad (IFS probationer), 'Letter to the Under-Secretary of PA Section, MEA', 22 January 1974, 'District Training of IFS Probationers of the 1974 Batch', F/Q/PA II/580/16/74, NAI; Interview 20; Interview 35.

to the practice of seasonal solidarity in the districts. The everyday indignities of poverty cannot be grasped by spending some months in a village, as a former Foreign Secretary wary of Nehru's sometimes performative Third Worldism pointed out.[116] After all, these future diplomats knew that they were about to become 'part of a profession that would never be forced to live in a tribal block'.[117]

Even worse, a self-conscious millennial cringed, 'you feel like a brown *saheb* touring around', the performativity of newfound rootedness only accentuating the distance.[118] Some officers from more disadvantaged backgrounds were sceptical that their privileged peers actually 'made a serious effort to change their perspective'[119]—decades of socialization could not be unwound in a matter of months. For many well-meaning officers from privileged households, a kind of homegrown self-orientalization of India seemed to colour their experience. One keen former participant of district training—an urbanite Stephanian—reported with an earnest expression of respect that the lesson he had learned was that 'you don't need much to live', and that in some parts of India, there was 'no need for civilization'.[120] The standard of civilization conditioned his own world but not that of the far-removed realities of India's exotically rural idyll, benignly left untouched by modernity. In fact, the Foreign Service seems to have displayed more anxiety about officers' ability to belong among an elite, Europeanized club of diplomats than about their ability to signal subaltern allegiance. As Shashi Tharoor, the quintessential prototype of the Anglophile Indian elite, chided in his doctoral dissertation in 1982: 'six months in the Indian countryside did not compensate for poor grounding in foreign life and customs'.[121]

Whatever 'Indianness' diplomatic training sought to instil in probationers was an Indianness of a very amorphous kind. The postcolonial compromise on Indian identity, scarred by Partition and shaped by Nehruvian renditions of secularism and liberalism, had relied on a purposefully ambiguous definition of what a postcolonial Indianness might actually involve. There was no one India, no true essence. This is why it had been a crucial tenet of district training and *Bharat Darshan* to expose future diplomats to as alien a part of India as possible. Diplomats repeatedly described their training as ensuring that future officers would be 'aware that you are representing a country that is very,

---

[116] Interview 39.
[117] Interview 27.
[118] Interview 71.
[119] Interview 49.
[120] Interview 27.
[121] Tharoor, *Reasons of State*, 175.

222 PEDAGOGY: MAKING DIPLOMATS IN INDIA

very diverse'[122] by 'exposing people to the diversity of India'[123] Even as many academic lessons eluded young probationers, they would 'have a concept of diversity'[124] Whatever the pathologies around 'authenticity', they were always expressed in a permissive plural. This, as the discussion of Hindu nationalist pedagogies will show in Chapter 6, is not the only way to express belonging in a postcolonial order founded on difference.

Democratization and its discontents

The democratization of the Foreign Service has shifted the burden of pedagogical proof. Once suspected of failing to bridge the cleft because they were unmoored from 'the people' of the Third World, probationers today find themselves defending their credentials as members of a sophisticated, worldly elite. The training of Indian diplomats, once insistent on rooting probationers deeper in Indian soil, has become more about ensuring that 'even' those from 'rural India' and 'deprived communities' can be made into 'excellent projectors of Indian culture', as one recently retired officer affirmed, the self-evidence in her voice suggesting that this culture had not been theirs before.[125]

Even if, as one Dean of the FSI emphasized in veiled defiance of the Service's elitist reputation, 'diplomats are made, not born',[126] who they were born as matters for how they are made. As Deepak Nair has observed, much of the work done under the IR rubric of 'international practice theory' is focused on the secondary socialization of practitioners—diplomats developing a generic 'diplomatic habitus'—while little is said of the kinds of formative environments, experiences, and early impressions that make up primary socialization.[127] The familial and educational environments that officers grew up in matter greatly for the kinds of diplomats they will grow into. One recently retired diplomat, looking at me as though he was formulating an open secret, referred to the undiminished utility of 'family-type training'—training that the more representative cohorts would have been in desperate need of.[128] Even if everybody has met the same official criteria to gain entry into the Service, 'the contacts you have had, the readings you have done growing up' distinguish you

[122] Interview 48.
[123] Interview 19.
[124] Interview 20.
[125] Interview 81.
[126] Interview 32.
[127] Nair, 'Saving Face in Diplomacy: A Political Sociology of Face-to-Face Interactions in the Association of Southeast Asian Nations', 675.
[128] Interview 67.

from your colleagues, posited one millennial officer who had grown up with neither.[129] 'Democratization' was a worthwhile ideal for a postcolonial Service, but it brought with it a set of cultural anxieties that constitute a pedagogical turn in Indian diplomacy.

To the manner born

Preparing to take their UPSC exams, traditional diplomats of older generations were often persuaded by those around them that their resumes of Anglophone elite schooling and a pair of urban professionals for parents made them better fits for the Foreign Service than for any of the Home Services, with their vulgar power games and disregard for the sophisticated art of persuasion.[130] They would grow more naturally into their roles than others, not because of an innate talent for international negotiation but because of their inherited endowment of cultural capital. One senior Stephanian considered diplomacy a 'natural' choice for somebody like himself[131]—a Cambridge graduate of English literature—although officially, of course, such biographical anecdotes were not supposed to matter in the bold new world under creation in postcolonial India.

Habitus first becomes inculcated in childhood, as children of the upper classes—and the upper castes—not only 'derive from their background of origin habits, skills, and attitudes which serve them directly in their scholastic tasks, but they also inherit from it knowledge and know-how, tastes, and a "good taste" whose scholastic profitability is no less certain for being indirect', Bourdieu believed.[132] Diplomats who seemed to most effortlessly fit the old-school European trope of a suave, eloquent envoy spoke of their parents sitting them down as children for BBC News to perfect their English elocution, growing up around copies of the *Times Literary Supplement* scattered around their living rooms, or discovering *Esprit de Corps,* a 1957 Wodehouse-like novel about the follies of diplomatic life by Indian-born British diplomat Lawrence Durrell, at the tender age of 11 in a household led by two 'big history buffs'.[133] These children were at home among a domestic elite that existed in

---

[129] Interview 65.

[130] Interview 7; Interview 9; Interview 10; Interview 28; Interview 29; Interview 35; Interview 37; Interview 39; Interview 50; Interview 52; Interview 57; Interview 67; Interview 40; Interview 70; Interview 79.

[131] Interview 23.

[132] Pierre Bourdieu and Jean Claude Passeron, *The Inheritors: French Students and Their Relation to Culture* (Chicago: University of Chicago Press, 1979), 13.

[133] Interview 12; Interview 35; Interview 52; Interview 56.

India but could present itself as compatible with a 'worldly' elite made in the image of Europe.

It was this inculcation that later made the offspring of privileged milieus a good 'fit' in the elite institutions educating them. Certain schools 'inculcated' ways of behaviour, dress, and basic norms 'since you were four'—'normal public-school traits which you used to get from Harrow and Eton', as one beneficiary of such institutions from an early 1970s batch outlined with a pride that suggested that such an education could only be considered a benign advantage that saved the Service a lot of pedagogical trouble further down the line.[134] Most iconic among such institutions was the Doon School, an all-boys boarding school in Dehradun modelled on Eton, where—as its alumni reminisced with palpable fondness—practice in public speaking, extracurricular exercises like writing, debating, and acting, as well as talks from visiting ambassadors from across the world were gently rearing a generation of future elites, secluded amidst the mountains of Uttarakhand and among their own social class.[135] 'Following the maxim of the elites', who had a notion of public service and the familial funds to frown upon the open pursuit of wealth, 'the brightest went to the Foreign Service', explained a prominent alumnus—bringing with them 'a very superior conception of ourselves' which provoked those who were not themselves 'Doon School boys'.[136]

In *Dominance without Hegemony: History and Power in Colonial India*, Ranajit Guha observed that by the last quarter of the nineteenth century, education had established itself as 'the most distinctive aspect of Westernization in our culture'.[137] In this pedagogical environment, 'what most of the first beneficiaries of education imbibed from it as a code of culture was a superficial Anglicism amounting to a mimicry of the vigorous liberalism of metropolitan England'.[138] Probationers who had studied at Oxbridge were perceived by their peers as more worldly than their Indian-educated colleagues and were sometimes mimicked to reportedly comical effect.[139] Yet education in India could impart such manners and ideals with equal ardour, as products of elite boarding schools and selective colleges named after Christian saints found upon reaching Western universities. In a phrase repeated across

---

[134] Interview 33.
[135] Interview 37; Interview 40; Interview 43; Interview 79.
[136] Interview 43.
[137] Guha, *Dominance without Hegemony*, 167.
[138] Guha, 167.
[139] Interview 17; Interview 43.

several conversations, there was a 'natural transition' from St Xavier's College in Mumbai to Oxford, from St Stephen's College in Delhi to Cambridge.[140]

Much like their predecessors in the ICS, the Stephenians who dominated the culture of the IFS, too, were mostly liberal arts graduates.[141] They, too, cultivated a belief in the supremacy of the liberal arts, staying true to the definition from classical antiquity which defined as liberal arts all those subjects which were required for a person to be a worthy participant in public life.[142] One young liberal arts graduate believed her kind to 'have a head-start' over pedantic engineers and scientists, for whom diplomacy is a problem to be solved rather than a complex web of meanings to be managed and marvelled at.[143] The 'peer pressure' at colleges like St Stephen's—'Have you read Orwell? Have you read Huxley? Have you read Fanon?'[144]—prepared future diplomats for a world in which the Western canon still constituted a common frame of reference but in which postcolonial readings were also *en vogue*. 'We were very well groomed to understand issues', concluded one proud alumnus of the 1960s.[145] Liberal arts graduates, with Stephenians at the helm, felt 'at home' rather than 'out of place' during training, as Bourdieu might have read them:[146] they were entering an institution moulded, in many ways, in their image. In fact, with their wild overrepresentation in Government Services, 'Mussoorie was like an extension of St Stephen's College', an alumnus rejoiced.[147]

The pedagogies of elite belonging functioned as a social sieve, signalling to privileged probationers that they had arrived among their own.[148] Others, a self-described outsider contrasted, were 'worried about how they will cope with diplomatic entertaining', because 'their families are not used to that kind of lifestyle'.[149] Indeed, there may have been little need to teach etiquette to those who had enjoyed 'family-type training' or the formative experience of Convent Schools and urban liberal arts colleges, because 'we all came from a pretty homogenous class'[150] and 'our background being what it is, about forks and knives and all, we knew'.[151] There would be no need for English lessons—or

---

[140] Interview 9; Interview 31; Interview 43.
[141] Interview 57.
[142] Ernst Robert Curtius, *European Literature and the Latin Middle Ages (1948)*, trans. Willard R. Trask (Princeton: Princeton University Press, 1973), 37.
[143] Interview 82.
[144] Interview 33.
[145] Interview 10.
[146] Bourdieu and Passeron, *The Inheritors*, 13–14.
[147] Interview 43.
[148] Interview 74.
[149] Interview 51.
[150] Interview 6.
[151] Interview 35.

226 PEDAGOGY: MAKING DIPLOMATS IN INDIA

often, as retired diplomats liberally quoting works in the 'lingua franca of the diplomatic world'[152] exhibited, even French classes.[153] Indeed, 'the fragrance of French permeated our Foreign Service' in arguable disproportion to its professional payoff—in 1980, the Service had 70 French speakers, almost twice the figure for Arabic and more than three times that for Chinese.[154]

Instead, such probationers required pedagogical chastening and, if anything, some counterbalancing of just how deeply comfortable they were in the dated conventions of an elite, white European world. The figure of a young probationer steeped in Western culture but not equally conversant in Indian history, literature, and art has haunted pedagogical debates in the Foreign Service since its founding.[155] Ambassador K.M. Panikkar, representing the IFS on the UPSC Selection Board, echoed Nehru's lament about probationers' disproportionate comfort with European history and thought when he suggested that the Service run an intensive training course intended to impart a sense of both Indian and pan-Asian identity on future diplomats.[156]

District training, too, took on such elevated relevance precisely because of the social make-up of the early cadres. The products of urban milieus, upper-class households, and elite education would need a crash course on how to represent a developing, rural nation.[157] 'Since most of such officers come from urban backgrounds', as one apologetic diplomat explained in a ministerial letter to his IAS colleague in 1982, they would need to be taught what most Indians instinctively knew about the villages in which the majority of them had once lived.[158] So revelatory was district training for the sheltered recruits of the Foreign Service that many considered their months in the villages the most formative spell of their training.[159] Convinced that their elite education had endowed them with an understanding of the world that ordinary Indians could never match, probationers were met in the districts by District Collectors who were convinced that 'these guys don't know anything about India', as

---

[152] Interview 52.

[153] Interview 6; Interview 37; Interview 41; Interview 52; Interview 51.

[154] Raman, *Indian Diplomatic Service*, 27.

[155] 'Circular Letters Issued by N.R. Pillai Chairman, IFS Committee, B.K. Nehru, Foreign Secretary and Other Papers Relating to ICS/IFS Services Matters', 1966, SF/14, T.N. Kaul papers, NMML; 'Oral History Transcript: B.K. Acharya', 10; Dixit, *Indian Foreign Service*, 53–55; Rana, *Inside Diplomacy*, 40.

[156] Dixit, *Indian Foreign Service*, 55.

[157] Interview 4; Interview 12; Interview 19; Interview 29; Interview 31; Interview 36; Interview 41; Interview 48; Interview 54; Interview 63; Interview 66.

[158] C. Narayanaswamy (IFS), 'Letter to I.J.S. Khurana (Collector in Koraput, IAS)', 20 October 1982, 'District Training of IFS of 1982 Batch', F/Q/PA II/580/25/82, NAI.

[159] Interview 1; Interview 9; Interview 26; Interview 27; Interview 46; Interview 36; Interview 48; Interview 41; Interview 72.

one self-effacing officer of a 1970s batch recalled.[160] These District Collectors would not have been entirely wrong, some diplomats conceded, since many harboured 'a lot of prejudice about what other Indians are like'.[161] Bureaucrats in the Home Services saw their colleagues in the Foreign Service as prodigal sons 'sheltered from the hurly-burly of Indian life in the districts',[162] thinking they could 'reconnect with who you are' by returning to what were supposed to be their roots under government supervision.[163] It was, in other words, precisely because of the elite character of early diplomatic batches that Indian diplomatic pedagogies developed such a strong anti-elite tone.

Democratization as appropriation

With the push for democratization came very different kinds of cohorts, and along with them, very different pedagogical challenges. Although it coincided with a personnel crunch during which training was condensed across the board, the cancellation of district training for diplomatic probationers in 2014 also told of a milestone: with many more probationers joining the Service from India's peripheries, district training had, for much of the batch, rendered itself pedagogically obsolete.[164] A rising star of the late-1990s batches conceded that much of his training would probably have felt superfluous 'if you are in Delhi, your father is a diplomat, your sister is in the IAS', but pointed out, with some understated defiance, that diplomatic training was no longer built around the needs of the Delhi elite.[165]

As the cadres have become more representative of India at large, the question of representability has come to occupy the Service's traditional elites. The newly 'uneven' quality of officers, one former Grade I diplomat phrased with a pregnant pause—presumably to let the various meanings of the word register—exerts a different kind of 'pressure on training'.[166] In the words of a former Dean of the FSI, the 'dilution of competence' had to be rectified before probationers became diplomats.[167] It was easy to celebrate democratization,

---

[160] Interview 22.
[161] Interview 45.
[162] Interview 10.
[163] Interview 1.
[164] Interview 12; Interview 24; Interview 32; Interview 61; Interview 65; Interview 66; Interview 74; Interview 78; Interview 83.
[165] Interview 83.
[166] Interview 36.
[167] Interview 30.

228   PEDAGOGY: MAKING DIPLOMATS IN INDIA

a self-ascribed liberal now in retirement admonished—'but then you have to train them'.[168]

The pedagogical imperatives most eagerly discussed among the elites of the Foreign Service today demarcate clear boundaries to the project of producing Indian diplomats for a postcolonial world, supposedly marked by its celebration of the subaltern and its disregard for the undemocratic mores of the old regime. The linguistic leverage endowed on the Foreign Service through colonial rule and its Anglophile elites has always dictated that it was imperative not only to speak English, as one recently retired Ambassador emphatically specified, but to '*think* in that language, *dream* in that language'.[169] The need for diplomats to be 'articulate' was repeatedly emphasized in interviews with the sort of vehemence that suggested that the term conveyed a much wider set of cultural demands than the mere ability to formulate arguments with care.[170] It has therefore been with subdued horror that India's traditionally dominant diplomatic elites have witnessed a deterioration in the English skills of their juniors, often schooled in Hindi Mediums rather than at English Convent Schools.[171] The stigma around poor English has been such that the optional after-hours English training guardedly introduced at the FSI has met with indignation from those who have been asked to attend it.[172]

Yet it is not only the technicalities of language that concern the Foreign Service elite but rather the conceptions of the world that language gives expression to. The entire worldview endowed by a liberal arts education has been felt to be at stake. Socializing the ever-growing constituencies of engineers, in particular, has been understood by historically dominant liberal arts graduates as an exercise in intellectual damage control.[173] 'We were actually at a loss for what diplomacy was all about', admitted one serving officer with an engineering degree, touching on one of the peculiar challenges of Indian diplomatic training: the Service attracts officers who may never have engaged with foreign affairs at all.[174] Engineers (who often seem to stand as placeholders for all kinds of non-liberal arts entrants in the imaginations of liberal arts graduates) lack 'a sense of international history'[175] and struggle to 'imbibe the language

---

[168] Interview 52; Also Interview 5; Interview 6; Interview 30; Interview 35; Interview 36; Interview 48; Interview 54.
[169] Interview 55.
[170] Interview 3; Interview 25; Interview 41; Interview 55; Interview 63; Interview 69; Interview 85.
[171] Interview 30; Interview 36; Interview 51; Interview 58; Dixit, *Indian Foreign Service*, 48.
[172] Interview 32; Interview 38; Interview 45.
[173] Interview 56; Interview 64.
[174] Interview 72.
[175] Interview 14.

of diplomacy', with its idiosyncratic 'tenor' and 'manners'.[176] One lecturer suggested that those accustomed to repetitive rote-learning and singular scientific truths could not be taught critical thinking.[177] A retired diplomat recalled his lecturing experience at the FSI with melancholy dread, with probationers 'parroting answers' the reading material suggested, 'their bearing, the way they answer questions' inferior to the interventions from independent-minded liberal art graduates.[178] Another veteran of the Service who has taught at the FSI since retirement was worried that the diverse educational backgrounds of incoming officers meant that a basic 'understanding of the national interest' was lacking because of the difficulty of internalizing abstract concepts such as sovereignty and power.[179] Only 'those who don't affect the *esprit de corps*' are welcome,[180] one of the earliest entrants into the Service specified about engineers. That is: assimilation into a liberal arts mindset remains a prerequisite for acceptance in a Service whose evolving demographic composition no longer matches the continued cultural dominance of liberal arts graduates.[181]

At its most fundamental level, however, 'democratization' presents a challenge to diplomatic pedagogy because of an overarching sense of cultural incompatibility. This is the realm of polite euphemisms. A commonly expressed imperative revolved around the need to 'polish up their social skills'.[182] It is no coincidence that this imperative has been felt more keenly since the mid-1980s,[183] as the reforms proposed by the Kothari Committee began to alter the social face of the Service. For rural recruits in particular, one millennial officer noted in a matter-of-fact-way, 'basic etiquette and all is not there'.[184] It is said of those from non-traditional backgrounds that problems of 'social integration' and 'behavioural patterns' have meant that 'it needed a great effort to get them to settle themselves' into the Service.[185] The 'learning of social graces, even simple things like table manners' has become a pedagogical priority.[186] Well-born elderly bureaucrats conceded under their breath that whatever the pedagogical effort to 'make us all the same', it was usually

---

[176] Interview 16.
[177] Interview 44.
[178] Interview 36.
[179] Interview 22.
[180] Interview 16.
[181] Interview 14; Interview 82.
[182] Interview 12; Also Interview 6; Interview 12; Interview 14; Interview 19; Interview 35; Interview 39; Interview 58; Interview 60; Interview 78.
[183] Interview 19.
[184] Interview 60.
[185] Interview 40.
[186] Interview 48.

possible to tell reservation recruits apart right until retirement.[187] One presumes, then, that it is no coincidence that 'communication skills' have become an independent component of FSI training over the past decade.[188]

Old imageries of a white-dominated world order legitimate these readings of the Service's internal cultural hierarchies. With repeated references to the culture of elite diplomacy, the welcome extended to the beneficiaries of the Service's democratization has been conditional on whether 'a person can be trained and polished', becoming capable of 'interacting with foreigners'.[189] 'A certain kind of behaviour is expected of you when you go abroad', and so there is 'a greater responsibility on the Ministry to train people accordingly', a young officer explained.[190] Even if the nature of Foreign Service intake may have changed, the quasi-aristocratic conventions of international diplomacy, with 'a style in which modulation is important',[191] apparently had not.

Democratization, in other words, required appropriation. After an impassioned moral case for democratizing the Service, one former Foreign Secretary noted that the increasing diversity of recruits posed no threat, because 'once they have joined the Service, there is also the existing culture in the Service which they imbibe', so that non-traditional probationers could begin 'making up for whatever disabilities they have', as though markers of a non-traditional background were best seen as malfunctions to paint over.[192] The language of appropriation employed a vocabulary of normalcy and self-evidence. For example, one recently retired self-ascribed Nehruvian suggested that although some 'imbibe correctly' the appropriate manners and mores, it was often 'difficult to integrate them in a way where everything is normal'.[193] To allow for this 'normalization', mentorship was elevated from an unspoken convention to an official arrangement: since 2018, the Foreign Service's mentorship programme has been pairing probationers with a Joint-Secretary for the first five years of their career, to smoothen socialization.[194] Mentoring officers from non-traditional backgrounds 'in the correct way' 'in social graces' had to be done, one particularly unrepentant believer in the exclusivity of diplomacy spelled out, 'by people like us', referring to an undefined but evidently elite collective of diplomats.[195] Many who themselves had slid effortlessly into the desired

---

[187] Interview 7; Also Interview 3.
[188] Interview 51.
[189] Interview 29.
[190] Interview 60.
[191] Interview 74.
[192] Interview 48.
[193] Interview 85.
[194] Interview 32.
[195] Interview 7.

habitus defended their rural, socioeconomically disadvantaged, or lower-caste colleagues with the well-intentioned compliment that after some years in the Service, one could barely tell where they came from.[196] Elite belonging required a social cleansing ritual, through which alternative biographies were rendered imperceptible in the diplomatic habitus. Diplomatic pedagogies in the wake of democratization have been premised on cultural assimilation rather than on any significant reconsideration of the meaning of diplomatic representation.

The diplomatic autodidacts

Those who felt out of place in the Service struggled to produce an air of effortless to suggest they belonged everywhere and anywhere, like good cosmopolitans. They were anxiously seeking to imbibe the effortlessness that K.P.S. Menon and M.C. Chagla, too, had sought to attain under the Raj. Most of those marked out as internal Others to be socialized and standardized understood their place in the Service's hierarchy through a cultural inversion: through what the ideal was against which they seemed to fail. One impossibly eloquent, widely read, and witty millennial recruit, who had only pushed himself through an undergraduate degree in order to sit the CSE while working night shifts at a call centre, joked that 'some of your St Stephen's types would be aghast: not only am I not a St Stephen's graduate, I am not even a classical graduate' at all, before conscientiously subscribing to the dominant narrative about socialization: 'you can't be an outlier without the entire system changing itself, so you tweak your own mental blocks to fit the system'.[197] Peering at his interlocutor through a pair of edgy glasses and clad in a crisp white shirt under a beige Nehru jacket, another millennial recruit from a rural family of teetotallers who ate with their hands professed to no longer be the same person who joined the Service as the first IFS officer from his district: 'from the place that I come from, I have changed my lifestyle', 'dress', 'personality'—'I tried to desperately change myself on how I looked, I talked'.[198] An ST batchmate from a tribal region declared that 'the Foreign Service has made me a completely different person: I have moved up a notch', meaning he could now 'speak about history and art' and 'enjoy a good drink' like those around him.[199] His background, which so obviously spoke to the vast diversity of the country which

---

[196] Interview 48; Interview 52; Interview 63; Interview 82.
[197] Interview 65.
[198] Interview 78.
[199] Interview 77.

the training otherwise pathologized, was, to him, something that fortunately 'evens out' in the long run.[200]

Caste also comes into play in the autodidactic socialization of diplomatic recruits from non-dominant groups. A term coined by the Indian anthropologist M.N. Srinivasan, *Sanskritization* describes a process of cultural upward mobility whereby lower castes attempt to adopt practices and beliefs of a higher caste in order to climb up the social ladder[201]—a process that Bourdieu surely would have recognized. One retired Dalit diplomat—a sociology major with little patience for academic niceties—took on Srinivasan's vocabulary, jeering that 'Sanskritization is a nice term for hiding your caste.'[202] Instead of the culture growing to accommodate different castes, different castes were to accommodate themselves into Foreign Service culture. If they felt discriminated, it was up to them to change, for 'it means that they have not yet assimilated themselves'.

This produces a pedagogy of 'passing': the ability of an individual to be perceived as a member of an identity group other than their own.[203] 'Passing'— whether as a member of a different class, race, gender, or caste—is a strategy often adopted by those lower in a social hierarchy for purposes of self-protection, social advancement, or the escaping of stigma. A Dalit diplomat, for example, may strive to 'pass' as upper-caste, by adopting purportedly upper-caste habits, ways of speaking, cultural tastes, or a different surname. Passing, when successful, goes unnoticed by the outside world. A striking example—one I am keeping anonymous since it is not my place to 'out' people's caste—would be a former, very prominent and senior diplomat, who made it into the Service as a 'general category' candidate and, through familial connections, cultural capital, and the adoption of a new name, spent an entire career 'passing' as upper-caste in the eyes of everyone but a few fellow Dalit officers.

The very existence of the 'creamy layer' reminds us that reservoirs of cultural capital and networks of social capital are not deterministically tied to caste status. A lower caste diplomat, because of their class status, may 'pass' as cosmopolitan in the eyes of colleagues. Conversely, much as with the

---

[200] Interview 77; Similar attempts at growing out of one's own background were, often heartbreakingly, described in Interview 58; Interview 49; Interview 71; Interview 74.

[201] M.N. Srinivas, *Religion and Society among the Coorgs of South India (1965)* (Bhopal: J.K. Publishers, 1978), ix.

[202] Interview 54.

[203] Elaine K Ginsberg and Donald E Pease, *Passing and the Fictions of Identity* (Duke University Press, 1996); Daniel G. Renfrow, 'A Cartography of Passing in Everyday Life', *Symbolic Interaction* 27, no. 4 (2004): 485–506.

upper-caste but lower-class engineering students at IITs studied by Ajantha Subramanian, whose 'unfamiliarity with English and open embrace of regionalism run counter to the cosmopolitanism that is supposed to distinguish upper from lower',[204] so too there are upper-caste diplomats whose habitus fails the cosmopolitan standard of civilization. They, too, would be called upon to adopt autodidactic self-help tactics to fit in, if only to 'pass' as belonging to a different social class, more aligned with their high-caste status.

Although one serving Dalit officer protested that the very term 'social graces' was 'upper-caste code' meant to alienate the lower castes,[205] there was no meaningful contestation of upper-caste renditions of the diplomatic habitus. A retired officer emphasized that Dalits in particular made conscious attempts at emulating what had been presented to them as the universal language of diplomacy: 'we learn to speak and articulate so that others will understand us'.[206] A millennial Dalit officer confirmed that all throughout training, 'you try and imitate the higher castes' because diplomacy is all about cultural codes which few Dalits have exposure to growing up.[207] The 'Dalit-Bahujans'[208] quietly look for mentors to fit in, hoping to 'obfuscate' their caste background as an attempt at 'keeping up with the Joneses'.[209] And yet caste is not something one trains oneself out of through rigorous practice. Speaking of the senior diplomat who had made it into the Service through the general merit list but was in fact a Dalit, the millennial recruit with his war chest of academic theories noted dryly that, whatever seniority or polish might give an officer, they 'will still be a Dalit [...] it's not like you take a dip in the Ganga and you come out with a different caste'.[210] If it is true that diplomats are made, not born, they cannot be reborn either. Diplomatic training may foster homogeneity, but it cannot guarantee equality.

Some autodidactic Dalits went to desperate lengths to belong. The cultural interpretations of diplomacy as an elite space came not only with a heavy homogenizing imperative but also with considerable personal sacrifice. Most men were already married upon entering the Service, usually to 'some

---

[204] Subramanian, *The Caste of Merit: Engineering Education in India*, 25.

[205] Interview 75.

[206] Interview 54.

[207] Interview 71.

[208] The interviewee used a political term which describes both Dalits and OBC communities as belonging to a shared, lower-caste collective. See e.g. Kancha Ilaiah Shepherd, *Post-Hindu India: A Discourse in Dalit-Bahujan, Socio-Spiritual and Scientific Revolution* (New Delhi: SAGE Publications India, 2009).

[209] Interview 71.

[210] Interview 71.

234 PEDAGOGY: MAKING DIPLOMATS IN INDIA

illiterate village girl', as one former Foreign Secretary noted,[211] but sensing their unsuitability for diplomatic life, many opted to divorce and re-marry supposedly more presentable wives, so as to fit in with their colleagues.[212] A few now retired officers spoke quietly of colleagues whose untimely deaths they attributed either to alcoholism brought on by their deep alienation in the Service, or even to suicide. Impressions such as these never make it into the annals of diplomatic history or even into mainstream internal debates inside the Foreign Service. Yet the very fact that these stories of deep marginalization circulate among some officers speaks to the extreme—and often devastating— strategies of belonging adopted by some officers of lower-caste backgrounds. If upper-caste diplomats don't 'see caste' inside the Foreign Service, this is in no small part because lower-caste diplomats work very hard to make theirs invisible.[213]

Becoming a female diplomat also calls for autodidactic methods. 'Institutions themselves (and not just the people working within them) are bearers of gender', as Ann Towns writes about the gendering of diplomatic work—'They contain gender symbols and norms that create and reproduce gender divisions of labour, ideas about femininity and masculinity, and what are appropriate tasks for men and women.'[214] The arduous pedagogical project for the women of the Indian Foreign Service is to tease out these implicitly gendered rules and to adjust their habitus to meet their demands. This autodidactic process is particularly fraught because the stage directions for how women ought to behave toward the dominant habitus have often proven internally contradictory. For Bourdieu, caught up in a startlingly un-reflexive and almost entirely domesticized understanding of women's roles, existing in a gendered world implied that women were expected to exhibit their submission in ways corresponding with orthodox notions of 'femininity'—'smiling', 'demure', 'restrained', 'self-effacing'.[215] And yet, fitting in in the male-dominated world of diplomacy was often premised on supressing these very practices. If anything, such 'so-called

---

[211] Interview 45.

[212] Interview 43; Interview 45.

[213] These subtle sociological cues, while perhaps indicative of discriminatory attitudes or hierarchical distance, are a kind of social sorting which can only happen in a nominally post-caste, relatively liberal space like the Foreign Service. By contrast, the rich literature on caste-based discrimination in Indian education documents very explicit discriminatory practices against Dalit students by peers and educators alike. See e.g. Geetha B. Nambissan and S. Srinivasa Rao, 'Structural Exclusion in Everyday Institutional Life', in *Sociology of Education in India*, ed. Geetha B. Nambissan and Srinivasa Rao (New Delhi: Oxford University Press, 2012), 199–223; Thorat Committee, 'Caste Discrimination in AIIMS', *Economic and Political Weekly* 42, no. 22 (2 June 2007): 7–8.

[214] Towns and Niklasson, 'Gender, International Status, and Ambassador Appointments', 525.

[215] Pierre Bourdieu, *Masculine Domination* (Cambridge, UK: Polity Press, 2001), 66.

feminine qualities', as one retired officer remembered, went against the perceived hallmarks of professionality in diplomacy—and so, among the first generations in particular, women made sure 'their personalities lined up to this image' that permitted few marks of feminine presentation or appearance.[216] The imagery of women as wives and homemakers, unaccustomed to the power intrigues of international diplomacy, nurtured a belief among male colleagues that women were less politically savvy and easier to manipulate by fellow diplomats and politicians alike.[217] The female autodidact's lessons in socialization, therefore, involved learning to imbibe a habitus that negated gendered stereotypes about women.

And so, to be taken seriously, women sought to adjust themselves to what they believed was a masculinized diplomatic habitus in a male diplomatic world. Female officers dressed down, lowered their voices, and adopted an accentuated serious demeanour.[218] 'There was this perception that there has to be a profile', marked by hard or politically sensitive postings, and women, in a vicious circle of gendered readings of both womanhood and diplomacy, were rarely granted such positions, as one female officer who joined the Service in the early 1980s explained.[219] 'We have this discussion quite a lot: how should we project ourselves?', a female officer from the mid-2010s batches asked.[220] Engaging in practices like lowering one's voice or avoiding practices like smiling are small, perceptible attempts at rendering the diplomatic Self less stereotypically female. One officer recalled wishing against conventional beauty standards that her hair would soon turn grey, so that perhaps the visible signs of seniority might make male colleagues take her more seriously.[221] A contemporary declared triumphantly: 'I became a highly successful officer because I became like one of the boys', going out for drinks with superiors after hours and downplaying any maternal responsibilities, so that male colleagues would 'defeminize you mentally'.[222]

Yet there is also a lot of autodidactic work that women found it difficult to even locate in themselves. Bourdieu, too, warned of the difficulties of trying to give voice to embodied knowledge, himself arguing in gendered but supposedly universal language: 'As soon as he [sic] reflects on his practice, adopting a quasi-theoretical posture, the agent loses any chance of expressing the truth of

---

[216] Interview 42.
[217] Interview 52.
[218] Interview 42.
[219] Interview 50.
[220] Interview 80.
[221] Interview 15, March 2019.
[222] Interview 81.

236 PEDAGOGY: MAKING DIPLOMATS IN INDIA

his [sic] practice.'[223] Perhaps female diplomats knew this kind of subconscious learning was constantly apace, however: a frustrated Under-Secretary felt that moulding herself for the job of a diplomat as a woman 'is so much a part of my existence that I don't even know where to start.'[224]

As the previous chapter discussed, those women who have traditionally made it into the Foreign Service have tended to be products of upper-class, liberal households even more often than their male colleagues. Therefore, they have also had recourse to the cultural capital that their primary socialization has provided, greatly facilitating their approximation of the dominant habitus. What is striking, then, is how little acknowledgement there was among more privileged female officers of how their autodidactic methods had necessarily involved less work than those of female colleagues whose socialization attempts were marked not only by a gender gap but also the inequalities of class and caste. If the unacknowledged pedagogical ideal was male, then then the conversations about socialization and gender tended to implicitly revolve around the pedagogical anxieties of women of upper-class, upper-caste backgrounds.

Conclusion

The education of an Indian diplomat is not a mere series of lectures, reading lists, and facts and figures. It imparts its most precious lessons between the lines. This is what Bourdieu called *implicit pedagogy*—the underlying ambitions and unspoken assumptions of training. Diplomatic training, too, should be considered an instrument of legitimation which valourizes certain forms of cultural capital over others. These pedagogies, therefore, also reflect and interact with the various intersections of class, caste, gender, family background, and education that have structured the social process of making the Indian diplomat.

Over the past seven decades, Indian diplomatic training has sought to socialize Foreign Service probationers into embodying the idealized diplomatic cleft habitus. It has endeavoured to create an Indian diplomat conversant in the old elite circles of European international society yet also attuned to the demands of postcolonial 'authenticity' and subaltern sensibility. In these sometimes competing pedagogical processes, the relationship between international and domestic hierarchies has been reversed. Measured against the imagery of an

---

[223] Bourdieu, *The Logic of Practice*, 91.
[224] Interview 59.

old, aristocratic, and European world, the domestic elite has been anxious to obfuscate their marginal position in the historically white club of international diplomacy. By contrast, measured against the ideals of a postcolonial vision of order, the same elite has sought to obfuscate its elite character at home so as to claim sufficient 'authenticity' as representatives of the subaltern or the Third World. The gradual democratization of the Service has shifted the pedagogical accent on how the cleft habitus is constructed. A Service once anxious to have its probationers reflect 'authentic Indianness' and a sensibility to the Third World subaltern is now adamant that this authenticity be disciplined into a more presentable whole.

While democratization was the prevalent form of change that Indian officers themselves talked about as they discussed the evolution of diplomatic training, changes external to the Service have also begun to unsettle diplomatic convention. These shocks have prised open the very question of what an Indian diplomat ought to represent and who this task of representation can be entrusted with. They are also the topic of the final empirical chapter, which puts in question much of the foundational dogma that the Foreign Service has abided by for much of the history of postcolonial India.

6

Interregnum

The end of the cosmopolitan elite?

The interregnum that follows a fracture in the old order is always precarious. It anticipates a new world that has yet to re-order itself. One is much too tempted to quote Gramsci's well-worn precept: 'The crisis consists precisely in the fact that the old is dying and the new cannot be born; in this interregnum a great variety of morbid symptoms appear.'[1] In the new millennium, India stands differently in relation to the world around it, and differently in relation to itself. The dawn of a 'post-Western world' of rising powers and declining Western pre-eminence is elevating India into a new position in the global order. Meanwhile, the evolving balance of social and political relations within India is producing new forms of 'authenticity', as a Hindu nationalist reading of Indian difference displaces much of what once defined the Nehruvian consensus on secularism and diversity.[2]

This twin transformation pushes against established wisdom on what it ought to look like to represent India in the world. 'We are all creatures of our circumstances [...] and the circumstances of India' and 'you cannot separate the human from the professional', a retired diplomat ruminated, concluding that perhaps a new kind of global order and a new kind of India called for a new kind of diplomat.[3] In Bourdieu's vocabulary, the interregnum produces 'misfires': occasions on which the habitus seems to have outlived the conditions in which it was originally assembled.[4] As the cultural credibility and political salience of existing imageries of the world are fracturing, so too are the social arrangements by which they once legitimated particular domestic hierarchies. Ideological departures must be read through sociological fault lines: it

---

[1] Antonio Gramsci, *Selections from the Prison Notebooks of Antonio Gramsci*, ed. Quintin Hoare and Geoffrey Nowell-Smith (New York: International Publishers, 1971), 276.

[2] Hindu nationalism itself has roots in pre-Independence India, as does the *Hindutva* brand that is at issue in this chapter. Vinayak Damodar Savarkar wrote the seminal work defining the contours of *Hindutva* as early as 1923—a pamphlet which is better known as *Hindutva: Who is a Hindu?*, reissued in 1928. However, it cannot be meaningfully argued that Hindu nationalism or *Hindutva* impinged on the workings of the Foreign Service before the election of Prime Minister Modi in 2014.

[3] Interview 12.

[4] Bourdieu, 'Habitus', 31.

Cosmopolitan Elites. Kira Huju, Oxford University Press. © Kira Huju (2023). DOI: 10.1093/oso/9780198874928.003.0007

is not only the contested ideals of cosmopolitanism that are under challenge, but the cosmopolitan elite with whom these ideas are associated. Out of these fractures, a new kind of elite may yet be born.

The first part of this chapter considers changes brought about by the dawn of an ever-more unmistakably 'post-Western' world. It considers how this shift is a challenge to the inherited imageries of international society that Indian diplomats have operated by. I ask what this transformation might do to the social reproduction of the cosmopolitan elite and whether it might provide a social opening for a more genuine democratization of the Foreign Service. The second part presents a first draft of a moving target, still finding its institutional shape: the saffronization of the Foreign Service. Saffronization—a process which takes its name from the colour saffron that adorns Hindu nationalist symbols—involves imagining India as a Hindu nation, both by reconstructing an imaginary past defined by Hindu unity and by refashioning political institutions to reflect majoritarian ideals.[5] In its contemporary garb, it was introduced inside state bureaucracy following the election of Hindu nationalist Prime Minister Narendra Modi in 2014 and has gathered pace since his re-election in 2019. The chapter details how diplomats have personally experienced, adjusted to, and resisted the gradual saffronization of their Service, and how they have sought to navigate their engagements with international society under a new domestic reality. It places the processes of saffronization against a broader set of debates about elites, difference, and the postcolonial governance of global order. The chapter suggests that the dominance of India's cosmopolitan elite is increasingly challenged by both international and domestic change: a post-Western world which might outgrow the elite's Europeanized disposition and Hindu nationalism which is hostile to its liberal inflections.

Misfires in a post-Western world

Three-piece Savile Row suits and a penchant for imperially born 'social graces' always looked a little misplaced in a postcolonial Foreign Service charting its Third Worldist course in the wake of empire. Yet the diplomatic practices of old European international society look ever more out of place in a complex and increasingly multipolar world, whose cultural practices are less

---

[5] See e.g. Edward Anderson and Christophe Jaffrelot, 'Hindu Nationalism and the "Saffronisation of the Public Sphere": An Interview with Christophe Jaffrelot', *Contemporary South Asia* 26, no. 4 (2018): 468–482.

240 INTERREGNUM: THE END OF THE COSMOPOLITAN ELITE?

forcefully underwritten by Western conventions posing as universal ideals. Since decolonization failed its more radical promise of challenging Western dominance, perhaps there was no structural basis for a sustained challenge to this dated imagery, however old-fashioned it soon grew in its aristocratic garb. Yet since the early twenty-first century, following on the heels of the end of the Cold War and the liberalization of the Indian economy in the early 1990s, narratives of a 'rising India' have complicated the imageries of international society that the Foreign Service has lived by, positioning India as a leading power in a post-Western world.[6] As Tarra Yosso notes, chastising Bourdieu for assuming a natural hierarchy of capital, it is not that marginalized groups lack cultural resources but that their forms of capital are not recognized as such in particular social orders.[7] Markers of distinction are only rendered desirable within a given social context. Even the most normalized hierarchies of capital can be contested and rearranged when the world changes. The possibilities of a post-Western era provide occasions for precisely these kinds of rearrangements.

In an age of seemingly declining Western hegemony and rising non-Western powers like India and China,[8] the insistence on India's outsider identity, some diplomats felt, no longer lent it the kind of moral authority it once had.[9] A few diplomats tied a sense of 'greater confidence' in their own everyday behaviour with the liberalization of the Indian economy in the early 1990s, which had allowed India to assume a 'footing of equality' with the West.[10] 'I belong to an India that contributes a lot to the IMF', one millennial recruit from a mid-2010s batch noted, contrasting his experience with his seniors' memories of the balance of payments crisis that presaged India's 1991 bailout by the International Monetary Fund—he was, consequently, 'more confident in flaunting the things that your culture has.'[11] Power undergirds cultural self-confidence.

A much-belated elegy

Diplomacy has long ceased to be a vocation for European nobility—and yet the resilient imagery of Europeanized international society has lived its

---

[6] Rajesh Basrur and Kate Sullivan de Estrada, *Rising India: Status and Power* (London: Routledge, 2017).

[7] Yosso, 'Whose Culture Has Capital?', 76.

[8] Though for some healthy scepticism regarding the scale and nature of this shift into a post-Western world, see e.g. Michael Cox, 'Power Shifts, Economic Change and the Decline of the West?', *International Relations* 26 (1 December 2012): 369–88.

[9] Interview 3; Interview 8; Interview 11.

[10] Interview 22; Also Interview 14.

[11] Interview 65.

cultural afterlife in the beliefs and behaviours of Indian diplomats. The elitism that came with the imagery was always racialized. Yet insofar as elite Indian diplomats could buy second-class belonging in its cultural hierarchies through the performance of an Anglophile, elite-educated habitus, it held its own charms. These charms are fading. Increasingly, the worldly diplomat, comfortable in elite circles across the world and thinly conversant in a wide range of fields, is an endangered species. In an ever more complex and globalized world, foreign ministries operate among non-state and supranational actors and are rushing to attract technical and specialist talent to manage climate change or cyber security.[12] As a consequence, 'the luxury of being a generalist is gone', as one proud Stephanian liberal arts graduate mourned.[13] This is a luxury whose hastened demise at the hands of political committees and public commentators the Service has long disdained. Perhaps most prominently, the Lok Sabha Parliamentary Standing Committee on External Affairs, chaired by Shashi Tharoor in 2016, made a new push for lateral hires at Joint-Secretary-level from the Home Services as well as fixed-term consultants from the private and academic sectors.[14] The technicalization and specialization of diplomacy are not only questions of changing foreign-policy priorities. They also reflect a shifting sense of who should get to manage the affairs of the world.

The traditional stature of old-school generalists was intimately tied to diplomatic 'glamour'—a word that kept longingly reappearing in conversations as diplomats described their reasons for joining the Service and lamented its gradual vanishing.[15] The idealized Indian diplomat had been defined by what one Delhiite liberal arts graduate Joint-Secretary, in grieving, remembered as 'the colourful, expansive, old-world figures' who had 'that kind of wit'.[16] Yet now, a certain 'aura' around these erudite, well-read elites was receding, one retired officer observed with some melancholy.[17] The age of the cosmopolitan elite seemed to be coming to a close.

In fact, the arrival of a post-Western world holds a promise of a double democratization: a democratization of who gets to define the high culture of international society and a concomitant possibility that this rethinking may yet turn the Service's internal Others into insiders, throwing out the old elite.

---

[12] See e.g. Sending, Pouliot, and Neumann, 'The Future of Diplomacy'.

[13] Interview 27.

[14] Lok Sabha Standing Committee on External Affairs, 'Recruitment, Structure and Capacity-Building of IFS Cadre, Including Need for a Separate UPSC Examination for Cadre, Mid-Career Entry and in-Service Training and Orientation—Twelfth Report', August 2016, http://164.100.47.193/lsscommittee/External%20Affairs/16_External_Affairs_12.pdf.

[15] Interview 3; Interview 12; Interview 15, March 2019; Interview 17; Interview 29; Interview 38; Interview 52; Interview 57.

[16] Interview 57.

[17] Interview 55.

242   INTERREGNUM: THE END OF THE COSMOPOLITAN ELITE?

There may be some truth to the remark of a retired multilateralist looking at the generations growing up after him: instead of globalization rendering the world more homogenous by the generation, young Indian diplomats joining the Service now have 'far less in common with the West' than their seniors.[18] And yet this change need not be read, as it so often has been, as a form of terminal decline, leaving Indian diplomats less capable of meeting their foreign counterparts on an equal footing.[19] On the contrary, one recently retired multilateralist read this change as a broader sign of a global democratization: there was no longer one dominant 'Anglicized' model to follow in the world of diplomacy.[20]

A powerful everyday expression of these fractures is the evolving role of English—a repository of cultural capital once jealously guarded by the Foreign Service, whose place is being rethought in an increasingly diverse, post-Western world. If their superiors believed that English was an end in itself, millennial officers were partial to a more pragmatist argument. A British-educated member of the mid-2010s batches was pleased to observe 'a growing recognition that English serves a functional purpose, it does not buy you esteem'—'diplomacy is not just about speaking good English and having a certain background'.[21] 'People in New York speak bad English!', one early 2010s batch officer once stationed at the UN exclaimed—'the world has changed'.[22] To drive this point home, her and some younger colleagues would sometimes smuggle intentionally incorrect English expressions into communications with Stephanian superiors to toy with their 'obsession' with the language.[23] In this 'new paradigm' of diplomacy, one Additional-Secretary with a management background noted with evident glee, there was less need for eloquent generalists with an embellished English vocabulary and a liberal arts repertoire of cultural references.[24]

The habits of the cosmopolitan class can also evolve to match a new cultural grammar of a post-Western world. If the old arrangement reflected an old Europeanized hierarchy of tastes, and the Foreign Service has historically

---

[18] Interview 11.

[19] The point about a post-Western world can be overblown, however. As many frustrated officers discussed, a European posting continues to be seen as a sign of merit on one's resume even as Europe's importance to India continues its arguable decline. Interview 7; Interview 12; Interview 25.

[20] Interview 11.

[21] Interview 76; also Interview 63.

[22] Interview 80.

[23] How much the attitudes are actually shifting is a complicated question: one eloquent Stephanian who in an interview had made similar arguments about language elitism and the purely functional role of English was himself a target of these pranks. The ideals and cultural capital that animate Indian diplomats may not always meet the modernizing impressions they feel compelled to relay to outsiders.

[24] Interview 70; Also Interview 36; Interview 73.

equated 'social graces' with customs in its most-coveted 'A-postings', then the notion of social graces might change as beliefs about what constitutes A-postings evolve.[25] China's ascendancy might mean the expansion of an etiquette of forks and knives to chopsticks. Diplomatic manners, in the twenty-first century, are 'not just French food and wine, it's also not just Westernized', as one Francophile Stephanian Additional-Secretary hastened to add to his description of diplomatic skills.[26] The 'wine-drinking liberal classes' are not naturally more cosmopolitan than anybody else, as a fellow Additional-Secretary from outside their circles pointed out with some defensive undertones.[27] Indeed, it is notable that the more representative batches have brought more teetotallers into the Service.[28] One retired Stephanian noted with some alarm in his voice that they were even beginning to frown upon etiquette training on wines.[29] Those for whom indulgences like wine were an alien marker of Indian urbanity and foreign custom were convinced that the insistence on creating wine connoisseurs out of Indian diplomats was a vestige of the old school of diplomacy, shackled to the West, which modern Indian diplomats need not abide by.[30] Views and habits that once marked diplomats from more traditional households as hopeless outsiders could now be presented as reflective of an India that had outlived its desire for Western approval.

Some even ventured to turn the habitus on its head: the insularity cultivated by Anglophone education and elite backgrounds, once legitimated by its family resemblance with dominant European culture, was an obstacle in a world edging into post-Western order.[31] Younger diplomats who themselves fit all the appropriate elite markers had learned a most millennial performance: they kept 'recognizing their own privilege' when giving what they feared may sound like elitist answers, 'called out' the insufficient progressivism of their superiors, and self-policed their own descriptions for 'essentializing markers' when talking about less privileged colleagues.[32] Their liberal seniors were careful to acknowledge that the more representative new batches were 'far more attuned to realities of life' outside the Anglophile circles.[33] A young Under-Secretary from outside India's traditionally dominant classes assumed a more

[25] Interview 44.
[26] Interview 56.
[27] Interview 70.
[28] Interview 33; Interview 58; Interview 59; Interview 65; Interview 73.
[29] Interview 33.
[30] Interview 58.
[31] Interview 17; Interview 33; Interview 38; Interview 45; Interview 49; Interview 62; Interview 70.
[32] Interview 56; Interview 59; Interview 82.
[33] Interview 28.

244   INTERREGNUM: THE END OF THE COSMOPOLITAN ELITE?

combative tone: 'those that used to form part of an elite club—their monopoly is broken.'[34]

Those who do not fit a dominant habitus, Bourdieu has been telling us all along, tend to seek to imbibe the manners and practices of those who do. However, he pointed out, they also tend to resent the pretensions which they associate with the dominant, however much they feel compelled to mimic them.[35] With the desirability of the dominant habitus with its 'worldly' performances now in question, this resentment has finally found a functional justification. This allows for the possibility of cultural rebellion: should the dominated seek to join the dominant group without abiding by the prevailing definitions of distinction, they put in play the very principles by which the habitus is assembled. And should such rebellions become more systematized, 'dominant individuals may fall into the dominated poles of the field.'[36] In such moments, new ideals can be fashioned to delegitimate old hierarchies and to forge new ones. This novel valorization of previously frowned upon practices resembles the Tamil Dalit intellectual Raj Gauthaman's project of reordering the markers of Indian modernity: instead of being cast outside the civilizational fold, practices like speaking in dialect, consuming non-vegetarian food, or moving outside urban *savarna* circles are resignified as worthy, even desirable.[37] That which used to attract stigma is reinterpreted as indicating status.

The changing social face of the Indian Foreign Service might well be the perfect diplomatic match for a post-Western world, in fact. One rising star of a late-1990s batch believed that the more representative batches brought with them a different set of professional priorities and skills which were far more in tune with the evolving modalities of diplomatic practice.[38] The emblematic dichotomy of European international society which divided the world into spheres of 'high' and 'low' diplomacy struggled to stand the test of time. If India was to compete for status in the uncertain age of rising powers, it needed technological and commercial diplomacy to leverage its strengths. These kinds of daily responsibilities are often taken more seriously by the more representative batches, who have had less time to imbibe the Service's classical disdain for matters of 'low diplomacy'. 'Down-to-earth people' from India's interior did not consider the project of material advancement a cultural taboo, a Dalit

---

[34] Interview 65.
[35] Reed-Danahay, *Locating Bourdieu*, 111.
[36] Steinmetz, 'Bourdieusian Field Theory', 612.
[37] Gauthaman cited in M.S.S. Pandian, 'One Step Outside Modernity: Caste, Identity Politics and Public Sphere', *Economic and Political Weekly* 37, no. 18 (2002): 1739.
[38] Interview 83.

officer argued in celebration of the Service's democratization—'a person like me could grasp that commercial work was important.'[39] The elite performances of anti-materialism once matched the social demands of an Indian diplomatic corps seeking to prove its enlightened credentials. Now, they look ever more alien in a shifting world in which India seeks to outgrow, rather than to mirror, the West.

Postcolonial afterlives

Those studying India's rise have tended to read the geopolitical shift as a sign of the growing irrelevance of India's insistence on postcolonial world-making. The debate about 'normalizing' Indian diplomacy seems to have consumed most of the analytical oxygen in the debate on India's rise, as India's self-ascribed realists have sought to convince the world that India has closed the chapter on its postcoloniality, exchanging protest for power.[40] And yet, if anything, the imagery of postcolonial international society matches the moment: the post-Western world could be its much-delayed incarnation.

When seeking to convince the world of its worth and promise, it was rarely arguments about material capabilities or institutional capacity that Indian diplomats have relied upon. Instead, there was a sense that Nehruvian secularism, postcolonial syncretism, and Third World diversity could themselves be thought of as legitimating India's leading role. India's ingrained diversity made it 'inherently equipped to handle diversity' in an increasingly multipolar order, its plurality of religions and cultures 'the calling card of India in a troubled world', as one devout Hindu officer, wary of the weaponization of his religion, insisted.[41] This diversity, aligning as it does with the supposed spirit of the contemporary era, to Dixit constituted one of India's 'greatest strengths in a globalized age'.[42] This discourse turns Samuel Huntington on his head: instead of containing dangerous fault lines that will become theatres of cultural conflict in the new century, India can find common ground with diverse cultures across the globe because of the repeatedly learned lessons of its domestic diversity.[43]

---

[39] Interview 49; Also Interview 78.
[40] See, again, e.g. Ganguly, 'India's Foreign Policy Grows Up'; Mohan, *Crossing the Rubicon*.
[41] Interview 4.
[42] Dixit, *Indian Foreign Service*, 285.
[43] Rana, *Inside Diplomacy*, 424.

Postcolonial visions clash, of course, with some of the external expectations of what it ought to look like for India to 'rise'. The tenacity of visions of a postcolonial world, founded on anti-imperialism and Third World solidarities, has made it difficult for many diplomats to accept the imported visions of 'rising India'. The loaded notion of India as a 'responsible power' was a quiet invitation to abandon the political projects of postcoloniality. One stalwart of climate diplomacy made the disconnect explicit, insisting that while since about the early 1990s, and certainly after the global financial crisis began in 2008, a great transformation of international economic power relations had occurred, this ought to change very little for, say, Indian climate diplomacy— 'no, India does not need to change its traditional stance', because amid all the punditry and lobbying, for Indian diplomats, 'development is the *sine qua non*'.[44]

Among the old hands in particular, 'superpower' was a suspect category precisely because it has been framed as signalling a closure of India's postcolonial project. A diplomat interviewed by Manjari Chatterjee Miller in 2013 declared that the very idea of India's rise was an imposed Western construct, designed to lure India out of its insistence on prioritizing development and poverty alleviation, and weaved into 'a rope to hang ourselves'.[45] During my interviews in 2019, too, there were few committed takers for the narrative of India's rise— even if, as is to be expected by now, Miller's article on India 'resisting its own rise' had been widely read by diplomats and some were rather irritated by quotes from their own colleagues.[46] 'I never felt comfortable' with it, declared a former Indian Consul-General in San Francisco, charged with promoting emerging Indian technologies in the United States—the narrative of a rise was preserved for 'investment bankers in Las Vegas', with few true believers inside the Service.[47] A retired Nehruvian officer described the ideal Indian diplomat as somebody who 'understands India's placement in the international order' and was unswayed by the rhetoric of a rise, which was 'all non-sense'.[48] A former diplomat who later served in an advisory governmental capacity called the narrative a derivative of 'the India Shining Syndrome', in reference to the magniloquent marketing slogan of the Indian Government in 2004, which drew

---

[44] Interview 15, March 2019.

[45] Manjari Chatterjee Miller, 'India's Feeble Foreign Policy: A Would-Be Great Power Resists Its Own Rise', *Foreign Affairs* 92, no. 3 (2013): 14.

[46] Interview 1; Interview 6; Interview 12.

[47] Interview 22.

[48] Interview 25.

widespread ridicule for portraying India as a land of prosperity.[49] 'Not everyone is in a position of privilege like us', the officer chastised, noting that India was not the sole preserve of 'your IITs, your IIMs' but also belonged to 'the 200 million [who] go to bed hungry'. It is as though senior officers felt it an offense to go against the pedagogies of their district training.

In a changing India which experiments with free markets and finds itself more comfortable in the company of incumbent powers, the old guard of the Foreign Service has become a carrier for India's postcoloniality. Mélissa Levaillant has argued that the continued insistence on postcolonial nonconformity and the discourses of Non-Alignment, in the face of an increasingly more laissez-faire, reformist tone in the Home Services, has shown the Foreign Service to act, in Iver Neumann's vocabulary, as a 'discourse police',[50] keeping diplomatic practices 'compatible with the inherited culture' of the Service.[51] Perhaps this is also why political leaders have needed to circumvent the Service when planning on diverging from the postcolonial Nehruvian mould: when the Indian Government sought to adopt a more conciliatory stance towards Western demands at the 2009 Copenhagen climate summit, it had to explicitly side-line senior IFS officers and replace them with Government-appointed negotiators.[52]

What may sound like a generational divide—old-school Nehruvians versus pragmatist millennials—often seemed, rather, to be a debate between those who fit the traditional dominant habitus and those who did not. The narrative of a rise sat most uneasily precisely among the urban liberal arts graduates with left-leaning sympathies at the cultural helm of the Service, one of whom chided the uncouth status-consciousness among some of his supposedly power-hungry colleagues drawn to the materialist rhetoric of 'rising India'.[53] Even shifts that are usually read in the register of political ideologies—such as the battles between socialism and capitalism—were felt as an internal sociological divide. One frustrated Additional-Secretary who joined the Service after some overtures in the business world declared that the batches of the 1960s and 1970s had 'destroyed' the Service, because 'everything had to be socialist' and 'everyone had to adhere to certain norms and ideals' simply

---

[49] Interview 52.

[50] Iver B. Neumann, 'Returning Practice to the Linguistic Turn: The Case of Diplomacy', *Millennium: Journal of International Studies* 31, no. 3 (July 2002): 648.

[51] Levaillant, 'The Contribution of Neo-Institutionalism to the Analysis of India's Diplomacy in the Making', 154.

[52] Navroz K. Dubash, 'The Politics of Climate Change in India: Narratives of Equity and Co-Benefits', *Wiley Interdisciplinary Reviews: Climate Change* 4, no. 3 (May 2013): 194; Interview 8.

[53] Interview 6.

because this was, he insisted, the kind of Nehruvian propaganda that had been endemic at their elite liberal arts colleges.[54] If diplomatic attitudes are slowly evolving on the question of India's rise, this might be in response not only to India's changing geopolitical coordinates but also the changing balance of cultural power inside the Foreign Service.

Against this backdrop of a possible double-democratization—of the cultures of global order and the culture inside the Service—cosmopolitanism, too, might become something bigger, almost emancipatory. 'Cosmopolitanism itself has changed', one recently retired multilateralist declared—a 'new kind of cosmopolitanism' could perhaps not only come to embrace the Global South, but, with the decline of Western hegemony, even revolve around it.[55] True, the term had once by historical necessity bounded itself within a heavy Western-centrism. However, Indian diplomats today were 'less diffident in following the stereotype' which once governed a habitus 'Westernized in approach and habits', one former Foreign Secretary gauged.[56] Could there be space for more inclusive practices of cosmopolitanism, unbound from an adherence to a Western aesthetic and an acquiescence to its political supremacy? And yet, just as the arrival of a post-Western world with its shifting hierarchies might have made it possible to rethink cosmopolitanism, a political ideology that rejects cosmopolitanism outright has captured the highest office in the land.

Saffronizing the Foreign Service

Hindu nationalism sits uneasily with the cultural inheritance of the Indian Foreign Service. In the diplomatic everyday, saffronization touches on all aspects of diplomatic performance, from discourse and protocol to the training of probationers. It is debatable whether Prime Minister Modi's supposedly transformative tenure has defied any basic tenets of India's long-running foreign policy doctrines since he came into office in 2014.[57] Yet change is apace elsewhere: among the cadre of the Indian Foreign Service to whom it falls to

---

[54] Interview 70.
[55] Interview 11.
[56] Interview 45.
[57] Rajesh Basrur, 'Modi's Foreign Policy Fundamentals: A Trajectory Unchanged', *International Affairs* 93, no. 1 (2017): 7–26; Sumit Ganguly, 'Has Modi Truly Changed India's Foreign Policy?', *The Washington Quarterly* 40, no. 2 (2017): 131–143; Ian Hall, 'Is a "Modi Doctrine" Emerging in Indian Foreign Policy?', *Australian Journal of International Affairs* 69, no. 3 (2015): 247–252; Manjari Chatterjee Miller and Kate Sullivan de Estrada, 'Pragmatism in Indian Foreign Policy: How Ideas Constrain Modi', *International Affairs* 93, no. 1 (1 January 2017): 27–49.

conduct everyday diplomacy under Hindu nationalist rule. The gradual saffronization of the Foreign Service is but the diplomatic rendition of a broader pattern of Hindu nationalism's long march through the institutions of the Indian state.[58] Inside the Foreign Service, however, saffronization creates a very particular crisis of the Self. The traditionally dominant officers of the Service are caught in a double bind. First, *Hindutva* represents a rejection of much of the foundational dogma that the Service has operated by since Independence. Secondly, many among the diplomatic corps feel personally excluded from the Hindu nationalist narrative of 'authentic' Indianness. In fact, the traditional upper echelons of the Foreign Service represent precisely the kind of Anglophone, cosmopolitan, westernized, upper-class India that Modi's populist rhetoric has sought to discredit in the eyes of the nation.

Trading solidarity for saffron

Nehru cast his shadow long and wide, and the core ideals of his India—secular, diverse, egalitarian—went virtually unchallenged after his passing.[59] Even the BJP Prime Minister A.B. Vajpayee (1998–2004) once described himself as a Nehruvian—meaning, argued one former diplomat, that officers wedded to the founding principles of the Service were not challenged in their beliefs in any significant way until very recently.[60] The election of a Hindu majoritarian, nationalistic government under the Premiership of Modi has, however, put these commitments in question. And if Nehru was a towering figure, Modi, too, has striven to become one: while the Foreign Service's influence on foreign-policy making has long ebbed and flowed in tandem with changing governments,[61] the uncharacteristically rapid concentration of powers in the Prime Minister's Office under Modi has been notable.[62]

Despite protestations to the contrary from diplomats themselves, politicization is not an inherently novel phenomenon for the Foreign Service. Jawaharlal Nehru's intimate involvement tied the executive branch to the Service from its very beginnings. The Emergency, a period in 1975–1977 during which

---

[58] Christophe Jaffrelot, *Modi's India: Hindu Nationalism and the Rise of Ethnic Democracy* (Princeton and Oxford: Princeton University Press, 2021), 253–298.

[59] Pratap Bhanu Mehta, 'Still under Nehru's Shadow? The Absence of Foreign Policy Frameworks in India', *India Review* 8, no. 3 (13 August 2009): 209–33.

[60] Interview 43.

[61] Benner, *Structure of Decision*, 202; Dixit, *Indian Foreign Service*, 199, 241, 252; Tharoor, *Reasons of State*, 117.

[62] James Manor, 'A Precarious Enterprise? Multiple Antagonisms during Year One of the Modi Government', *South Asia: Journal of South Asian Studies* 38, no. 4 (2015): 737.

Prime Minister Indira Gandhi suspended the normal functioning of India's democratic apparatus, introduced the concept of 'committed bureaucracy' to the institutional lexicon of the Foreign Service, and diplomats have often strategically aligned themselves with the Congress Party or, more recently, the BJP.[63] Indeed, if Modi represents a deviation from a democratic norm, then the Emergency may offer a parallel: in interviews, diplomats who witnessed the Emergency rationalized their decision to stay within a compromised state machinery despite a crisis of conscience by emphasizing their belief that the suspension of a democratic, broadly tolerant 'idea of India'[64] would be a temporary aberration and that the outward-facing Foreign Service would be better insulated against political pressure than the Home Services.[65] In fact, if politicization of the bureaucracy is 'the substitution of political criteria for merit-based criteria in the selection, retention, promotion, rewards, and disciplining of members of the public service',[66] then one may legitimately wonder about the very possibility of an entirely non-political bureaucracy.

What does stand out by historical comparison is the official insistence on a secular creed, which has not faced a systematic challenge inside the Service before. To combat exoticized western impressions of India as inherently Hindu in the 1970s, Indian diplomats even took to correcting the convention in Spanish-speaking countries of referring to Indian nationals as 'Hindu', with Indian Ambassador to Argentina B.K. Sanyal requesting in 1971 that the Ministry of External Affairs instruct all Foreign Offices in countries where India had missions to limit use of the term only to instances describing religion, not nationality, having already written to the Spanish Royal Academy of Letters to discuss the term's description in Spanish dictionaries.[67] In line with such anxieties of association, diplomats who entertain religious figures at embassies have traditionally received a reprimand from their superiors.[68] In other words, Indian diplomats have spent decades consciously countering a conception of India as a Hindu *rashtra*, or Hindu nation.

---

[63] Dixit, *Indian Foreign Service*, 177.

[64] For a long-running debate on 'the idea of India', see Sunil Khilnani, *The Idea of India* (Penguin Books India, 2004); Perry Anderson, *The Indian Ideology* (London: Verso Books, 2013); Partha Chatterjee, Sudipta Kaviraj, and Nivedita Menon, *The Indian Ideology: Three Responses to Perry Anderson* (New Delhi: Permanent Black, 2015).

[65] Interview 4; Interview 22; Interview 24.

[66] B. Guy Peters and Jon Pierre, 'Politicization of the Civil Service: Concepts, Causes, Consequences', in *The Politicization of the Civil Service in Comparative Perspective*, ed. B Guy Peters and Jon Pierre (London: Routledge, 2004), 2.

[67] B.K. Sanyal (Ambassador to Argentina), 'Letter to the MEA', 3 March 1971, 'Use of the word "Hindu" in Argentina when referring to Indian nationals', FW(II) 307/3/71, NAI.

[68] Interview 7, 7; Interview 45; Interview 85.

With its intellectual roots in the writings of thinkers like V.D. Savarkar, M.S. Golwalkar, and Deendayal Upadhyaya, *Hindutva*—the predominant expression of Hindu nationalism in India—builds on the spiritual superiority and universal truth of Hinduism, believes in a conservative imperative of natural authority under unified Hindu domination, and is politically invested in a narrative of Hindu victimization at the hands of Muslims as an internal Other.[69] In its diplomatic garb, the Hindu majoritarian turn challenges the diplomatic imperative to represent a diverse, secular India, which stands as a beacon of a syncretic postcoloniality. What it offers instead is a political investment in civilizational greatness, hypermasculine conceptions of international security, and anti-western ideologies of Hindu revivalism.[70]

Slowly, the blurry edges of ambiguous Indian identity, traditionally more civic than ethnic or religious in nature among India's ruling elites, are being drawn in sharper strokes: a once almost ethereal conversation about 'Indian culture' is, one Muslim officer argued, becoming a conversation about 'blood and soil'.[71] At its core, *Hindutva* therefore represents a jingoistic rejection of all things foreign as well as a revision of how to demarcate Indian difference in the world. Nehruvian postcolonial Indianness premised on elite-managed diversity is giving way to a saffronization of the Indian Self, insistent on uniform civilizational and religious identity. In a global age of identitarian movements, former Ambassador Paramjit Sahai writes, India too, is faced with a reactionary challenge to the 'cherished values of democracy, pluralism and secularism, which has come to be defined as the "Idea of India"'.[72] These reactionary tendencies are also an assault on much of what Indian diplomats have been expected to stand for.

Hindutva rejects both visions of the world that the Foreign Service has operated by. It cares little for elite, colonially tainted imageries perpetuated by India's Anglophile classes, but it also rejects the narratives of a diverse postcolonial society bound together by cross-cutting solidarities. *Hindutva* also rejects the traditional diplomatic elite itself. Under the *Hindutva* regime, this elite is scorned both because its Anglophile inflections are interpreted as *insufficiently* Indian and because the left-wing sympathies and resolute secularism of the 'St Stephen's type' are seen as the *wrong kind* of Indianness.

---

[69] Thomas Blom Hansen, *The Saffron Wave: Democracy and Hindu Nationalism in Modern India* (Princeton University Press, 1999).

[70] Ian Hall, *Modi and the Reinvention of Indian Foreign Policy* (Bristol University Press, 2019), 41.

[71] Interview 7.

[72] Paramjit Sahai, *Indian Cultural Diplomacy: Celebrating Pluralism in a Globalized World* (New Delhi: Indian Council of World Affairs, 2019), 39.

252 INTERREGNUM: THE END OF THE COSMOPOLITAN ELITE?

Hindutva as everyday diplomatic practice

The *Hindutva* accents on everyday diplomatic life involve, in the words of one recently retired senior Ambassador, 'going back to more quote-unquote Indian aspects' of diplomacy: a reassertion of India's 'civilizational' identity and Hinduism, expressed in annual diplomatic practices like the celebration of *Kumbh Mela*, a major religious festival.[73] Since 2014, there has been a proliferation of Hindu events held at or sponsored by Indian embassies, including those organized by the paramilitary Hindu-nationalist organization *Rashtriya Swayamsevak Sangh* (RSS)[74]—even though such events have met with 'immediate backlash' from the Service's religious minorities and secular-minded Hindus, one officer noted.[75] In the polemical rendering of the BBC foreign affairs correspondent Ashis Ray, after 2014, 'senior diplomats began to look over their shoulders, RSS activists were planted at Embassies and High Commissions and local loyalists of Modi started bossing over pliant or petrified Heads of Mission.'[76] One officer who had once been lectured on the importance of a secular Service by Nehru himself considered it 'almost demolished'.[77]

The soft end of saffronization overlaps with a seemingly innocuous celebration of Indian culture. Prime Minister Modi insists on visits to Hindu and Buddhist temples as part of his itinerary on foreign trips and chooses Hindu artefacts such as the religious tract the *Bhagavad Gita* as gifts to political counterparts.[78] We might entertain some scepticism about the relevance or novelty of Modi's cultural and religious accents such as the promotion of yoga or Ayurveda. After all, yoga has an illustrious history as an Indian cultural export. The Indian Council of Cultural Relations, founded in 1950 to promote Indian culture, has long been a 'soft power' arm of Indian diplomacy.[79] It is certainly possible to overstate the cultural cache of diplomatic practices of this kind. And yet the tenor in which Indian culture is pushed is significant, since the very possibility of fronting 'soft' aspects of Indian culture is what allows *Hindutva* to find international respectability. The 'soft power'

---

[73] Interview 3.

[74] The RSS ('National Volunteer Organisation') is a mass Hindu nationalist, paramilitary organization with close links to the governing BJP-party. See e.g. Walter Andersen and Shridhar D Damle, *Messengers of Hindu Nationalism: How the RSS Reshaped India* (London: Hurst & Company, 2018).

[75] Interview 52.

[76] Ashis Ray, 'Has the "Foreign Service" Declined?', National Herald, 14 July 2020, https://www.nationalheraldindia.com/opinion/has-the-foreign-service-declined.

[77] Interview 25.

[78] S.D. Muni, 'Modi's "Neighbourhood First" Initiative', in *Modi and the World: Reconstructing Indian Foreign Policy*, ed. Sinderpal Singh (Singapore: World Scientific, 2017), 126.

[79] Rajesh Basrur, 'Modi, Hindutva, and Foreign Policy', *International Studies Perspectives* 20, no. 1 (2018): 10.

emphasis on yoga—at India's initiative, the UN has observed International Yoga Day since 2014—portrays India as a 'benign and beneficial cultural force in global affairs' while also employing a globally popular phenomenon to normalize tenets of cultural-nationalist discourse.[80] What even these supposedly soft aspects betray is a departure from a time when ambassadors would negotiate with Spanish dictionary makers to combat impressions of India as a Hindu *rashtra*.

With the Modi administration has also come an aggressive push to marginalize English in diplomatic communications, in favour of Hindi. This may be framed to foreign audiences as a delayed 'decolonization of the mind', as India sheds the language of the former colonizer at the dawn of a post-Western age. However, it also serves the domestically controversial end of cementing Hindi, most prevalent in Northern India's 'Hindi belt', as the country's one 'authentic' language in a diverse country of over a thousand languages, out of which the Constitution recognizes 22.[81] At the time of the interviews in the first half of 2019, the very first Hindi-language book for the Indian Council of World Affairs was about to be published, the first Hindi-language foreign policy conference was being organized, and the Prime Minister's conference for Heads of Mission had been held in Hindi, during which even ambassadors uncomfortable in the language had been made to speak in it.[82] These changes form part of a wider bureaucratic shift, with heads of various government ministries called to appear in front of official language committees to testify on how Hindi is being brought into ministerial work. Should these efforts be deemed insufficient, you 'get quite a scolding', one serving officer from a mid-1990s batch warned.[83]

The linguistic question is also a sociological one. English might have given Indian diplomats a strategic edge in committee work and drafting at the United Nations, as Chapter 3 outlined, but it also connoted the supremacy of a class whose very dominance the Hindu nationalist reading of Indianness rejects. It will not do, however, to suggest that a once purely pragmatic preference is now being politicized by the forces of *Hindutva*. For, as Chapter 4 analysed, English was always a Rorschach test onto which cultural anxieties, hierarchies,

---

[80] Aavriti Gautam and Julian Droogan, 'Yoga Soft Power: How Flexible Is the Posture?', *The Journal of International Communication* 24, no. 1 (30 October 2017): 18.

[81] On the complex language politics of English versus vernacular languages in India, see e.g. D. L. Sheth, 'The Great Language Debate: Politics of Metropolitan versus Vernacular India', in *At Home with Democracy: A Theory of Indian Politics*, ed. D.L. Sheth and Peter Ronald deSouza (Singapore: Springer, 2018), 169–95, https://doi.org/10.1007/978-981-10-6412-8_10.

[82] Interview 61.

[83] Interview 61.

254   INTERREGNUM: THE END OF THE COSMOPOLITAN ELITE?

and class-based preferences have been projected. No side in the language wars can claim pragmatism in their defence. For all of the talk of Modi as the quintessential pragmatist,[84] his disapproval of officials using their expressive English to maximal diplomatic effect is driven by a cultural-linguistic preference for Hindi as the 'authentically' Indian idiom over English as a tainted language of the foreigner.

Diplomatic pedagogies, too, are acquiring hues of saffron. Culturally, many of the changes in diplomatic training are 'an offshoot of this Government', as one sympathetic diplomat phrased it,[85] following the mandate of the 'Ayush' Ministry established in 2014, which among other indigenous modalities promotes Ayurveda and homeopathy, with yoga acquiring a particular centrality as both academic and physical classes prepare future diplomats to promote the International Day of Yoga.[86] While protocol attachments have usually involved probationers attending international summits or conferences, in 2019, future diplomats were dispatched to the *Kumbh Mela* religious festival in the recently renamed city of Prayagraj (a Sanskrit word replacing the Islamic Mughal name, Allahabad).[87] In February 2020, what had been known as the Foreign Service Institute since its founding in 1986 became the Sushma Swaraj Institute of Foreign Service, in honour of the late BJP Minister of External Affairs (2014–2019).[88] Many diplomats once known for decrying the mimicry of Western diplomatic practice during diplomatic training now wondered how to advocate for more Indian culture in training without sanctioning a pedagogy of 'aggressive superiority' which exalts a parochial Indianness while rejecting all things 'foreign' as culturally corrupt.[89]

(Inter)nationalism reconsidered

There is a paradox at the heart of Modi's quest for global recognition. Although he is socially invested in personal rapport with world leaders[90] and his increasingly authoritarian moves at home are widely interpreted as damaging India's

---

[84] See e.g. Harsh V. Pant and Yogesh Joshi, 'Indo-US Relations under Modi: The Strategic Logic Underlying the Embrace', *International Affairs* 93, no. 1 (1 January 2017): 133–46; Surupa Gupta et al., 'Indian Foreign Policy under Modi: A New Brand or Just Repackaging?', *International Studies Perspectives* 20, no. 1 (2019): 1–45.

[85] Interview 38.

[86] Interview 32.

[87] Interview 32.

[88] 'Home - Sushma Swaraj Institute of Foreign Service', accessed 23 August 2020, https://ssifs.mea.gov.in/.

[89] Interview 4.

[90] Hall, *Modi and the Reinvention of Indian Foreign Policy*, 150.

global status ambitions,[91] his prescription for diplomatic representation rejects the importance of cross-cultural communicability. During an address to IFS probationers in the presence of media on 12 June 2014, the newly elected Prime Minister, seemingly intending to reach both Indian and international audiences, compared foreign nations to a haughty aunt, never as deserving of diplomats' loyalty as *Bharat Mata* (Mother India): '*Apni ma phate purane kapdon mein bhi toh bhi ma hoti hain, aur mausi agar ache kapdon mein ho toh bhi mausi hi rehti hain*' ('Your mother is still your mother even in old and torn clothes, whereas your aunt, even in her best finery, is still an aunt').[92] The worldly diplomat, conversant in international practices of diplomatic etiquette, was no longer an ideal to be imbibed: '*Chammach kahan rahkna hain [...] in sab baton se hatke kaam karo*' ('Where your spoon has to be laid [...] ignore that kind of issue and do your work'). For the UN veteran, Congress politician, and former Minister of State for External Affairs Shashi Tharoor, the taunt was emblematic of 'the Modi notion of stoutly resisting the siren call of foreign countries while haranguing others about the strengths of your own.'[93] It was a declaration of closure for the once-dominant Anglophone elite, in place of which a no less narrow Indianness, predicated on Hinduism, Hindi, and nationalistic price, would come to define the contours of an alternative diplomatic ideal.

Commenting on the tide against the liberal intelligentsia sweeping through Delhi, the essayist Pankaj Mishra has suggested in sharp tones that a 'cleansing of rootless cosmopolitans is crucial to realizing Modi's vision.'[94] The Service has felt this, too—one retired Muslim officer offered that 'five years ago all of us were cosmopolitan', but that 'in today's polarized environment, narrower assertions of identity have come to the surface.'[95] 'Not once' having had to explicitly justify his cosmopolitan beliefs or interpretation of his own Indianness in his almost forty years in the Service, 'now I own ten books on the topic of culture and identity', he exclaimed. Moments of change have a tendency of unmasking received wisdom, shattering its self-evidence.

Hindutva does not allow for the compatibility of internationalist commitments and nationalist preoccupations. In this negation, it stands at odds with

---

[91] Manjari Chatterjee Miller, 'India's Authoritarian Streak: What Modi Risks with His Divisive Populism', *Foreign Affairs* 30 (May 2018); Kate Sullivan de Estrada, 'In the World's Eyes, the Indian State May Be Declining but Its Citizenry Is Rising', The Wire, 25 December 2019, https://thewire.in/rights/india-citizenship-protests-narendra-modi.

[92] Shashi Tharoor, *India Shastra: Reflections on the Nation in Our Time* (New Delhi: Aleph Book Company, 2014), 59.

[93] Tharoor, 59.

[94] Pankaj Mishra, *Age of Anger: A History of the Present* (London: Macmillan, 2017), 162.

[95] Interview 7.

Foreign Service tradition. One passionate multilateralist, now in retirement, thought back to his Civil Service entry interview in the late 1960s, when the interviewer representing the Indian Police Service told him that the correct answer to a question about a diplomat's most important quality would in fact have been 'patriotism': 'it's the opposite that is true; you need to attenuate your pursuit of the national interest', he argued in response to his own question about how to define cosmopolitanism.[96] In his reading, the ideals of cosmopolitanism became a sophisticated version of 'patriotism through a different lens'.[97]

Since 2014, patriotism through a different lens is giving way to diplomacy as nationalism by other means. As one former Foreign Secretary noted, there is now an expectation that diplomats perform 'a strong assertion of national identity' in the discharge of their duties.[98] Fluidity and ambivalence are antithetical to the *Hindutva* construction of Self and Other. A BJP-affiliated contract employee of the MEA declared that the old-fashioned regard for cosmopolitan niceties had only ever tied India's hands as it fended for itself abroad.[99] If India once sought to envision a postcolonial international society founded on diversity, depicting this as a break from the uniformity imposed by colonial international society, the *Hindutva* reading of Indian difference represents it as a religious, civilizational distinction which rejects the diversity creed supposedly imposed on India by its postcolonial liberal elites. In his book on the evolution of Indian foreign policy, former Foreign Secretary Shyam Saran (2004–2006) warns that 'India is in danger of being reduced to a mere agglomeration of narrowly conceived communities with closed minds', and anticipates that since '[h]ow Indians relate to one another influences how the country handles interstate relations', a 'shrinking vision at home cannot sustain an expansive vision abroad'.[100] Or, in the phrasing of a devoted multilateralist who served under Modi's first term: 'If India looks narrowly at itself, it will look narrowly at the world'.[101] Much as Nehru's postcolonial nationalism was the basis of his Third Worldist internationalism, so too Modi's Hindu nationalism is intimately tied to India's diplomatic existence. In the shadow of saffron, India's rise, too, must be scripted anew.

[96] Interview 28.
[97] Interview 28.
[98] Interview 45.
[99] Interview 2.
[100] Shyam Saran, *How India Sees the World: Kautilya to the 21st Century* (New Delhi: Juggernaut Books, 2017), 291.
[101] Interview 27.

The desire to rescue a concept which promises tolerance and diversity—even when culturally and historically, it has done so within paradoxically elitist bounds—has also evoked reconsiderations of the Service's brand of cosmopolitanism. 'The idea is to make it accessible', one impeccably dressed Stephanian Joint-Secretary implored, believing that cosmopolitanism was 'often mistaken for elitism' but ought not be abandoned in a moment of crisis.[102] 'I wouldn't self-identify as a cosmopolitan, but then again, what's the choice?', a weary Dalit officer posed as a rhetorical question, weighing his options between the elitism of upper-caste, upper-class cosmopolitanism against the cultural absolutism of *Hindutva*, which to him signified not empowerment but another form of exclusion.[103] The choice between a faux embrace of diversity and the forced embrace of oneness, to him, was no choice at all.

Adaptation and resistance

The role of the Indian diplomat, too, is shifting. Building on Rebecca Adler-Nissen's four-way typology, Geoffrey Wiseman has sought to make sense of the politicization of diplomatic services under the global tide of populism through a taxonomy of ways in which diplomats relate to government policy: the diplomat as messenger, the diplomat as policy shaper, the diplomat as policy producer, and the diplomat as policy resister.[104] In the early years of a severely understaffed Indian Foreign Service in particular, one encountered many policy shapers and producers. Under the heavy centralization of foreign policy in the Prime Minister's Office in the Modi administration, the diplomat is assigned the passive role of messenger—a role many have proven themselves either eager or at least willing to perform. Yet under the cultural pressures of saffronization, others have assigned themselves a different role: that of a resister. Policy resisters attempt to 'deflect, slow-walk or kill what they see as ill-judged policies', in the style of *Yes, Minister*[105]—a British comedy series that many diplomats referenced in either fond or ironic tones during our conversations.

---

[102] Interview 56.
[103] Interview 71.
[104] Geoffrey Wiseman, 'Expertise and Politics in Ministries of Foreign Affairs: The Politician-Diplomat Nexus', in *Ministries of Foreign Affairs in the World: Actors of State Diplomacy*, ed. Christian Lequesne (Brill Nijhoff, 2022), 119–149.
[105] Wiseman, 127–128.

258   INTERREGNUM: THE END OF THE COSMOPOLITAN ELITE?

While few outsiders have ventured to invite career diplomats to share their experience of Hindu nationalist rule, it has been suggested that Modi derives backing for his religiously tinted diplomacy not from Foreign Service officers but from functionaries of his own BJP party.[106] This seems to be broadly true of the Service's historically dominant Anglophile elites, socialized into broadly Nehruvian worldviews. At the same time, responses to Modi's reign often reflect a sociological dividing line, pitting traditional elites against a more demographically representative officer intake in recent years. The saffron challenge has divided the Service, whose former and current members debate the essence of majoritarianism, the diplomatic purchase of *Hindutva*, and the new foreign policy overtures under Modi on an ongoing basis in a closed Google group of about a thousand members.[107]

Modi's reign is too recent for there to exist publicly available archival material recording diplomats' attitudes towards his *Hindutva* regime. The NMML does, however, hold exchanges between some of the Service's earliest officers responding to the infamous Hindu nationalist violence unleashed at the illegal demolition of the Babri Masjid, a contested mosque, in the Northern city of Ayodhya in 1992. In letters from December 1992 and February 1993, the retired Ambassador Arthur Lall writes in a personal capacity to the retired Ambassador B.K. Nehru to denounce the 'stupid lack of civilized restraint displayed first at Ayodhya and subsequently in many parts of the country',[108] rhetorically asking if the BJP has 'taken into account the regional and international consequences of its actions, not just its actions, but the interpretation that Ms [sic] around the world will give to them?', following political statements which, to Lall, were 'so prehistorical as to make one despair'.[109] Beyond such scattered archival finds, interviews become a rare opportunity to let Indian diplomats speak for themselves.

Allegiance or acquiescence to Hindu nationalist rule can take many forms. There are officers who have professionally benefited from it: Modi has surrounded himself with retired and seconded diplomats, appointing former Foreign Secretary Subrahmanyam Jaishankar as his Minister of External Affairs in 2019 and filling senior positions in the Prime Minister's office with

---

[106] Ian Hall, 'Narendra Modi's New Religious Diplomacy', *International Studies Perspectives* 20 (2018): 13.

[107] Interview 1; Interview 10; Interview 15, March 2019; Interview 35.

[108] Arthur S. Lall, 'Letter from Arthur Lall to B. K. Nehru, December 8th 1992. B. K. Nehru Individual Papers. Manuscript Section of the Nehru Memorial Library', 8 December 1992, 'Individual Correspondence' between B.K. Nehru and Arthur Lall, B.K. Nehru papers, NMML.

[109] Arthur S. Lall, 'Letter to B. K. Nehru', 3 February 1993, 'Individual Correspondence' between B.K. Nehru and Arthur Lall, B.K. Nehru papers, NMML.

trusted Foreign Service appointees.[110] At the same time, many of those willing to align themselves with aspects of Modi's reign sought hard to distinguish between a 'modernizing' Modi and the regressive expressions of *Hindutva* in whose name he governs. In many conversations with diplomats, there was a sense that the sheer fact of Modi's accentuated interest in foreign affairs elevated the status of the Foreign Service, too, offering opportunities for officers to prove themselves—even if this focus has come with an exceptionally swift devolution of foreign-policy making into the orbit of the Prime Minister's Office.[111] Most diplomats who were complimentary of the new accents on Indian diplomacy spoke not of *Hindutva* but business, lauding the right-wing BJP's aspirational emphasis on economic diplomacy, exemplified by the 'Make in India' manufacturing and branding campaign which diplomats were expected to champion abroad.[112]

In daily diplomatic praxis, the Foreign Service, one senior diplomat who served under the first Modi administration explained, had been 'quick to read-just to his style', toning down its left-leaning Nehruvian rhetoric and adopting what he called a 'modern-world approach to things'.[113] A more visibly concerned retired officer was convinced that the growing number of RSS affiliates within the Service signified a cultural project of re-education, which could not be adequately described through the modernizing language of business but only be captured in the nationalist argot in which *Hindutva* is most commonly articulated.[114] Indeed, the BJP-affiliate working as a contractor for the Ministry of External Affairs sounded confident in the slow churn of promotion patterns, suggesting that it might take about one and a half decades for the attitudinal change to find indigenous roots within the Service, as liberal Nehruvian diplomats retire out of the Service and more nationalistically minded colleagues assume their place.[115] As I discuss in the Epilogue, this estimate may, in fact, prove to be conservative.

---

[110] See e.g. Sreemoy Talukdar, 'S Jaishankar's Appointment as Foreign Minister Reveals Narendra Modi's Mindset on Trust, Acumen and Leadership', Firstpost, 31 May 2019, https://www.firstpost.com/politics/s-jaishankars-appointment-as-foreign-minister-reveals-narendra-modis-mindset-on-trust-acumen-and-leadership-6737001.html; Press Trust of India, 'Sanjeev Kumar Singla Appointed Private Secretary to PM Narendra Modi', Livemint, 20 July 2014, https://www.livemint.com/Politics/xHmdQIS03l9bDHFmD10rxJ/Sanjeev-Kumar-Singla-appointed-private-secretary-to-PM-Naren.html; Press Trust of India, 'IFS Officer Vivek Kumar Appointed Private Secretary to PM Narendra Modi', *Business Standard India*, 19 July 2019, https://www.business-standard.com/article/pti-stories/ifs-officer-vivek-kumar-appointed-private-secretary-to-pm-modi-119071900678_1.html.

[111] Interview 1; Interview 2; Interview 3; Interview 4; Interview 5.

[112] Interview 2; Interview 3; Interview 32; Interview 39; Interview 45.

[113] Interview 3.

[114] Interview 7.

[115] Interview 2.

260 INTERREGNUM: THE END OF THE COSMOPOLITAN ELITE?

There was some disagreement among officers on the sincerity with which some seemed willing to shed established diplomatic ideals to embrace saffronization. One retired Muslim diplomat suggested that certain colleagues would 'wear their culture on their sleeve' only to win political favour with the current government.[116] In the words of a staunchly secular-minded Hindu colleague: nationalism 'plays well now'.[117] Many, a former Foreign Secretary relayed, had joined the ruling BJP party before the 2014 and 2019 elections—a pattern not too dissimilar to the once highly prized allegiance to the Congress Party, which has elevated many former diplomats into ministerial positions and has long incensed the Indian right.[118] Others speculated that the permissive political environment would continue revealing 'closet RSS' diplomats[119] and those newly emboldened to 'be proud of being Hindu'[120], once socially pressured into burying their predilections under a performative veneer of secular internationalism.

And yet, although diplomats were keen to identify others as potential *Hindutva* advocates, few offered themselves up as such. Partly, this was perhaps because the notions espoused by Modi so ill-fitted the Service's traditional outlook which officers still thought it best to uphold, partly because of the self-perpetuating sociology of interview 'snowballing', whereby like-minded officers would put me in touch with each other for further interviews. I suspect that there may have been officers who chose to downplay or conceal their admiration of *Hindutva* in the presence of a young European interlocutor such as myself, on the assumption that mine did not look like the biography of somebody who would be sympathetic to their politics. By and large, in the most senior circles, sincerely held *Hindutva* allegiances seemed to be considered a fringe occupation of some 'less bright' members of the Service.[121] 'I slept through the rise of the *Hindutva* movement', a retired Muslim diplomat frowned, because to diplomats, it had always seemed like 'something that happened on the side', not inside their Service.[122] This inertia in the face of deviations from established culture underlines the stickiness of old ideological arrangements and the social sanctions for violating them.

Much of the critique of *Hindutva* was courteously cryptic, even when the demeanour, tone, or context may have betrayed more conviction than the

---

[116] Interview 53.
[117] Interview 85.
[118] Interview 45; Dixit, *Indian Foreign Service*, 241.
[119] Interview 85.
[120] Interview 45.
[121] Interview 3; Interview 43.
[122] Interview 7.

utterance alone. 'Loyalty or patriotism is not the monopoly of any religion', one diplomat of a mid-1960s batch noted;[123] 'you can't make it a fetish to be Indian', a recently retired Ambassador mentioned, as though in passing.[124] One young officer, seemingly *apropos* nothing, suggested that 'there is a broad consensus' among his colleagues 'that we want to represent a modern, rising, progressive India', and since 'broadly the ethos remains intact', 'we will survive as it is'.[125] Others suggested discreetly that most of their colleagues have been 'compelled to compromise' on their values since 2014.[126] Many spoke of the importance of distinguishing between a brand of enlightened patriotism and narrower forms of religious nationalism.[127] The intellectual historian Quentin Skinner is insistent that 'anyone issuing a serious utterance will always be doing something as well as saying something'.[128] The pointed talk among officers of a more inclusive patriotism, offered with knowing eyes and raised eyebrows, or indeed the sheer frequency of unsolicited commentary on the sacrosanctity of Indian diversity, too, seemed to be doing something: they seemed designed to invite a parallel with *Hindutva* between the lines.

Since their capacity for free speech is wider than that of serving colleagues, retired officers were often less guarded: one incensed diplomat who had retired by 2014 scoffed that it would have required considerable 'self-discipline' on his part to 'represent this wretched country even now'.[129] 'The current regime represents a completely contradictory value system' to the one the older batches had been socialized into, a left-leaning officer from a 1960s batch argued, claiming that even those who did not speak up had 'their worldviews challenged' in the discharge of their duties.[130] An elderly Sikh officer broke into tears describing a battle to uphold the values of diversity and secularism that he had spent a career defending as an Indian diplomat.[131]

Sometimes, dissent need not be vocalized at all. One junior diplomat spoke to me from across the coffee table in his office, on which were placed nothing but our cups of *chai* and a copy of the most recent issue of *The Caravan*—an investigative Indian magazine known for its distinctly anti-government disposition. Even as I made sure not to interrogate him on anything that would

---

[123] Interview 1.
[124] Interview 3.
[125] Interview 66.
[126] Interview 14.
[127] Interview 1; Interview 3; Interview 42; Interview 45; Interview 48; Interview 52.
[128] Quentin Skinner, *Visions of Politics: Volume 1, Regarding Method* (Cambridge: Cambridge University Press, 2002), 106.
[129] Interview 37.
[130] Interview 43.
[131] Interview 26.

262 INTERREGNUM: THE END OF THE COSMOPOLITAN ELITE?

compromise the status and security of a serving junior diplomat, I could not help but wonder whether the magazine had been placed between us as some sort of signal—an emblem of his silent rebellion, which certainly would not have been casually thrown across the table for a visit by a superior.

In testimony to the resilience of received Service culture, the scepticism towards *Hindutva* extends to many devout Hindus who had previously objected to what they perceived as a suppression of Indian culture within their Anglophile Service. With India's reading of secularism as religious equidistance rather than rejection, it is entirely possible to identify as a 'secular Hindu', in the sense of espousing a politics of secular toleration while personally practising religion. One former Foreign Secretary once critical of his internationalist colleague's disinterest in Indian tradition considered the 'endless talk' about India's '5000-year-old civilization' overblown—'you don't challenge China by doing yoga'.[132] A famously nationalistically minded former Foreign Secretary thought that the rejection of foreign influences could be overemphasized, decrying the 'fake resistance' to the '*savoir-faire*' of Western diplomatic custom.[133] Similarly, a diplomat who had publicly spoken for the importance of engaging with Hinduism in diplomatic representation took a wary tone, insisting that he had—perhaps falsely—imagined that this could be done 'without jingoism'.[134] We must, therefore, distinguish between Hinduism and Hindutva[135]—the former theoretically compatible with secularism and internationalism, the latter rejecting them altogether.

At the same time, changing demographics may yet make the Foreign Service more receptive to its own saffronization. Democratization has meant that the diplomatic corps is gradually becoming more reflective of India at large—and thus also more likely to reflect the popular support for a Hindu nationalist platform. 'Rural India, small towns have started exerting themselves and their values' in the Service, one Delhiite from a 1970s batch noted,[136] although the shift had as much to do with class and caste as with geography. These batches, in the words of a senior retired Ambassador, are showing 'more consciousness of who they are', religiously and culturally.[137] Geoffrey Wiseman, analysing

---

[132] Interview 45.
[133] Interview 39.
[134] Interview 4.
[135] There are, however, political limits to the extent to which insisting on this distinction can yield a more liberal religious polity. The project of 'reclaiming' Hinduism from *Hindutva* has its detractors, for example. Pratap Bhanu Mehta, 'The Limits of the Hindu vs Hindutvavadi Debate', *The Indian Express* (blog), 16 December 2021, https://indianexpress.com/article/opinion/columns/limits-of-hindu-vs-hindutvavadi-debate-rahul-7675010/.
[136] Interview 33.
[137] Interview 3.

the particular forms of politicization that befall diplomatic services under populist-nationalist leadership, is right to suggest that charges of symbolizing society's 'elite', detached and insulated from 'the people', can be countered by making these services more representative of the respective countries' citizenry.[138] What the case of India suggests, however, is that such 'democratization' may simultaneously render the diplomatic community itself more open to populism and nationalism.

This is not to say that only sociocultural elites can hold broadly internationalist views—indeed, it seems to be part of the social schism inside a changing Foreign Service that many unfounded cultural anxieties are projected by the traditional elite onto diplomats from less privileged backgrounds. And yet it is precisely this apparent resentment that may also be pushing some junior colleagues towards a more assertive Hindu nationalist disposition. 'Secularism is not born out of denial' was the retort of a conservative-leaning millennial officer for whom India's 'composite culture' owed its pluralistic nature to Hinduism's universalism, making it entirely appropriate for Indian institutions to centre around 'a Hindu perspective' which his urban, elite-educated superiors derided.[139] In his answers, opinions and ideologies were always tied back to the kinds of people who held them: 'real' Indians joining the Service from the country's rural heartlands and vernacular schools, juxtaposed against the out-of-touch Indians who looked upon their junior colleagues with elitist disdain. This points towards a larger pattern, whereby internationalism is resisted at least in part because of a social resentment against the internationalists themselves.

The cosmopolitan elite turned domestic Other

With the saffronization of the Foreign Service, the ideational cannot be separated from the sociological. There is a twin rejection afoot: of both internationalist, liberal principles and the elites who claim to hold them. The *Hindutva* vision of Indianness rejects ideological strands of the Foreign Service's Nehruvian vision, but it also stands at odds with the very being of many Indian diplomats themselves. These two forms of rejection are not happening at the same time by accident, but perhaps always had to come together. It has been more politically palatable for the Indian right to represent an ideological

---

[138] Wiseman, 'Expertise and Politics in Ministries of Foreign Affairs: The Politician-Diplomat Nexus', 141.
[139] Interview 65.

264   INTERREGNUM: THE END OF THE COSMOPOLITAN ELITE?

rejection of secularism and internationalism as a principled stance against out-of-touch elites rather than to openly declare their rejection in the language of religious nationalism. In other words, it matters not only what Indian diplomats *think* but who they *are*.

Ideas are not free-floating entities without social moorings, as Bourdieu reminds us at every turn. As such, it is perhaps no surprise that, when it comes to Nehruvian secularism, as a former Foreign Secretary noted of older generations, 'people felt a sense of comfort, because the social background of the diplomats was not religious themselves [sic]'.[140] Indeed, the dominant conception of Indian secularism has been, in Bourdieu's words, a 'worldmaking power', allowing the upper-caste postcolonial elite to set the 'legitimate vision of the social world and of its divisions'.[141] 'The idea of India that "Lutyens Liberals" have is that India is a secular country', an officer who left the Service mid-career argued, juxtaposing popular sentiment against the elite progressivism that supposedly confined itself to the governing quarters of central Delhi designed by the colonial architect Edwin Lutyens.[142] Even the most committed secularists often felt that there was a tinge of condescension to the stigmatization of religion in the Service, and few were surprised to see a growing sense of Hindu pride emerge amongst the new cohorts, whose rural roots and provincial education were interpreted as signalling a more conservative, religious predisposition.[143] Hindu nationalism emerges against this secular consensus, like Faisal Devji argued over two decades before Modi's national ascendence, 'as the only credible, organized form of alternative politics in a country where the ruling elite has appropriated secular nationalism so completely as to allow no room for dispute in its terms'.[144] In this constellation of cultural power, even a majoritarian push for a singular religion can dress itself up as emancipation, whereby 'real' India is released to express its 'authentic' Self.

In our conversations, the Service's traditional elites tended to invest much explanatory power in a binary between enlightened elites and irrational masses. In the words of one St Stephen's College and Oxford-educated diplomat from a 1960s batch: 'you can't be a semi-literate person and be expected to understand the beauty and richness of our country'.[145] When respect for diversity becomes a clarion call of the elites against a broader population

---

[140] Interview 45.
[141] Bourdieu, 'What Makes a Social Class?', 13.
[142] Interview 10.
[143] Interview 10; Interview 16; Interview 45; Interview 65.
[144] Devji, 'Hindu/Muslim/Indian', 5.
[145] Interview 37.

of Indians, who are deemed incapable of appreciating it prima facie, the ideological and the sociological intersect in ways that make the rejection of a cosmopolitan ethic appear like a principled stance in the name of some suppressed, subaltern Indianness. That two Dalit officers distinguished themselves as particularly articulate supporters of the current regime and its purported anti-elitism[146] might jar against a political logic which assumes that marginalized castes will feel most at ease in secular, liberal circles. Yet it made sense when set against decades of lived experience of social condescension at the hands of upper-caste liberal colleagues.[147]

The personal, then, is political. The contrast between an English-educated Kashmiri Pandit like Nehru and a supposed 'man of the masses' like Modi who, in the political mythologies of the BJP, rose from a lower-caste tea-selling *chaiwallah* to become Prime Minister, symbolizes a laudatory 'de-elitification' to his sympathizers.[148] The BJP's recent General Secretary Ram Madhav, whose omnipresence on the Delhi think tank scene suggests an increasing interest in diplomacy and foreign policy, in 2017 mapped Nehru and Modi onto opposing sides of a transnational class divide: while the Harrow and Cambridge-educated Nehru espoused ideas that 'were transmitted by the colonisers of the West', the 'mob, humble people of the country are behind Modi', being 'finally at ease with a government that looks and sounds familiar'.[149] One former Foreign Secretary believed that Modi's personal brand itself 'is giving a message: you must not be cosmopolitan by upbringing' to join the Indian elite, or ever be 'apologetic' about not meeting classical elite markers.[150]

In this personification of Indian political debate, the traditional elites of the Foreign Service become part of the general *Hindutva* threat perception which singles out 'a powerful foreign Other *within* India in the form of a pseudosecular, neocolonial, and illegitimately powerful establishment that colludes with dangerous minorities who, in turn, have links to India's external enemies'.[151]

---

[146] Interview 38; Interview 67.

[147] There is a thriving literature on Dalit mobilization and the complex caste politics of *Hindutva*. See e.g. Christophe Jaffrelot, 'Class and Caste in the 2019 Indian Election: Why Have So Many Poor Started Voting for Modi?', *Studies in Indian Politics* 7, no. 2 (1 December 2019): 149–160; Sukhadeo Thorat, 'Dalits in Post-2014 India: Between Promise and Action', in *Majoritarian State: How Hindu Nationalism Is Changing India*, ed. Angana P. Chatterji, Thomas Blom Hansen, and Christophe Jaffrelot (Oxford: Oxford University Press, 2019), 217–236; Badri Narayan, *Fascinating Hindutva: Saffron Politics and Dalit Mobilisation* (New Delhi: SAGE Publications India, 2009).

[148] Interview 1; Interview 3.

[149] Ram Madhav, 'Coming Full Circle at 70', *The Indian Express* (blog), 15 August 2017, https://indianexpress.com/article/opinion/columns/independence-day-coming-full-circle-at-70-atal-bihari-vajpayee-hamid-ansari-muslims-india-insecure-modi-nehru–4796919/.

[150] Interview 45.

[151] Thorsten Wojczewski, 'Populism, Hindu Nationalism, and Foreign Policy in India: The Politics of Representing "the People"', *International Studies Review* 22, no. 3 (2020): 415.

The traditional elites of the Foreign Service are imagined as belonging to the same class of Indians as members of the left-leaning Congress Party, who are depicted in *Hindutva* discourse as a comprador class, steeped in a 'neo-colonialist mindset' and insistent on harnessing the language of the colonizer to engage in political, social, and cultural gate-keeping against the Indian masses who do not speak it.[152] In *Hindutva* discourse, there is a purposeful conflation of Westernized Indian elites and foreign Others, both of whom pose a 'collaborative threat to "the people"' and stand in the way of 'the realization of a strong and monolithic Hindu identity'.[153] Because of the outward-facing nature of diplomacy, the Service's traditional Anglophone elites are a particularly convenient object of Othering, blurring as they do by profession the lines between the domestic and the foreign. In other words, it is precisely the porousness of the boundary between Self and Other that makes the globetrotting cosmopolitans of the Foreign Service culturally and socially suspect in the eyes of a Prime Minister like Narendra Modi. What ensues is, as I have argued, a double rejection: both of an internationalism whose sense of Self is purposefully ambivalent, and of the Indian elites who so willingly indulge in this ambivalence.

The saffronization of the Foreign Service has crystallized how all identities are politically perceived and ordered into a social hierarchy. Even if many seemed to share the concern of a Sikh officer about a contemporary 'tendency to politicise identity',[154] the politicization of identity is precisely what the cleft habitus, too, always revolved around. It was just that this identity, in all its cultural syncretism and amorphous Indianness, signalled a very different *kind* of politics. As with the two dominant imageries of international society, so too with the emerging alternative visions of *Hindutva*: appeals to higher principles of universalism always create an internal Other and legitimate a set of hierarchies within.

The cultural exclusions and social practices of the old guard complicate conversations about postcoloniality in the Indian Foreign Service. These have allowed the Hindu right to portray saffronization as a true, delayed democratization of a once exclusive club. It has enabled them to discursively tie saffronization to a postcolonial project of liberation,

---

[152] Taruna Vijaya, *Saffron Surge: India's Re-Emergence on the Global Scene and Hindu Ethos* (New Delhi: Har Anand Publications, 2008), 32.

[153] Wojczewski, 'Populism, Hindu Nationalism, and Foreign Policy in India: The Politics of Representing "the People"', 406.

[154] Interview 20.

whereby an unrepresentative, colonially tainted interpreter class of diplomats is replaced by a more 'authentic', truly postcolonial elite. Thus, the push for an increasingly Hindu nationalist Service is not presented as an anti-pluralist move, in the traditional populist fashion,[155] but rather as an anti-elite move which seeks to champion true pluralism. The emancipatory discourse of postcoloniality is appropriated to serve a nationalistic, conservative cause. However politically disingenuous, the populist appeals to anti-elitism are empirically grounded in a demographic reality of a historically insular Foreign Service—complicating any political defence of it.

Conclusion

At the dawn of a post-Western world, are we about to witness the birth of a de-elitified cosmopolitanism or rather the rise of a non-cosmopolitan elite? Points of fracture create what Bourdieu called 'misfires': moments in which changes in the social order render particular performances of a habitus asynchronous and out of place. The old-school European imagery of international society looks ever more old-fashioned and ill-fitting. The fractures to this imagery involve the potentially declining roles of the English language and European 'social graces' as well as the heightened salience of non-traditional 'low diplomacy', the evolution of diplomatic tastes, and a democratization of sorts of diplomatic culture.

Internally, fissures have begun to appear in the kind of India that will be demanding a seat at the negotiating table as its power grows. After seven decades of aspiring to represent a diverse, secular India, the Indian Foreign Service has been dealt a very different set of diplomatic instructions since the Hindu nationalist Prime Minister Modi came into office in 2014. The gradual—and often resisted—saffronization of the Foreign Service is putting in play the very question of what its diplomats are expected to represent. The traditionally amorphous sense of Indianness, insistent on authenticity but purposefully vague on its definition, is giving way to a narrower assertiveness, which sees Indian diplomats representing not a postcolonial coalition, the Third World, or a secular state, but a Hindu *rashtra*. This saffronized rendition sits awkwardly both with the Nehruvian, postcolonial conception of secular, liberal India, and the cultural conceptions of the Service's self-appointed cosmopolitans. Saffronization is emblematic of the analytical need

---

[155] Johannes Plagemann and Sandra Destradi, 'Populism and Foreign Policy: The Case of India', *Foreign Policy Analysis* 15, no. 2 (2019): 283.

268   INTERREGNUM: THE END OF THE COSMOPOLITAN ELITE?

to understand populist challenges to conventional diplomacy not merely as ideological critiques of internationalism but as sociological responses to the elites with whom these ideologies are associated. The sharpened debates around cosmopolitanism crystallize dynamics that underpin the global backlash against the demonised rootless 'elite' who stands apart from a romanticized reading of the rooted 'people'.

As the inherited legacy of a secular, internationalist India fractures, so do the social ideals which once legitimated the dominance of an elite-educated, Anglophone class of Indians as its diplomatic representatives. Cosmopolitanism has always been an elite aesthetic for the Foreign Service—a Bourdieusian form of distinction which assigns members their status in its cultural hierarchies. We may now be witnessing the birth of a new elite. This birth must be understood against both an international backdrop of reconfigurations of global order and an internal context of shifting political alliances. It must also be thought of sociologically: not only in terms of the political challenges to the ideologies of internationalism but in terms of the resentment against the cosmopolitan elites who hold those commitments.

Our story of change, then, is complex. It is too early to gauge how rapid, deep, permanent, or sincere many of the points of fracture are. Just as the colonial, white imagery of a Europeanized world outlived the material conditions in which it was born, so it would be premature to declare the old arrangements dead when we are still enmeshed in the disorientations and false starts of the interregnum. Heavy quotation marks must be placed around any notion of an 'end' to various things: the classical trappings of diplomacy, the deep-seated culture of the Foreign Service, Indian diplomats' philosophical commitment to representing a diverse country, and their concomitant insistence on valuing the Service's social exclusivity.

The changes apace form neither a straightforward teleology of liberal progress nor a simple storyline of a more 'assertive' India, be that geopolitically or culturally. Rather, change has come to the Indian Foreign Service in various guises, to be read differently depending on the reader. More demographic diversity among diplomatic cadres can coincide with, or even abet, a narrowing vision of Indianness. The 'democratization' of diplomatic cadres— theoretically allowing for a more pluralistic Service—has also meant the entry of officers who may reject the liberal values of Nehruvian secularism—thus making the Service less pluralistic. 'Modernization' in the guise of a business-oriented diplomacy can be presented as part of a political agenda which at its core rejects much of what we might usually think of as 'modern'. The gradually diminishing role of English is similarly ambiguous: it is losing value because diplomats who speak vernacular languages are becoming more prevalent and the emphasis on English has come to be seen as excessively elitist, but also because it is part of the *Hindutva* project to impose Hindi on a country of striking linguistic diversity. The 'de-elitification' of the Service can either be celebrated as a win for democracy, mourned as a decline of diplomatic standards, or feared as a Trojan horse that erodes the supposedly elite liberal values that have shaped the Service since its founding. There is no single narrative arch that captures these changes. Much as with every question asked in a reflexive sociological manner, each possible answer reveals something important about where each interpreter stands in the hierarchies they are commenting on.

For now, what can be offered is a tentative evaluation of changes in the making, still to reveal themselves in full. And yet the changes already speak to something: not only to possible future trajectories but just as crucially to the liberal exclusions, underlying resentments, and internal contestations which have accompanied Indian world-making for decades. They reveal cracks in the compromises historically forged in the making of postcolonial India. In so doing, they prise open some of the ostensible consensus around cosmopolitan elites and diplomatic representation that has governed India's engagement with the world since decolonization.

Epilogue

A world of difference

Neither the colourless vagueness of cosmopolitanism, nor the fierce self-idolatry of nation-worship, is the goal of human history. And India has been trying to accomplish her task through social regulation of differences on the one hand, and the spiritual recognition of unity on the other.

She has made grave errors in setting up the boundary walls too rigidly between races, in perpetuating in her classifications the results of inferiority; often she has crippled her children's minds and narrowed their lives in order to fit them into her social forms, but for centuries new experiments have been made and adjustments carried out.

[...]

The worldflood has swept over our country, new elements have been introduced, and wider adjustments are waiting to be made.

Rabindranath Tagore, *Nationalism* (1917)

There is nothing natural or obvious about the existence of the cosmopolitan elite, or the way that very particular readings of worldliness and inclusion in international society have come to captivate our imagination. It is the normalization of dominant Westerncentric, post-aristocratic narratives that make the social constitution of the cosmopolitan elite seem commonsensical, even inevitable. Denaturalizing and contextualizing the elite aesthetic of cosmopolitanism allows us to analyse the oxymoron inherent in the very notion of a 'cosmopolitan elite'—and to understand how this elite reproduces itself in the face of global and local change. In 'worlding' cosmopolitanism, we are asking how 'actually existing cosmopolitanism' animates, regulates, and shapes social life in particular places at particular moments in world-historical time.

How we imagine the world is not an esoteric question of high theory. Culture and power are intertwined: imageries of cosmopolitanism produce and reproduce the social hierarchies of global order. Who gets to belong among the cosmopolitan elite depends on how we believe such 'actually existing cosmopolitanism' to operate in the world. This, in turn, calls our attention to the kinds of imageries that are produced about what it means to be and be

Cosmopolitan Elites. Kira Huju, Oxford University Press. © Kira Huju (2023). DOI: 10.1093/oso/9780198874928.003.0008

seen as a cosmopolitan—about how belonging in the cosmopolitan club is performed. Imageries make themselves felt in a very real sense—by shaping how we behave, how we see the world, what we understand our place in its hierarchies to be, and who we think best represents us in it. They become institutionalized, hardening into self-evident facts of social life we rarely question—thus also calling forth a dominant habitus, a rewarded way of *being* in the world. This habitus becomes an embodied form of social gatekeeping, adjudicating membership in the cosmopolitan elite. Cosmopolitanism is not innocent of power—either at home or in the world. Understanding it as a social phenomenon throws a host of power constellations and hierarchies into sharp relief.

The curious postcolonial afterlives of exclusive worldliness are particularly striking in India, whose diplomacy has been predicated on the ideological rejection of Western supremacy and gatekeeping. The case of Indian diplomats shows how embodied standards of civilization survive formal decolonization even in spaces dedicated to passionately countering imperial influence. This standard also creates and disciplines thought patterns, social hierarchies, and forms of behaviour in diplomacy. Understanding these processes, however, requires moving away from the neutralizing, universalizing, and technocratic language of liberal international order.

India never really believed itself to operate under a liberal rules-based international order governed by a benign class of cosmopolitans. There was never anything particularly liberal, rules-based, or orderly to India about the way that the world was remade after 1947. Measuring Indian diplomacy against the ideals of this order is a category error of sorts. Instead, what the representatives of India believed themselves to be facing was the long conservative shadow of colonialism's aftermath and a radical postcolonial moment of reshaping the world in the image of its former margins. The colonial and postcolonial are not neatly sequenced as chronologically distinct epochs; they coexist in the way that marginalized members of global order envision their place in the world.

This world-historical lag is the backdrop to India's dual project of proving its belonging, at the same time, inside an exclusive club and an equal world. For most of the existence of independent India, its diplomats have been awkwardly suspended between two very different imageries—on the one hand, an archaic imagery built in the old image of aristocratic and colonial Europe; on the other, a postcolonial international society founded on anti-imperialism and Third World difference. I have sketched out the constitution, genealogy, institutionalization, outward projection, reproduction, and contestation of the cleft habitus that this duality has produced. It has been the difficult task of

India's representatives to both attain some form of distinction *within* an old conception of Eurocentric order and to simultaneously distinguish India *from* it. This balancing act has produced a complex performance of worldliness: the world-embracing inflections of Third World solidarity have intermingled with colonially tinted forms of transnational class signalling and a desire not to flatten global hierarchies but to do some social climbing within them. The performance of actually existing cosmopolitanism among postcolonial elites is a complex affair, fraught with ethical dilemmas and political trade-offs.

The tension in diplomatic performances in the everyday of the Indian Foreign Service has been enabled by the deep, globally felt ambivalence about just how much of a transition has truly occurred in the social codes of international society following the formal breakdown of empire. The respective rules, codes of conduct, forms of desirable capital, and ways of behaving look very different between these two worlds. Thus, they also constrain and enable different modes of diplomatic practice and thought. Both imageries reflect various international hierarchies—of race, colonial relationships, material wealth—and are also intimately tied to domestic hierarchies—of caste, class, gender, religion. They justify the existence of a particular kind of *domestic* elite, who is entrusted with seeking status for the nation out there in the world, as part of a *global* elite.

Driving this performance is a desire to belong. The question, therefore, is: what do standard liberal internationalist narratives about inclusion under global order leave out? Or, asked in reverse: where do the narrow rules of belonging in the cosmopolitan elite come from? Describing the shifting rules of membership in international society in the wake of decolonization, Barry Buzan was found arguing in an earlier chapter that '[w]ith the right of independence and sovereign equality becoming almost unconditional, questions of membership in, and conditions of entry to, international society largely disappeared.'[1] This procedural reading puts great faith in official rules of admission as a way of solving questions of identity and voice.

By contrast, I have argued that recognition is more than formal accession into a club of nations—it is a continuous, quotidian performance of belonging, status, and distinction. It does not end, but rather begins at the point of formal admission. Technically, postcoloniality signalled the birth of a new authenticity—an idiom of difference that sought to secure equality by rejecting old hierarchies and speaking from a marginal, moralistic position of Third World solidarity. In this reading, India was not a permission-seeking

---

[1] Buzan, 'The "Standard of Civilization"', 585.

outsider of a European-dominated order but a culture-setting founder of a new postcolonial world. Yet social misrecognition creates world-historical trauma. Patterns of behaviour are not unlearned overnight; the indignities of mimicry linger. The most stable social expressions of order are maintained neither by ideological imposition nor physical force; they live on in the everyday, subtle elevation of certain dispositions, behaviours, and ways of being. In this way, Indian diplomats learned to master the social codes of two very different imageries of global order.

I have argued that the 'actually existing cosmopolitanism' of the Indian Foreign Service serves a dual function. It takes on features of both an international audition and a domestic social sorting mechanism. On the one hand, elite performances of the cosmopolitan aesthetic have allowed Indian diplomats to prove their belonging by imbibing the habits and tastes of an old, transnational insider club abroad. That is, elite members of the Indian Foreign Service have put their command of the cosmopolitan aesthetic to use in order to ameliorate the inherent inequalities that underpin formally pluralistic but socially stratified global order. Cosmopolitan capital—even with all its classist, colonial, casteist baggage—can be leveraged to purchase belonging in the eyes of a Western-centric world. This suggests that some of the most resilient re-enactments of elite cosmopolitanism are not merely expressions of hegemonic policy regimes, nor are they necessarily Western impositions. Rather, they are performances that a postcolonial elite may themselves reproduce to find recognition and status in the social hierarchies of global order.

Recognition among a global class of cosmopolitans comes easier to postcolonial local elites with inherited exposure to internationally convertible forms of social and cultural capital. This is also what explains the seemingly asynchronous continuing dominance of the typically upper-caste and upper-class 'St Stephen's type', which in so many ways still dominates the Indian Foreign Service, both organizationally (by disproportionately occupying higher posts) and culturally (by continuing to demarcate what an ideal diplomat looks like). The continued admiration for Stephenians attests to Bourdieu's intuition that cultural capital in all its forms is valued most highly when it is at its most scarce.

On the other hand, the elite's monopoly over the cosmopolitan performance in India has perpetuated and legitimated its dominant status at home. The elite has leveraged its cosmopolitan credentials to justify domestic forms of social, institutional, and cultural domination within the inherited institutions of the Indian body politic. The elite cosmopolitanism of the Foreign Service functions through quotidian exclusionary practices and embodied habitus in the diplomatic everyday, which order social relations and grant diplomats status according to their familiarity with cosmopolitan mores. Elite cosmopolitanism becomes a social sorting mechanism. This shows how postcolonial elites become socially invested in self-perpetuating visions of elite cosmopolitanism that legitimate their own continued domestic dominance.

This is a crucial part of why we see the continued phantom existence of a colonially inflected performance of elite cosmopolitanism in India. Even as the world transitions past Western domination and European signals of class and status have lost their charm, historically dominant Indians of a particular social class and caste are culturally invested in reproducing facets of a Europeanized habitus that once granted people like them their elite status. Those whose capital—eloquent English, elite education, social networks—fit old ideals of a cosmopolitan class have an interest in reproducing these ideals. The social codes of the cosmopolitan elite may ostracize most kinds of Indians, but they do empower a small Indian constituency to belong. The nominal elite commitment to diversity has had an almost therapeutic effect on India's cosmopolitan diplomats: it has allowed them to thrive as celebrated pluralists abroad while perpetuating an elitist diplomatic culture within.

In this respect, the narratives of a standard of civilization, once imposed on the world outside Europe, resemble the rationalizations of dominant diplomats within the Indian Foreign Service, defending their continued dominance over a now much more diverse Service. Under colonial rule, it was European powers who employed the standard of civilization to legitimate their dominance over those whose social practices they deemed inferior. In a formally postcolonial order, a rendition of this judgement has been harnessed by postcolonial elites against their compatriots. In this rationalization, a particular conception of international society, defined by European aristocratic and colonially born conventions, is used against internal Others—lower-caste or lower-class Indians, rural recruits, vernacular speakers, sometimes women—not seen as adhering to the codes of comportment, manners, and etiquette expected of an ideal diplomat. This throws up a question about what we mean, precisely, when we talk about representation: the ideals of being *representative* jar against the ideals of being *representable*. All in all, the social reproduction of an exclusive cosmopolitan elite is the result of both colonial traumas of misrecognition and the postcolonial incentives of domestic elite reproduction.

Heirs and pretenders in Naya Bharat

The cleft around which Indian diplomacy cohered for almost seven decades is fraying at both ends. However unsteady the tension between the two visions of international society that Indian diplomats have operated by, at least it was a familiar tension—institutionalized, practised, and imbibed over decades. Today, many diplomats no longer recognize either the diplomatic world they used to be a part of or the India they ought to represent. The emerging forms of being differently in the world are yet to fully form themselves. A reflexive sociological sensibility allows us to get at these uncertainties even as new institutional arrangements, global power shifts, and evolving diplomatic allegiances are still in flux. A focus on the diplomatic habitus, reflecting social orders through 'the body of the diplomat',[2] shows us how much of the unsteadiness of the fraying order is rooted in social estrangement. In the interregnum, the Foreign Service, too, becomes a battleground 'between the heirs and the pretenders'.[3]

The battles of estrangement are fought on two fronts. There are those for whom the Foreign Service's allegiance to an old aristocratic world has been experienced, day to day, through the social arrogance and cultural distance that traditional elites have practised towards their less polished colleagues. There are also those for whom the official insistence on a pluralist, Third Worldist vision felt like a modernist straitjacket imposed on India by the cultural tastes of its secular, socialist elites. Sometimes these groups include the same people—say, in the case of diplomats from 'non-traditional' vernacular backgrounds drawn to the promises of recognition offered by *Hindutva*. Neither rejection comes from ignorance, but rather from deep intimacy. They do not reflect a misunderstanding but a misrecognition: a felt marginalization in a prevailing order that one knows closely, but always as an outsider. As such, these tensions often point not to future breaks but to long-suppressed resentments that the interregnum forces to the surface.

In fact, there is nothing inherently indigenous about the basic structure of Hindutva's representational claims either. If anything, its civilizational-religious reading of global order is deeply reminiscent of late-nineteenth-century discourses which legitimated forms of domination by recourse to notions of religious unity, racial purity, and hegemonic nationalism. Under colonialism, civilizational thinking was harnessed to argue for the supremacy

---

[2] Neumann, 'The Body of the Diplomat'.
[3] Bourdieu quoted in Bigo, 'Pierre Bourdieu and International Relations', September 2011, 240.

276   EPILOGUE: A WORLD OF DIFFERENCE

of white Christianity and European civilization. In Modi's India, instead of being categorically rejected, this civilizational logic is reappropriated to speak for the supremacy of an ancient Indian civilization expressed in a Hindu *rashtra*, set against its internal barbarians.

There are also parallels with deeply European readings of the nation. From the early 1920s and into the final years of World War II, leading figures of the main historical organizations of *Hindutva*, primarily the RSS and the Hindu Mahasabha, drew ideological and organizational inspiration from Italian fascism under Mussolini and German Nazism under Hitler, sometimes facilitated by direct contacts between *Hindutva* figures and European fascist leadership.[4] Vinayak Damodar Savarkar's thinking on national unity and racial purity repeatedly drew explicit comparisons between the Jews in Germany and the Muslims of India. Thus, describing a Hindu nationalist India as post-Western or anti-Western—while politically and rhetorically resonant—can understate the entanglements between *Hindutva* ideologies and quintessentially European strands of political thought on nation, nationalism, and the international.

With the re-election of Prime Minister Modi in the spring of 2019 and the government's hardening line on academic and political freedom,[5] one is left to wonder whether the kinds of open and critical interviews that made this book possible will take place in the future. At the time of writing, serving officers have officially been banned from speaking to academics. The internal battle lines are also hardening among diplomats: there is less space for ambivalence, for travelling between different worlds, for code switching depending on the audience, and for holding multiple allegiances that cut across strict identity boundaries. If their public statements and fiery Twitter forays are anything to go by, some conservative-leaning former officials who at the time of the interviews were still rather measured in their assessments of Modi have since proven themselves as unconditional advocates, who engage in colourful and categorical dismissals of any critique of the Indian Premier. On the other side of this battle line are interviewees now organizing under the banner of the 'Constitutional Conduct Group', comprised of former government officials

---

[4] Marzia Casolari, 'Hindutva's Foreign Tie-up in the 1930s: Archival Evidence', *Economic and Political Weekly* 35, no. 4 (2000): 224.

[5] See e.g. Academic Freedom Monitoring Project, 'Scholars at Risk Reports on Jawaharlal Nehru University', Scholars at Risk, 2019, https://www.scholarsatrisk.org/report/2019-12-09-jawaharlal-nehru-university/; Sobhana K. Nair, 'India Again Placed at 142nd Rank in Press Freedom', *The Hindu*, 21 April 2021, sec. National, https://www.thehindu.com/news/national/india-again-placed-at-142nd-rank-in-press-freedom/article34377079.ece; Reporters without Borders, 'India: Modi Tightens His Grip on the Media', *Reporters without Borders*, 2021, https://rsf.org/en/india.

concerned about executive overreach and anti-constitutional instincts under Modi's reign.

When I was first sharpening my arguments around saffronization in 2019, I thought that the Foreign Service would need to undergo a generational shift for *Hindutva* to cement itself inside the institutional architecture of Indian diplomacy. I believed that the old guard would need to vacate their positions en route to permanent retirement for the cultural, social, and political priorities of *Hindutva* to find any sustainable footing; for an entire young generation to be socialized into a new way of being a diplomat from the very beginning. However, saffronization is unfolding across India's governing apparatus in a manner so systematic and pervasive that this prediction may prove to have been too conservative. Mid-level officers may well choose not to jeopardize half of their careers in service of strong principles loosely held. The distinction between a principle and a preference may collapse. Even retired officers might find it easier to yield to the political will of the current sovereign. Most Indian diplomats retire in their early 60s and, with another few decades ahead of them on government pensions that cannot furnish an upper-middle class lifestyle, are economically reliant on the kinds of think tank work, NGO affiliations, and academic collaborations that increasingly collect a demonstration of one's *Hindutva* sympathies as a price of entry.

When I published a journal article in *International Affairs* on the topic of the Service's saffronization in early 2022,[6] perhaps the most common pushback I received—barring some rather unimaginative social media trolling from *Hindutva*-supporting Twitter accounts—was on this very question. Scholars, practitioners, and journalists reached out with anecdotes and pieces of news about a Foreign Service transforming before their very eyes. There were, for example, instances conveyed in confidence by a young journalist of academic conferences on Indian diplomacy abroad being monitored and censored by Indian Missions.

There were also mentions of an undiplomatically worded scolding by the Indian Ambassador to Australia in 2021, which sought to discipline Australia's free press for questioning Modi's handling of the Covid pandemic in India. While Indian diplomats have a proud and admirable tradition of countering simplistic Western narratives, the exchange represented a stark departure from standards of evidence and language that one has come to expect from Foreign Service officers. In a bombastically worded official letter reproduced

---

[6] Kira Huju, 'Saffronizing Diplomacy: The Indian Foreign Service under Hindu Nationalist Rule', *International Affairs* 98, no. 2 (2022): 423–441.

278   EPILOGUE: A WORLD OF DIFFERENCE

for a broader audience on the Indian High Commission to Australia's Twitter account, the Indian Deputy High Commissioner, P.S. Karthigeyan, lambasted an Australian newspaper for its critical coverage.[7] In categorical language that did not bring to mind a liberal democracy engaging in a diplomatic exchange, the letter claimed that *The Australian*'s coverage had been produced 'with the sole objective of undermining the universally acclaimed approach taken by the Government of India'. Calling The *Australian*'s richly researched article 'baseless and malicious', the Deputy High Commissioner arrives at a chilling proposal to Australia's free press: it ought to 'refrain' from publishing such critical commentary in the future. The social media age perhaps incentivizes such grandstanding, and the letter was merely the most eye-catching fallout from Minister of External Affairs S. Jaishankar's orders to Indian diplomats to counter negative coverage of Modi's pandemic politics in international media.[8] At the same time, one is left to wonder how tightly journalists and academics may be watched behind the scenes if the tone has shifted to this extent in public.

Should a Hindu nationalist government continue to hold the reins of power in Delhi for several election cycles to come, I now believe that the cultural conventions and institutional practices of the Foreign Service, which this book, too, has detailed, will not endure. In 2018, the government launched a scheme of lateral entry into Indian bureaucracy, under which nine Joint-Secretaries from outside the elite services joined key ministries, while two years later, a government proposal emerged to source 400 Directors and Deputy Directors from the private sector to run state agencies.[9] Similar departures from the conventional aversion to lateral entry in the Ministry of External Affairs would undoubtedly come to serve not merely as a means of attracting meritorious private sector talent, as the official government line suggests, but as an opportunity to paint the Ministry in saffron. In their analysis of what, exactly, is 'new' about 'new *Hindutva*' in its contemporary expression, Thomas Blom Hansen and Srirupa Roy go as far as suggesting that 'the present Hindutva regime

---

[7] India in Australia [@HCICanberra], 'Urge @australian to Publish the Rejoinder to Set the Record Straight on the Covid Management in India and also Refrain from Publishing Such Baseless Articles in Future. @cgisydney @CGIPerth @cgimelbourne @MEAIndia Https://T.Co/4bgWYnKDlB', Tweet, *Twitter*, 26 April 2021, https://twitter.com/HCICanberra/status/1386678297665314827.

[8] 'Counter "One-Sided" World Media Narrative on Govt's Pandemic "Failure", Jaishankar Tells Indian Diplomats', *The Indian Express* (blog), 30 April 2021, https://indianexpress.com/article/india/counter-one-sided-world-media-narrative-on-govts-pandemic-failure-jaishankar-tells-indian-diplomats-7296036/.

[9] Thomas Blom Hansen and Srirupa Roy, 'What Is New about "New Hindutva"?', in *Saffron Republic: Hindu Nationalism and State Power in India* (Cambridge: Cambridge University Press, 2022), 6.

relies almost exclusively on ideological and loyalty criteria' in appointments, so that positions and promotions are decided 'on the basis of a shared *Hindutva* worldview and personal loyalty to Prime Minister Narendra Modi'.[10] I can think of officers I interviewed who certainly do not fit this description but have since our meeting nonetheless assumed prestigious postings abroad. However, to argue against patterns with anecdotes is not the kind of evidence one can use to form firm convictions either way.

Perhaps a kind of tipping point is being reached—or has been reached—as I write. One would need more sustained and pervasive elite access than I could ever claim during my time in New Delhi to confirm to what extent and in which ways, precisely, the MEA is yet another example of how the RSS acts as 'a penumbral authority in the contemporary regime, a shadowy and unaccountable presence that insists on its non-political identity even as it facilitates an organized ideological *gleichschaltung* or a coordinated homogenization across multiple state institutions'.[11] To think that its alternative reading of India will not or cannot permeate a historically relatively liberal or insular community like the Foreign Service, however, would be naïve.

We know very little, partly because the scholarly community that works on Indian IR has so far largely evaded *Hindutva* in favour of more conventional foreign-policy analysis under Modi's Premiership. There are also senior scholars both in India and abroad whose work has had the effect of normalizing, elevating, or trivializing *Hindutva* by treating foreign-policy thinking in government circles as 'muscular', 'bold', or 'transformative', without much nuance as to what kinds of associations these terms invoke, how they are rooted in Hindu nationalist imageries, and what, precisely, is being transformed in the Indian body politic. Any researcher must balance questions of career progress, political access, and personal safety against questions of academic integrity—especially so in the case of researchers with Indian passports, whose pursuit of their vocation today requires compromises and vigilance of an entirely different magnitude to those of us who work on India 'from outside'. It is nonetheless striking that the service of publicly available analysis on the saffronization of Indian diplomacy has been taken up primarily by more junior researchers, many without the protective cover of elite social networks, tenured and permanent university positions, or the comforts of a foreign passport.[12] This is

---

[10] Hansen and Roy, 7.
[11] Hansen and Roy, 7.
[12] Mohamed Zeeshan, 'The Indian Foreign Service Must Speak Out Against Growing Politicization', *The Diplomat*, accessed 11 October 2022, https://thediplomat.com/2021/05/the-indian-foreign-service-must-speak-out-against-growing-politicization/; Angshuman Choudhury, 'As India

work on which I hope the larger researcher community will build in the years to come, finding ways of writing without fear or favour.

As the cultural salience of inherited imageries of international society is fraying, so too is the cultural dominance of the Indian Foreign Service's self-appointed cosmopolitans. What the book has captured, then, are perhaps the last moments of institutional reign for a self-professedly cosmopolitan but peculiarly parochial class of Indian diplomats, 'at home in the world'. Precisely when political power in India is shifting, a portrait of this once dominant diplomatic elite must be drawn for posterity, capturing a postcolonial elite whose cultural ideals have for decades been pushing into world-historical overtime, living a sort of cultural afterlife in the wake of formal decolonization. Theirs was often a socially exclusive way of conceiving of their own Service. Yet in their role as representatives of postcolonial India out in the world, they distinguished themselves as fierce, eloquent defenders of global solidarity, secular toleration, and an international society much larger and more diverse than the West ever dared to imagine.

Difference and recognition in global order

The experience of Indian diplomats navigating a Western-dominated global order is emblematic of broader processes of representation, diversity, and exclusion in international relations. It is also emblematic of the social limits of a cosmopolitan creed that was supposed to bind this order together.

The Bourdieu-inspired exercise inside the Indian Foreign Service shows what is gained by thinking about questions of membership and belonging as sociological processes of recognition. It has shown the limits of an understanding of recognition that focuses purely on formal admission. Instead, recognition is a deeply social affair. It is about governing the social rules of belonging, and thus also about enabling, constraining, shaping, and legitimating various forms of difference. The case of India also shows why, precisely, the mere presence of minorities or marginalized groups does not in and of itself render an organization, system, community, or order diverse—neither

---

Hurtles Towards a Terrifying Endgame, Foreign Policy Community Cannot Remain Silent', *The Wire*, accessed 27 October 2022, https://thewire.in/diplomacy/as-india-hurtles-towards-a-terrifying-endgame-foreign-policy-community-cannot-remain-silent; Sumit Ganguly and Nicolas Blarel, 'Modi's Burning Bridge to the Middle East', 12 July 2022, https://www.foreignaffairs.com/articles/india/2022-06-30/modis-burning-bridge-middle-east; Wojczewski, 'Populism, Hindu Nationalism, and Foreign Policy in India: The Politics of Representing "the People"'; Sullivan de Estrada, 'In the World's Eyes, the Indian State May Be Declining but Its Citizenry Is Rising'; Miller, 'India's Authoritarian Streak: What Modi Risks with His Divisive Populism'.

inside the Indian Foreign Service nor in the supposedly pluralist and culturally neutral order envisioned by liberal internationalists. The 'democratization' of an elite culture is no numbers game, because cultural codes and social ideals are not determined by numerical majorities. An order can formally welcome new kinds of entrants without altering its ideals and behaviours, making late-entrants second-class members in its social hierarchies of recognition. It can socially punish newcomers for non-conformity or discipline their expressions of identity to fit its own ideals.

This, I argue, is a shallow form of diversity, which produces precisely the kind of estrangement that is now corroding the social foundations of existing order. Inclusion through assimilation is hardly an act of great tolerance or diversity; for assimilation is always assimilation into dominant culture. Winning formal recognition as a sovereign member does not settle a deeper struggle for recognition as a diplomatic peer and cultural equal. What matters for understanding the supposed diversification of international society is, rather, the significance or space afforded to the difference and diversity that members from new, different, non-dominant backgrounds embody. Genuine presence and voice are predicated on one's ability to 'win a place in the social order'.[13]

Seeing the varied performances of belonging in all their complexity requires us to take an expansive view of hierarchy in IR. If we think about hierarchy primarily through conventionally international binaries—colonizer/colonized, West/non-West, incumbent/challenger—two things become difficult to study. Firstly, we lose any sense of hybridity. Indian diplomats have sought to navigate different imageries of order, seeking membership in a white elite club while also daring to imagine parallel possibilities of postcoloniality. They transgress boundaries, show fluency in the codes of different readings of international society, and are torn between them. We will not get far by assuming that mimicry of 'Western' mores can only be countered by a wholesale embrace of an altogether different, exotic form of non-Western authenticity.[14] Secondly, a conventional focus on international hierarchy obscures other forms of ordering. The Indian diplomatic habitus is also a reflection of domestic inequalities, which are discursively tied in the rationalizations of a domestic elite to the perceived 'demands' of international society. In our analysis of the social hierarchies of global order, we must study an array of intersecting hierarchies:

[13] Bourdieu, *Distinction*, 483.
[14] On this point, again, see Nandy, *The Intimate Enemy: Loss and Recovery of Self under Colonialism*, 73.

282 EPILOGUE: A WORLD OF DIFFERENCE

colonial, material, and racial imbalances of international life matter, but so do those of class, gender, religion, and caste.

The complex hierarchies that produce a cosmopolitan elite also inform how we ought to debate its future. A mere rejection of the West does not democratize membership in the cosmopolitan club. The debate must move beyond the question of whether cosmopolitanism is Western-centric—for it is not merely Western-centrism that has allowed an elite reading of cosmopolitanism to consolidate itself. Pratap Bhanu Mehta has suggested that individuals from outside the West make better, more genuine cosmopolitans, since 'it is only in these parts of the world, where living deeply in two cultures—the modern "Occidental" and the vernacular—translating back and forth between them, negotiating their contradictory demands and incommensurable outlooks, is not a matter of choice but a deeply internalized practice that makes the complacencies of the West, or even its gestures towards multiculturalism, seem decidedly settled and provincial.'[15] Yet there are also complacencies shared between elites across the divide between West and non-West. These complacencies order themselves not so much around lines of nationality but of class, caste, education, and familial background. Indian diplomats can practise a 'decidedly settled and provincial' cosmopolitanism, too. Cosmopolitans are a community—even if much of their self-identification revolves around a stubborn insistence that they alone have found a way of transcending the parochial confines of their own roots. Understanding the intersecting boundary conditions and transnational codes of belonging in the cosmopolitan elite is crucial for any critical analysis of it.

Similarly, understanding the entangled origins of India's turn inwards is one way of getting at broader processes of nationalism, populism, and anti-cosmopolitanism that define so much of the discourse on our global order in peril. The nativist turn is not peculiar to India alone and neither is the rejection of cosmopolitanism as a vain occupation of a cultural elite. Ultimately, the case of internationalist Indian diplomats adjusting to life under Hindu nationalist rule is emblematic of processes of diplomatic accommodation, as self-ascribed cosmopolitans the world over seek to make sense of their role as representatives of nations turning inwards. In our conversations, Indian diplomats recognized this, drawing parallels to a global tide of revolts against perceived elites from Trump in the United States to Brexit in the United Kingdom, and the *gilets jaunes* protests sweeping across France—currents which had rendered the notion of cosmopolitanism 'a very loaded question' the world

---

[15] Mehta, 'Cosmopolitanism and the Circle of Reason', 632.

over, as a retired officer anxiously put it.[16] Saffronization is a rendition of a trend whose roots are primarily domestic but whose basic characteristics are, in many ways, global. The social dynamics of misrecognition, resentment, and outsider status, too, undergird political processes across the world. We may not want to speak of universal conditions, but we can certainly identify transnational patterns.

Yet unlike the more vulgar example of former President Donald Trump's United States or the miscellaneous collection of conspiracies that underwrite former Brazilian President Jair Bolsonaro's critiques of the West, what India's case brings to the fore is how even those wedded to facets of a global order and beholden to many of its social ideals can grow wary of it. India's resistance and resentments are not easily caricatured, not least because they are articulated from a place of deep intimacy and knowledge of this order. There is no easy binary that places India on one side of a clean divide—'us' versus 'them', 'upholders' against 'challengers'. Therefore, India's case points to the futility of much of the binary thinking that characterizes contemporary debates on liberal order.

Going against the liberal internationalist instinct that nationalism and internationalism must always be at odds, India also shows that there is nothing intrinsic to nationalism that makes it a corrosive substance to global justice and order. The nationalism of the freedom struggle against the Raj was a world-shifting force that rightly demanded sovereign equality for the dispossessed. Third World nationalism opened up avenues for postcolonial nations to build bonds of solidarity across the world. What is a threat is the essentialist demand for a hermetically sealed non-Western authenticity, which is wary of internal diversity and dissent, making cultural and political acquiescence to a particular political programme a condition for proving true national allegiance.

Finally, recent developments in India display the ethical dilemmas of studying contemporary reactions to Western-centric order at the intersection of politics and academia. It is imperative that we identify a sustainable line between understanding legitimate grievances and justifying regressive responses to them. A critique of Westerncentric world-ordering is easily appropriated by nationalist regimes and theoreticians, who can justify their domestic project of exclusions by deceptively articulating it in the postcolonial language of liberation. Indeed, the appropriation of postcolonial language is a discursive method of considerable popularity among India's Hindu right, as all foreign critique is read as an imperial incursion. Contemporary regimes of

---

[16] Interview 7.

284 EPILOGUE: A WORLD OF DIFFERENCE

domestic exclusion are legitimated by reference to past forms of colonial marginalization: the 'anticolonial' fight against foreign domination becomes a fight against 'anti-national' citizens critical of the government. This is not an equation that critical scholarship can afford to let itself be intellectually appropriated for. As Sankaran Krishna has warned fellow academics providing 'non-Eurocentric' explanations in the case of nationalist China, 'enhancing the soft power of emerging hegemons by supporting, wittingly or otherwise, their derivative histories does not augur well for pacific futures'.[17] In theory, of course, there could be something democratizing or liberating about a repurposed civilizational discourse, which speaks of civilizations in the plural, instead of conceiving of one civilization threatened by a multitude of barbarians. Yet in claiming civilizational standing under the banner of *Hindutva*, this call for a new, more disciplined, and closely monitored Indianness makes internal barbarians of all those Indians who do not fit the majoritarian mould. Replacing colonially inherited notions of enforced sameness with domestic ones does nothing to democratize India or the world.

The once and future cosmopolitans?

Where does this leave the historically embedded and hierarchically ordered process of making and unmaking cosmopolitan elites? How this elite has been envisioned in India tells us about the power imbalances of international and Indian society, about the clash between worldly mores and post-colonial ideals, the longing for parity in similarity and pride in difference, and the pushback now underway against the ostensibly (but never quite) liberal order. For all this sociological baggage, it is important to study the backlash against cosmopolitan elites not only as a backlash against a supposedly world-embracing ethic, but also as a rejection of the elite-reproducing social exclusions that 'actually existing cosmopolitanism' has facilitated across the world.

One legitimate interpretation of the foregoing chapters is to see the processes of colonial assimilation and class-based socialization of diplomatic probationers into elite manners and etiquette as a making of a cosmopolitan elite. This cosmopolitan elite would, then, be in a process of its own unmaking—both because the more diverse incoming cadres fail to imbibe the correct elite habitus and because the nativist turn in Modi's India rejects all

---

[17] Sankaran Krishna, 'China Is China, Not the Non-West: David Kang, Eurocentrism, and Global Politics', *Harvard Journal of Asiatic Studies* 77, no. 1 (2017): 109.

things cosmopolitan as culturally suspect. This is the kind of story that the Service's traditional elite tells of itself.

Another way of reading the story of this book is to see in it an unfinished journey towards a cosmopolitan elite that never truly existed. If the cosmopolitan ethic is supposed to be about celebrating difference and diversity, then this celebration is at odds with the historically homogenous group of diplomats who have sought to assimilate vernacular elements and marginalized officers into a dominant habitus. This cosmopolitan elite could perhaps have finally been in the making now, with the move towards a post-Western world and the gradual shift among younger generations towards a more inclusive imagery of what 'worldliness' means. Yet here, too, the ethnocentric turn stops the process in its tracks: *Hindutva* may reject the mimicry of elitist standards of 'worldliness', but its narrow insistence on Indian authenticity, Hindi, and Hinduism sets its own punishing standard that rejects plurality.

I have argued throughout this book that the practices of 'actually existing cosmopolitanism' among Indian diplomats draw the circle of tolerance much smaller than normative theory would tell us. Cosmopolitanism is not evoked to advocate for global equality, diversity, or inclusion but to legitimate the dominance of a sociocultural elite inside the Service and to barter for a higher social status for India's representatives in a deeply unequal world. It has been precisely the desire to be recognized as equal in international society that has legitimated the stigmatization of difference within the Foreign Service. Cosmopolitanism, as it is lived out in the everyday lives of Indian diplomats navigating the social hierarchies of global order, functions more as a class marker of elite distinction inside a club. And instead of transcending private loyalties, as political theory says cosmopolitanism does, cosmopolitanism in the Indian diplomatic imagination is tied to hierarchies of class and caste. Self-described cosmopolitans speak the language of diversity while engaging in practices of social exclusion, in which internal Others are marked by their inability to imbibe the cosmopolitan aesthetic, and thus also by the impossibility of being recognized as worthy members of international society. Much like the prizes after which post-liberalization 'aspirational India' clamours, so too the markers of an effortless cosmopolitan are out of reach for many, even within India's diplomatic corps.

The belief among India's traditional diplomatic elite that diversity equals decline speaks to this exclusionary reading of cosmopolitan belonging. Perversely, this reading mirrors the cultural anxiety that once defined the white Western response to decolonization: a homogenous elite now being forced to

286 EPILOGUE: A WORLD OF DIFFERENCE

welcome an unruly expansion in its membership interprets this change as a threat to the integrity of the institution that the elite once presided over alone. Ultimately, then, the exclusionary social logics of 'actually existing cosmopolitanism' signify the political failure of a postcolonial project of solidarity, democratization, and diversity.

The reduction of cosmopolitanism to a social marker of elite distinction betrays the normative failure of its radical egalitarian potential in the wake of decolonization, the Non-Aligned Movement, and the transnational solidarities indicated in Third Wordlist diplomatic projects. The performative demands of this kind of cosmopolitanism have compromised the postcolonial project of democratizing the Foreign Service and thinking past Western diplomatic convention. They have normalized a politically unambitious and heavily hierarchal reading of cosmopolitanism. From the very beginning, Indian diplomats spoke with authority and conviction against racial inequality and global economic injustice, but borrowed a thin conception of cosmopolitanism from a deeply hierarchical, colonial, and aristocratic European tradition. Despite the heavy emphasis on solidarity in India's postcolonial diplomatic parlance, the discourse on cosmopolitanism itself has been strangely unmoored from solidarist thinking. The absence of any elaborations on an alternative 'postcolonial cosmopolitanism' in Indian diplomatic discourse shows both a certain social investment on the part of dominant officers in cosmopolitan capital as it expresses itself in domestic elite status, and the difficulties of thinking past Western hegemonic concepts. The paradox between the world-embracing ambitions of 'cosmopolitanism' and the narrow confines of any 'elite' invites us to think about the very existence of a cosmopolitan elite as a kind of political failure.

Perhaps it was precisely the officers' disappointment at discovering the power imbalances of cosmopolitanism as they found it in the world—at just how little space it actually held for difference and diversity—that shrunk cosmopolitanism into a domestic elite marker in the first place. Even for the most ardent espousers of elite liberal cosmopolitanism, the most painful facet of the cosmopolitan creed was, in fact, the unspoken power asymmetry one was not supposed to speak out loud. There was no genuinely international cosmopolitan praxis which Indian diplomats could propagate from a place of equal standing. It is almost as though Indian diplomats knew that cosmopolitanism could realistically only be expected to function as a domestic elite identity, never as a practicable principle of international life. Cosmopolitanism could not buy much by way of genuine equality in the world, and so it settled into a scarce personal resource that individual diplomats could use to purchase

THE ONCE AND FUTURE COSMOPOLITANS? 287

social standing within the Service and, so they hoped, among the global club of cosmopolitan elites.

We have grown accustomed to using broadly liberal terms such as 'diversity' and 'cosmopolitanism' as virtually interchangeable, as different descriptors of the same political project. Yet diversity and cosmopolitanism are not by necessity natural allies. Sometimes an outward-facing cosmopolitanism has required a negation of diversity within. This is precisely what has occurred with the elevation of 'actually existing cosmopolitanism' into a personalized standard of civilization: the disciplining effects of its elite performance discourage expressions of difference and subalternity. In fact, they encourage traditional elites in India to neutralize internal diversity through the pedagogies of diplomatic training and socialization. In many ways, this rendition of cosmopolitanism actually shares its stated ideals of neutrality and sameness with Ikenberrian liberal internationalism: as Calhoun has argued, '[s]tarting from the perspective of abstract equivalence, seeing essential similarities as the main ground for cosmopolitanism tends to make differences appear as potential problems.'[18] This is also how a language of diversity can exist alongside practices of exclusion. The performance of elite cosmopolitanism, imbibed through the diplomatic body, could buy esteem and belonging in the diplomatic club—not *despite* the fact that cosmopolitanism was never as inclusionary as it claimed to be, but precisely *because it was not.*

This raises the awkward question of whether prevalent interpretations of cosmopolitanism are actively working against principles of diversity and difference. Cosmopolitanism, as long as it is practised as an elite marker of social distinction, will do little to hold together a fractious world. Cosmopolitanism is cheap if it asks nothing in return—if it does not necessitate a critical evaluation of the basic political and cultural structures within which it is practised. In this sense, as Calhoun cautions:

> Much of its appeal comes from the notion that cosmopolitanism (a version of ethical goodness) can be achieved without much deeper structural change. But cosmopolitanism is not simply a free-floating cultural taste, equally accessible to everyone; it is not just a personal attitude or a political choice, although it can inform these. Cosmopolitanism is also a matter of material conditions that are very unequally distributed. What seems like free individual choice is often made possible by capital—social and cultural as well as economic.[19]

[18] Calhoun, 'A Cosmopolitanism of Connections', 195.
[19] Calhoun, 189.

288 EPILOGUE: A WORLD OF DIFFERENCE

Is it even possible to sever the ties between cosmopolitanism and elitism? Those hoping to counter the charge that cosmopolitanism is irretrievably elitist have tended to turn to a 'cosmopolitanism from below', studying migrants, seafarers, or translators.[20] Rahul Rao, acknowledging that cosmopolitanism has often been 'at best, a normative world view that would be beneficial for subalterns if adopted by elites', turns to social movements for alternative practices of cosmopolitanism.[21] But can there be a cosmopolitanism *inside elite spaces* that makes room for perspectives that are not articulated in a dominant idiom? Can the cosmopolitan elite itself evolve into something different?

As we struggle to make sense of the global revolt against the cosmopolitan elite, we must critically interrogate the socially expressed hierarchies and everyday exclusions that underlie a formally pluralistic world. 'Actually existing cosmopolitanism' has a social context. As cosmopolitanism comes under challenge, it is imperative to ask whose sense of belonging is legitimated by a commitment to it. If we want to keep some of the professed ethical virtues of cosmopolitanism in a fracturing world, we need to not only query its material basis but to abandon much of the attendant cultural expectations. It is this elitist imagery, which diplomats embody so well, that makes the nativist appeals to 'authenticity' so personally palatable to those left out of the cosmopolitan club. One might, at an earlier point in time, have assumed that such appeals would go unheeded by diplomats—after all, they surely count among global elites by professional default. Yet the case of the Indian Foreign Service, in large part owing to caste reservations, shows that those who govern the world through diplomacy need not be made up of 'elites' in a conventional sense of the word. It reminds us that diplomats, too, are carriers of a multiplicity of identities, in an intersectional web of social hierarchies.

Ideals and values are not randomly held preferences, as Bourdieu continually reminds us, and so we ought not divorce a consideration of cosmopolitanism from the social structures that sustain its various interpretations. Cosmopolitanism, too, is to some degree about power—not only the power that comes with being able to set the dominant definition of the term, but also the power that expresses itself through the unequal cultural and material resources available to actors to meet the demands of this definition. Perhaps it too easily escapes those who fit the cosmopolitan aesthetic that for cosmopolitanism to manifest itself as genuine openness and hybridity, power and resources must be relatively equally distributed.[22]

---

[20] Robbins and Horta, 'Introduction', 2017, 9.
[21] Rao, *Third World Protest*, 199.
[22] Bender, 'The Cosmopolitan Experience', 120.

What would it look like for the world to 'learn to live with, accept, celebrate, and operationalise its own diversity'?[23] A cosmopolitanism which celebrates difference—instead of ridiculing it when it appears vernacular—is a cosmopolitanism that can be embodied irrespective of one's status in a social order. A politics of diversity, as Srirupa Roy writes about India, is a politics that recognizes 'the distinctiveness of group identity' not through ghettoization or assimilation, but by allowing these identities 'to flourish within the context of a single institutional framework'.[24] Crucially, inclusion must mean more than formal accession to a society of states and recognition must mean more than the right to have your difference neutralized to fit a dominant ideal. This would require relaxing, rethinking, and democratizing notions of who is recognized as a cosmopolitan worthy of the moniker.

Finally, our conversation about a liberal order in crisis must move beyond the liberal internationalist insistence on dividing the world into either 'cosmopolitan' or 'closed'. We must investigate the forms of closure inherent in elite cosmopolitanism itself. Liberal readings of global order have understood cosmopolitanism as delivering us from parochialisms and ensuring diversity, pluralism, and tolerance. Yet it is precisely the imperative to fit into this rarefied 'cosmopolitan' fold, free of cultural baggage and political strife, that has thwarted many initiatives at the global margins that might have expressed ideals of openness. Ultimately, performances of sameness and difference—as alternative strategies of belonging—force us to consider what and whom we are willing to sacrifice to be truly seen. There are various ways in which actors might self-sensor their supposed difference to be seen as equal members of international society—or police those around them in order to have their collective as a whole be more acceptable, more knowable, more recognizably 'cosmopolitan', and comfortably similar in the gaze of others.

The conversation about governing difference in the twenty-first century cannot be a simple sorting exercise between defenders and detractors of cosmopolitanism—about governing entry into the cosmopolitan elite. Instead, it but must be an honest debate about the very nature of cosmopolitanism in a fractious and volatile world, shifting shape before our eyes.

Cosmopolitanism is not a professional perk, served with canapes and identical opinions. It ought to be a constant challenge, practised with patience—for 'the world of difference, the foundation of cosmopolitanism, is a domain of inevitable uncertainties and recalculations about oneself and of people and

---

[23] O.P. Dwivedi, 'The Challenge of Cultural Diversity for Good Governance', *Indian Journal of Public Administration* 48, no. 1 (2002): 28.

[24] Roy, 'Instituting Diversity', 81.

places.'[25] Thus, a cosmopolitan is not, in fact, 'comfortable anywhere in the world', as Indian diplomatic elites often argued. Rather, a cosmopolitan is 'always slightly uncomfortable, even at home.'[26] A cosmopolitan is, if anything, the very antonym of Bourdieusian effortlessness. Cosmopolitanism in an unequal world is hard work.

[25] Bender, 'The Cosmopolitan Experience', 116.
[26] Bender, 119.

Bibliography

Archival sources

National Archives of India, New Delhi: Ministry of External Affairs Section

Nehru Memorial Library and Museum (restricted archival section), New Delhi:

Individual papers

- M.C. Chagla
- Subimal Dutt
- Y.D. Gundevia
- P.N. Haksar
- T.N. Kaul
- Mohan Sinha Mehta
- K.P.S. Menon
- V.V. Krishna Menon
- R.K. Nehru
- B.K. Nehru
- Vijaya Lakshmi Pandit
- Apa B. Pant
- Gopal Singh

Oral history transcripts

- B.K. Acharya (1976)
- J.N. Dixit (2000)
- K.P.S. Menon (1976)
- Lakshmi N. Menon (1971)
- R.K. Nehru (1971)
- Apa B. Pant (1973)

First-hand accounts and collected speeches

Bandaranaike, S.W.R.D. 'The Majlis in the Mid-Twenties'. *Hilary Term 1986, The Majlis Magazine, Oxford*, 1986.

Bandyopadhyaya, Jayantanuja. *The Making of India's Foreign Policy: Determinants, Institutions, Processes, and Personalities*. Bombay: Allied Publishers, 1970.

292 BIBLIOGRAPHY

Bedekar, G.V. 'Not Many but Much'. In *The Civil Servant in India, by Ex-Indian Civil Servants*, edited by Kewalram Laichand Panjabi, 270–277. Bombay: Bharatiya Vidya Bhavan, 1965.

Bhaduri, Madhu. *Lived Stories*. New Delhi: Orient BlackSwan, 2021.

Bhandari, P. L. *How Not to Be a Diplomat: Adventures in the Indian Foreign Service Post-Independence*. London: The Quince Tree, 2013.

Chagla, M.C. *Roses in December: An Autobiography*. 9th ed. Bombay: Bharatiya Vidya Bhavan, 1990.

Curzon of Kedleston, George Nathaniel Curzon. *Speeches by Lord Curzon of Kedleston, Viceroy and Governor General of India (Vol. 3)*. Calcutta: Office of the Superintendent of Government Printing, India, 1899.

Dayal, Rajeshwar. *A Life of Our Times*. New Delhi: Orient Longman, 1998.

Deshmukh, C.D. 'Looking Back on My Service Days'. In *The Civil Servant in India, by Ex-Indian Civil Servants*, edited by Kewalram Laichand Panjabi, 3–7. Bombay: Bharatiya Vidya Bhavan, 1965.

Dixit, J. N. *My South Block Years: Memoirs of a Foreign Secretary*. New Delhi: UBS Publishers, 1996.

Dixit, J. N. *Indian Foreign Service: History and Challenge*. Delhi: Konark Publishers, 2005.

Dubey, Muchkund. *India's Foreign Policy: Coping with the Changing World*. New Delhi: Orient BlackSwan, 2016.

Dutt, R.C. 'The Civil Service before and after Independence'. In *Memoirs of Old Mandarins of India*, edited by Raj Kumar Nigam, 58–74. New Delhi: Documentation Centre for Corporate & Business Policy Research, 1965.

Dutt, Subimal. *With Nehru in the Foreign Office*. Calcutta: South Asia Books, 1977.

Gundevia, Y. D. *Outside the Archives*. Hyderabad: Sangam Books, 1984.

Iengar, H.V.R. 'My Life in the ICS'. In *The Civil Servant in India, by Ex-Indian Civil Servants*, edited by Kewalram Laichand Panjabi, 119–129. Bombay: Bharatiya Vidya Bhavan, 1965.

Isvaran, V. 'The Indian Civil Servant'. In *The Civil Servant in India, by Ex-Indian Civil Servants*, edited by Kewalram Laichand Panjabi, 247–259. Bombay: Bharatiya Vidya Bhavan, 1965.

Kaul, Triloki Nath. *Ambassadors Need Not Lie: Some Aspects of India's Foreign Policy*. New Delhi: Lancer International, 1988.

Kirpalani, S.K. *Fifty Years with the British: Memoirs of an Indian Civil Servant*. Hyderabad: Sangam Books, 1993.

Lall, Shamaldharee. 'An Indian Civil Servant'. In *The Civil Servant in India, by Ex-Indian Civil Servants*, edited by Kewalram Laichand Panjabi, 7–22. Bombay: Bharatiya Vidya Bhavan, 1965.

Macaulay, Lord Thomas Babington. 'Minute on Indian Education (1835)'. In *Archives of Empire, Volume I: From the East India Company to the Suez Canal*, edited by Mia Carter and Barbara Harlow, 227–239. Duke University Press, 2003.

Mangat Rai, E. N. *Commitment, My Style: Career in the Indian Civil Service*. Delhi: Vikas Publishing, 1973.

Mathai, M.O. *Reminiscences of the Nehru Age*. New Delhi: Vikas Publishing, 1978.

Mehta, Jagat S. *The Tryst Betrayed: Reflections on Diplomacy and Development*. Gurgaon: Penguin Random House India, 2015.

Menon, K.P.S. 'My Life and Work in the ICS'. In *The Civil Servant in India, by Ex-Indian Civil Servants*, edited by Kewalram Laichand Panjabi, 29–59. Bombay: Bharatiya Vidya Bhavan, 1965.

Menon, K.P.S. *Many Worlds Revisited: An Autobiography*. Bombay: Bharatiya Vidya Bhavan, 1981.

Mukherjee, Bhaswati. *India and the EU: An Insider's View*. New Delhi: Vij Books, 2018.

Muthamma, C. B. Slain by the System: India's Real Crisis. New Delhi: Viveka Foundation, 2003.

Nehru, Braj Kumar. *Nice Guys Finish Second: Memoirs*. New Delhi: Viking, 1997.

Nehru, Jawaharlal. *An Autobiography*. Bombay: Allied Publishers, 1962.

Nehru, Jawaharlal. *Selected Works of Jawaharlal Nehru, Volume 19: 16th July–18th October 1952*. Edited by Sarvepalli Gopal. New Delhi: Jawaharlal Nehru Memorial Fund, 1966.

Nehru, Jawaharlal. *Jawaharlal Nehru: Thoughts*. New Delhi: Jawaharlal Nehru Memorial Fund, 1985.

Nehru, Jawaharlal. *The Discovery of India (1946)*. New Delhi: Penguin Books, 2004.

Nehru, Jawaharlal. *Letters for a Nation: From Jawaharlal Nehru to His Chief Ministers, 1947–1963*. Edited by Madhav Khosla. Gurgaon: Allen Lane, 2014.

Nehru, Jawaharlal. *Jawaharlal Nehru's Speeches, Vol. 3: 1953–1957*. New Delhi: Publications Division of the Ministry of Information and Broadcasting of the Government of India, 1958.

Pandit, Vijaya Lakshmi. *The Scope of Happiness: A Personal Memoir*. London: Weidenfeld and Nicolson, 1979.

Panikkar, K. M. Common Sense about India. London: Macmillan, New York, 1960.

Prabhu, J.M. Lobo. 'My Work in the ICS'. In *The Civil Servant in India, by Ex-Indian Civil Servants*, edited by Kewalram Laichand Panjabi, 223–233. Bombay: Bharatiya Vidya Bhavan, 1968.

Rana, Kishan S. *Inside Diplomacy*. New Delhi: Manas, 2000.

Rasgotra, Maharaja Krishna. *A Life in Diplomacy*. Gurgaon: Penguin/Viking, 2016.

Saran, Shyam. 'India and Multilateralism: A Practitioner's Perspective'. In *Shaping the Emerging World: India and the Multilateral Order*, edited by Waheguru Pal Singh Sidhu, Pratap Bhanu Mehta, and Bruce D. Jones, 43–56. Washington, D.C.: Brookings Institution Press, 2013.

Singh, Balwant. An Untouchable in the I.A.S. Saharanpur: B. Singh, 1997.

Tyabji, Badr-ud-Din. *Indian Policies and Practice*. Delhi: Oriental Publishers, 1972.

Secondary source books and journal articles

Abbas, Ackbar. 'Cosmopolitan De-Scriptions: Shanghai and Hong Kong'. In *Cosmopolitanism*, edited by Carol A. Breckenridge, Dipesh Chakrabarty, Sheldon Pollock, and Homi K. Bhabha, 209–228. Durham, NC: Duke University Press, 2002.

Abraham, Itty. *How India Became Territorial: Foreign Policy, Diaspora, Geopolitics*. Palo Alto: Stanford University Press, 2014.

Acharya, Amitav. 'Advancing Global IR: Challenges, Contentions, and Contributions'. *International Studies Review* 18, no. 1 (2016): 4–15.

Acharya, Amitav. 'Race and Racism in the Founding of the Modern World Order'. *International Affairs* 98, no. 1 (2022): 23–43.

Acharya, Amitav, and Barry Buzan, eds. *Non-Western International Relations Theory: Perspectives on and beyond Asia*. London: Routledge, 2010.

Adler, Emanuel, and Peter M Haas. 'Conclusion: Epistemic Communities, World Order, and the Creation of a Reflective Research Program'. *International Organization* 46, no. 1 (1992): 367–390.

BIBLIOGRAPHY

Adler-Nissen, Rebecca. 'The Diplomacy of Opting out: A Bourdieusian Approach to National Integration Strategies'. *Journal of Common Market Studies* 46, no. 3 (2008): 663–684.

Adler-Nissen, Rebecca. 'On a Field Trip with Bourdieu'. *International Political Sociology* 5, no. 3 (2011): 327–330.

Aggestam, Karin, and Ann Towns. 'The Gender Turn in Diplomacy: A New Research Agenda'. *International Feminist Journal of Politics* 21, no. 1 (2019): 9–28.

Andersen, Walter, and Shridhar D. Damle. *Messengers of Hindu Nationalism: How the RSS Reshaped India.* London: Hurst & Company, 2018.

Anderson, Benedict. *Imagined Communities: Reflections on the Origin and Spread of Nationalism.* London: Verso, 1991.

Anderson, Edward, and Christophe Jaffrelot. 'Hindu Nationalism and the "Saffronisation of the Public Sphere": An Interview with Christophe Jaffrelot'. *Contemporary South Asia* 26, no. 4 (2018): 468–482.

Anderson, Perry. *The Indian Ideology.* London: Verso Books, 2013.

Anievas, Alexander, Nivi Manchanda, and Robbie Shilliam. *Race and Racism in International Relations: Confronting the Global Colour Line.* Interventions (Routledge (Firm)). London; New York, NY: Routledge, Taylor & Francis Group, 2015.

Appadurai, Arjun. 'Is Homo Hierarchicus?' *American Ethnologist* 13, no. 4 (1986): 745–761.

Appiah, Kwame Anthony. 'Cosmopolitan Patriots'. *Critical Inquiry* 23, no. 3, (1997): 617–639.

Appiah, Kwame Anthony. *Cosmopolitanism: Ethics in a World of Strangers.* London: Penguin, 2007.

Babu, D. Shyam. 'Caste and Class among the Dalits'. In *Dalit Studies,* edited by Ramnarayan, 233–247.

Barik, R.K. 'Social Background of Civil Service: Some Depressing Trends'. *Economic and Political Weekly* 39, no. 7 (February 2004): 625–628.

Baru, Sanjay. 'Strategic Consequences of India's Economic Performance'. In *Globalization and Politics in India,* edited by Baldev Raj Nayar, 321–345. New Delhi: Oxford University Press, 2007.

Basrur, Rajesh. 'Modi's Foreign Policy Fundamentals: A Trajectory Unchanged'. *International Affairs* 93, no. 1 (2017): 7–26.

Basrur, Rajesh. 'Modi, Hindutva, and Foreign Policy'. *International Studies Perspectives* 20, no. 1 (2018): 7–11.

Basrur, Rajesh, and Kate Sullivan de Estrada. *Rising India: Status and Power.* London: Routledge, 2017.

Basu, Subho. 'The Dialectics of Resistance: Colonial Geography, Bengali Literati and the Racial Mapping of Indian Identity'. *Modern Asian Studies* 44, no. 1 (2010): 53–79.

Bayly, C.A. *The Local Roots of Indian Politics: Allahabad, 1880–1920.* Oxford: Clarendon Press, 1975.

Bayly, Martin J. 'Lineages of Indian International Relations: The Indian Council on World Affairs, the League of Nations, and the Pedagogy of Internationalism'. *The International History Review* 44, no. 4 (4 July 2022): 819–835.

Beaglehole, Tim Holmes. 'From Rulers to Servants: The ICS and the British Demission of Power in India'. *Modern Asian Studies* 11, no. 2 (1977): 237–255.

Behera, N. C. 'Re-Imagining IR in India'. *International Relations of the Asia-Pacific* 7, no. 3 (21 May 2007): 341–368.

Bell, Duncan. *Reordering the World: Essays on Liberalism and Empire.* Princeton: Princeton University Press, 2016.

Bender, Thomas. 'The Cosmopolitan Experience and Its Uses'. In *Cosmopolitanisms*, edited by Bruce Robbins and Paulo Lemos Horta, 116–127. New York: University Press, 2017.

Benner, Jeffrey. *Structure of Decision: The Indian Foreign Policy Bureaucracy.* New Delhi: South Asian Publishers, 1984.

Bennett, Tony. 'Introduction to the Routledge Classics Edition'. In *Distinction: A Social Critique of the Judgement of Taste*, by Pierre Bourdieu, xvii–xxiv. Routledge, 2010.

Berg, Dag Erik. 'Sovereignties, the World Conference against Racism 2001 and the Formation of a Dalit Human Rights Campaign'. Ceri Sciences Po, 2007. Research in question, No. 20, April 2007.

Béteille, André. *Caste, Class and Power: Changing Patterns of Stratification in a Tanjore Village.* New Delhi: Oxford University Press, 2012.

Béteille, André. 'The Peculiar Tenacity of Caste'. *Economic and Political Weekly* 47, no. 13 (March 2012): 41–48.

Bhagat, Ram. 'Census and Caste Enumeration: British Legacy and Contemporary Practice in India'. *Genus* 62, no. 2 (2006): 119–134.

Bhagavan, Manu. *India and the Quest for One World: The Peacemakers.* Basingstoke: Palgrave Macmillan, 2013.

Bhagavan, Manu. 'India and the United Nations, or Things Fall Apart'. In *The Oxford Handbook of Indian Foreign Policy*, edited by David M. Malone, C. Raja Mohan, and Srinath Raghavan, 596–608. New Delhi: Oxford University Press, 2015.

Bhambra, Gurminder K. 'Whither Europe? Postcolonial versus Neocolonial Cosmopolitanism'. *Interventions* 18, no. 2 (2016): 187–202.

Bhargava, G.S. 'The Ills of the Indian Foreign Service'. *Economic and Political Weekly* 1, no. 10 (October 1966): 407–410.

Bhatia, Gautam. 'Horizontal Discrimination and Article 15(2) of the Indian Constitution: A Transformative Approach'. *Asian Journal of Comparative Law* 11, no. 1 (2016): 87–109.

Bigo, Didier. 'The Globalization of in(Security)'. *Cultures Conflits* 58, no. 2 (2005): 3–3.

Bigo, Didier. 'Pierre Bourdieu and International Relations: Power of Practices, Practices of Power'. *International Political Sociology* 5, no. 3 (September 2011): 225–258.

Bilgin, Pinar. 'Thinking Past "Western" IR?' *Third World Quarterly* 29, no. 1 (2008): 5–23.

Blaney, David, and Naeem Inayatullah. 'International Relations from Below'. In *The Oxford Handbook of International Relations*, edited by Christian Reus-Smit and Duncan Snidal, 663–674. Oxford: Oxford University Press, 2008.

Bourdieu, Pierre. *The Algerians.* Boston: Beacon Press, 1962.

Bourdieu, Pierre. 'The Specificity of the Scientific Field and the Social Conditions of the Progress of Reason'. *Information (International Social Science Council)* 14, no. 6 (1975): 19–47.

Bourdieu, Pierre. *Outline of a Theory of Practice.* Cambridge: Cambridge University Press, 1977.

Bourdieu, Pierre. 'What Makes a Social Class? On the Theoretical and Practical Existence of Groups'. *Berkeley Journal of Sociology* 32, no. 1 (1987): 1–17.

Bourdieu, Pierre. 'Social Space and Symbolic Power'. *Sociological Theory* 7, no. 1 (1989): 14–25.

Bourdieu, Pierre. *The Logic of Practice.* Palo Alto: Stanford University Press, 1990.

Bourdieu, Pierre. *The Craft of Sociology: Epistemological Preliminaries.* Berlin: Walter de Gruyter, 1991.

296 BIBLIOGRAPHY

Bourdieu, Pierre. 'Rethinking the State: Genesis and Structure of the Bureaucratic Field'. Translated by Samar Farage and Loïc Wacquant. *Sociological Theory* 12, no. 1 (1994): 1–18.

Bourdieu, Pierre. *The State Nobility: Elite Schools in the Field of Power*. Palo Alto: Stanford University Press, 1996.

Bourdieu, Pierre. *Masculine Domination*. Cambridge: Polity, 2001.

Bourdieu, Pierre. 'Habitus'. In *Habitus: A Sense of Place*, edited by Jean Hillier and Emma Rooksby, 43–52. Aldershot: Ashgate, 2002.

Bourdieu, Pierre. *Sketch for a Self-Analysis*. Translated by Richard Nice. Cambridge: Polity, 2007.

Bourdieu, Pierre. *The Bachelors' Ball: The Crisis of Peasant Society in Béarn*. Chicago: University of Chicago Press, 2008.

Bourdieu, Pierre. *Distinction: A Social Critique of the Judgement of Taste (1984)*. Translated by Richard Nice. London: Routledge, 2010.

Bourdieu, Pierre. 'The Forms of Capital (1986)'. In *Cultural Theory: An Anthology*, edited by Imre Szeman and Timothy Kaposy, 81–94. Oxford: Wiley-Blackwell, 2010.

Bourdieu, Pierre. *On the State: Lectures at the Collège de France, 1989–1992*. Translated by David Fernbach. Cambridge: Polity Press, 2014.

Bourdieu, Pierre, and Jean Claude Passeron. *The Inheritors: French Students and Their Relation to Culture*. Chicago: University of Chicago Press, 1979.

Bourdieu, Pierre, and Jean Claude Passeron. *Reproduction in Education, Society and Culture (1977)*. London: Sage, 1990.

Bourdieu, Pierre, Derek Robbins, and Rachel Gomme. 'Colonialism and Ethnography: Foreword to Pierre Bourdieu's "Travail et Travailleurs En Algérie"'. *Anthropology Today* 19, no. 2 (2003): 13–18.

Bourdieu, Pierre, and Abdelmalek Sayad. 'Colonial Rule and Cultural Sabir'. *Ethnography* 5, no. 4 (2004): 445–486.

Bourdieu, Pierre, and Loïc Wacquant. *An Invitation to Reflexive Sociology*. Chicago: University of Chicago Press, 1992.

Brennan, T.J. *At Home in the World: Cosmopolitanism Now*. Cambridge, Mass.: Harvard University Press, 1997.

Bull, Hedley. *The Anarchical Society: A Study of Order in World Politics*. London: Macmillan, 1977.

Bull, Hedley. *Hedley Bull on International Society*. Edited by Kai Alderson and Andrew Hurrell. Basingstoke: Macmillan, 2000.

Bull, Hedley, and Adam Watson. *The Expansion of International Society*. Oxford: Clarendon Press, 1984.

Buzan, Barry. 'The "Standard of Civilisation" as an English School Concept'. *Millennium: Journal of International Studies* 42, no. 3 (June 2014): 576–94.

Buzan, Barry, and Richard Little. 'The Historical Expansion of International Society'. In *Guide to the English School in International Studies*, edited by Daniel M. Green and Cornelia Navari, 59–74. New Jersey: John Wiley & Sons, 2013.

Cabrera, Luis. *The Humble Cosmopolitan: Rights, Diversity, and Trans-State Democracy*. Oxford Scholarship Online. New York, NY: Oxford University Press, 2020.

Calhoun, Craig. 'The Class Consciousness of Frequent Travelers: Toward a Critique of Actually Existing Cosmopolitanism'. *The South Atlantic Quarterly* 101, no. 4 (2002): 869–897.

Calhoun, Craig. 'A Cosmopolitanism of Connections'. In *Cosmopolitanisms*, edited by Bruce Robbins and Paulo Lemos Horta, 189–201. New York: NYU Press, 2017.

Callahan, William A. 'Nationalising International Theory: Race, Class and the English School'. *Global Society* 18, no. 4 (October 2004): 305–323.

Cannadine, David. *Ornamentalism: How the British Saw Their Empire*. Oxford: Oxford University Press, 2001.

Casolari, Marzia. 'Hindutva's Foreign Tie-up in the 1930s: Archival Evidence'. *Economic and Political Weekly* 35, no. 4 (2000): 218–228.

Chacko, Priya. *Indian Foreign Policy: The Politics of Postcolonial Identity from 1947 to 2004*. London: Routledge, 2013.

Chacko, Priya. 'New "Special Relationship"? Power Transitions, Ontological Security, and India–Us Relations'. *International Studies Perspectives* 15, no. 3 (August 2014): 329–346.

Chakrabarty, Dipesh. 'Legacies of Bandung: Decolonisation and the Politics of Culture'. *Economic and Political Weekly* 40, no. 46 (2005): 4812–4818.

Chakrabarty, Dipesh. *Provincializing Europe: Postcolonial Thought and Historical Difference*. Princeton: Princeton University Press, 2008.

Chakraborty, Arpita. '"Symbolic Violence" and Dalit Feminism: Possibilities Emerging from a Dalit Feminist Standpoint Reading of Bourdieu'. *International Feminist Journal of Politics*, 21 October 2021, 1–19.

Chan, Stephen. 'Seven Types of Ambiguity in Western International Relations Theory and Painful Steps towards Right Ethics'. In *The Zen of International Relations: IR Theory from East to West*, edited by Stephen Chan, Peter Mandaville, and Roland Bleiker, 69–78. London: Palgrave Macmillan UK, 2001.

Charsley, S.R., and G. K. Karanth. *Challenging Untouchability: Dalit Initiative and Experience from Karnataka*. New Delhi: Sage, 1998.

Chatterjee, Partha. *Nationalist Thought and the Colonial World: A Derivative Discourse?* London: Zed Books, 1986.

Chatterjee, Partha. *The Nation and Its Fragments: Colonial and Postcolonial Histories*. Princeton: Princeton University Press, 1994.

Chatterjee, Partha. *I Am the People: Reflections on Popular Sovereignty Today*. New York: Columbia University Press, 2019.

Chatterjee, Partha, Sudipta Kaviraj, and Nivedita Menon. *The Indian Ideology: Three Responses to Perry Anderson*. New Delhi: Permanent Black, 2015.

Chauhan, DS. 'India's Underprivileged Classes and the Higher Public Service: Towards Developing a Representative Bureaucracy'. *International Review of Administrative Sciences* 42, no. 1 (1976): 39–55.

Chowdhry, Geeta. 'Edward Said and Contrapuntal Reading: Implications for Critical Interventions in International Relations'. *Millennium* 36, no. 1 (1 December 2007): 101–116.

Chowdhry, Geeta, and Sheila Nair. *Power, Postcolonialism and International Relations: Reading Race, Gender and Class*. London: Routledge, 2002.

Cohen, Antonin. 'Pierre Bourdieu and International Relations'. In *The Oxford Handbook of Pierre Bourdieu*, edited by Thomas Medvetz and Jeffrey J. Sallaz, 200–246. New York: Oxford University Press, 2018.

Cohen, Stephen P. *India: Emerging Power*. Washington, D.C.: Brookings Institution Press, 2001.

Cox, Michael. 'Power Shifts, Economic Change and the Decline of the West?' *International Relations* 26 (1 December 2012): 369–388.

Crenshaw, Kimberle. 'Mapping the Margins: Intersectionality, Identity Politics, and Violence against Women of Color'. *Stanford Law Review* 43, no. 6 (1990): 1241–1299.

298 BIBLIOGRAPHY

Curtius, Ernst Robert. *European Literature and the Latin Middle Ages (1948)*. Translated by Willard R. Trask. Princeton: Princeton University Press, 1973.

Curzon of Kedleston, George Nathaniel Curzon. *Speeches by Lord Curzon of Kedleston, Viceroy and Governor General of India (Vol. 3)*. Calcutta: Office of the Superintendent of Government Printing, India, 1899.

Darwin, J. 'Imperialism and the Victorians: The Dynamics of Territorial Expansion'. *English Historical Review* 112, no. 447 (1997): 614–642.

Datta-Ray, Deep K. *The Making of Indian Diplomacy: A Critique of Eurocentrism*. Oxford: Oxford University Press, 2015.

Davenport, Lauren. 'The Fluidity of Racial Classifications'. *Annual Review of Political Science* 23, no. 1 (2020): 221–240.

Davis, Alexander E., and Vineet Thakur. '"An Act of Faith" or a New "Brown Empire"? The Dismissal of India's International Anti-Racism, 1945–1961'. *Commonwealth & Comparative Politics* 56, no. 1 (2018): 22–39.

Der Derian, James. *On Diplomacy: A Genealogy of Western Estrangement*. Oxford: Basil Blackwell, 1987.

Deshpande, Satish. *Contemporary India: A Sociological View*. New Delhi: Viking, 2004.

Deshpande, Satish. 'Pass, Fail, Distinction: The Examination as a Social Institution'. In *Marjorie Sykes Memorial Lecture*. Regional Institute of Education, Ajmer: National Council for Educational Research and Training, 2010.

Deshpande, Satish, and Mary E John. 'The Politics of Not Counting Caste'. *Economic and Political Weekly* 45, no. 25 (2010): 39–42.

Devji, Faisal. 'Hindu/Muslim/Indian'. *Public Culture* 5, no. 1 (1992): 1–18.

Dirks, Nicholas B. *Castes of Mind: Colonialism and the Making of Modern India*. Princeton: Princeton University Press, 2001.

Dormandy, Xenia. 'Is India, or Will It Be, a Responsible International Stakeholder?' *Washington Quarterly* 30, no. 3 (2007): 117–130.

Dubash, Navroz K. 'Copenhagen: Climate of Mistrust'. *Economic and Political Weekly* 44, no. 52 (2009): 8–11.

Dubash, Navroz K. 'The Politics of Climate Change in India: Narratives of Equity and Co-Benefits'. *Wiley Interdisciplinary Reviews: Climate Change* 4, no. 3 (May 2013): 191–201.

Dunne, Tim. *Inventing International Society: A History of the English School*. Basingstoke: Palgrave Macmillan, 1998.

Dwivedi, O.P. 'The Challenge of Cultural Diversity for Good Governance'. *Indian Journal of Public Administration* 48, no. 1 (2002): 14–28.

Eagleton-Pierce, Matthew. *Symbolic Power in the World Trade Organization*. Oxford: Oxford University Press, 2013.

Elias, Norbert. *The Civilizing Process (Vol. 1: The History of Manners)*. Oxford: Basil Blackwell, 1978.

Elias, Norbert. *The Germans: Power Struggles and the Development of Habitus in the Nineteenth and Twentieth Centuries*. Cambridge: Polity, 1996.

Enloe, Cynthia H. *Bananas, Beaches and Bases: Making Feminist Sense of International Politics*. Berkeley: University of California Press, 2014.

Fernandes, Leela. 'Restructuring the New Middle Class in Liberalizing India'. *Comparative Studies of South Asia, Africa and the Middle East* 20, no. 1 (2000): 88–104.

Fukuyama, Francis. *The End of History and the Last Man*. London: Hamish Hamilton, 1992.

Ganguly, Sumit. 'India's Foreign Policy Grows up'. *World Policy Journal* 20, no. 4 (2004): 41–47.

Ganguly, Sumit. 'Has Modi Truly Changed India's Foreign Policy?' *The Washington Quarterly* 40, no. 2 (2017): 131–143.

Ganguly, Sumit, and Nicolas Blarel. 'Modi's Burning Bridge to the Middle East', 12 July 2022. https://www.foreignaffairs.com/articles/india/2022-06-30/modis-burning-bridge-middle-east.

Gautam, Aavriti, and Julian Droogan. 'Yoga Soft Power: How Flexible Is the Posture?' *The Journal of International Communication* 24, no. 1 (30 October 2017): 18–36.

Getachew, Adom. *Worldmaking after Empire: The Rise and Fall of Self-Determination.* Princeton University Press, 2019.

Ginsberg, Elaine K, and Donald E Pease. *Passing and the Fictions of Identity.* Duke University Press, 1996.

Go, Julian. 'Decolonizing Bourdieu: Colonial and Postcolonial Theory in Pierre Bourdieu's Early Work'. *Sociological Theory* 31, no. 1 (March 2013): 49–74.

Godrej, Farah. *Cosmopolitan Political Thought: Method, Practice, Discipline.* Oxford University Press, 2011.

Gong, Gerrit W. *The 'Standard of Civilization' in International Society.* Oxford: Clarendon Press, 1984.

Gong, Gerrit W. 'Standards of Civilization Today'. In *Globalization and Civilizations,* edited by Mehdi Mozaffari, 77–97. London: Routledge, 2002.

Gopal, Sarvepalli. *Jawaharlal Nehru: A Biography, Volume 3 (1956–1964).* New Delhi: Oxford University Press, 1975.

Gramsci, Antonio. *Selections from the Prison Notebooks of Antonio Gramsci.* Edited by Quintin Hoare and Geoffrey Nowell Smith. New York: International Publishers, 1971.

Guha, Ranajit. *Dominance without Hegemony: History and Power in Colonial India.* Cambridge, Mass.: Harvard University Press, 1997.

Gupta, Akhil, and Kalyanakrishnan Sivaramakrishnan, eds. *The State in India after Liberalization: Interdisciplinary Perspectives.* London: Routledge, 2010.

Gupta, Dipankar. *Interrogating Caste: Understanding Hierarchy and Difference in Indian Society.* New Delhi: Penguin Books, 2000.

Gupta, Dipankar. 'Caste and Politics: Identity over System'. *Annual Review of Anthropology* 34, no. 21 (2005): 409–427.

Gupta, Sisir. *India and the International System.* New Delhi: Vikas Publishing, 1981.

Gupta, Surupa, Rani D Mullen, Rajesh Basrur, Ian Hall, Nicolas Blarel, Manjeet S Pardesi, and Sumit Ganguly. 'Indian Foreign Policy under Modi: A New Brand or Just Repackaging?' *International Studies Perspectives* 20, no. 1 (2019): 1–45.

Guthrie, Anne. *Madame Ambassador: The Life of Vijaya Lakshmi Pandit.* New York: Harcourt, 1962.

Guyot-Réchard, Bérénice. 'Stirring Africa towards India: Apa Pant and the Making of Post-Colonial Diplomacy, 1948–54'. *The International History Review* 44, no. 4 (2022): 892–913.

Hall, Ian. 'Is a "Modi Doctrine" Emerging in Indian Foreign Policy?' *Australian Journal of International Affairs* 69, no. 3 (2015): 247–52.

Hall, Ian. 'Narendra Modi's New Religious Diplomacy'. *International Studies Perspectives* 20 (2018): 11–14.

Hall, Ian. *Modi and the Reinvention of Indian Foreign Policy.* Bristol University Press, 2019.

Hall, Stuart. *Familiar Stranger: A Life between Two Islands.* London: Penguin Books, 2017.

Hall, Stuart. 'The West and the Rest: Discourse and Power (1996)'. In *Race and Racialization: Essential Readings,* edited by Tania Das Gupta, Carl E. James, Chris Andersen,

300 BIBLIOGRAPHY

Grace-Edward Galabuzi, and Roger C. A. Maaka, 2nd edition, 85–93. Toronto: Canadian Scholars' Press, 2018.

Hansen, Thomas Blom. *The Saffron Wave: Democracy and Hindu Nationalism in Modern India*. Princeton University Press, 1999.

Hansen, Thomas Blom, and Srirupa Roy. 'What Is New about "New Hindutva"?' In *Saffron Republic: Hindu Nationalism and State Power in India*, edited by Thomas Blom Hansen and Srirupa Roy, 1–24. Cambridge: Cambridge University Press, 2022.

Harvey, David. *Cosmopolitanism and the Geographies of Freedom*. New York: Columbia University Press, 2009.

Heimsath, Charles Herman, and Surjit Mansingh. *A Diplomatic History of Modern India*. Bombay: Allied Publishers, 1971.

Held, David. *Cosmopolitanism: Ideals, Realities and Deficits*. Cambridge: Polity, 2010.

Helliwell, Christine, and Barry Hindess. 'Kantian Cosmopolitanism and Its Limits'. *Critical Review of International Social and Political Philosophy* 18, no. 1 (2015): 26–39.

Henderson, Errol A. 'Hidden in Plain Sight: Racism in International Relations Theory'. *Cambridge Review of International Affairs* 26, no. 1 (2013): 71–92.

Hobson, John M. 'Re-Embedding the Global Colour Line within Post-1945 International Theory'. In *Race and Racism in International Relations*, edited by Alexander Anievas, Nivi Manchanda, and Robbie Shilliam, 81–97. Routledge, 2014.

Hoffmann, Stanley. 'An American Social Science: International Relations (1977)'. *Daedalus* 106, no. 3 (1977): 41–60.

Huju, Kira. 'Saffronizing Diplomacy: The Indian Foreign Service under Hindu Nationalist Rule'. *International Affairs* 98, no. 2 (2022): 423–441.

Hurrell, Andrew. *On Global Order*. Oxford: Oxford University Press, 2007.

Hutchings, Kimberly. 'Dialogue between Whom? The Role of the West/Non-West Distinction in Promoting Global Dialogue in IR'. *Millennium* 39, no. 3 (2011): 639–647.

Ikenberry, G. John. *Liberal Leviathan: The Origins, Crisis, and Transformation of the American World Order*. Princeton: Princeton University Press, 2011.

Ikenberry, G. John. 'Reflections on "After Victory"'. *The British Journal of Politics and International Relations* 21, no. 1 (1 February 2019): 5–19.

Jackson, Peter. 'Pierre Bourdieu, the "Cultural Turn" and the Practice of International History'. *Review of International Studies* 34, no. 1 (2008): 155–181.

Jaffrelot, Christophe. 'The Impact of Affirmative Action in India: More Political than Socioeconomic'. *India Review* 5, no. 2 (2005): 173–189.

Jaffrelot, Christophe. *Religion, Caste and Politics in India*. London: Hurst, 2011.

Jaffrelot, Christophe. 'Class and Caste in the 2019 Indian Election: Why Have so Many Poor Started Voting for Modi?' *Studies in Indian Politics* 7, no. 2 (1 December 2019): 149–160.

Jaffrelot, Christophe. *Modi's India: Hindu Nationalism and the Rise of Ethnic Democracy*. Princeton and Oxford: Princeton University Press, 2021.

Jahn, Beate. 'Liberal Internationalism: From Ideology to Empirical Theory - and Back Again'. *International Theory* 1, no. 3 (2009): 409–438.

Jeffers, Chike. 'Appiah's Cosmopolitanism'. *The Southern Journal of Philosophy* 51, no. 4 (2013): 488–510.

Jodhka, Surinder S. 'Ascriptive Hierarchies: Caste and Its Reproduction in Contemporary India'. *Current Sociology* 64, no. 2 (2015): 1–16.

Jones, Branwen Gruffydd. '"Good Governance" and "State Failure": The Pseudo-Science of Statesmen in Our Times'. In *Race and Racism in International Relations*, edited by Alexander Anievas, Nivi Manchanda, and Robbie Shilliam. Routledge, 2014.

Kale, Sunila S. 'Inside out: India's Global Reorientation'. *India Review* 8, no. 1 (2009): 43–62.

BIBLIOGRAPHY   301

Kapur, Devesh. 'Why Does the Indian State Both Fail and Succeed?' *Journal of Economic Perspectives* 34, no. 1 (2020): 31–54.

Karnad, Bharat. *Why India Is Not a Great Power (Yet)*. New Delhi: Oxford University Press, 2015.

Kauppi, Nikko. 'Transnational Social Fields'. In *The Oxford Handbook of Pierre Bourdieu*, edited by Thomas Medvetz and Jeffrey J. Sallaz. Oxford: Oxford University Press, 2018.

Kautilya. *The Arthashastra*. New Delhi: Penguin Classics India, 2000.

Keene, Edward. *Beyond the Anarchical Society: Grotius, Colonialism and Order in World Politics*. Cambridge: Cambridge University Press, 2002.

Kennedy, Andrew B. 'Nehru's Foreign Policy: Realism and Idealism Conjoined'. In *The Oxford Handbook of Indian Foreign Policy*, edited by David M. Malone, C. Raja Mohan, and Srinath Raghavan, 92–103. Oxford: Oxford University Press, 2015.

Khan, Shamus. *Privilege: The Making of an Adolescent Elite at St. Paul's School*. Princeton and Oxford: Princeton University Press, 2012.

Khan, Shamus. 'The Sociology of Elites'. *Annual Review of Sociology* 38, no. 1 (2012): 361–377.

Khan, Shamus, and Colin Jerolmack. 'Saying Meritocracy and Doing Privilege'. *The Sociological Quarterly* 54, no. 1 (February 2013): 9–19.

Khare, Ravindra S. *The Changing Brahmans: Associations and Elites among the Kanya-Kubjas of North India*. Chicago: Chicago University Press, 1970.

Khilnani, Sunil. *The Idea of India*. Penguin Books India, 2004.

Kochanek, Stanley A. 'India's Changing Role in the United Nations'. *Pacific Affairs* 53, no. 1 (1980): 48–68.

König, Lion. *Cultural Citizenship in India: Politics, Power, and Media*. Oxford: Oxford University Press, 2016.

Krais, Beate. 'Gender, Sociological Theory and Bourdieu's Sociology of Practice'. *Theory, Culture & Society* 23, no. 6 (November 2006): 119–134.

Krastev, Ivan, and Stephen Holmes. *The Light that Failed: A Reckoning*. London: Penguin Books, 2020.

Krishna, Sankaran. 'Race, Amnesia, and the Education of International Relations'. *Alternatives* 26, no. 4 (1 October 2001): 401–424.

Krishna, Sankaran. 'IR and the Postcolonial Novel: Nation and Subjectivity in India'. In *Postcolonial Theory and International Relations: A Critical Introduction*, edited by Sanjay Seth. London: Routledge, 2013.

Krishna, Sankaran. 'A Postcolonial Racial/Spatial Order: Gandhi, Ambedkar, and the Construction of the International'. In *Race and Racism in International Relations: Confronting the Global Colour Line*, edited by Alexander Anievas, Nivi Manchanda, and Robbie Shilliam, 151–168. London: Routledge, 2014.

Krishna, Sankaran. 'Colonial Legacies and Contemporary Destitution: Law, Race, and Human Security'. *Alternatives* 40, no. 2 (2015): 1–17.

Krishna, Sankaran. 'China Is China, Not the Non-West: David Kang, Eurocentrism, and Global Politics'. *Harvard Journal of Asiatic Studies* 77, no. 1 (2017): 93–109.

Latham, Andrew. 'Constructing National Security: Culture and Identity in Indian Arms Control and Disarmament Practice'. *Contemporary Security Policy* 19, no. 1 (1998): 129–158.

Leander, Anna. 'The Promises, Problems, and Potentials of a Bourdieu-Inspired Staging of International Relations'. *International Political Sociology* 5, no. 3 (2011): 294–313.

302 BIBLIOGRAPHY

Levaillant, Mélissa. 'The Contribution of Neo-Institutionalism to the Analysis of India's Diplomacy in the Making'. In *Theorizing Indian Foreign Policy*, edited by Mischa Hansel, Raphaëlle Khan, and Mélissa Levaillant, 160–181. Abingdon: Taylor & Francis, 2017.

Linklater, Andrew. 'Process Sociology and International Relations'. *The Sociological Review* 59, no. 1 (2011): 48–64.

Luce, Edward. *In Spite of the Gods: The Rise of Modern India*. Abacus Books, 2007.

Macaulay, Lord Thomas Babington. 'Minute on Indian Education (1835)'. In *Archives of Empire, Volume I: From the East India Company to the Suez Canal*, edited by Mia Carter and Barbara Harlow, 227–239. Duke University Press, 2003.

Madan, T. N. 'Whither Indian Secularism?' *Modern Asian Studies* 27, no. 3 (1993): 667–697.

Maitra, Sankar N. 'Ills of the Indian Foreign Service: A Comment'. *Economic and Political Weekly* 1, no. 13 (1966): 549–551.

Malone, David M. *Does the Elephant Dance? Contemporary Indian Foreign Policy*. Oxford: Oxford University Press, 2011.

Malone, David M., C. Raja Mohan, and Srinath Raghavan. *The Oxford Handbook of Indian Foreign Policy*. New Delhi: Oxford University Press, 2015.

Manor, James. 'A Precarious Enterprise? Multiple Antagonisms during Year One of the Modi Government'. *South Asia: Journal of South Asian Studies* 38, no. 4 (2015): 736–754.

Markey, Daniel. 'Developing India's Foreign Policy "Software"'. *Asia Policy* 8, no. 1 (2009): 73–96.

Martin-Mazé, Médéric. 'Returning Struggles to the Practice Turn: How Were Bourdieu and Boltanski Lost in (Some) Translations and What to Do about It?' *International Political Sociology* 11, no. 2 (1 June 2017): 203–220.

Mayer, Adrian C. 'Public Service and Individual Merit in a Town of Central India'. In *Culture and Morality: Essays in Honour of Christoph von Fürer-Haimendorf*, 153–173, 1981.

Mearsheimer, John J. 'Bound to Fail: The Rise and Fall of the Liberal International Order'. *International Security* 43, no. 4 (2019): 7–50.

Mehta, Pratap Bhanu. 'Cosmopolitanism and the Circle of Reason'. *Political Theory* 28, no. 5 (2000): 619–639.

Mehta, Pratap Bhanu. 'Still under Nehru's Shadow? The Absence of Foreign Policy Frameworks in India'. *India Review* 8, no. 3 (13 August 2009): 209–233.

Metcalf, Thomas R. *Ideologies of the Raj*. Cambridge: Cambridge University Press, 1997.

Michelutti, Lucia. '"We (Yadavs) Are a Caste of Politicians": Caste and Modern Politics in a North Indian Town'. *Contribution to Indian Sociology* 38, no. 1–2 (2004): 43–71.

Miller, Manjari Chatterjee. 'India's Feeble Foreign Policy: A Would-Be Great Power Resists Its Own Rise'. *Foreign Affairs* 92, no. 3 (2013): 14–19.

Miller, Manjari Chatterjee. 'The Un-Argumentative Indian? Ideas about the Rise of India and Their Interaction with Domestic Structures'. *India Review* 13, no. 1 (2 January 2014): 1–14.

Miller, Manjari Chatterjee. 'India's Authoritarian Streak: What Modi Risks with His Divisive Populism'. *Foreign Affairs* 30 (May 2018).

Miller, Manjari Chatterjee, and Kate Sullivan de Estrada. '1'. *International Affairs* 93, no. 1 (1 January 2017): 27–49.

Mohan, C. Raja. *Crossing the Rubicon: The Shaping of India's New Foreign Policy*. New Delhi: Viking, 2003.

Mishra, Pankaj. *Butter Chicken in Ludhiana: Travels in Small-Town India*. Pan Macmillan, 2006.

Mishra, Pankaj. *Age of Anger: A History of the Present*. London: Macmillan, 2017.

Mohan, C. Raja. 'India and the Balance of Power'. *Foreign Affairs*, August 2006, 17–32.

Mohan, C Raja. 'Rising India: Partner in Shaping the Global Commons?' *The Washington Quarterly* 33, no. 3 (2010): 133–148.

Mondal, Seik Rahim. 'Social Structure, OBCs and Muslims'. *Economic and Political Weekly* 38, no. 46 (2003): 4892–4897.

Moore, Robert J. *Third World Diplomats in Dialogue with the First World: The New Diplomacy.* London: Macmillan, 1985.

Muni, S.D. 'Modi's "Neighbourhood First" Initiative'. In *Modi and the World: Reconstructing Indian Foreign Policy,* edited by Sinderpal Singh, 117–138. Singapore: World Scientific, 2017.

Nair, Deepak. 'Saving Face in Diplomacy: A Political Sociology of Face-to-Face Interactions in the Association of Southeast Asian Nations'. *European Journal of International Relations* 25, no. 3 (2019): 672–697.

Nair, Deepak. 'Sociability in International Politics: Golf and ASEAN's Cold War Diplomacy'. *International Political Sociology* 14, no. 2 (1 June 2020): 196–214.

Nair, Parameswaran N. *The Administration of Foreign Affairs in India with Comparative Reference to Britain.* New Delhi: School of International Studies, 1963.

Najiullah, Syed. 'Representation of Minorities in Civil Services'. *Economic and Political Weekly* 41, no. 8 (2006): 688.

Nambissan, Geetha B., and S. Srinivasa Rao. 'Structural Exclusion in Everyday Institutional Life'. In *Sociology of Education in India,* edited by Geetha B. Nambissan and Srinivasa Rao, 199–223. New Delhi: Oxford University Press, 2012.

Nandy, Ashis. *The Intimate Enemy: Loss and Recovery of Self under Colonialism.* New Delhi: Oxford University Press, 1983.

Narayan, Badri. *Fascinating Hindutva: Saffron Politics and Dalit Mobilisation.* New Delhi: SAGE Publications India, 2009.

Narlikar, Amrita. 'Peculiar Chauvinism or Strategic Calculation? Explaining the Negotiating Strategy of a Rising India'. *International Affairs* 82, no. 1 (2006): 59–76.

Narlikar, Amrita. 'Is India a Responsible Great Power?' *Third World Quarterly* 32, no. 9 (2011): 1607–1621.

Narlikar, Amrita, and Aruna Narlikar. *Bargaining with a Rising India: Lessons from the Mahabharata.* Oxford: Oxford University Press, 2014.

Natarajan, Kalathmika. 'The Privilege of the Indian Passport (1947–1967): Caste, Class, and the Afterlives of Indenture in Indian Diplomacy'. *Modern Asian Studies* First View, no. Online (11 July 2022): 1–30.

Nayudu, Swapna Kona. '"India Looks at the World": Nehru, the Indian Foreign Service & World Diplomacy'. *Diplomatica* 2, no. 1 (2020): 100–117.

Neumann, Iver B. 'Returning Practice to the Linguistic Turn: The Case of Diplomacy'. *Millennium: Journal of International Studies* 31, no. 3 (July 2002): 627–651.

Neumann, Iver B. 'The Body of the Diplomat'. *European Journal of International Relations* 14, no. 4 (2008): 671–695.

Neumann, Iver B. 'Entry into International Society Reconceptualised: The Case of Russia'. *Review of International Studies* 37, no. 2 (2011): 463–484.

Neumann, Iver B. *At Home with the Diplomats: Inside a European Foreign Ministry.* Ithaca: Cornell University Press, 2012.

Neumann, Iver B. *Diplomatic Sites: A Critical Enqiry.* Oxford: Oxford University Press, 2013.

Nicolaidis, Kalypso, Claire Vergerio, Nora Fisher Onar, and Juri Viehoff. 'From Metropolis to Microcosmos: The EU's New Standards of Civilisation'. *Millennium* 42, no. 3 (1 June 2014): 718–745.

Nicolson, Harold. *Diplomacy*. 3rd ed. Oxford University Press: Oxford, 1963.

O'Hanlon, Rosalind. 'Recovering the Subject: Subaltern Studies and Histories of Resistance in Colonial South Asia'. *Modern Asian Studies* 22, no. 1 (February 1988): 189–224.

O'Hanlon, Rosalind, and David Washbrook. 'After Orientalism: Culture, Criticism, and Politics in the Third World'. *Comparative Studies in Society and History* 34, no. 1 (1992): 141–167.

Omvedt, Gail. *Dalit Visions: The Anti-Caste Movement and the Construction of an Indian Identity*. Hyderabad: Orient Blackswan, 2006.

Onar, Nora Fisher, and Kalypso Nicolaïdis. 'The Decentring Agenda: Europe as a Post-Colonial Power'. *Cooperation and Conflict* 48, no. 2 (2013): 283–303.

Pagden, Anthony. 'Stoicism, Cosmopolitanism, and the Legacy of European Imperialism'. *Constellations* 7, no. 1 (2000): 3–22.

Paliwal, Avinash. 'Colonial Sinews of Postcolonial Espionage—India and the Making of Ghana's External Intelligence Agency, 1958–61'. *The International History Review* 44, no. 4 (2022): 914–934.

Pandey, Gyanendra. 'The Secular State and the Limits of Dialogue'. In *The Crisis of Secularism in India*, edited by Anuradha Dingwaney Needham and Rajeswari Sunder Rajan, 157–177. Duke University Press, 2007.

Pandey, Gyanendra. *A History of Prejudice: Race, Caste, and Difference in India and the United States*. Cambridge University Press, 2013.

Pandian, M. S. S. 'One Step Outside Modernity: Caste, Identity Politics and Public Sphere'. *Economic and Political Weekly* 37, no. 18 (2002): 1735–1741.

Panini, M.N. 'The Social Logic of Liberalization'. *Sociological Bulletin* 44, no. 1 (1995): 33–62.

Pant, Harsh V. 'A Rising India's Search for a Foreign Policy'. *Orbis* 53, no. 2 (2009): 250–264.

Pant, Harsh V., and Yogesh Joshi. 'Indo-US Relations under Modi: The Strategic Logic underlying the embrace'. *International Affairs* 93, no. 1 (2017): 133–146.

Parmar, Inderjeet. 'The US-Led Liberal Order: Imperialism by Another Name?' *International Affairs* 94, no. 1 (2018): 151–172.

Perkovich, George. 'Is India a Major Power?' *Washington Quarterly* 27, no. 1 (2003): 129–144.

Peters, B. Guy, and Jon Pierre. 'Politicization of the Civil Service: Concepts, Causes, Consequences'. In *The Politicization of the Civil Service in Comparative Perspective*, edited by B Guy Peters and Jon Pierre, 1–13. London: Routledge, 2004.

Phule, Jyotirao. *Slavery in the Civilised British Government under the Cloak of Brahmanism (1873)*. Translated by P.G. Patil. Bombay: Education Department of the Government of Maharashtra, 1991.

Pinto, Ambrose. 'UN Conference against Racism: Is Caste Race?' *Economic and Political Weekly* 36, no. 30 (28 July 2001): 2817–2820.

Plagemann, Johannes, and Sandra Destradi. 'Populism and Foreign Policy: The Case of India'. *Foreign Policy Analysis* 15, no. 2 (2019): 283–301.

Pogge, Thomas W. 'Cosmopolitanism and Sovereignty'. *Ethics* 103, no. 1 (1992): 48–75.

Pollock, Sheldon, Homi K. Bhabha, Carol A. Breckenridge, and Dipesh Chakrabarty. 'Cosmopolitanisms'. *Public Culture* 12, no. 3 (2000): 577–589.

Porter, Patrick. *The False Promise of Liberal Order: Nostalgia, Delusion and the Rise of Trump*. Hoboken (New Jersey): John Wiley & Sons, 2020.

Potter, David C. *India's Political Administrators: From ICS to IAS*. Delhi: Oxford University Press, 1996.

Pouliot, Vincent. *International Security in Practice: The Politics of NATO-Russia Diplomacy*. Cambridge: Cambridge University Press, 2010.

Pouliot, Vincent. 'Methodology: Putting Practice Theory into Practice'. In *Bourdieu in International Relations: Rethinking Key Concepts in IR*, edited by Rebecca Adler-Nissen, 45–59. London: Routledge, 2012.

Pouliot, Vincent, and Jérémie Cornut. 'Practice Theory and the Study of Diplomacy: A Research Agenda'. *Cooperation and Conflict* 50, no. 3 (2015): 297–315.

Pourmokhtari, Navid. 'A Postcolonial Critique of State Sovereignty in IR: The Contradictory Legacy of a 'West-Centric' Discipline'. *Third World Quarterly* 34, no. 10 (2013): 1767–1793.

Prashad, Vijay. *The Karma of Brown Folk*. University of Minnesota Press, 2000.

Price, Pamela. 'Ideology and Ethnicity under British Imperial Rule: "Brahmans", Lawyers and Kin-Caste Rules in Madras Presidency'. *Modern Asian Studies* 23, no. 1 (1989): 151–177.

Raghavan, Pallavi. 'Establishing the Ministry of External Affairs'. In *The Oxford Handbook of Indian Foreign Policy*, edited by David Malone, C. Raja Mohan, and Srinath Raghavan, 82–91. Oxford: Oxford University Press, 2015.

Raghavan, Pallavi, Martin Bayly, Elisabeth Leake, and Avinash Paliwal. 'The Limits of Decolonisation in India's International Thought and Practice: An Introduction'. *The International History Review* 44 (2022): 1–7.

Raghavan, Srinath. *War and Peace in Modern India*. Basingstoke: Palgrave Macmillan, 2010.

Rajamani, Lavanya. 'Differentiation in the Emerging Climate Regime'. *Theoretical Inquiries in Law* 14, no. 1 (1 January 2013): 151–172.

Raman, N. V. *Indian Diplomatic Service: The First Thirty-Four Years*. Delhi: Chanakya Publications, 1986.

Ramanathan, Vaidehi. *The English-Vernacular Divide: Postcolonial Language Politics and Practice*. Clevedon: Multilingual Matters LTD, 2005.

Rana, Kishan S. *Inside Diplomacy*. New Delhi: Manas, 2000.

Rana, Kishan S. *The 21st Century Ambassador: Plenipotentiary to Chief Executive*. New Delhi: Oxford University Press, 2005.

Rana, Kishan S. *The Contemporary Embassy: Paths to Diplomatic Excellence*. Basingstoke: Palgrave Macmillan, 2013.

Rao, Nirupama. *The Fractured Himalaya: India, Tibet, China 1949–62*. New Delhi: Penguin Viking, 2021.

Rao, Rahul. *Third World Protest: Between Home and the World*. Oxford: University Press, 2010.

Rao, Rahul. 'The Diplomat and the Domestic: Or, Homage to Faking It'. *Millennium* 45, no. 1 (1 September 2016): 105–112.

Rao, Rahul. *Out of Time: The Queer Politics of Postcoloniality. Out of Time*. Oxford University Press, 2020.

Rawat, Ramnarayan S., and K. Satyanarayana. 'Dalit Studies: New Perspectives on Indian History and Society'. In *Dalit Studies*, edited by Ramnarayan S. Rawat and K. Satyanarayana, 1–31. Durham: Duke University Press, 2016.

Ray, Tridip, Arka Roy Chaudhuri, and Komal Sahai. 'Whose Education Matters? An Analysis of Inter-Caste Marriages in India'. *Journal of Economic Behavior & Organization* 176 (2020): 619–633.

Reddy, Deepa S. 'The Ethnicity of Caste'. *Anthropological Quarterly* 78, no. 3 (2005): 543–584.

306 BIBLIOGRAPHY

Reed-Danahay, Deborah. *Locating Bourdieu*. Bloomington: Indiana University Press, 2005.

Renfrow, Daniel G. 'A Cartography of Passing in Everyday Life'. *Symbolic Interaction* 27, no. 4 (2004): 485–506.

Reus-Smit, Christian. 'Cultural Diversity and International Order'. *International Organization* 71, no. 4 (2017): 851–885.

Robb, Peter. *The Concept of Race in South Asia*. New Delhi: Oxford University Press, 1995.

Robbins, Bruce, and Paulo Lemos Horta. 'Introduction'. In *Cosmopolitanisms*, edited by Bruce Robbins and Paulo Lemos Horta, 1–21. New York: New York University Press, 2017.

Roy, Arundhati. *The Ministry of Utmost Happiness*. London: Hamish Hamilton, 2017.

Roy, S.L. *Diplomacy*. New Delhi: Sterling, 1984.

Roy, Srirupa. 'Instituting Diversity: Official Nationalism in Post-independence India'. *South Asia: Journal of South Asian Studies* 22, no. 1 (1999): 79–99.

Rudolph, Lloyd I., and Susanne Hoeber Rudolph. 'The Political Role of India's Caste Associations'. *Pacific Affairs* 85, no. 2 (2012): 5–22.

Rushdie, Salman. *Midnight's Children*. London: Penguin Vintage Edition, 2008.

Sabir, Sharjeel. 'Chimerical Categories: Caste, Race, and Genetics'. *Developing World Bioethics* 3, no. 2 (2003): 170–177.

Sahai, Paramjit. *Indian Cultural Diplomacy: Celebrating Pluralism in a Globalized World*. New Delhi: Indian Council of World Affairs, 2019.

Said, Edward. 'Representing the Colonized: Anthropology's Interlocutors'. *Critical Inquiry* 15, no. 2 (1989): 205–225.

Sapiro, Gisèle. 'Field Theory from a Transnational Perspective'. In *The Oxford Handbook of Pierre Bourdieu*, edited by Thomas Medvetz and Jeffrey J. Sallaz, 161–182. New York: Oxford University Press, 2018.

Saran, Shyam. *How India Sees the World: Kautilya to the 21st Century*. New Delhi: Juggernaut Books, 2017.

Scott, John, and Gordon Marshall. 'Caste'. In *A Dictionary of Sociology*. Oxford: Oxford University Press, 2009, 64.

Seal, Anil. *The Emergence of Indian Nationalism: Competition and Collaboration in the Later Nineteenth Century*. Vol. 1. Cambridge: Cambridge University Press, 1971.

Sending, Ole Jacob, Vincent Pouliot, and Iver B. Neumann. 'The Future of Diplomacy: Changing Practices, Evolving Relationships'. *International Journal* 66, no. 3 (2011): 527–542.

Shankar, Shobana. *An Uneasy Embrace: Africa, India and the Spectre of Race*. London: Hurst & Company, 2021.

Shanthakumari Sunder, L. *Values and Influence of Religion in Public Administration*. Los Angeles: SAGE, 2011.

Shepherd, Kancha Ilaiah. *Why I Am Not a Hindu: A Shudra Critique of Hindutva Philosophy, Culture and Political Economy (1996)*. Calcutta: Samya, 2002.

Shepherd, Kancha Ilaiah. *Post-Hindu India: A Discourse in Dalit-Bahujan, Socio-Spiritual and Scientific Revolution*. New Delhi: SAGE Publications India, 2009.

Shepherd, Kancha Ilaiah. *Buffalo Nationalism: A Critique of Spiritual Fascism*. Calcutta: Samya, 2012.

Sheth, D. L. 'The Great Language Debate: Politics of Metropolitan versus Vernacular India'. In *At Home with Democracy: A Theory of Indian Politics*, edited by D.L. Sheth and Peter Ronald Desouza, 169–195. Singapore: Springer, 2018. https://doi.org/10.1007/978-981-10-6412-8_10.

Shilliam, Robbie. *International Relations and Non-Western Thought: Imperialism, Colonialism and Investigations of Global Modernity*. London: Routledge, 2010. https://doi.org/10.4324/9780203842126.

Singer, Milton B. *Traditional India: Structure and Change*. Philadelphia: American Folklore Society, 1959.

Singh, Tripurdaman, and Adeel Hussain. *Nehru: The Debates That Defined India*. London: William Collins, 2021.

Skinner, Quentin. *Visions of Politics: Volume 1, Regarding Method*. Cambridge: Cambridge University Press, 2002.

Slate, Nico. 'Translating Race and Caste'. *Journal of Historical Sociology* 24, no. 1 (2011): 62–79.

Spivak, Gayatri Chakravorty. 'Can the Subaltern Speak?' In *Marxism and the Interpretation of Culture*, edited by Gary Nelson and Lawrence Grossberg, 271–313. Basingstoke: Macmillan, 1988.

Spivak, Gayatri Chakravorty. 'Scattered Speculations on the Subaltern and the Popular'. *Postcolonial Studies* 8, no. 4 (2005): 475–486.

Srinivas, M.N. *Social Change in Modern India*. Berkeley: University of California Press, 1966.

Srinivas, M.N. *Religion and Society among the Coorgs of South India (1965)*. Bhopal: J.K. Publishers, 1978.

Steinmetz, George. 'Bourdieusian Field Theory and the Reorientation of Historical Sociology'. In *The Oxford Handbook of Pierre Bourdieu*, edited by Thomas Medvetz and Jeffrey J. Sallaz, 602–628. New York: Oxford University Press, 2018.

Stern, Henri. 'Power in Modern India: Caste or Class? An Approach and Case Study'. *Contributions to Indian Sociology* 13, no. 1 (1979): 61–84.

Still, Clarinda, ed. *Dalits in Neoliberal India: Mobility or Marginalisation?* London: Routledge, 2015.

Subramanian, Ajantha. *The Caste of Merit: Engineering Education in India*. Cambridge, Mass.: Harvard University Press, 2019.

Sullivan, Kate. 'India's Ambivalent Projection of Self as a Global Power: Between Compliance and Resistance'. In *Competing Visions of India in World Politics: India's Rise Beyond the West*, edited by Kate Sullivan, 15–33. London: Palgrave Macmillan UK, 2015.

Sullivan de Estrada, Kate. 'Exceptionalism in Indian Diplomacy: The Origins of India's Moral Leadership Aspirations'. *South Asia: Journal of South Asian Studies* 37, no. 4 (2014): 640–655.

Sullivan de Estrada, Kate. 'In the World's Eyes, the Indian State May Be Declining but Its Citizenry Is Rising'. The Wire, 25 December 2019. https://thewire.in/rights/india-citizenship-protests-narendra-modi.

Sullivan de Estrada, Kate. 'The Liberal World Order Is Yet to Free Itself from Imperial Bias, as a Report that Dubs India a "Difficult" Country Reveals'. *The Indian Express*, 15 January 2021. https://indianexpress.com/article/opinion/columns/the-liberal-world-order-is-yet-to-free-itself-from-imperial-bias-as-a-report-that-dubs-india-a-difficult-country-reveals–7146640/.

Suri, K. C. 'Competing Interests, Social Conflict and the Politics of Caste Reservations in India'. *Nationalism and Ethnic Politics* 1, no. 2 (1995): 229–249.

Symonds, Richard. 'Indians at Oxford before Independence'. *Synopsis of a Lecture Delivered at the Oxford Majlis, Trinity Term 1985. Majlis Magazine, Oxford*, 1986.

Symonds, Richard. *Oxford and Empire: The Last Lost Cause?* Oxford: Clarendon Press, 1986.

Tagore, Rabindranath. *Home and the World*. Penguin Books India, 2005.

Tangirala, Maruthi. 'Language Choice and Life Chances: Evidence from the Civil Services Examination'. *Economic and Political Weekly* 44, no. 39 (2009): 16–20.

Tanham, George. 'Indian Strategic Culture'. *The Washington Quarterly* 15, no. 1 (1992): 129–142.

Taylor, Charles. *Multiculturalism and the Politics of Recognition*. Princeton: Princeton University Press, 1992.

Tellis, Ashley J. 'India as a New Global Power: An Action Agenda for the United States'. *Carnegie Endowment for International Peace*, 2005, Washington, DC.

Teltumbde, Anand. 'Race or Caste, Discrimination Is a Universal Concern'. *Economic and Political Weekly* 44, no. 34 (2009): 16–18.

Thakur, Vineet. 'The Colonial Origins of Indian Foreign Policy-Making'. *Economic and Political Weekly* 49, no. 32 (August 2014): 58–64.

Thakur, Vineet. *India's First Diplomat: V.S. Srinivasa Sastri and the Making of Liberal Internationalism*. Bristol: Bristol University Press, 2021.

Thapar, Romila. *Early India: From the Origins to AD 1300*. London: Allen Lane, 2002.

Tharoor, Shashi. *Reasons of State: Political Development and India's Foreign Policy under Indira Gandhi, 1966-1977*. New Delhi: Vikas PubHouse, 1982.

Tharoor, Shashi. *India Shastra: Reflections on the Nation in Our Time*. New Delhi: Aleph Book Company, 2014.

Thorat, Sukhadeo. 'Dalits in Post-2014 India: Between Promise and Action'. In *Majoritarian State: How Hindu Nationalism Is Changing India*, edited byAngana P. Chatterji, Thomas Blom Hansen, and Christophe Jaffrelot, 217–236. Oxford: Oxford University Press, 2019.

Thorat Committee. 'Caste Discrimination in AIIMS'. *Economic and Political Weekly* 42, no. 22 (2 June 2007): 7–8.

Towns, Ann, and Birgitta Niklasson. 'Gender, International Status, and Ambassador Appointments'. *Foreign Policy Analysis* 13, no. 3 (2017): 521–540.

Vaid, Divya. 'Caste in Contemporary India: Flexibility and Persistence'. *Annual Review of Sociology* 40, no. 1 (2014): 391–410.

Vijaya, Taruna. *Saffron Surge: India's Re-Emergence on the Global Scene and Hindu Ethos*. New Delhi: Har Anand Publications, 2008.

Visvanathan, Shiv. 'The Race for Caste: Prolegomena to the Durban Conference'. *Economic and Political Weekly* 36, no. 27 (July 2001): 2512–2516.

Vitalis, Robert. *White World Order, Black Power Politics: The Birth of American International Relations*. United States in the World. Ithaca: Cornell University Press, 2015.

Vittachi, Tarzie. *The Brown Sahib*. London: Andre Deutsch, 1962.

Vittachi, Tarzie. 'Bureaucrats Who Won't Lie Down'. *The Guardian*, 10 April 1978.

Waghmore, Suryakant. 'Community, Not Humanity: Caste Associations and Hindu Cosmopolitanism in Contemporary Mumbai'. *South Asia: Journal of South Asian Studies* 42, no. 2 (2019): 375–393.

Watson, Adam. *The Evolution of International Society: A Comparative Historical Analysis*. London: Routledge, 1992.

Weber, Heloise, and Poppy Winanti. 'The "Bandung Spirit" and Solidarist Internationalism'. *Australian Journal of International Affairs* 70, no. 4 (2016): 391–406.

Wenger, Etienne. *Communities of Practice: Learning, Meaning, and Identity*. Cambridge: Cambridge University Press, 1999.

Wight, Martin. *Systems of States*. Leicester: Leicester University Press, 1977.

Wiseman, Geoffrey. 'Expertise and Politics in Ministries of Foreign Affairs: The Politician-Diplomat Nexus'. In *Ministries of Foreign Affairs in the World: Actors of State Diplomacy*, edited by Christian Lequesne, 119–149. Brill Nijhoff, 2022.

Wojczewski, Thorsten. 'Populism, Hindu Nationalism, and Foreign Policy in India: The Politics of Representing "the People"'. *International Studies Review* 22, no. 3 (2020): 396–422.

Wolf-Phillips, Leslie. 'Why "Third World"? Origin, Definition and Usage'. *Third World Quarterly* 9, no. 4 (1987): 1311–1327.

Woodruff, Philip. *The Men Who Ruled India: The Guardians (Vol I and II)*. New York: St Martin's Press, 1954.

Woodward, Kerry. *The Relevance of Bourdieu's Concepts for Studying the Intersections of Poverty, Race, and Culture*. Edited by Thomas Medvetz and Jeffrey J. Sallaz. Vol. 1. Oxford: Oxford University Press, 2018.

Yengde, Suraj. *Caste Matters*. New Delhi: Penguin Random House India, 2019.

Yosso, Tara J. 'Whose Culture Has Capital? A Critical Race Theory Discussion of Community Cultural Wealth'. *Race, Ethnicity and Education* 8, no. 1 (March 2005): 69–91.

Zelliot, Eleanor. 'India's Dalits: Racism and Contemporary Change'. *Global Dialogue* 12, no. 2 (Summer 2010): 1–9.

SELECTED REPORTS AND ONLINE SOURCES

Academic Freedom Monitoring Project. 'Scholars at Risk Reports on Jawaharlal Nehru University'. Scholars at Risk, 2019. https://www.scholarsatrisk.org/report/2019-12-09-jawaharlal-nehru-university/.

Basu, Nupur. 'Chonira Muthamma, India's First Woman Career Diplomat'. NewsBlaze, 8 December 2009. https://newsblaze.com/world/south-asia/chonira-muthamma-indias-first-woman-career-diplomat_11341/.

Chauhan, KS. 'How the EWS Judgment Has Failed the Indian Constitution'. *The Indian Express* (blog), 10 November 2022. https://indianexpress.com/article/opinion/columns/how-the-ews-judgment-has-failed-the-indian-constitution–8259525/.

Choudhury, Angshuman. 'As India Hurtles towards a Terrifying Endgame, Foreign Policy Community Cannot Remain Silent'. The Wire. Accessed 27 October 2022. https://thewire.in/diplomacy/as-india-hurtles-towards-a-terrifying-endgame-foreign-policy-community-cannot-remain-silent.

Dhingra, Sanya. '5% Muslims among New Civil Services Recruits, Only One in Top 100'. ThePrint, 4 August 2020. https://theprint.in/india/governance/5-muslims-among-new-civil-services-recruits-only-one-in-top-100/474488/.

Ganeshan, Balakrishna. 'Interview: Dalit Woman Appointed UN Special Rapporteur Says Caste a Global Phenomenon'. The News Minute, 10 October 2022. https://www.thenewsminute.com/article/interview-dalit-woman-appointed-un-special-rapporteur-says-caste-global-phenomenon–168746.

Ghose, Sagarika. 'At Home on Foreign Affairs'. Outlook Magazine, 15 January 2001. https://www.outlookindia.com/magazine/story/at-home-on-foreign-affairs/210681.

The Hindu. 'Top IFS Posts Still Out of Bounds for SCs, STs', 5 December 2015. https://www.thehindu.com/news/national/top-ifs-posts-still-out-of-bounds-for-scs-sts/article7950262.ece.

The Indian Express. 'Counter "One-Sided" World Media Narrative on Govt's Pandemic "Failure", Jaishankar Tells Indian Diplomats', 30 April 2021. https://indianexpress.com/

article/india/counter-one-sided-world-media-narrative-on-govts-pandemic-failure-jaishankar-tells-indian-diplomats–7296036/.

Jayakumar, Nivedita. 'C B Muthamma: India's First Woman IFS Officer'. Feminism In India, 16 December 2019. https://feminisminindia.com/2019/12/16/c-b-muthamma-indias-women-ifs-officer/.

Madhav, Ram. 'Coming Full Circle at 70'. *The Indian Express* (blog), 15 August 2017. https://indianexpress.com/article/opinion/columns/independence-day-coming-full-circle-at-70-atal-bihari-vajpayee-hamid-ansari-muslims-india-insecure-modi-nehru–4796919/.

Mehta, Pratap Bhanu. 'The Limits of the Hindu vs Hindutvavadi Debate'. *The Indian Express* (blog), 16 December 2021. https://indianexpress.com/article/opinion/columns/limits-of-hindu-vs-hindutvavadi-debate-rahul–7675010/.

Nair, Sobhana K. 'India Again Placed at 142nd Rank in Press Freedom'. *The Hindu*. 21 April 2021, sec. National. https://www.thehindu.com/news/national/india-again-placed-at-142nd-rank-in-press-freedom/article34377079.ece.

Niblett, Robin. 'Global Britain, Global Broker'. Chatham House, 11 January 2021. https://www.chathamhouse.org/2021/01/global-britain-global-broker.

Ray, Ashis. 'Has the "Foreign Service" Declined?' National Herald, 14 July 2020. https://www.nationalheraldindia.com/opinion/has-the-foreign-service-declined.

Reporters without Borders. 'India: Modi Tightens His Grip on the Media'. Reporters Without Borders, 2021. https://rsf.org/en/india.

Singh Rathore, Khushi. 'Where Are the Women in Indian Diplomacy?' The Diplomat, 12 November 2020. https://thediplomat.com/2020/11/where-are-the-women-in-indian-diplomacy/.

Yengde, Suraj. 'Race, Caste and What It Will Take to Make Dalit Lives Matter'. The Caravan, 3 July 2020. https://caravanmagazine.in/essay/race-caste-and-what-it-will-take-to-make-dalit-lives-matter.

Yengde, Suraj. 'Dalit Panthers Was an Ideology and a Sight of the Dalit Response to Injustice'. *The Indian Express* (blog), 29 May 2022. https://indianexpress.com/article/opinion/columns/dalit-panthers-black-panthers-maharashtra-br-ambedkar–7941737/.

Zeeshan, Mohamed. 'The Indian Foreign Service Must Speak Out against Growing Politicization'. The Diplomat. Accessed 11 October 2022. https://thediplomat.com/2021/05/the-indian-foreign-service-must-speak-out-against-growing-politicization/.

Index

For the benefit of digital users, indexed terms that span two pages (e.g., 52–53) may, on occasion, appear on only one of those pages.

A

Abraham, Itty 116
adaptation and resistance 257
Adivasis 57–58, 177–179; *see also* Scheduled Tribes.
Adler, Emanuel 3
Adler-Nissen, Rebecca 53, 257
Africa
  African Americans 149–150
  East Africa 119–120, 145–146
  South Africa 151–152
Ali, Asaf 106–107, 116, 120
Allahabad 158, 254
Ambedkar, B.R. 58–59, 149, 152
America, United States of 4, 62–63, 65–66, 74–75, 81–82, 89, 105–106, 110–111, 116, 118, 122–123, 125, 127, 132, 138–139, 145–146, 149–150, 165–166, 209–210
Anderson, Benedict 30
Anglophiles 11, 14–15, 43, 51, 127–128, 132–134, 214, 221, 228, 240–241, 243–244, 251, 258, 262
Anglophones 43, 49–50, 79, 133–135, 143, 154, 171, 182, 193–197, 209–210, 223, 243–244, 248–249, 254–255, 265–266, 268
Apartheid 119, 145–146, 151–152
Appiah, Kwame Anthony 20–23
Appleby, Paul H. 212
Arthashastra 41
assimilation 9, 12, 38, 43, 98, 143–144, 229–231, 281, 284–285, 289
Austen, Jane 49
Australia 200, 277–278
Australian (newspaper) 277–278
Ayurveda 252–254

B

Babri Masjid, demolition of 258
Bachchan, H.R. 134–135
Bajpai, G.S. 81–82, 106–109, 126, 138, 159–160, 165–168, 211–212
Bajpai, K.S. 159–160
Bajpai, Uma Shankar 159–160
Balliol College 70–71, 78, 210–211
Bandaranaike, S.W.R.D. 92–93
Bandung 78, 119, 130
Bandyopadhyaya, Jayantanuja 97–98, 138–139, 190
Banerjee, N.C. 126
  "Random Thoughts on Office Routine" (circular letter) 126
Banerjee, R.N. 81, 105–106
Bayly, Martin 23–24
Bedekar, G.V. 88–89
belonging
  boundaries of 114, 202
  codes and rules of 5, 8–11, 30, 32–33, 38, 41–42, 44, 192, 280–282
  elite 5, 8–9, 13, 20, 38, 76–77, 125, 127–128, 138–139, 143, 153–154, 157, 192, 225–226, 230–231, 272
  performance of 139–140, 272–273, 281–282
  project of 9, 28, 271–272
  purchasing 273, 287
  race and 76–77, 91
  strategies of 233–234, 289
  unequal 6–7, 11
Bengal 96–97, 218
Benner, Jeffrey 67–68
Bhabha, Homi K. 20
Bhaduri, Madhu 67
  Lived Stories 67
Bhandari, P.L. 189

312 INDEX

Bhanu Mehta, Pratap 202
Bharat Darshan 215–216
Bharatiya Janata Party (BJP) 11–12,
    249–250, 254, 256, 258–260, 265
Bigo, Didier 53
Bihar 58–59, 88–89, 172–173, 217–218
Blaney, David 154
Bombay; *see* Mumbai.
boundary-making 23, 116
Bourdieu, Pierre 29, 31, 43–49, 51–56,
    60–63, 73–74, 76–80, 83, 90–93, 103,
    151, 180–181, 184, 185–187, 189,
    194–195, 197–198, 225, 234–236, 264,
    267, 273, 280–281, 288
    Cosmopolitan Elites 12–13
    *Distinction: A Social Critique of the
        Judgement of Taste* 52
    State Nobility 204
    symbolic violence, theorizing of 52
Brahmins 56–57, 60–61, 63, 66, 86,
    110–111, 151–152, 160–161, 166–167,
    177–179
Breckenridge, Carol 20
Brennan, Timothy 111
Bretton Woods 10
Britain 35–36, 86–87, 89, 92–93, 95–96,
    105–106, 109–111, 131–132, 145–146,
    209–210, 282–283
British Civil Service 94, 107–108, 167–168
British Commonwealth 80–81, 93,
    105–106, 116, 132, 209–210
British Indian Armed Forces 81–82
British Raj 23–24, 27–28, 49, 79–80, 82,
    99, 105, 119–120, 124, 126, 132, 146,
    151–152, 155, 160–161, 205–206, 208
Bull, Hedley 143
Buzan, Barry 39, 139–140, 272

C
Cabrera, Luis 147
Calcutta 158–159
Calhoun, Craig 193, 287
Cambridge 81, 86–89, 92–93, 98, 104–105,
    109–110, 128, 130–132, 134–135,
    165–166, 189–190, 209–211, 223,
    224–225, 265
capital
    cultural 1–2, 18, 28, 46, 49–50, 52,
        63–64, 84–86, 92–93, 99, 125–126,

        129–132, 154, 180–181, 186, 196–197,
        203, 204, 223, 232–233, 236, 242, 273
    hierarchies of 132
    social 28, 46, 49–50, 76, 89, 101,
        105–106, 116, 130, 132, 156, 160,
        168–169, 177, 181, 186, 189, 203,
        206–207, 232–233
Caroe, Sir Olaf 105–106, 109–110
caste 18, 25, 55–56, 70, 140, 146–147, 156,
    164, 176, 183, 232, 281–282
    anti-casteism 146, 154
    casteism 24–25, 84–85, 146, 153
    castelessness 62–63, 185
    discrimination 62, 102, 148, 150–154
    Economic & Educational Development
        of Scheduled Castes 148
    hierarchies of 60–61, 66, 157, 166
    high-caste status 11, 232–233
    Indian Foreign Service (IFS), caste
        relations in 18, 61–62, 182, 185–186
    lower 8–9, 16–17, 28–29, 160–161,
        177–178, 185, 233
    meritocracy and 184
    "Other Backward Castes" (OBCs)
        58–59, 172, 177–178, 181–182,
        197–198
    race and, parallels between
        144–145, 147–148
    Scheduled Castes (SC) 56–58, 146, 148,
        150, 160–161, 177–179, 185–186, 190;
        see also Dalits *and* Untouchables.
    upper 14–15, 58–59, 81, 110–111,
        152–154, 156, 159–161, 176–177, 182,
        185–187, 202–203, 232–233
censorship 64–66
Chacko, Priya 117–118
Chagla, M.C. 89–91, 93, 118, 231–232
Chakrabarty, Dipesh 20–21, 35–36,
    113–114, 136
Chakraborty, Arpita 52
Chandra Bose, Subhas 81–82
Chandrasekar, Maragatham 148
Chatterjee Miller, Manjari 246–247
Chatterjee, Partha 37
Chib, A.S. 211–212
China 81–82, 138, 242–243
Chinese language 183, 225–226
Chowdhury, Geeta 1
Christ Church College 86–89, 91

INDEX 313

Christianity 41–42, 275–276
Christians 72, 163–164, 166–167, 176, 190
Churchill, Winston 105
civil service; *see* Indian Civil Service (ICS).
civilization, standard of 9–11, 18, 31–33,
   39–41, 44, 76–77, 96–97, 124,
   128–129, 139–140, 143, 154, 192–193,
   199–200, 214–215, 221, 232–233, 274,
   287
class
   "depressed" 85–86
   hierarchies of 18, 157, 166
   lower 10, 59–60, 68, 75, 196–197,
      232–233, 274
   middle 18, 96–97, 153, 160, 165–166,
      171–173, 175, 193–194, 277
   upper 9–11, 21–22, 27–28, 43, 49–51,
      60–61, 66, 81, 89, 91–93, 99, 101–102,
      107–110, 143–144, 154, 157–158, 165,
      176–177, 193–194, 196–197, 199,
      201–203, 223–224, 236, 249, 257, 273
cleft habitus 47, 51–52, 76–77, 79–80,
   86, 89, 97, 109, 111–112, 153–154,
   202–205, 208, 214, 236–237, 266,
   271–272
climate
   diplomacy 4, 15, 121–122, 246
   summits 135–136, 247
Cold War 6, 139, 239–240
colonial
   mimicry 92
   standard of civilization 31–32, 76–77,
      96–97, 214–215
colonialism 44, 47–48, 79–80, 85–86,
   92–95, 99, 107, 114, 142, 145–146,
   275–276
Commonwealth 80–81, 93, 105–106, 116,
   132, 209–210
Congress Party 62, 80–81, 110–111, 148,
   249–250, 260, 265–266
constructive ambiguity, cultural capital
   of 132
cosmopolitanism
   "actually existing cosmopolitanism" 1,
      140–141, 144, 151, 157, 196–197,
      199–200, 203, 270–273, 284, 285–288
   aesthetic 1–2, 11, 22, 28, 42, 195,
      196–197, 199–200, 203, 273, 285, 288
   elite aesthetic 1–2, 192, 200

metonym, as 201–202
standard of civilization 9–11, 18,
   31–33, 39–41, 44, 76–77, 96–97, 124,
   128–129, 139–140, 143, 154, 192–193,
   199–200, 214–215, 221, 232–233, 274,
   287
"worlding" 1, 13, 22, 270
Covid pandemic 277–278
cultural
   capital 1–2, 18, 28, 46, 49–50, 52, 63–64,
      84–86, 92–93, 99, 125–126, 129–132,
      154, 180–181, 186, 196–197, 203, 204,
      223, 232–233, 236, 242, 273
   Cultural Relations, Indian Council
      of 252–253
   hierarchies 11, 49–50, 139–140, 156,
      192, 200, 203, 230, 240–241, 268
   identity, analysis of 44
culture
   brahminical 85–86
   bureaucratic 84
   diplomatic 17, 128, 267, 274
   global 21, 50
   Indian 152, 222, 251–254, 262
   institutional 48, 65, 156
Curzon, Lord 87–88

D
Dalits 17, 25, 56–60, 63, 66–67, 73, 85–86,
   146–152, 160–161, 166–167, 172,
   177–178, 182, 190–191, 195, 197–198,
   202, 232–234, 244; *see also* Scheduled
   Castes *and* Untouchables.
Damodar Savarkar, Vinayak 276
Datta-Ray, Deep K. 23–24
Davis, Lyn 122–123
Dayal, H. 127
Dayal, Rajeshwar 92–93
decolonization 6–7, 14, 30–32, 39, 41–42,
   79, 103, 107, 111–114, 122–125, 139,
   145–146, 155, 199–200, 210, 239–240,
   253, 269, 271, 272, 280, 285–286
Delhi 98, 134, 138, 158–159, 162–163, 173,
   177–178, 180–181, 191–192, 195, 197,
   212–213, 224–225, 227, 265, 278–279
   University 46, 49–50, 158–159

314   INDEX

democratization 31–32, 156–157, 160–
    161, 167, 176–177, 180–181, 199–200,
    202–205, 222, 227, 239, 241–242, 248,
    262–263, 266–269, 280–281, 285–286
  appropriation, as 227
  civil services 155
  democracy promotion 15
  demographic 156, 177
  diplomatic cadres 268–269
  discontents and 222
  elite culture 280–281
  fatigue 169–170
  global governance 31–32
  Indian Foreign Service (IFS) 28,
    65, 155, 204–205, 222, 236–237,
    239
  institutional culture 156
  international society 42
  process 167, 176–177
demographics 170–171, 177, 203, 262–263
Desai, Kiran 96–97, 199
Desai, M.J. 81
Deshpande, Satish 183–184
Deudney, Daniel 33
Devji, Faisal 264
Dhamija, Ambassador 104–105
difference
  ethical good, elevated to 118
  Indian, expression of 98
  liberal neutrality and the question of 32
  postcolonial expression of 116
  rethinking 11
Discovery of India 56, 109, 214
discrimination
  anti-discrimination measures 20,
    145–147
  caste 62, 102, 148, 150–154
  gender 25
  International Convention on the
    Elimination of all Forms of Racial
    Discrimination 148
  political 61
  racial 146–148, 150–152
district training 205–206, 216–220,
    226–227, 246–247
diversity 14–15, 29, 70, 156, 199, 238, 245,
    274, 285–286
  decline 199
  domestic 245

rethinking 11
  "talk" 119
Dixit, J.N. 65, 67–68, 81–82, 107–108,
    119–120, 122–123, 126, 166, 208–209,
    211–212, 245
  Indian Foreign Service: History and
    Challenge 65
domestic elite 11, 62–63, 114, 127–128,
    138–139, 223–224, 236–237, 272, 274,
    281–282, 286–287
doxa 12–13, 73–74
Du Bois, W.E.B. 149, 152
Dubey, Muchkund 146–147, 178–179
Dulles, John Foster 65–66
Durrell, Lawrence 223–224
Dutt, R.C. 125–126
Dutt, Subimal 81, 94–95, 102, 149,
    162–163, 169–170

E
Eagleton-Pierce, Matthew 54–55
  Symbolic Power in the World Trade
    Organization 54–55
Economic & Educational Development of
    Scheduled Castes 148
Economic and Political Weekly
    (journal) 185–186
economy, Indian, liberalization of 156,
    171–172, 239–240
education
  Anglophone 195–197, 243–244
  elite 27–28, 46, 75–76, 86, 89, 158–159,
    186, 195–197, 223, 226–227, 274
egalitarianism 1–2, 8, 9, 22–23, 51, 75, 84,
    102–103, 109–112, 153–154, 165, 192,
    200, 249, 286
  cosmopolitanism as egalitarian
    ethic 1–2, 9, 22–23, 192, 200
  Nehru and 84, 109, 111, 165, 249
  postcolonial ethic of 8, 51, 102–103,
    111–112, 165, 286
Eisenhower, Dwight D. 65–66
Elias, Norbert 45
elite
  aesthetic 1–2, 9, 11, 192, 200
  anti-imperial, education of 84
  belonging 5, 8–9, 13, 20, 38, 76–77, 125,
    127–128, 138–139, 143, 153–154, 157,
    192, 225–226, 230–231, 272

domestic 11, 62–63, 114, 127–128, 138–139, 223–224, 236–237, 272, 274, 281–282, 286–287
education 27–28, 46, 75–76, 86, 89, 158–159, 186, 195–197, 223, 226–227, 274
global 125–126, 272, 288
postcolonial 119, 152, 256, 266–267
upper-caste 152–154
whiteness and, equation between 7
Ellayaperumal, L. 148
English language
declining roles of 267
eloquent 274
evolving role of 242
examination, language of 168
"link language" 132
marginalization of 253–254
schools 79, 97, 171, 228
significance of 134
skills 228
socioeconomic status, as marker of 168
Estrada, Kate Sullivan de 23–24
ethnicity 75, 119, 146–147, 155, 164, 251
etiquette 128–129, 181, 212, 242–243
aristocratic 40–41
diplomatic 119, 254–255
European 125–126
foreign 213
international 165–166
manners 1, 11, 21–22, 40–42, 45–46, 49, 76–77, 79, 82, 84–85, 91, 102–103, 106–107, 138, 154, 212–213, 224–225, 228–231, 242–244, 274, 284–285
"social graces" 43–44, 96–97, 106–107, 131–132, 208, 212–213, 229–231, 233, 239–240, 242–243, 267
Western 143
Europe
culture 243–244
diplomacy 124–125
provincialization of 113–114
Renaissance 40–41
European international society 80, 91, 136–137, 204
exclusion
selection as 165
social 285

exclusivity, social 268
Exeter College 88–89

F
familial
background 70, 282
social capital 160
fascism 276
females and femininity; *see* women.
Financial Times 4, 194
First World War 80–81
Foreign Service; *see* Indian Foreign Service (IFS).
France 52, 282–283
French language 16–17, 225–226
Fukuyama, Francis 6

G
Gandhi, Indira 85–86, 128–129, 249–250
Gandhi, Mohandas 61–62, 81–82, 93–95, 149, 151–152, 174, 177, 215, 220, 289–290
Ganguly, Sumit 4
Gauthaman, Raj 244
gender 70, 140, 156, 176, 188–189, 232, 281–282
balance 175
diplomatic habitus, neutral 187
diplomatic services, practices across 180
"double-standards" 188
inclusion 176
parity 178–179
socialization and 236
stereotypes 234–235
Geneva 136–137, 164–165
German Nazism 276
Ghosh, Amitav 199
Gibbon, Sir Edward 106–107
gilets jaunes protests 282–283
Girard, René 6
global elite 125–126, 272, 288
Global North 17–18, 36–37, 125, 143
global order 2–3, 13–14, 76–77, 248
debate on 5, 13–14
difference and recognition in 280
social hierarchies of 16–17, 270–271
Western-dominated 2–3, 121–123, 203
Global South 7–8, 14n26, 36–37, 125, 141, 143, 248
globalization 171–172, 241–242

316 INDEX

Golwalkar, M.S. 251
Gorewala, A.D. 212
Gramsci, Antonio 238
Guantanamo 147
Guha, Ranajit 143, 224–225
  *Dominance without Hegemony: History
    and Power in Colonial India* 224–225
Gupta, Sisir 125, 133
Guyot-Réchard, Bérénice 69
Gymkhana Club 189–192

H
Haas, Peter M. 3
Haksar, P.N. 85–86, 214
Hall, Stuart 47–48
Harijans; *see* Dalits.
Hastings, Warren 80–81
hierarchies
  caste, of 18, 60–61, 66, 85–86, 157, 166
  class, of 18, 157, 166
  cultural 11, 49–50, 139–140, 156, 192,
    200, 203, 230, 240–241, 268
  global order, of 16–17, 270–271
  race, of 84–86, 144–145, 272
  religious 156–157
  social 17, 164–165, 193, 270–271, 288
High Altitude Warfare School 216
Hindi 253–255, 285
  Medium Schools 171
  "proficiency" 134–135
Hindu
  Hinduism 251–252, 254–255, 262–263,
    285
  nationalism 2, 14–17, 29, 72, 134–135,
    221–222, 238–239, 248–249, 251,
    252–254, 256, 258–259, 262–264,
    266–268, 276, 278–280, 282–283
  officers 72, 195, 245
  revivalism, anti-western ideologies
    of 251
Hindutva 251, 255–256, 258–266, 275–280
History, End of 6
Hitler, Adolf 276
Hobson, John 35
Hughes, William 200
human rights 10, 132–133, 140–141,
  145–147

I
Ikenberry, John 33
Ilaiah Shepherd, Kancha 151
Imitation, Age of 6
imperialism 114, 119, 145–146
  anti-imperialism 28, 84, 98, 209–210,
    246, 271–272
  bureaucracy, glamourizing 88–89
  language 220–221
Inayatullah, Naeem 154
inclusion 11, 33–34, 60–63, 144, 146, 150,
  154, 156, 165, 167–168, 175–176, 181,
  193–196, 202–203, 270, 272, 281, 285,
  287, 289
India
  colonial 85–86, 165–166
  Constitution 57–58, 148, 155
  diplomacy 5, 38, 50, 52, 53–56, 64–69,
    79–81, 122, 128–130, 134, 146,
    153–154, 174, 222–223
  discovery of 214
  diversity 119, 134–135
  economy, liberalization of 156, 171–172,
    239–240
  Emergency, The 249–250
  famines 93–94
  Foreign Service Research
    Bureau 145–146
  Hindu nation, as 250
  "Idea of India" 251
  Independence 27–28, 31–32, 47–48, 60,
    78–79, 94, 97–98, 107–108, 111, 114,
    124–125, 168–169, 209–210, 219
  "Indianness" 54, 62–63, 119, 221–222,
    236–237, 248–249, 251, 253–255,
    263–269, 283–284
  international society, membership
    in 139–140
  National Archives of India (NAI) 11–12
  National Army 81–82
  National Congress Party 110–111
  nuclear capabilities, right to 122–123
  Partition 61–62, 162–163, 195–196
  postcolonial creation of 220–221, 223
  saffronization of 251
  self-orientalization of 221
  "Shining Syndrome" 246–247
  "Third World leader", role as 119–120
  UN Security Council, case for permanent
    seat on 121–122

INDEX 317

Indian Administrative Service (IAS)
66–67, 170–171, 174, 176, 190,
206–207, 219, 226–227
Indian Civil Service (ICS) 27–28, 57, 65,
78, 79–97, 99, 101–112, 118, 124–128,
151–152, 158, 159–160, 162–163,
165–170, 200–201, 205–206, 208–214,
219, 225
Civil Service Examination
(CSE) 170–171, 231–232
"civil service families" 57, 159–160,
167–168, 186, 189–190
postcolonial recruits 108–109
syllabus 86–87
Indian Foreign Service (IFS) 2–3, 16–17,
20, 207
caste relations in 18, 61–62, 185–186
class, caste, and gender, hierarchies
of 18
Conduct Rules 106–107
"democratization" of 28, 65
hierarchies of 18
Institute (FSI) 205–207, 212–213,
222–223, 227–230
Interview Board 83
marriage, rules on 175–176
Nehruvian vision 263–264
saffronization of 248–249
"type" 54
women, ascent in hierarchies of 178–179
Indian Institute of Management (IIM) 173,
246–247
Indian Institute of Technology (IIT) 173,
183–184, 232–233, 246–247
Indian Police Service (IPS) 174, 176,
255–256
inequality 114, 186
inferiority complex 95–96
International Monetary Fund (IMF) 240
International Relations (IR) 7, 13, 17–20,
24–25n63, 27, 31–35, 40, 42, 51–56,
70, 76–77, 107, 141, 156, 199, 222–223,
279–282
international security 15, 251
international society 12–13, 30–31, 75,
76–77
caste and race in 143
colonial history of 40–41
democratizing 115
European 80, 91, 113–114, 136

postcolonial 114–115
internationalism 115, 254, 263–264
Italian fascism 276
Iyer, Chokila 178–179
Iyer, Krishna 175–176

J

Jackson, Peter 46–47
Jaishankar, Subrahmanyam 258–259,
277–278
Jha, L.K. 81
Jharkhand 195
Jodhka, Surinder S. 52
Jowett, Benjamin 86–87

K

Kalathmika Natarajan 18
Kale, Sunila 4
Kalimpong, hill station of 96–97
Kalingas of Andhra Pradesh 58–59
Kant, Immanuel 20–21, 168–169
Kapur, Ashok 64
Karnataka, state of 168–169
Karthigeyan, P.S. 277–278
Kashmir 216
Kashmiri Pandits 66, 110–111, 265
Kathmandu 129–130, 136–137
Kaul, T.N. 26, 101–107, 118, 136–138, 214
Kautilya 41
Kenyan nationalists 145–146
King, Martin Luther 149
Kirpalani, K.S. 88–89
Kirpalani, S.K. 93–94
Kissinger, Henry 123
Kona Nayudu, Swapna 23–24
Kothari Committee 170–171, 229–230
Krastev, Ivan 6
Krishen, Prem 104
Krishna, Sankaran 17–18, 36–37, 152, 199,
201, 283–284
Kshatriyas 56–57
Kumar, Pavan 18
Kumbh Mela (religious festival) 252, 254

318 INDEX

L

Lakshmi Pandit, Vijaya 65–66, 78, 80–81, 105, 109–111, 126, 130, 138, 197, 211–212, 220
   IFS Officers' Conduct Rules 65–66
Lal Bahadur Shastri National Academy of Administration in Mussoorie 212
Lall, Arthur 95–96
Lall, Shamaldharee 88–89
League of Nations 18, 60–61
liberal
   arts 240–241, 247–248
   neutrality 32, 76–77
   order 2, 10–11, 13–15
liberalization
   Indian economy 156, 171–172, 239–240
   post-liberalization 3–4
Lok Sabha 62, 158, 240–241
Luce, Edward 4
Lytton, Earl of 93

M

Macaulay, Lord Thomas Babington 78, 97, 106–108, 130
   Macaulay Report for the Indian Civil Service 167–168
   Minute on Indian Education 78
Madan, T.N. 61–62
Madhav, Ram 265
Mandal
   "amendments" 156
   Commission Report 58–59
   reforms 172
manners 1, 11, 21–22, 40–42, 45–46, 49, 76–77, 79, 82, 84–85, 91, 102–103, 106–107, 138, 154, 212–213, 224–225, 228–231, 242–244, 274, 284–285; *see also* etiquette.
Manusmriti 57
marginalized communities 186–187
marriage
   polygamous 163
   rules 67–68, 175–176
Martin-Máze, Médéric 54–55
Marx, Karl 21, 209–210, 215
masculinity 234–235
Mayur Vihar 76
Meenakshi Temple 216
Mehta family 161–162

Mehta, Jagat 83, 105–107, 159–162, 175–176, 179–180
Mehta, M.S. 83, 102
Menon Rao, Nirupama 178–179
Menon, K.P.S. 44–45, 65–66, 80–83, 86–91, 93–95, 101, 105, 109–110, 116, 120, 127–128, 159–160, 168–169, 208, 211–212, 231–232
   Flying Troika 65–66
   Many Worlds Revisited: An Autobiography 65
Menon, Krishna 209–210, 214
Menon, P.N. 159–160
Menon, Shankaran 159–160
merit 43–44, 92–93, 157–162, 165, 167–170, 172, 180–182, 189–192, 203, 233, 249–250, 278–279
Mill, John Stuart 87–88
   On Liberty 87–88
Milton, John 87–88
   Areopagitica 87–88
mimicry 2, 5–7, 12, 17, 23, 28, 31, 38, 92, 96–97, 116, 224–225, 254, 272–273, 281–282, 285
Ministry of External Affairs (MEA) 3, 11–12
Mishra, Pankaj 255
Modi, Narendra 11–12, 14–15, 72, 239, 249, 252–255, 258–260, 265–266, 275–278, 284–285
Moore, Robert J. 125
Moravcsik, Andrew 33
Moscow 102–104, 138, 197
Mountbatten, Lord 105
Mukherjee, Bhaswati
Mumbai 158–159, 224–225
Muslims 72, 118, 152, 162–164, 166–167, 176, 195–196, 251
   Muslim Personal Law (Shariat) Application Act 163
Mussolini, Benito 276
Mussoorie 206–207, 212, 215, 225
Muthamma, C.B. 118, 161–162, 175–176, 179, 188

N

Nair, Deepak 55–56, 139–140
Nandy, Ashis 38
National Archives of India (NAI) 11–12

National Association for the Advancement of Colored People 149
nationalism 256, 260, 262–263, 276, 282–283
NATO-Russia relations 53
Naya Bharat 275
Nazism 276
Nehru, B.K. 81, 84–85, 89–94, 110–111
Nice Guys Finish Last 65
Nehru, Jawaharlal 49–50, 56, 61–62, 65–66, 81–85, 89, 93, 98–100, 104, 106–107, 109–111, 115–118, 120, 123–124, 134–135, 157–158, 166–167, 195–196, 200, 220–221, 226, 249–250, 256, 265
   Discovery of India 56, 109, 214
   Jawaharlal Nehru University 205–206
   Nehru Memorial Museum and Library (NMML) 11–12
   Nehruvianism 15–16, 23–24, 27–28, 49–50, 80, 84, 115, 118, 123–124, 165, 214–215, 221–222, 230–231, 238, 245–249, 251, 258–259, 263–264, 267–269
Nehru, R.K. 101–102, 109–110, 116, 143
Neumann, Iver 53–54, 247
neutrality, liberal 32, 76–77
Nicolson, Harold 209–210
Northcote–Trevelyan Report 167–168
Nuclear Non-Proliferation Treaty 117–118

O
"Other Backward Castes" (OBCs) 58–59, 172, 177–178, 181–182, 197–198
Oxbridge 8–9, 16–17, 27–28, 48, 75–76, 78, 127–128, 158–159, 167–168, 189–190, 210–211, 224–225
Oxford 158, 165–166, 209–211, 224–225
   Handbook of Indian Foreign Policy 18
   Labour Club 214

P
Pakistan 62–63, 168–169, 177, 195–196
Pandian, M.S.S. 20, 62, 63–64, 66–67, 185–186
Pandits 66, 104, 110–111, 128–130, 191–192, 265
Panikkar, K.M. 43, 93, 226
Pant, Apa 119–120, 145–146

Pant, Harsh 4
Partition 162–163, 195–196
patriotism 162–163, 256
Phule, Jyotirao 146
Pillai Committee 83, 104–105, 162
Pillai, N.R. 81, 89–90, 94, 108–109, 165–166
Pogge, Thomas 20–21
political theory 2–3, 13, 22–23, 28, 32–33, 203, 285
Pollock, Sheldon 20
polygamy; *see* marriage.
populism 5, 257, 262–263, 282–283
postcolonialism 245
   egalitarianism, ethic of 8, 51
   elites 119, 152, 266–267
   international society 155, 271–272
   practice of 119
Pouliot, Vincent 53
prestige 23, 84–86, 95–96, 126, 129–131, 151, 155, 172, 185–186
provincialization 107–108, 113–114, 136

Q
Quit India Movement 81–82

R
race 91, 143, 232
   anti-racism 132–133, 145–146
   caste and, parallels between 144–145, 147–148
   discrimination 146–148
   equality 80, 145–146, 149, 152
   hierarchies of 84–86, 144–145
   international society 143
   Racial Discrimination, International Convention on the Elimination of all Forms of 148
   racialism 114, 145–146
   xenophobia 146–147
Radhakrishnan, Dr Sarvepalli 44–45
Raghavan, Pallavi 23–24
Raj, British 23–24, 27–28, 49, 79–80, 82, 99, 105, 119–120, 124, 126, 132, 146, 151–152, 155, 160–161, 205–206, 208
Rajya Sabha 11–12
Rana, Kishan 65, 161–162
rank 26, 81, 83, 94–95, 174, 180–181, 183–184, 195–196, 205–206

320 INDEX

Rao, Rahul 22–23, 143, 153
Rasgotra, M.K. 66, 81–82, 117–118, 123, 131–132, 209–210
Rashtriya Swayamsevak Sangh (RSS) 252
Ray, Deepak 218–219
reflexivity 73–74, 76–77
religion 70, 140, 281–282
  hierarchies of 156–157
  minorities 68–69
  representation 162–163
riots, anti-Hindi 220–221
Roy, Arundhati 86–87, 199
  God of Small Things (novel) 199
  Ministry of Utmost Happiness 86–87
Roy, Srirupa 278–279, 289
Rushdie, Salman 137–138
  Midnight's Children (novel) 137–138
Russia 126–127, 138
  "habitus" 53
  Soviet Union 6–7, 126–127, 138

S
Sachar Committee Report 176
saffronization 29, 239, 248–249, 251, 254, 262–264, 266–267, 277
Sahai, Paramjit 251
Said, Edward 1
Sanskrit 232, 254
Sanyal, B.K. 250
Saran, Shyam 256
Satow, Ernest 138, 211–212
  Diplomatic Practice 211–212
Savarkar, V.D. 251
Sayad, Abdelmalek 78
Scheduled Castes (SC) 56–58, 146, 148, 150, 160–161, 177–179, 185–186, 190; *see also* Dalits *and* Untouchables.
Scheduled Tribes (ST) 58–59, 160–161, 172, 178–179, 183, 185–186, 190, 195, 231–232; *see also* Adivasis.
Second World War 35, 143, 208–209, 276
secularism 61–63, 66, 115, 238, 245, 260, 261–264, 267–268
Sen, B.R. 81
sexism 24–25
Shah, Major A.S.N. 105–106
Shankar, Meera 178–179
Shudras 56–59, 160–161, 172
Sikhs 72, 163–164, 166–167, 176, 261, 266
Singh Rathore, Khushi 179
Singh, Avtar 175

Singh, Balwant 66–67
  Untouchable in the IAS 66–67
Singh, Sujatha 178–179
Sinha, Yashwant 147
Skinner, Quentin 260–261
Slaughter, Anne-Marie 33
social
  capital 28, 46, 49–50, 76, 89, 101, 105–106, 116, 130, 132, 156, 160, 168–169, 177, 181, 186, 189, 203, 206–207, 232–233
  "graces" 43–44, 96–97, 106–107, 131–132, 208, 212–213, 229–231, 233, 239–240, 242–243, 267; *see also* etiquette.
  hierarchies 17, 164–165, 193, 270–271, 288
socialism 214, 247–248
socialization 230–231, 234–235
  gender and 236
South Asia 55–57
South Block 48, 84, 130, 162–163, 200
Soviet Union; *see* Russia.
Srinivasa Shastri, V.S. 18, 60–61, 141–142, 200
Srinivasan, M.N. 232
St Paul's Boarding School 195
St Stephen's College 46, 49–50, 130–131, 158–159, 164–165, 182, 189–190, 195, 204, 224–225, 231–232
  St Stephen's "type" 251, 273
  Stephenians 158–159, 167–168, 177–178, 180–182, 189–190, 200, 221, 223, 225, 240–241, 251, 257, 273
St Xavier's College 158–159, 224–225
standard of civilization 9–11, 18, 31–33, 39–41, 44, 76–77, 96–97, 124, 128–129, 139–140, 143, 154, 192–193, 199–200, 214–215, 221, 232–233, 274, 287
status
  ambivalent 13–14, 144–145, 186–187
  caste 10, 59–60, 73, 152, 232–233
  elite 6–8, 12–13, 62–63, 125–126, 164–165, 274, 286
  outsider 26, 53–54, 117, 282–283
  social 114, 200, 285
  status consciousness 23–24, 247–248
stereotypes 53–54, 186, 188, 234–235, 248

stigma and stigmatization 10, 12, 17, 23, 66–67, 96–97, 101, 124, 185–187, 197–198, 228, 232, 244, 264, 285

Stoics 20–21

Subramanian, Ajantha 52, 183–184, 186–187, 232–233

Superior Civil Services 170–171, 212

"superiority complex" 95–96, 127–128

Sushma Swaraj Institute of Foreign Service 254

T

Tagore, Rabindranath 50

Tamil Nadu 76, 218, 220–221

Taylor, Charles 143

Teja, J.S. 146–147

Thakur, Vineet 18, 23–24, 60–61

Thant, U. 148

Tharoor, Shashi 126

Thatcher, Margaret 131–132

Third World 31–32, 48, 138–139, 143, 208, 214–215, 239–240

   difference 113, 115, 271–272

   diversity 245

   identities 98

   internationalism 125

   nationalism 283

   solidarity 28, 79–80, 98, 214, 246, 271–272

   Third Worldism 114–117, 286

Thumba Rocket Launching Centre 216

Towns, Ann 180

Trump, Donald 282–283

Tyabji, Badr-ud-Din 81, 124–125, 134, 207

U

Union Public Service Commission (UPSC) 167, 223, 226

United Kingdom; see Britain.

United Nations (UN) 132–133, 145–146, 149, 253–254

   General Assembly 148

   human rights bodies 147

   International Convention on the Elimination of all Forms of Racial Discrimination 148

   Security Council 117–118, 121–122

   World Conference Against Racism 147

United States; see America, United States of.

universality, politics of 31

Untouchables 56–57, 149; see also Dalits and Scheduled Castes (SC).

   Offences Act 148

   Committee on 148

Upadhyaya, Deendayal 251

V

Vaishyas 56–57

Vajpayee, A.B. 249

W

wars

   Cold War 6, 139, 239–240

   First World War 80–81

   Second World War 35, 143, 208–209, 276

Washington 138

Weber, Max 49

Weightman, Hugh 80–81

West

   anti-western ideologies 251

   dominance of 10, 15, 29

   post-Western world 29, 239

whiteness, equation between elites and 7

Wigram, Sir Clive 89

Wiseman, Geoffrey 257, 262–263

women

   anti-women bias 175–176

   diplomats 25, 67–68, 72, 75–76, 161–162, 175–176, 188–189, 191–192, 196–197, 234–237

   empowerment 176

   femininity 188–189, 234–235

   feminist domination 178–179

   Indian Foreign Service (IFS), ascent in hierarchies of 178–179

   officers 25, 68, 161–162, 175, 176, 179, 187–189, 196–197, 235–236

   stereotypes about 234–235

Woodruff, Philipp 87–88

   Men Who Ruled India 87–88

"worlding" cosmopolitanism 1, 13, 22, 270

"worldliness" 27–28, 48, 107–108, 111–112, 138–139, 270–272, 285

X

xenophobia 146–147

Y

Yengde, Suraj 63

yoga 252–254

Yosso, Tarra 239–240